The Rogue River Indian War
and Its Aftermath, 1850–1980

The Rogue River Indian War and Its Aftermath, 1850–1980

By E. A. Schwartz

University of Oklahoma Press
Norman and London

This book is published with the generous assistance of The McCasland
Foundation, Duncan, Oklahoma.

Library of Congress Cataloging-in-Publication Data

Schwartz, E. A., 1942–
    The Rogue River Indian War and its aftermath, 1850–1980 / by
E. A. Schwartz.
        p.   cm.
    Includes bibliographical references and index.
    ISBN 0-8061-2906-9 (alk. paper)
    1. Rogue River Indian War, 1855–1856.   2. Indians of North America—
Oregon—Government relations.   3. Siletz Indian Reservation (Or.)—
History.   I. Title.
    E83.84.S39   1997
    973.6'6—dc20   96-32767
                                                                        CIP

Text design by Cathy Carney Imboden. Text is set in Janson; display type
is set in Univers Medium.

The paper in this book meets the guidelines for permanence and durability
of the Committee on Production Guidelines for Book Longevity of the
Council on Library Resources, Inc. ∞

1 2 3 4 5 6 7 8 9 10

Kopa Konaway
Nika Tillicums

Contents

Contents

Illustrations

Figures

Maps

Preface

This study argues that in the case of certain western Oregon Indian peoples, local interests thwarted or subverted the ideals of stated federal Indian policy through the late nineteenth century. When those ideals were realized—to the extent that they could be, in an unpromising environment without the loss of social continuity and Indian identity—they were realized by the Indians themselves. But the Indians' relative success served only to make them seem good subjects for later policies based on crude assimilationism that were meant to dissolve their community and turn their resources over to non-Indians.[1]

This is not a tribal history. The Indian peoples whose experiences are considered have not belonged to any single tribal group. What they have shared is an association with the Coast Reservation in Oregon and its successors, the Alsea and Siletz Reservations. Nor is this an ethnohistory, though culture and cultural change have been considered. This is a study of the influences that have formed the economic, social, political, and physical environments of certain western Oregon Indians, with an emphasis on comparing the stated Indian policies of the federal government with the policies actually applied.

If stated federal policies have had little influence, or have been subject to substantial distortion in their application, then the traditional focus on the making of policy cannot provide a satisfactory picture of the broad significance of policies. We have to consider their diverse and complex outcomes, and the local as well as general sources of their failures.[2]

Moreover, if Indian people have had a substantial influence on the context of their own lives, there can be no understanding of the outcomes of policies without a corresponding understanding of that influence.

I have necessarily depended for the most part on ordinary historical sources—usually non-Indian sources, which frequently distort and even deliberately misrepresent Indian statements and actions. Such sources must be considered with a strong sense of their ironies, their self-contradictions, and their tendency to promote the interests of their authors. They should be understood as artifacts rather than statements of fact, to be dissected and, whenever possible, compared with similar artifacts.

The Rogue River War of 1855–56 takes up considerable space in this account because it is an unambiguous example of a war against Indians that was drummed up to attract public funds—a pork barrel war, successfully promoted by rival politicians who effortlessly thwarted the humane intentions of the new western reservation policy, notwithstanding the vociferous objections of both civil and military officials of the federal government.

The later experiences of the peoples involved in the war, and the others who were made to join them on the Coast Reservation, are especially useful because the Coast Reservation was among the first established under the western reservation policy, and each significant policy change was in some sense applied to them.

They were culturally unlike the Plains peoples about whom so much has been written, and so their experiences provide a different sense of the significance of federal policies. They never again went to war after 1856, which rules out violent conflict as an explanation for the outcomes of the government's policies. They showed a willingness to adapt and a desire to improve their material well-being, which made them ideal subjects for the transformation that the reservation policy was meant to work. Later, they seemed to be ideal subjects for the policies of allotment and termination.

The only scholarly book about the Rogue River War to date is *Requiem for a People: The Rogue Indians and the Frontiersmen*, by Stephen Dow Beckham (Norman: University of Oklahoma Press, 1971). Beckham was also the author of *The Indians of Western Oregon: This Land Was Theirs* (Coos Bay, Ore.: Arago Books, 1977), which deals broadly with the experiences of western Oregon Indians from precontact times to the 1970s, and *Land of the Umpqua: A History of Douglas County, Oregon* (Roseburg, Ore.: Douglas County Commissioners, 1986). More recently, Terence O'Donnell has produced *An Arrow in the Earth: General Joel Palmer and the Indians of Oregon* (Portland: Oregon Historical Society Press, 1991), the sole biography of Joel Palmer, who was among other things the founder of the Siletz Reservation. The present work asks different questions of the evidence than Beckham and O'Donnell asked and inevitably reaches different conclusions.

The research that went into this study, spanning about ten years, would not have been possible without the help of the staffs of the National Archives and its branches in Seattle and Laguna Niguel, the Oregon Historical Society Library, Ellis Library at the University of Missouri-Columbia, the Bancroft Library at the University of California at Berkeley, and the libraries of the University of Oregon, the University of California at San Diego, and the University of California at Los Angeles.

Members of the history faculty of the University of Missouri-Columbia read previous sections and versions of this book and helped with their comments. They include Susan Flader, who supervised my dissertation; John L. Bullion, my advisor; Winfield L. Burggraaff; and Eli Zaretsky. W. Raymond Wood, of the anthropology department, read my master's thesis, which was the first version of several chapters of this book. Lee Lyman, also an anthropology professor at Missouri, read my dissertation and added significantly to my knowledge of the anthropological literature concerning western Oregon, despite our past disagreement over certain aspects of archeology.

Clifford E. Trafzer, a professor of ethnic studies at the University of California at Riverside, read the penultimate version and helped sharpen both my writing and my thinking. Rick Harmon, editor of the *Oregon Historical Quarterly*, helped clarify my thinking about the Mitchell removal episode and published the results as the article "Sick Hearts: Indian Removal on the Oregon Coast, 1875–1881" in the fall of 1991.

I must also thank the anonymous second reader of the manuscript for the University of Oklahoma Press, who encouraged much necessary re-writing and reorganization, and Stephen Dow Beckham, already mentioned, whose work provided a sturdy scholarly foundation for my efforts and who unknowingly provoked me into undertaking an academic career.

The interest shown in my research by Selene Rilatos, Robert Kentta, and other members of the Confederated Tribes of Siletz Indians must also be acknowledged.

Through their experiences Darrelle Dean Butler and Gary Butler provoked my inquiry. Nilak Butler and Ishbel Butler encouraged me even though my initial efforts were unpromising. Grace Castle convinced me of the significance of the Siletz Reservation in the history of federal Indian policy. Larry Robey, my editor when I was a correspondent for the *Statesman-Journal* of Salem, was unfailingly supportive.

Sandra Baringer read and commented on many permutations of this work, and encouraged me to undertake graduate study. Frosine Kathy Brown, my former student at California State University, San Marcos, read an earlier draft of the manuscript. Cathy Johnston read the penultimate draft. Their comments made the final draft substantially more readable than it might have been.

My research was funded in part by Viles and Trenholme scholarships provided through the University of Missouri-Columbia history department, and by California State University, San Marcos.

E. A. SCHWARTZ

The Rogue River Indian War
and Its Aftermath, 1850–1980

1

Original Inhabitants

In 1852 the followers of a man called Tipsu Tyee went to war with a neighboring village of Shasta Indians in the Rogue River valley in southwestern Oregon.[1] Their war involved about one hundred men and took three days. A white newcomer named James Cardwell saw this fight. He said it developed out of Tipsu Tyee's refusal to pay compensation in horses for the killing of a Shasta. All kinds of disputes were ordinarily settled by payment in the Rogue River country.[2]

The two groups took positions facing each other. Their basic tactic was a charge made by a small group of men. Cardwell said that the attackers usually got within about fifty yards of their enemies, who then shot arrows at them and chased them back. No one was killed. The Shastas seem to have been satisfied when a few men had been wounded.[3]

The formalized and almost benign form of combat observed by Cardwell was not the only kind that might have been called traditional in the Rogue River country by 1852. There was also raiding. The Latgawas, for example, were said to have raided villages of the Takelmas, their neighbors and linguistic relatives, for slaves to trade with the people beyond the Cascades,[4] although slavery does not seem to have been significant anywhere in the Rogue River country itself.[5] Shastas made raids to settle private feuds, fighting until the raiders killed their designated victim or were driven off by his fellow villagers.[6]

By 1852 there was also a tradition, although only about one generation old, of exchanges of violence with transient trappers, drovers, miners, and soldiers. Military adaptations were among the first the peoples of the Rogue River country made to the persistent presence of groups of outsiders. They had taken up firearms; in 1850, the territorial governor counted about twenty firearms among the weapons carried by a group of men who came to watch a treaty negotiation.[7] And they had organized armies that must have included men from more than one village; in 1851, as many as three hundred men had come together to oppose a raid by a detachment of dragoons.[8]

Local traditions of warfare involved men clad in elk-hide armor who observed strict rules. Young women sometimes took part, going out with knives to cut their enemies' bowstrings. They were in no danger because a man who killed a woman would be despised. After a successful raid by Shastas, the man responsible had to begin peace negotiations, although not for at least one year, because no one could speak of the dead until then. Often two women were engaged as negotiators. Their efforts would conclude in a general confrontation of the parties, prepared as if for war but expecting peace and perhaps even a night of dancing and reconciliation.[9]

Reconciliation in the old sense was not possible with the Rogue River peoples' new, white enemies, who at that point were only passing through. These enemies, constantly growing more numerous toward the middle of the nineteenth century, did not see their indigenous antagonists as honorable people but rather as a species of predatory vermin. In 1847, the author of one guidebook to Oregon was so certain of their bad reputation that he condemned them sight unseen. He had been told that the Indians in southern Oregon and northern California traded little and were inclined to attack people driving cattle from California to Oregon. Although no cattle drivers had been killed for several years, he said, many cattle had been lost. Whites could not safely settle there, he said, until posts were established to protect them from "the depredations of these merciless savages."[10]

The guidebook author was Joel Palmer, who would become a decisive presence in the imposition of radical change on the Rogue River peoples. Although Palmer later took a more sympathetic attitude, neither he nor anyone else in the middle of the nineteenth century had a late-twentieth-century perspective on cultural differences. He would have rejected the idea that the complex of indigenous cultures he encountered in southwestern Oregon had any inherent significance or claim to respect. But the changes the Rogue River peoples underwent cannot be understood without some sense of their world as it was—a world as complete and full of meaning for them as our world is for us.

The original inhabitants of southwestern Oregon were members of a multilingual complex of interlocking cultures. They should probably be thought of as populations focused on streams and estuaries rather than tribes occupying territories that might be delineated by lines on a map. Although these populations spoke an uncertain number of dialects of languages belonging to three different groups, they shared most of the other elements of their cultures. A recent study of the ethnography of the Rogue River valley peoples suggests that boundaries between groups were vague. Many people spoke more than one language. Marriage between members of different groups was common. People thought of themselves as belonging to their villages rather than to tribes or ethnic groups defined by language and culture.[11]

The peoples whose contacts and conflicts with whites led to the Rogue River War lived along the Rogue and upper Umpqua Rivers and their tributaries. To get an idea of their territory, imagine that you are standing on the pinnacle of Mount McLoughlin, rising about 9,500 feet in the Cascade Range in southern Oregon, 180 miles due east of the mouth of the Rogue River on the coast of the Pacific Ocean and about thirty miles north of the present California border.

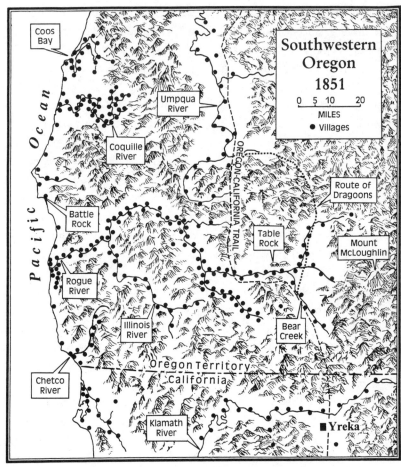

Southwestern Oregon, 1851. Non-Indians, with few exceptions, had never been more than transients in the Rogue River country as of 1851. But miners had penetrated nearby northwestern California, bringing the town of Yreka into being. One party had mined on the Illinois River in Oregon, and white people were establishing themselves in the Umpqua River valley. Village sites shown on this map are speculative, based loosely on lists of villages reported in *Indian Tribes of North America*, by John R. Swanton (Washington: Government Printing Office, 1952), and should be understood as reflecting population densities rather than precise locations. In areas not mentioned by Swanton, populations have been inferred on the basis of populations of similar groups. Based on Stephen Dow Beckham's estimate that 9,500 people lived in the Rogue River country at this time, each dot represents about 43 people. Actual village populations seem to have ranged from about 30 to 150.

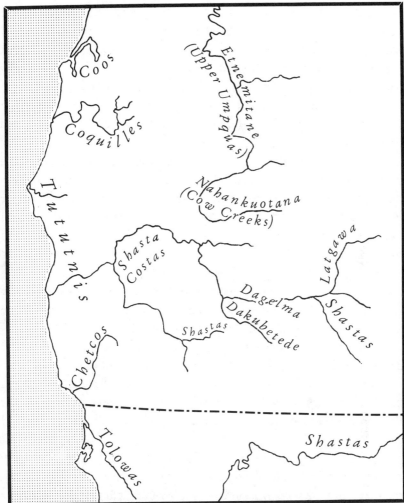

Indigenous Groups in Southwestern Oregon. Before intense contact, Indian populations were centered on river systems, although they used and lived in other parts of
their territories during their annual migratory movement, which began in the spring
and ended in the autumn. Ethnographers included several Athapascan-speaking
groups along on the coast on the lower Rogue River in the group called Tututni (or
Tututunne).

Face the ocean and you have at your back the country of the people now known as the Klamath Indians, in the basin of the two shallow Klamath lakes and at the edge of the immense sagebrush desert that stretches east from the leeward slope of the Cascades to the Rocky Mountains. On your right is the spine of the Cascades to the north. On your left are the starkly volcanic Siskiyou Mountains enclosing the high valley of the Klamath River, fifty miles south of Mount McLoughlin and fifty miles wide.

In front of you is the Rogue River valley, beginning thirty miles to the west and stretching seventy miles toward a broad, ragged southern continuation of the Coast Ranges called the Klamath Mountains. The Rogue River rises in the Cascades near Crater Lake, flows southwestward through the valley, and then continues into the Klamath Mountains and down to the Pacific.

Looking northwest beyond the main stem of the Rogue River is a series of ridges forming a barrier in the gap between the Coast Ranges and the Cascades. On the other side of those ridges, sixty miles north of the Rogue River valley, is the valley of the Umpqua River.[12]

The peoples who occupied this territory have been categorized by anthropologists as attached to the Northwest Coast culture area. In terms of economy, the coastal groups shared an emphasis on fishing for food and the use of wood for shelter. The peoples in the Umpqua and Rogue River uplands depended more than the coastal peoples on hunting deer and gathering roots and berries, but they still resembled the coastal peoples far more than they resembled peoples living to the east.[13]

Except in the relatively dry valleys of the Umpqua and the Rogue, with their chaparral, manzanita, and oaks, the environment was dominated by mountains, moisture, and evergreen forests. Along the coast was a zone of Sitka spruce. Western red cedar grew in swampy places. On the east was a zone dominated by western hemlock. Not far inland, the firs and pines were mixed with broadleaf evergreens in a moist mountainous zone stretching to the Cascades. The people used burning to modify their environment, encouraging the growth of grasslands. Douglas fir and western hemlock grow in burned-over places and red alder in disturbed sites near water.[14]

When contact with whites began on the coast, Athapascan-speaking peoples lived on most of the land from the Coquille River, immediately south of the Coos country, to what is now Humboldt Bay in California, along some 290 miles of coastline. Ethnologist J. Owen Dorsey, who studied the coastal cultures in the late nineteenth century, said they had a collective term for themselves, Tuqwetatunne, meaning "all the people."[15]

North of Humboldt Bay were the Tolowas, some of whom would be involved in the Rogue River wars, and then the Chetcos, who gave their name to a small river a few miles north of what is now the border between Oregon and California. The name is believed to mean "close to the mouth of the stream." J. Owen Dorsey listed nine villages on the Chetco River, counting both halves of the double village at the river's mouth, Chettanne on the south bank and Chettannene on the north side. "The Chetco belonged to the Athapascan linguistic stock and differed little in culture from the other Athapascan groups immediately north of them and the Tolowa to the south," according to ethnological compiler John R. Swanton.[16]

He listed the Tututnis, "meaning unknown," as the next people to the north, living in thirty-two villages, according to Dorsey. Anthropologist Philip Drucker's later, shorter list of Tututni villages includes one called Tututun, five or six miles upriver from the mouth of the Rogue River, where a vast meadow spreads along the right bank today. Tututun is said to have had two sections, Tatretun, "downriver," and Nagutretun, "upriver," and a suburb called Tagrilitun. Villages given the loose classification Tututni were located along a hundred-mile stretch of coast centered on the mouth of the Rogue and extending upstream at least fourteen miles to the village called Mikonotunne.[17]

Another Athapascan-speaking group, the Chastacostas, "from Shistak-wusta, their own name, significance unknown," lived on the Rogue River above the Tututunis. Thirty-seven villages have been listed, among them the town of Cistakwusta near the point where the Illinois River runs into the Rogue River, about halfway between the Rogue River valley and the

Pacific. It was divided into three sections called Tleattlintun, Tcetciwut, and Setlatun. Chastacosta villages were located along the Rogue as far east as the west end of the Rogue River valley and on the lower Illinois River.[18]

North of the Tututnis were the northernmost of the Athapascan speakers in the coastal region, the Mishikwutmetunne or Coquilles, the "people who live on the stream called Mishi," now known as the Coquille River. Thirty-three of their villages are listed. Their neighbors to the north were the Coos people.[19]

Population estimates for the Athapascan-speaking peoples who lived on or near the south coast of Oregon are vague, apparently because the whites who tried to count them were not sure who should be counted as what. Anthropologist James Mooney estimated in 1928 that the Tututunis and Chetcos had amounted to about thirty-six hundred people in prewhite times, but a 1986 estimate by Robert T. Boyd put their number at forty-five hundred before contact.[20]

Swanton divided the upland Athapascan speakers into four groups. The Dakubetede, "own name, significance unknown," lived along the upper Applegate River, a tributary of the Rogue River that flows into it from the south in the western or lower end of the Rogue River valley, near the point where the river plunges into the Klamath Mountains.[21] The people who lived on Galice Creek called themselves the Taltushtuntude, "own name, meaning unknown," and spoke the same dialect as the Dakubetede. The two divisions of Athapascan speakers in the Umpqua River valley were known to the whites collectively as the Umpqua or Upper Umpqua Indians (not to be confused with the Penutian-speaking Lower Umpquas or Kalawatsets). Swanton said the Athapascan speakers along the South Umpqua River called themselves the Etnemitane and were called Cictaq-wutmetunne, "Umpqua River people," by the Tututni. The people who lived on Cow Creek, a tributary of the South Umpqua rising between the Umpqua River valley and the Rogue River valley, were "often spoke of separately under the name Nahankhuotana," according to Swanton.[22] They spoke a Takelman language related to the language of their neighbors to the south.[23]

Original Inhabitants

The Shastas occupied some territory in southwestern Oregon, although which territory and how much is subject to argument. The Shastas spoke a Hokan language distantly related to the Siouan languages of the Great Plains. The conventional assumption is that they lived in the valleys of a major Rogue River tributary called Bear Creek and a lesser tributary known as Little Butte Creek.[24] Modern Shastas claim, however, that their relatives occupied most of the Rogue River valley and that the principal leaders in the years leading up to the 1855–56 war were their kin.[25]

Their argument is supported by early white accounts such as that of Elisha Steele, a lawyer and sometime Indian Service official who arrived in northern California in 1850. When he arrived, Steele said, "The Shasta, the Yreka, and the Rogue River Indians all Talked one Language and claimed to have been formerly under one chief." He identified Joe and Sam (or Apserkahar, translated as Horse Rider, and Toquahear, translated as Wealthy), who later signed treaties on behalf of the Rogue River valley peoples, as leaders of the Shasta-speaking people in the nearby Siskiyou Mountains in northern California as well as the people in the Rogue River valley.[26]

Sargent Sambo, a descendent of the Oregon Shastas, told ethnographer Catharine Holt in 1937 that they called themselves Ikirukatsu, that is, the people of the Ikiruk, their name for the Rogue River valley, meaning "back behind." The name reflected the location of the Oregon Shastas beyond the Siskiyou Mountains from the three Shasta divisions to the south, in California. Sambo claimed that the principal leader of the Oregon Shastas was also the leader of all four Shasta divisions.[27]

According to the conventional view the Takelmas, "those dwelling along the river," and their upland relatives, called the Latgawas, occupied much of the Rogue River valley proper. They spoke a language with Penutian affinities.[28] They do not seem to have gotten on well with their Shasta neighbors—their name for the Shastas was Wulx, which means enemies. Both the Latgawas and Shastas looked upon the Athapascan speakers on the upper Umpqua River system as enemies.[29]

The Takelmas and Latgawas do not seem to have been very numerous; James Mooney thought there were only about five hundred people in the two divisions as of 1780.[30] He estimated that the Takelmas and the inland Athapascan speakers together numbered about 5,700 before contact. Boyd estimated their population at about 6,750.[31]

No estimate is likely to give us more than a general idea of populations at a particular hypothetical moment, the last moment before significant contact. Contact was a process, not a point in time. People in southwestern Oregon seem to have been affected by smallpox, for example, long before they themselves were in regular contact with non-Indians.

Oregon historian Leslie M. Scott estimated that 80 percent of the Indian population of the Willamette valley, the focus of white settlement in Oregon in the middle of nineteenth century, died in epidemics. Writing in 1925, he said, "Always it will be a source of thanksgiving that the destruction of the Indians of the Pacific Northwest by diseases spared the pioneer settlers the horrors of a strong and malignant foe." He theorized that the southwestern Oregon peoples had escaped this destruction.[32]

He was mistaken. The inland peoples seem to have suffered through smallpox epidemics in the 1770s, 1801, 1824–25, and 1838, and epidemics of smallpox appear to have spread down the entire Oregon coast in 1775 and 1824.[33] Indian Service agent Josiah L. Parrish reported from Port Orford on the south coast in 1854 that the people there showed signs of having been through a smallpox epidemic about thirty years before and a measles epidemic eighteen years before.[34]

In the threatened world of the southwestern Oregon peoples at midcentury, villages were the basic social and political units, consisting of groups of related men and their families, led by head men who gained approval through wealth and prestige.[35] The people of more than one village might come together temporarily for specific purposes.[36] The number of people living in a village varied. Dennis J. Gray estimated that the average Athapascan village in the Rogue River valley amounted to four or five families. One village on the Applegate River included ten houses. Peter Skene Ogden, the leader of a Canadian fur brigade that passed through the valley in 1827, reported that the Latgawa village of Dilomi included six large houses that could have held as many as one hundred people.[37]

The closest thing to an Indian account of precontact culture not mediated by an ethnographer was written by Sam Van Pelt and published in the Portland *Oregonian* Sunday magazine in 1939. Van Pelt wrote that he had been born in 1866 and identified himself as a Chetco Indian, but the son of a white man, Thomas Van Pelt, who had settled at the mouth of the Winchuck River, a few miles south of the Chetco River, in 1852. Although Sam Van Pelt was not born until a decade after the Rogue River war ended, he grew up in the old Chetco country and had known elders who had managed to stay behind when most of the south coast peoples were sent north in 1856.

Before the whites came, Van Pelt said, houses in the Chetco country were built mostly of split redwood puncheons (boards). An excavation was made and puncheons seven or eight feet long were stood on end to form the walls. "Then a saddle comb roof was put on of the same stuff, with the exception of a hole three by six feet in the middle of the comb. This is where the smoke escaped."[38] The Takelmas built similar houses about twelve feet wide and fifteen to twenty feet long with gabled rooves, framed with posts, covered with split sugar-pine planks, and sunk into the ground eighteen to twenty-four inches deep.[39] Philip Drucker reported that houses built by Athapascan speakers on the lower Rogue River were similar, but builders used split western red cedar (common near the coast but not in the valley) and sometimes a thatched roof.[40]

Coastal Athapascan speakers had sweathouses, which were described to Drucker as serving as the sleeping quarters for men from early childhood. Takelma villages also commonly included sweathouses, which were built deep into the ground and covered with earth. They were big enough for six men. Hot stones were passed through an opening, and water was poured on them to fill the sweathouse with steam. Men often spent the night there after a sweat. Taltushtuntude sweathouses were similar, but the heat was produced by hardwood coals rather than water over rocks. Taltushtuntude men, unlike the coastal Athapascan speakers, do not seem to have used their sweathouses as their usual dwellings.[41]

Although people had substantial houses in permanent villages, they moved from place to place during about half the year to take advantage

Chetco Indians in 1855. This engraving, from the *Harper's New Monthly Magazine* for October 1856, illustrated a travel article by William V. Wells called "Wild Life in Oregon." Note that all of the people shown appear to be wearing at least some American-style clothing. (San Diego Public Library)

of varying food sources. Fish, especially salmon, was the most important food source. Drucker said that in early summer people came together along the rivers for the spring salmon run. The significance of the salmon was so great that the one ceremony common throughout the Pacific Northwest was what Drucker called the "first salmon rite." Although the ceremony was performed with many variations, the central idea was to treat the first salmon caught in each run as an honored guest, to be sprinkled with ritual substances and welcomed with an oration and songs.

Drucker provided a generalized Northwest salmon myth to explain the context of the ceremony. He said that some animal spirits were believed to live much as human beings did, and the salmon were thought to live in a huge house far under the ocean where they took on human

Typical Housing. This Kalawatset house on the lower Umpqua River, shown in an engraving accompanying an article published in 1857 in *Frank Leslie's Illustrated Weekly*, was typical in general terms of indigenous housing in southwestern Oregon.

form. When the time came for the annual runs, they clothed themselves in salmon flesh to become a voluntary sacrifice for the benefit of the human race. When their bones were returned to the rivers, they went back to the oceans where the fish came back to life.[42]

The Shastas considered fishing places to be a kind of private property, and they could be passed down as inheritances within the male line of a family. People who were not family members could demand a share of the fish, however, and might be given permission sometimes to fish for themselves.[43]

Plants provided many foods. People gathered ripening roots and berries along the rivers in early summer. Camas bulbs were common food. They were cooked in a pit with hot stones. The roasted bulbs might be mashed into cakes that could be kept for winter. People in the valley used sugar-pine bark and nuts for food, among other things, but cultivated only one crop, tobacco. Chetco men also cultivated tobacco. Sam Van Pelt said that tobacco was "sown in the shade of the myrtle bottoms along the rivers. The reason for planting in the shade was so it would be mild and pleasant to inhale."[44]

From the rivers the peoples near the coast went to the ocean, where they gathered shellfish and smelt and hunted sea lions. Van Pelt said that Chetco hunters killed seals and sea lions for their oil, which "was rendered out and put in dried sea calf skins to keep sweet until used up." The animals were easy to catch asleep along the shore.

By the time the fall salmon came up the rivers, the people had returned to their fishing sites to catch their winter supplies. Van Pelt said that when the *tonkalooka* (chinook salmon) ran in the river in September, the men "would take their canoes and a boat puller and just throw their spears at random and soon have all they wanted for the day." The salmon was dried "and put away for future use in large baskets called met-ton, which would hold about five hundred pounds."[45]

After the fall salmon run, the people moved into the mountains for the acorn harvest. Throughout the region, acorns were an important food source. They were shelled and mashed and leached with hot water to get out the bitterness. Van Pelt called them "the son-chon; this was the staff of life, made from the nut of the acorn. This was hulled and dried so it would keep without mildewing for winter use."

Fall was also the time for deer hunting, mainly using traps. The Chetcos trapped both elk and deer in pits the men dug ten or twelve feet deep and five to ten feet in diameter in soft clay. "All the young hunters would make drives across these pits," Van Pelt said. The meat "was all divided with the old first, then the rest would take their share. These drives would take place about two times a year or as was necessary."[46]

When winter came, according to Philip Drucker, the people were back in their towns along the rivers. Dances were held. The men, who did all the fishing, worked on their gear; they made everything used for fishing without the help of women, who were not even allowed to watch them work. There was gambling,[47] which among the Shastas, at least, was a contest among villages, often carried out at some neutral location. The sexes had separate versions of the stick game, in which the object is to determine the location of a particular stick. Men and women used different types and numbers of sticks.[48]

Men and women also had separate versions of a popular game resembling field hockey. The Taltushtuntude men's version involved a ball made of wood, moved between goals using sticks about three feet long with a bend at the end. Instead of a ball, Taltushtuntude women and Shasta women used two sticks tied together with a cord. The Takelma women's game involved teams of three women.[49]

Traditional relations between men and women may have favored men, but the evidence is equivocal. No source suggests village leaders were ever female. Men were said to have bought their wives, ordinarily from other villages, and taken them from their homes so that they could give birth to children who would belong to the villages of their husbands. This was the commonly accepted form of marriage, and children borne by an unbought woman had little status.[50]

As already mentioned, however, young Shasta women took an aggressive role in warfare, and women were usually chosen as negotiators to end Shasta feuds.[51] No group seems to have celebrated male adulthood, but the initial five menstruations of Shasta, Takelma, and inland Athapascan-speaking women were said to have been celebrated with ceremonial dancing and feasting. (The woman whose emergence was being celebrated, however, was not allowed much celebration herself.)[52]

Women were in conspicuously successful competition with men in the field of traditional medicine. Among the Athapascan speakers, doctors were usually women. After long training, they went through a ten-day initiation during which they got the guardian spirits that helped them and gave them power. Takelma doctors were at least as likely to be women as they were to be men.[53]

The Takelmas, whose name for doctors was *goyo*, believed that a doctor had the power to prevent, and cause, illness and bad weather. Illness resulted when someone or something sent pains to penetrate the victim's body. These pains were conceptualized as small material objects of different colors. Through song and dance, a goyo used the power of his or her guardian spirits to drive out pains. But pains were thought to respond to more physical methods of healing as well. People often preferred to call on a *somloholxa*, a more benign doctor who did not inflict pains as a goyo might but was capable of removing them by rubbing the afflicted parts of the body.[54]

Beyond the spirits that inhabited everything and sometimes became involved in human affairs, there were more significant but also more distant spirits or beings who were responsible for the condition of the earth and the people on it. A creation myth told to J. Owen Dorsey by an Athapascan speaker on the Siletz Reservation suggests a sense of profound alienation from "the great Being." According to this story, the creator Qawaneca or Kwawanesha rearranged the earth, learned from the birds how to make the sun shine, and created the serpent that is wrapped around the earth fives times and holds it together. But Qawaneca failed to become the father of the Indians because he had a companion, an immortal but lesser being who tricked the immortal Mother into marrying him; "All Indians return to her at death, and she sends them back to this world as infants. Her husband, too, is still alive. He never leaves this world; but Qawaneca now dwells in the sun and looks down on the people. The circumference of that upper world in which he dwells is curved upwards. No one who dies here can go to live with Qawaneca."[55]

Perhaps this sense of alienation from the creator was the product of what Sam Van Pelt described as almost a fall from grace some thirty years before Dorsey heard the story. Van Pelt said the Chetcos lived a good life in former times. They "lived to a great old age," he said. "I can't recall of hearing my ancestors having to pull any teeth, for those that were 80 and 90 years old would have every tooth, although some were worn very close to their gums." Before the white people came there were "no diseases of any kind," he said. Living on what nature provided meant "no taxes or interest to pay, hence we people had all kinds of time for every kind of pleasure, as dances of various kinds," some "carried on for days."

This golden age, probably a little too good to be entirely true, began to fade away in the spring of 1852, when whites began coming into the Chetco country. Van Pelt's father settled on the mouth of the Winchuck River, but first he went to the local headman for permission to build a house there. The Indian people decided that he could stay as long as he was friendly.[56]

The whites remained friendly for about a year. Peace broke down while the hunters and nut gatherers were upriver and the only people left in villages at the mouth of the river were the elderly and children too young to help with the work. Van Pelt said that the Chetcos had some confidence in their new neighbors "and did not dream anything would happen. But before a week or ten days passed the Indians were told that the white man had burned about forty houses and the old people in them."[57]

2

Expeditions

The destruction of the Chetco towns in 1854 was one incident in a long series of confrontations between Indians and non-Indians in southwestern Oregon. Some whites recognized that the excesses of certain of their compatriots fueled the chronic violence in the region. But the violence provoked white fear and promoted the reputation of the inhabitants for merciless savagery. The name that non-Indians gave to the principal river of southwestern Oregon, the Rogue River, signified the reputation of the peoples who lived there.

Jesse Applegate, a pathfinder for the American occupation of southwestern Oregon, claimed in 1851 that Canadian traders had begun calling the Indian peoples the "Rascals" because of "their disregard of the laws of property," hence the name of "the Rascal or Rogues river." But there was no killing, Applegate said, until they encountered a party led by the American trapper Ewing Young in 1834.[1]

Applegate was mistaken. Members of a Hudson's Bay Company party that passed through the valley not long before Young were the first outsiders known to have killed Rogue River valley people. They were led by Michel Laframboise, and they were said to have killed eleven Indians in a confrontation while suffering no losses of their own.[2]

In the case of the Young party, by Jesse Applegate's account, Young ordered his men to fire on Indians who had tried to take meat from a drying scaffold, and "terrible slaughter of the unprepared natives ensued." The sole injury among Young's men was "a *serious bite* received by one of the men while stripping the skin from the head of an Indian not yet dead." Only since the Young expedition, according to Applegate, had the Rogue River peoples been hostile to whites.[3]

One of Young's men told another version of the massacre. When the Young party reached the Rogue River, he said, several of its members were suffering from malaria. Two Indians who visited the camp were killed to keep them from telling others how vulnerable the sickness had made the trappers.[4]

The 1834 encounters of Indian people with murderous trappers followed at least forty-two years of contact during which no one was recorded killed, and no non-Indians would be killed until 1835.

The first recorded meeting of southwestern Oregon Indians and non-Indians took place on the coast and involved members of the expedition of British explorer George Vancouver. In the journal of his North Pacific voyage in the spring of 1792, Vancouver reported that the Indians paddled out in canoes to visit his ships "with the greatest confidence, and without any sort of invitation."

Vancouver said they were distinguished by "a pleasing and courteous deportment." Their complexions were "a light olive" and they "punctuated" their skin "in the fashion of the south-sea islanders." They were "under the middle size; none that we saw exceeding 5 feet, 6 inches in height." They were slender and clean and wore small ornaments of bone in their ears and noses, and clothing made of "the skins of deer, bear, fox and river otter."

They must have had previous contact with whites; Vancouver said they brought out "a few trifling articles to barter, and they anxiously solicited in exchange iron and beads." He said they were "scrupulously honest" and did not expect presents.[5]

A land-based Hudson's Bay Company expedition led by Alexander McLeod made contact with the peoples of the Umpqua River country in 1826 and then went down the coast to the Rogue River. The people whose parents had gone out to meet Vancouver's ships in 1792 fled their villages to avoid the McLeod party, though some were lured out of hiding by "trinkets" the company men offered as presents.[6] Perhaps their shyness was related to a smallpox epidemic two years before,[7] which they may have connected with the presence of non-Indians.

Direct contact between non-Indians and inland Rogue River peoples seems to have begun in early 1827. The outsiders were members of a Hudson's Bay Company fur brigade commanded by Peter Skene Ogden. His first encounter was with an Indian who came into his camp on upper Bear Creek on February 8 and gave him two fresh salmon and a beaver pelt. Soon, however, relations deteriorated. Indians took one of Ogden's horses and shot arrows into several more. Company trappers were harassed, and they complained that the beavers were very wild because of Indian hunting methods that had left marks on six out of ten beavers the trappers caught.

A peace delegation made up of about fifty Indians approached Odgen on February 21. When peace had been made, Ogden handed out what he said were two dozen buttons to show his goodwill. The Indians, he said, would have given him something in return but appeared to own nothing but their "bare coverings" and their bows and arrows.

The Indians were displeased, Ogden said, at seeing the company trappers take their beavers, "and say they will in consequence starve."[8] Historian Nathan Douthit argued that they were hostile to the Hudson's Bay Company men because the trappers disturbed their food-gathering routine, in part by hunting beavers the Indians wanted for food.[9]

Beaver, however, may not have been a common food in the Rogue River valley. Dennis J. Gray's ethnographic study of Takelman and inland

Expeditions

Athapascan speakers does not mention using beaver for food, although mention is made of yellow-jacket larvae, grasshoppers, boiled angleworms, salmon eggs, ground squirrel, ant eggs, crow, and caterpillars, as well as the predictable deer, elk, salmon, acorns, and camas bulbs. Catharine Holt's study of Shasta ethnography mentions in passing that the body of the beaver (as opposed, presumably, to the tail) was not eaten, but it could not be thrown on the ground and so was left in a tree.[10]

If beaver was not a common food, then why did the trappers take so many beavers showing signs of having been hunted by Indians? The Rogue River peoples may have had another trading arrangement. People in the western end of the valley, probably inland Athapascan speakers, told members of the Ogden party that they traded with people to the north of them. There may also have been trade through the people beyond the Cascades, the Klamaths, who seem to have tried to keep the Rogue River peoples from making direct contact with the Ogden party by spreading a rumor that it was a slave-catching expedition.[11]

The Rogue River peoples had items of non-Indian manufacture before Ogden arrived. When Ogden returned to the valley in March 1827, after examining the Rogue River above the valley, he found a large village deserted, its inhabitants apparently having fled from his men, taking their property with them. Left behind were a sickle and two china bowls.[12] Other things acquired in trade may well have been carried away by the villagers.

The very fact that Odgen could communicate with the Rogue River peoples suggests that they were part of an indigenous trading network. Their ineptness as beaver hunters, shown by the notable proportion of previously wounded beavers taken by Ogden's trappers, suggests that hunting beavers was a recent endeavor, perhaps undertaken so that Rogue River peoples could take part in the recently developed trade in imported goods.

Ogden's statement that Indians said they would starve because the trappers were destroying their beavers may reflect a misunderstanding; they may have been trying to tell him that his party was starving them of their stock in trade. They may also have been offended and concerned for their spiritual and thus physical well-being if Ogden's party threw leftover beaver parts on the ground rather than disposing of them in the right way. Moreover, they may have shown hostility because they had been through a smallpox epidemic some three years before.[13]

Hudson's Bay Company expeditions encountered inland Rogue River people again in 1829, and afterward, apparently without deadly violence being inflicted, though company men were harassed. Some Indians who lived in the valley seemed to be friendly: Ogden's first encounter was with an Indian bearing gifts; five Indians stayed in the camp of a party commanded by John Work in 1833 even as other Indians shot arrows into his horses, and the people killed by Young's men in 1834 do not seem to have come to his camp with hostile intentions.[14]

The year after Rogue River people came into contact with the homicidal Laframboise and Young expeditions, four members of an eight-man party of Americans going from Oregon to California were killed by Rogue River people.[15] The killers were doing about all that could be done to redress the balance of violence and assert sovereignty. The traditional legal system in the valley could not be used to put matters right. The people of the villages that lost men to transient trappers in 1834 could neither demand payment from the actual offenders nor raid their villages.

In 1836, the Hudson's Bay Company set up a permanent post, called Fort Umpqua, at the lower, northwestern end of the Umpqua River valley. Umpqua River people attacked the fort in 1840. In 1841, the manager of the post complained that they had made more attacks and had tried to burn the fort. The people were hostile, he said, because of a recent smallpox epidemic, which they blamed on company expeditions.[16]

Meanwhile, in 1837, a cattle drive from California to Oregon that had been organized by Ewing Young and others had passed through the Rogue River valley, stirring up more violence. Among the drovers were survivors of the 1835 clash, and they seem to have been set on getting revenge. The drovers had killed the first two Indians they met north of the Klamath River and were, in turn, harassed and then attacked when they got to the Rogue River valley. Although they seem to have lost many cattle on their way through the valley, none of them were killed, and only one man was wounded.[17]

The Rogue River peoples were not uniformly hostile to the whites who were passing through their country in increasing numbers in the 1840s. But their reputation could generate the perception of danger even when it was absent, as it did in at least one case in 1843. Warren Lansford Hastings, who was involved, described it in his widely read guide to the Oregon and California trails. Hastings was a young Ohio lawyer who became an Oregon Trail wagon train captain and then a noted promoter of American emigration to California. He was leading a party from Oregon to California when the incident happened at the crossing of the Rogue River.

The Americans had to rely on the Indians with their canoes to get across the river. Hastings was apprehensive. He had been told that other travelers had been robbed while crossing. The Indian people "thronged around us," he said, and more than once the emigrants gathered "in battle array against them, when we were under a necessity of discharging a gun or two occasionally in the open air." This made them "invariably fall back and flee in every direction, with the greatest confusion," but after a few minutes "they would again crowd and huddle around us in increased numbers, when we would again dispel them as before."

Hastings was certain they meant to rob his party and would have made a direct attack if they had seen an opportunity. Their real intent, he said, was "our indiscriminate extermination," but his party nonetheless crossed the river "in perfect safety."[18]

Hastings's description does not quite make sense. How could the Americans have formed "in battle array" if the Rogue River people were thronged around them? Why did the Rogue River people remain anywhere near whites firing guns? How was it that some Indians ferried the whites across the river in safety while others seemed intent on murdering them? Perhaps the people who worried Hastings were simply waiting their turn to be ferried across the river or came to the crossing out of curiosity. They may have looked upon these Americans as lunatics who, for reasons that were not quite clear, periodically became excited and fired guns in the air. Perhaps Hastings's account is a compound of posturing and hallucination. Whatever happened at the crossing, the Rogue River peoples cannot have been as hostile as they seemed to Hastings, primed as he was by stories of their savagery.

The following year two other travelers had a completely different experience at the same place. Overton Johnson and William H. Winter said that at the river crossing, "thirty of the Rascals came into camp, for the purpose of opening a trade." These people were shy and stopped about two hundred yards away, "regarding us closely, in order to ascertain, from our movements, whether we were disposed to be friends or foes." The whites finally persuaded them to come forward, though they came very slowly and cautiously. Members of the emigrant party had prepared a pipe and tobacco. They and the Indians arranged themselves in a circle and shared the pipe, passing it around to the left.

These shy people came back the next morning with a quantity of beaver skins and traded them to members of the party "for such trifling articles as they pleased to give them."[19]

Johnson and Winter, however, warned their readers about the fearsome reputation of the Rogue River peoples, even though that reputation contradicted their own experience. "From their extreme hostility and treachery, and from the great amount of damage they had done to the white man," the authors wrote, "they have been almost universally called the Rascals. They seldom allow a company to pass, without molestation."[20]

The chronic conflict along the Oregon-California trail intensified after news of the discovery of gold on the Sacramento River in California reached Oregon by way of a ship's captain toward the end of July 1848. Perhaps two out of three of the able-bodied white men in the territory soon set out for the California goldfields.[21]

Cyrenius Mulkey, a sixteen-year-old recent arrival in Oregon, was among them. He and his fellow "argonauts" had few problems until they came to Point of Rock, or Rocky Point, on the Rogue River. This, he said in an account written in his later years, "was a place that the Indians never allowed a white man to pass without a fight." Rogue River men were

26   Expeditions

waiting for Mulkey and his friends, but after a two-hour fight, according to Mulkey, the Indians were driven back, and the prospective miners continued their journey to California without any of them having been killed or wounded.[22]

While Mulkey was on his way back to the Willamette valley in 1849, he came down with a fever and was asleep when the camp of his small party was attacked in the Rogue River valley. He claimed about one hundred men charged the camp, raining arrows on the whites, but the attackers turned back when they were about twenty-five yards away. Mulkey, hit in the thigh with what he said was a poisoned arrow, fled north with his companions.[23]

In the spring of 1850, a group of Oregonians who had clashed with the Rogue River valley peoples appealed for help to the territorial governor, Joseph Lane. In Oregon City, a town on the lower Willamette River that was then the territorial capital, they complained to Lane that they had been robbed.[24]

Lane, who was about to become a miner himself, had been appointed the first governor of Oregon Territory in 1848 by a fellow North Carolina-born Democrat, President James K. Polk, who, the year before, had made Lane a major general of volunteers in Mexico.[25] A newspaper correspondent who saw General Lane (as he was frequently called) in the field during a confrontation with Rogue River valley people in 1853 said he was "a robust good-looking middle aged man" whose "rear extremities [were] cased in an old pair of grey breeches that looked as though they were the identical ones worn by Gen. Scott when he was 'exposed to fire in the rear.'" His tangled hair "would have frightened the teeth out of a curry comb," and it was "surmounted by the remains of an old forage cap, which, judging from its appearance, might have been worn at Braddock's defeat. This composed the uniform of the old hero who never surrendered."[26]

Lane was forty-eight, and aside from his Mexican War career, he was best known as a former leader of the Indiana legislature. He didn't arrive in his new jurisdiction until March 2, 1849, only three days before Polk left office. The new president, the last Whig who would be elected, was

Joseph Lane (*left*), shown in about 1856, was an ambitious pro-slavery Democratic politician from Indiana who had been a general in the Mexican-American War. Lane coerced in informal treaty in the Rogue River valley in 1850, returned three years later to lead volunteers against the Rogue River peoples, and argued in favor of war against them as territorial delegate to Congress. (Oregon Historical Society, neg. Or Hi 1703) Joel Palmer (*right*), shown in about 1860, was another Democratic politician from Indiana and had been captain of a wagon train in the 1845 emigration. As Oregon superintendent of Indian affairs, Palmer came under pressure for implementing the new reservation policy. He resigned in 1856, but returned to the Indian Service twenty years later for a brief stint as agent at Siletz. (Oregon Historical Society, neg. Or Hi 362)

Mexican War hero Gen. Zachary Taylor. Taylor was slow to name a Whig appointee, former Kentucky congressman John Gaines, to take Lane's place. By the time Gaines made his way to Oregon City, Lane had been gone from the territorial capital for more than two months.[27] He had left toward the end of May 1850 to try his luck in the California goldfields.[28]

Lane had made his resignation effective on June 18, giving himself time for one last accomplishment as governor.[29] He had probably looked upon Oregon from the beginning as a horse that could carry him to the presidency, and Indians meant constant opportunities to show off his aggressive statesmanship. He had begun his term by finding a relatively painless way to satisfy white desire for revenge for an 1847 attack on missionaries at the Whitman mission on the middle Columbia River, and he set out to conclude his term by putting an end to clashes with the Indians along the Rogue River by getting them under his control.

Lane's success in the Whitman case had been the result of extended negotiations through which Lane had persuaded the Cayuse Indians to give up five men who could be presented as the perpetrators of the massacre. After exciting a modest degree of admiration in their captors for their spirit of self-sacrifice, they were tried at the end of May 1850 in Oregon City and hanged on June 3, after Lane himself had left for the Rogue River country and points south.[30]

For an escort on his journey south to the goldfields beyond the summit of the Siskiyou Mountains in California, Lane recruited about fifteen whites and eleven Klickitat Indians.[31] The Klickitats were members of a group based north of the Columbia River who were go-betweens in the trade between whites and Indians in the Willamette and Umpqua valleys. In white eyes, they were "a superior race" among the Indians, according to Oregon historian Howard McKinley Corning.[32] The Klickitats were led by a man whom General Lane called Quatley.[33]

When Lane's party arrived in the Rogue River valley, Lane said, he sent a messenger to the Indians; two days later Apserkahar (or Horse Rider)[34] came into Lane's camp to parley, accompanied by as many as one hundred men. They were unarmed, as Lane had demanded. But after the talking began another party of perhaps seventy-five men arrived, and they carried not only bows but about twenty firearms.[35] The general seems to have understood this as a display of hostility.

Lane tried to chastise Apserkahar and the others, but the wait for translations broke his rhythm.[36] His words probably had to be translated first into Chinook Jargon, the common language of trade in the Northwest, and then into the local language, because few Rogue River people spoke Chinook Jargon.[37]

At length, as Lane would tell the story, Apserkahar stood up and called for a demonstration from his supporters, which stimulated Lane into giving a prearranged signal to some of the Klickitats. They, with malice aforethought, had taken positions near Apserkahar. On the general's signal, the Klickitats took hold of Apserkahar and threw him on the ground, and Quatley threatened to slit his throat. Through his high-ranking hostage, Lane ordered the Rogue River valley men to disperse and to come back in two days with the property stolen from the miners. They did as they were told, Lane would recall, except that they claimed to have dumped the miners' gold dust out for the sake of the bags it was in, having had no idea the gold dust was valuable.[38]

The general seems to have swallowed this story whole; it would be, after all, an enormous joke on the Indians. But it was unreasonable to believe that the Rogue River valley peoples did not know what gold dust was even though Americans had been tramping through their country for almost two years for the express purpose of going to California to get gold dust.[39]

Lane recalled that after Apserkahar had been for a time in captivity, he asked to speak to Lane, and they had an exchange in Chinook Jargon: "He asked the interpreter the name of the white chief and requested me to come to him as he wanted to talk. As I walked up to him he said, 'Mika name Jo Lane?' I said, 'Nawitka,' which is 'Yes.' He said, 'I want you to give me your name, for,' said he, 'I have seen no man like you.' I told the interpreter to say to him that I would give him half my name, but not all; that he should be called Jo. He was much pleased, and to the day of his death he was known as Jo." A little later, the general would claim, he and Apserkahar made a pact; Apserkahar would let the whites pass through the valley unhindered, and Lane (although a lame duck) promised to send an agent to protect the Indians and to see that gifts were distributed annually thereafter.[40]

Lane's forceful negotiations were the first official contact between southwestern Oregon peoples and the federal government, and in some ways they foreshadowed what was to come. Lane was only the first official to come to them hoping to use them to promote his personal ends.

At about the same time that Jo Lane was negotiating with Apserkahar, a band of miners moved into the Illinois River valley, halfway across the Klamath Mountains between the Rogue River valley and the coast. Reports of their coming and going amounted to little more than rumors. They did not talk much about their accomplishment, which was the first discovery of gold in southwestern Oregon. They are supposed to have worked placer deposits—that is, gold-bearing gravels that can be mined with simple devices such as pans and sluice boxes. The river got its name, so the story goes, because several of the miners were from Illinois.[41] Their silence gave the Rogue River peoples a little more time than they might have had to learn how to deal with white outsiders, because no gold rush followed the Illinois River discovery. But it was only a little time.

The peace Jo Lane extorted from Apserkahar disappeared with the increase in traffic on the Oregon-California trail that came with the next spring. The growing tension did not embroil all whites, however. It was at about this time that Thomas Smith pitched a tent at what he called "the head" of the Rogue River valley (probably on Bear Creek) and began raising vegetables to sell to the miners in Yreka.[42] Smith took care to get the permission of the leader of the Indian people in the neighborhood, the man known as Tipsu Tyee.[43] This name was really a description in Chinook Jargon—it meant Bearded Chief. Although Typsu Tyee dealt with Smith to their apparent mutual satisfaction, he would soon become a symbol of Indian intransigence. Smith said he was "a half-Breed 5 feet and 6 or 7 inches high heavy Set and Compact built Powerfully musseled dark hazle eyes Brown hair and Sandy Chin whiskers which caused his People to call him Typsee Tyee or the bearded chief—he was brave but caushious and had more good trates than was common among Indians."[44]

Smith's peaceful integration into the valley by means of a personal treaty was nothing like the experience of the transients who kept insisting on the bad character of the native residents. The *Oregon Statesman*, a strongly Democratic newspaper that Massachusetts-born, twenty-six-year-old Asahel Bush had begun publishing in Oregon City in March,[45] reported on June 20, 1851, that Jacob Parsons, a blacksmith from Illinois, had been killed by the Indians in the vicinity of Rogue River. "Some pretended friendly Indians obtained permission to camp with him and his two comrades for the night," the paper said. "When the party fell asleep, they arose, stole the guns and shot Mr. Parsons." But this report was followed immediately by a postscript informing the readers that Parsons was alive and the man who had been killed was probably a man named David Dilley.[46]

Undeterred by the imprecision of his sources, Bush also reported a series of Indian attacks on the first, second, and third of June on travelers camped on Bear Creek at Willow Springs, about twenty miles south of the crossing of the Rogue River. According to the most dramatic and incredible of the accounts Bush offered, a party of thirty-two Oregonians led by one Dr. James McBride had been attacked at daybreak on June 3 by one hundred to three hundred Indians.

Each side, the newspaper reported, had about seventeen guns, and the rest of the Indians had bows and arrows. The fight had lasted four and one-half hours, until the leader of the Indians, whose name was given as Chucklehead, was killed. Six or seven Indians were said to have been killed and several wounded, whereas no one in McBride's party was killed and only one was wounded. The Indians got away with three of the party's horses, however, and also a pack mule carrying about fifteen hundred dollars' worth of property and gold dust.[47]

This account begs several questions, among them how, given the long-distance character of the fight, the members of the McBride party knew that they had been attacked by the chief Chucklehead (who is unmentioned elsewhere in the literature of conflict on the Rogue River), and precisely how they had avoided massacre against such fabulous odds.

The clashes reported in early June 1851 may have been related to the death of young David Dilley on the Rogue River the month before, which was not as illusory as the reported killing of Parsons.[48] After Dilley was killed, a punitive expedition made up of about thirty miners rode out of Yreka. The miners crossed the Siskiyous into the Rogue River valley and attacked a band of Indians at the Rogue River crossing,[49] then cut back across the mountains into California to make their mark on the Shastas and Tolowas.[50] Perhaps the McBride party had run afoul of a party of Rogue River men who were hunting these Yreka vigilantes.

Later that month two incidents took place, one on the coast and the other in the valley, which were far more serious and deadly than the McBride affair. Both grew from the desire of whites to control the routes between Oregon and California. The first involved a band of men who had been put ashore on the coast to set up a town.

According to the nineteenth-century Oregon historian Frances Fuller Victor, the operators of the Pacific Mail steamship line decided in 1851 that they wanted an Oregon port nearer to San Francisco than Astoria, on the Columbia River. So the company hired William Tichenor, a thirty-six-year-old New Jersey-born miner turned sea captain, to establish a settlement at a place to be called Port Orford, twenty-eight miles north of the mouth of the Rogue River.[51] Tichenor and four other men, among them craggy-faced, forty-five-year-old William G. T'Vault, who seven years before had been the first editor of Oregon's first newspaper, the *Spectator*,[52] would be the proprietors of Port Orford.[53]

There are two distinctly different versions of what happened next. According to the story told by J. M. Kirkpatrick, who described himself as captain of the landing party, the inhabitants of the country who oberved Tichenor's initial landing on June 9 of nine men and a four-pound cannon were somewhat friendly and seemed to want to trade, but their attitude changed after the steamer left. Then, Kirkpatrick said, the Indians "grew saucy and ordered us off." The would-be colonizers planted themselves on "a small island or rock" and the next morning repulsed about forty Indians, killing half of them. In the afternoon, a leader of the

Indians came to have a conference, and Kirkpatrick supposed that he had communicated by signs that his party would leave in fourteen days.

No one came to take them away, however, and on the morning of the fifteenth day, according to Kirkpatrick, the Indians attacked again. But after an ineffectual exchange of shots and arrows at three hundred yards, the Indians went away. The would-be colonizers decided the time had come to escape from their perch on what would become known as Battle Rock.

The nine Americans walked for two days and nights to what Kirkpatrick told the readers of the *Statesman* was the mouth of the Rogue River[54] but probably was the Coquille[55]; the fugitives were going north toward the Coquille, not south toward the Rogue. After five more days they reached the mouth of the Coos River, where, Kirkpatrick said, they found friendly Indians who gave them food. But to get these Indians to ferry them across the mouth of the river, he said, "we had to give them the shirts off our backs."

Kirkpatrick had mistaken the Coos for the Umpqua River, which is about twenty miles north of the Coos, and spent a futile day on a twenty-mile hike looking for two newly established white towns on the Umpqua. On the following day, the eighth day after they had fled from Port Orford, Kirkpatrick and his men finally reached the white settlements on the Umpqua.[56]

The alternative to Kirkpatrick's story was written by Anson Dart, who was superintendent of Indian affairs for Oregon in 1851.[57] Dart did not write his somewhat garbled account until more than twenty years after the Port Orford fight. It was published in the *San Francisco Chronicle* during the Modoc War in northern California when that paper was taking a position sympathetic to Indian people. Dart said he went to Port Orford (which he misplaced about twenty miles north of the California border) aboard the steamer *Sea Gull* about two weeks after learning of what had been represented to him as the massacre of a white settlement. "The first fact that I learned was, instead of an Indian massacre of a white settlement, it was an atrocious massacre of peaceable and friendly Indians," he said.

The landing party had included about sixty Californians. Eight men were sent immediately to look for a route into the Rogue River country. About thirty Indians came down to the shore and helped unload the boat that had brought the landing party. Dart said the whites brought ashore two brass six-pound cannon, "one of which, with the assistance of the Indians, was taken to the top of a large rock, standing three sides in the water. The only approach to it was a narrow way from the land side."

The cannon was pointed down the narrow path, and the Indians were told "a little before dark" to go to the rock to get their pay. "When all the Indians were on the narrow way," Dart said, "the piece of cannon was discharged by one of the parties who came up on the schooner." Twenty-two Indians were killed, and the rest escaped by jumping into the ocean. The next morning "more than two hundred Indians, all painted for war, appeared in the vicinity and exhibited unmistakable signs of hostility." The Californians "hastened on board of the schooner and put out to sea, leaving the eight men of the exploring party to take care of themselves."

Dart went on to confuse the trek made by Kirkpatrick and his comrades with an expedition led by T'Vault from the interior later in the year. Garbled though his account was, he was clear about the heart of the matter concerning the "battle" of what would soon be known as Battle Rock; the cause was not an Indian effort to drive off the foreigners, as Dart saw it, but rather a deliberate and unprovoked attack by the foreigners.[58]

Kirkpatrick's own description of Captain Tichenor's attitude toward the Indian peoples supports the Dart version. When Tichenor recruited him in Portland, Kirkpatrick said, "He told me that there was not a particle of danger from the Indians, that he had been ashore among them many times and they were perfectly friendly." When Kirkpatrick asked for arms for defense against them, Tichenor insisted again that there was no danger and gave the men only three flintlock muskets and a rusty sword. Kirkpatrick and some of his men had brought their own weapons, however; Kirkpatrick had an army-issue rifle bought at the last minute that "proved to be a magnificent shooting gun," plus a pair of derringers.[59]

When they landed on the beach at Port Orford, Kirkpatrick said, the few Indians in sight appeared friendly. Nonetheless, Kirkpatrick told

Tichenor that he "did not like the looks of things at all and those Indians meant mischief." Kirkpatrick asked Tichenor for the cannon on the *Sea Gull*. "He laughed at us at first for wanting it, but when we told him we wouldn't stay without it he studied a bit and then said all right he would send it ashore."[60]

On June 17, eight days after the landing at Port Orford, a detachment of regular army dragoons commanded by Maj. Philip Kearny was reported by the *Statesman* to have been attacked by a party of Indians near Table Rock in the Rogue River valley. Two officers were killed together with about twenty Indian people. The attack had come during an exploration to find a new route through the Umpqua canyon directed by the pathfinders Jesse Applegate and Levi Scott.[61] This account in the *Statesman*, accurate as far as it went, did not include significant information disclosed in Kearny's report.

Kearny was a one-armed millionaire who had ridden with French chasseurs in North Africa and served as bodyguard to General Winfield Scott in the Mexican War. He would die in combat in 1862 at Chantilly, Virginia, as a major general in the Union army.[62] According to his report, he and his dragoons were the aggressors, not the Rogue River Indians.

The major said that when the dragoons and the road surveyors they were escorting from Fort Vancouver to San Francisco Bay reached the north end of the Umpqua Canyon, where the trail southward began its climb through the sixty hardest miles between the Columbia and the Siskiyous, he was met by a deputation of citizens who gave him a petition asking him to clear the trail southward of Indians they considered hostile. Kearny agreed.

He said he decided to surprise the Indians in the Rogue River valley "at their fisheries if possible." He sent his baggage train through the canyon by the usual route and swung around to the east. Kearny said, "I penetrated the mountain by a new route, placing myself in the rear of the presumed situation of this Tribe. I thus hoped with my small force of 67 men to break them up before they could combine in numbers or disperse entirely." After a five-day march, Kearny's cut-down squadron arrived at the Rogue River on June 17.

Kearny failed to catch the Indian people unaware. "Signals and Cries Convinced us that we had been expected and our movements watched," he reported. "Our Column took the gallop trusting to anticipate the Indian Scouts." Kearny was not clear about what happened next, but he apparently sent a detachment under Captain James Stuart across the river to intercept a few Indians who were crossing to escape from the dragoons at the head of the column. Stuart got into "a brisk skirmish. . . . A charge brilliant in itself, but most costly to us, as it resulted in the death of its most distinguished leader who fell mortally wounded whilst heading his men."

A detachment under Captain I. G. Walker that had crossed the river just in time to see Stuart killed kept moving down the opposite bank. Kearny set up camp for the wounded and then pressed on with the seventeen men still available to him, intending to make a diversion to help Walker's men. "After passing on some miles," Kearny said, "a smoke at a distance, which proved to be a signal fire, led me to suppose that Captain Walker had destroyed some village."

Kearny prepared to catch the refugees from the attack he thought Walker had made, but he found himself facing instead of refugees "a powerful war party of 250 to 300 Indians." The major's description of his response was coy: "Fortunately a small isolated clump of trees gave me a strong position and concealed my numbers."

Having declined to fight, Kearny retreated southward. Walker's detachment and the baggage train Kearny had left behind at the north end of the Umpqua canyon joined the major at his camp two days after Stuart's fatal skirmish. The major sent Lieutenant C. E. Irvine together with the local guides Levi Scott and Jesse Applegate to the Shasta mines in California for volunteers. Kearny stayed in camp waiting for the reinforcements from the mines, but "the desultory bonds of a mining community caused a comparatively small number to volunteer." He had only about one hundred more men when he led his force out on the night of June 22 hoping to catch his enemies in the dark, but he failed because the sun rose too soon.

Kearny's men spent the next two days attacking such Indians as they could find and destroying Indian camps. Jo Lane arrived in the valley on

June 24 to lend his support. "We spent the next three days in making a circuit around the stronghold near Table Rock," Kearny reported. He had taken more than thirty women and children prisoner and predicted, "They will prove useful in effecting a treaty or holding the Indians in check." He added, "It was impossible to spare the men as they combat with desperation to the last—meeting any advances with treachery."[63]

Joseph Lane claimed that the Indian people were "completely whipped in every fight" and that about fifty were killed and many others wounded. Lane also told of "a conversation with a considerable number of Indians, across the river, who gave me a terrible account of the invasion of their country by our people." Lane said they told him "that they now were afraid to lay down to sleep, for fear the white people would be on them before they could wake—that they were tired of war, and now wanted peace."

An entirely different view of the temper of the Indian people after Kearny's invasion appeared opposite Lane's account on the facing page of the *Statesman*. A correspondent signing himself Ewald, in a letter dated July 12 from the recently established village of Scottsburg on the lower Umpqua River, said that Governor Gaines had camped on the Rogue River and was negotiating with some of the Indians, but those who wanted to make peace "receive abuse from the war party. It is hoped by some that the Governor will accomplish his object, because the majority of Indians are desirous of giving battle to the whites." The *Statesman* also reported that packers who had visited Gaines's camp had reported that "several chiefs have come in, but the leader was not among them. . . . It was reported that he had gone up the coast to rally the Indians for the purpose of retaking the prisoners."[64]

The clashes that led up to Kearny's expedition against the Rogue River people had been predicted some three months before by Anson Dart, the Oregon superintendent of Indian affairs. Dart had tried to head them off by ordering Indian Service agent H. H. Spalding to take up a station on the Umpqua River where he could intercept the Oregonians on their way to the mines in California "and urge upon them the necessity of not molesting the Indians on Rogue river or elsewhere." Dart was persuaded that clashes could be avoided with "a more conciliatory course" and hoped that Spalding could prevent "that state of things transpiring in Oregon that had produced so much bloodshed and misery in Northern California."[65]

Dart would complain later that Spalding had failed to get to his post on time, but the superintendent also admitted, "I do not suppose, however, that it would have been in the power of one man to entirely prevent the difficulty amongst men who look upon Indians as intruders and having no more rights in this country than wild beasts."[66] Governor Gaines, while camped on the Rogue River, wrote to Dart that an agent was needed there to deal with "infamous white men" because "all the difficulties here are justly attributable to the latter class of persons if my information can be relied upon."[67]

Alonzo Skinner, a thirty-seven-year-old lawyer from Ohio[68] who went to the Rogue River as Indian agent in November, reported to Dart that he had met with Jo—that is, Apserkahar—and Apserkahar's brother Sam—that is, Toquahear.[69] "I have been very favorably impressed," Skinner said. "They appear entirely friendly, and to have sufficient intelligence to see that neither they nor their people have anything to gain by hostility with the whites."[70]

On the coast, the second invasion of the site of Port Orford, about two weeks after the clash at Battle Rock, was more successful than the first. Captain Tichenor had been delayed by creditors in San Francisco who seized the *Sea Gull*.[71] After resolving his financial difficulties, Tichenor steamed back to the site and landed seventy men and four cannon.[72]

In the Rogue River valley, meanwhile, Governor Gaines was making what Frances Fuller Victor called an "altogether informal" treaty by which some one hundred men supposedly "placed themselves under the jurisdiction and protection of the United States." They agreed to restore property taken from whites and in return "received back their wives and children and any property taken from them."[73]

Asahel Bush of the Democratic *Statesman* condemned the Whig governor and his treaty and quoted an unnamed person, "one of the most intelligent and reliable citizens of Umpqua," who objected to the treaty provision giving the Indians restitution for horses and mules taken from

Toquahear, or Wealthy, identified as "Sam, Shasta chief," is shown in a sketch made on the Grande Ronde Reservation in April 1856 by E. Girardin. Toquahear took part in treaty negotiations in 1853 and 1854 and, in October 1855, became the leader of the Rogue River valley peoples who declined to go to war in October 1855 and were moved to Grande Ronde in early 1856. (National Archives of Canada)

Mary, a Shasta girl, was also sketched by Girardin in 1856. She was probably Toquahear's niece, the daughter of his brother Apserkahar, who was called Jo by white people. Joseph Lane said in his autobiography that he had held Mary and her brother as hostages during treaty negotiations in 1853. The marks on her chin are tattoos. (National Archives of Canada)

them by white people. He said, "It is a well known fact that these Indians have come into the possession of such property only by robbery and theft."[74]

The conflict on the coast was not entirely finished. In pursuit of the route to the interior that was needed to make Port Orford a success, coowner William G. T'Vault set out with either eighteen or twenty-three men, depending upon the account, on August 24. The inept explorers rode south to the Rogue River on the beaches and then tried to find their way through the mountains by way of the river canyon. When their rations ran out, thirteen men turned back. T'Vault and the remainder of his company reached the Big Bend of the Rogue River, killed an elk, and found a trail that T'Vault apparently believed they could take north to the Umpqua River.[75]

On the way north they lost their horses, but they made their way to the middle fork of the Mishikhwutme (the Coquille River), where they found Indians whom they somehow got to take them downriver in canoes. But when the party got to a village near the mouth of the river on September 14, the Americans were attacked. Five of the ten remaining Americans were killed. T'Vault was one of the survivors.[76]

Neither of the two accounts of this event, one by T'Vault and the other by another survivor, Lorin L. Williams, suggests why the people who found them on the middle fork of the Coquille would have voluntarily taken them perhaps fifty miles downstream before attacking them. Like Lansford Hastings and the men in the McBride party, T'Vault and Williams seem to have left out some element necessary to make sense of the rest of the story. Perhaps T'Vault had compelled the cooperation of the people who took him downstream and the attack was made to free them. Perhaps there was no attack at all but only a misunderstanding in the minds of the fatigued and frightened white men.

On the same day that T'Vault's band fought with the Coquilles, Anson Dart arrived in Port Orford with Lt. August Kautz and twenty dragoons sent to establish an army post.[77] Dart made two treaties on September 20. In the treaty with four "chiefs and headmen of the Yoyotan, Youqueechee, and Qua-ton-wah bands of Indians," Dart promised twenty-five hundred dollars' worth of clothing and other goods every year for ten years. In return the "chiefs and headmen" were said to have ceded all the land between the Rogue and Coquille Rivers up to the crest of the Coast Range (roughly six hundred square miles). According to Article 2, "the said bands of Indians shall have free and unmolested possession of the ground now occupied by their houses, and upon which they now reside, during the ten years in which they receive their annuities." They were also to be free "to fish as they have heretofore done."[78]

Dart's second treaty of September 20, similarly written, purchased the land for twenty miles south of the Rogue (about four hundred square miles) from five "chiefs and headmen of the Ya-su-chah band of Indians" for the delivery of goods worth $350 every year for ten years.[79]

There was no peace, however, for the Mishikhwutmetunne—that is, the Coquille Indians, who were accused of attacking the T'Vault party. In late October, 130 soldiers and 87 horses and mules were brought to Port Orford aboard the *Columbia* and the *Sea Gull*. They had been sent from San Francisco Bay by the commanding general of the Department of the Pacific, Ethan Allen Hitchcock, to punish the Coquilles for the attack.[80]

After a failed attempt to land troops at the mouth of the Coquille delayed the expedition, Col. Silas Casey got about 60 men to the river's mouth by land from Port Orford. An unidentified soldier wrote in a letter later published in the *Statesman* that the march took four days and the soldiers "met with nothing but deserted lodges, swamps and mountains almost impassable."[81]

At the mouth of the Coquille were boats the colonel had ordered sent by sea from Port Orford. He split his command, sending one boat up the middle fork and the other boat up the south fork. On November 21, a few miles up the south fork, the troops finally found Indians to punish, and the following day the whole command attacked their camp, Casey supposedly shouting, "Boys, take good sight, throw no shots away, give them hell!" Two privates were mortally wounded. The soldier who had written the letter drowned a few days afterward while acting as a messenger.[82] The casualties suffered by the Mishikhwutmetunne were estimated as fifteen.[83]

The history of the beginnings of intense contact between Americans and the southwestern Oregon Indian peoples can be interpreted as being about pioneering Americans fighting back irrational savages to secure lines of communication necessary for the expansion of civilization. That reading, however, requires putting complete faith in the accounts of the likes of J. M. Kirkpatrick, who went looking for trouble and found it.

A more reasonable interpretation suggests that the Indian peoples were generally willing to tolerate white people coming among them, but also that they were quick to respond when trouble came. Johnson and Winter found them eager to trade. Hastings, notwithstanding his suspicions and his use of firearms to frighten them, found them willing to ferry travelers across the Rogue River. Thomas Smith found the supposedly most recalcitrant of their leaders, Tipsu Tyee, honorable and friendly. The experienced Captain Tichenor did not expect the people at Port Orford to oppose his town-building scheme. According to Anson Dart, they were even willing to help Tichenor's men, up to a point.

It would seem, then, that the Indian peoples were adapting to the new world closing in around them, but their adaptation had two faces. They might be friendly and take encounters with whites as opportunities to acquire articles of white manufacture by trading or working for them. Or, under different circumstances, they might gather in small armies and use the white-manufactured firearms they had been able to get to try to drive off people who threatened them, perhaps acquiring white goods, and horses and beef, by capture. Their reputation among non-Indians, however, had only one face, the face of a dangerous predator.

3

Invasion in Force

The clashes with travelers, the conflict with the dragoons, the confrontations at Port Orford, and the subsequent attack on the Coquilles all grew out of white efforts to control lines of communication. Until the beginning of 1852, southwestern Oregon was important to white people only because it lay between two areas occupied by them. Only a few whites, such as Thomas Smith, went there to stay. Then came the discovery of gold, followed by an influx of miners. That influx was distinct from the California gold rush only in that it took place north of the forty-second parallel, the border between California and Oregon.

The whites who would invade the Rogue River valley over the next few years belonged to a class that sometimes called themselves "argonauts," after the crew that hunted the Golden Fleece in Greek mythology. They were not typical or representative of the American society they had left behind. One of their modern chroniclers has said that the gold rush that brought them to the West "was a heroic exercise of wit and will, and reference to the dawn world of Greek myth was as good a way as any to suggest that there was something primal and immemorial going on." In the California of the gold rush, "the bottom fell out of the 19th century" and Americans "returned en masse to primitive and brutal conditions, to a Homeric world of journeys, shipwreck, labor, treasure, killing and chieftainship."[1]

In this makeshift society, Indian people were frequent targets of vigilantes. In the spring of 1852, an Indian Service agent, Redick McKee, got into an acrimonious exchange with Gov. John Bigler of California over the behavior of certain miners in northern California. The governor had remonstrated against McKee's charge that killings of Indian people by vigilantes near Eureka, on the northern California coast, had "brought lasting disgrace on the American name."[2]

McKee responded that the governor must have been aware that "if a pack-train is attacked or robbed, if a corral in one of the valleys is broken into and robbed, the conclusion is instantly reached that the Indians are the aggressors: the Oregon rifle or the Pike county revolver is at once called into requisition, and the first red skins met with are made to pay the penalty."

McKee said that in the Shasta country the previous autumn, a series of robberies had almost provoked a war of extermination before the miners discovered that the Shastas had been holding talks with him when the robberies were committed. At that point, "the idea was broached, apparently for the first time, that *possibly* they were not *guilty*." Pursuers later caught up with the robbers, who were white, on the road to Salt Lake.

McKee argued that much of the problem grew out of the presence on the California frontier of "great numbers of *Mexicans, Chilians, Sydneyites, and renegades from justice in the old States*, wholly undeserving to be classed with American citizens."[3] About the best the governor could do by way of a rejoinder was to deny that the United States government was responsible for the behavior of foreigners or that renegades from justice could disgrace the American name.[4]

The California legislature had given its support to privately organized campaigns against Indian peoples by ordering state bonds sold to pay wages to the "volunteers" and reimburse their suppliers. By 1852, the legislature had authorized the sale of $1.1 million in bonds. The state had built up an Indian-fighting debt of more than nine hundred thousand dollars by 1854 (the equivalent of about eighteen million dollars in current terms). This debt would eventually be paid by the federal government.[5] In effect, the state had authorized pork-barrel wars, providing work to miners when mining was going poorly or or when the miners were bored with it.

Even as Redick McKee and Governor Bigler argued over violence against Indians, the rough-cut, heroic-minded society that had produced the outrages that troubled McKee was being carried across the forty-second parallel into Oregon by young men hungry for gold. The details of the discovery of gold in the Rogue River valley are disputed. One historian said it was found by a man named Sykes in February 1852. Another credited a man named Cluggage, who was said to have found it in January while chasing two missing mules. According to yet another version, it was first found in December 1851 near a campsite on the Oregon-California trail that would soon become the site of the town of Jacksonville.[6]

The largest conflict between the miners and the original inhabitants in the first summer after the discovery originated in the northern California mining districts. Indian Service agent Alonzo Skinner said that the murder of a white man there on July 8, 1852, provoked "a war of extermination" against the Shastas in California. When Indians in the Rogue River valley heard about what was happening, they were excited and alarmed.

A sometime physician named George Ambrose had set himself up in the Rogue River valley about two miles from Big Bar on the Rogue River, near the village of Sam, or Toquahear. Skinner described Toquahear as "the principal war-chief of the Indians of this valley." At about the same time that the white man was killed in northern California, Toquahear was said to have gone to Ambrose and ordered him to leave because Toquahear had already sold the land there to William G. T'Vault. He also frightened Ambrose by proposing "to trade two Indian children and a horse and some money for a little girl of Dr. Ambrose, about two years of age," Skinner said.

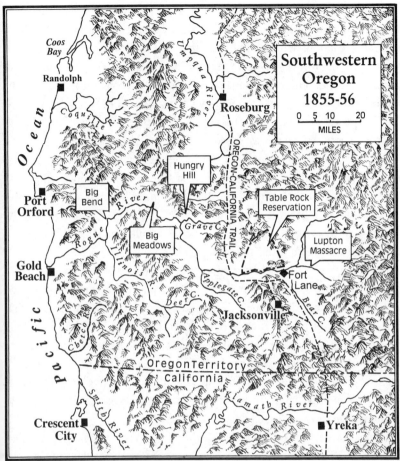

Southwestern Oregon, 1855–56. In October of 1855, self-styled volunteers led by James Lupton attacked a group of Indian people on Butte Creek, in the east end of the Rogue River valley, setting off the Rogue River War. By the middle of 1856 most Indian people in southwestern Oregon had been forcibly removed to the Coast Reservation.

On July 15, the agent added, some white travelers camped near Ambrose's house were confronted by a party of angry Indians who were said to have complained about whites killing Indians in California. They added that whites in the Rogue River valley had also done wrong by the Indian people and they intended to make the whites do right in the future. The whites who heard these statements went into Jacksonville and told what had happened in such a way that "great excitement" was felt, and a company of about 80 men was raised to fight the Indians.

Skinner went to Jacksonville to persuade the prospective Indian fighters to hold back until he could speak to the Rogue River people. The Jacksonville men nonetheless rode out to the Ambrose house but gave Skinner a little time to talk with Toquahear before attacking. Toquahear said he was not angry with the whites. He said he would send for all his people to come to a meeting the following day.

At about 9 A.M. on the morning of July 16, Skinner was confronted at his camp near Big Bar by a party of ten or twelve Californians who had a Rogue River man with them. They said they had come to demand that the Rogue River people turn over to them the Indian who had killed the white man in California. The alleged killer was supposed to have fled to the Rogue River valley. Learning that they had "arrested" the Rogue River man who was with them, Skinner demanded his release. The Californians refused. An hour later, the company raised in Jacksonville came into Skinner's camp.

Skinner said he crossed the river and went up to the camp of Apserkahar and Toquahear, a mile and a half away, where he persuaded them to go back with him. But at the crossing, they found the whites "all mounted and drawn up in a line, facing the river, and in range of the Indians as they crossed the river. Joe and Sam immediately inquired why the men were drawn up in that order."

Skinner somehow talked the whites into stacking their arms and sitting on the ground, and Toquahear and Apserkahar crossed, but few of the Rogue River people who had followed them to the crossing were willing to follow them across the river. The whites, said Skinner, seemed restless and determined to attack. Toquahear, and then the agent, crossed back to persuade the rest of the Rogue River people to go to the other side, and Toquahear told Skinner they would all cross to where the whites were waiting as soon as some late arrivals reached the crossing from his camp upriver.

At that point, two friends of Skinner crossed the river and told him that the whites were about to attack. When he went back across the river, he found most of the white men mounted. They refused his request for further delay and proposed to begin by shooting down the twenty or twenty-five Indians who had come across to their side of the river. Skinner had convinced them to settle for making the Indians prisoners, when one Indian tried to escape and a Californian fired at him.

"The firing now became pretty general upon both sides," Skinner said. Four of the prisoners were killed. No whites were injured. Skinner himself, "not being disposed to take part in hostilities commenced under circumstances such as herein related," went home. He informed Indian Service superintendent Anson Dart that when the Indians fled down the river they were pursued for about twenty-five miles. He was told that the vigilantes had attacked and dispersed several small parties and killed two or three people.

Toquahear took up a position in "an almost impenetrable thicket on the bank of the river near Table Rock," but on July 21 he came into the Indian Service agency and agreed to end the fighting. Four days later, most of Toquahear's people were still camped near the agency and seemed to Skinner to be friendly.[7] If they felt murderous impulses, they kept them to themselves, but the same could not be said of their white neighbors. More than a hundred men, and twenty-two women, honored the Jacksonville volunteers at a dinner held July 25, where J. W. Davenport offered a toast that concluded with a wish that his listeners would "live to see the time when the Indians of Rogue River are extinct."[8] By honoring men for hunting people as if they were wolves, the community was suggesting that little if any provocation would be needed to set in motion the inevitable next action against the Rogue River people.

In the spring of 1853 the federal government gave the Indian people a new protector. He was the one-time guidebook author Joel Palmer. His appointment as federal superintendent for Indian affairs in Oregon would test whether a well-liked, conscientious, competent man with links to the dominant Democratic leadership could make federal policy an influence on the course of Indian affairs in the territory. A former canal builder and twice a member of the Indiana legislature, Palmer had, at the age of thirty-five, become captain of one of the wagon trains that traveled to Oregon in 1845. He had been commissary-general of volunteers in the Cayuse War, an Indian war fought east of the Cascades by Oregon's provisional government, and thus was often called General Palmer. He was a town founder and a capitalist.[9]

The new western reservation policy that Palmer would try to carry out was still being formed, although it had been emerging since the Mexican War. Indian affairs commissioner William Medill presented a tentative version of the reservation concept in his 1848 report. Medill suggested that the government set up two Indian colonies on the Great Plains, one on the headwaters of the Mississippi River and the other on the western borders of Missouri and Arkansas. This would leave a corridor for white expansion in the middle of the Plains. The peoples restricted to the two colonies would be moved toward assimilation through training in agriculture and other aspects of civilization. The government would save money because fewer agents would be needed when the Indian peoples were concentrated on less land.[10]

Sen. Stephen A. Douglas, looking toward clearing a route for a transcontinental railroad, asked at the end of 1849 for a Senate Indian affairs committee inquiry into the reservation idea. Indian affairs commissioner Luke Lea said in his 1850 report that tribes should be compelled to settle in permanent, well-defined territories where the government would encourage their members to take up farming. By the summer of 1851, officials responsible for Indian affairs had developed what historian Robert A. Trennert, Jr., called "a definite reservation psychology," and the concept had broad support throughout the West.[11] Tentative efforts to put the idea into practice quickly failed in Texas, but another attempt was made in New Mexico beginning in the spring of 1852.[12]

Invasion in Force

George Manypenny, who succeeded Lea as Indian affairs commissioner, set out the principles of the new reservation policy in his 1853 annual report. His plan was a development of the proposal made by Lea, adding the principle of isolation from whites and putting more stress on promoting agriculture. Manypenny planned to place western Indians "in suitable locations, limited in extent and distant as possible from white settlements, and to teach and aid them to devote themselves to the cultivation of the soil and the raising of stock."

Manypenny recognized that the reservation approach to resolving the government's problems with Indians "would be attended with considerable cost at the outset, as will any other that can be suggested for their safety and permanent welfare," but he expected them to become self-supporting and argued that "the expenses would diminish from year to year." Moreover, no other plan would save the western Indians "from dire calamities, if not entire extermination."[13]

Earlier colonizers had tried similar systems. The Puritan "Apostle to the Indians," John Eliot, began establishing his system of missions or "praying towns" in Massachusetts in 1646. Eliot intended to train Indian people in "visible civility." One of Eliot's missionary colleagues said that by 1674, the system included fourteen towns with eleven hundred residents. But "praying Indians" were among the first to fight the Puritans in 1675 in the conflict the Puritans called King Philip's War.[14]

In 1769, Franciscans set up the first of their missions in Alta California. Colonial authorities expected these missions to serve the usual purpose of missions in the Spanish empire—that is, they would bring the Indian peoples and their lands under Spanish control and eventually make the Indians into ordinary colonial subjects, speaking Spanish, practicing Catholicism, and eschewing the traditions of their ancestors.

The missionaries forced Indians to live in poor conditions and often brutalized them. Epidemic diseases prospered. Mission inmates frequently rebelled and escaped. And the Mexican colonial government of California pulled the system apart in 1834 after years of pressure from non-Indians who wanted mission lands for themselves.[15]

The theorists who developed the American reservation concept ignored the poor results of these earlier efforts. Neither Indian resistance nor non-Indian land hunger was significant in their ruminations. Commissioner Manypenny even supposed that the reservation system would stabilize the Indian land base. He said in 1855 that reservations would soon be recognized as "an inevitable necessity." American settlers would soon understand that the Indians' new homes were "settled, fixed, and permanent" and would come to consider the Indians their friends and neighbors. Indians, in turn, would "cease to regard the white man with that restless doubt and distrust which has been so disastrous to [their] comfort and peace and so fatal to [their] civilization and improvement."[16]

Joel Palmer signified his agreement with the reservation policy in a letter dated June 23, in which he said the "aborigines" should be given "a home, remote from the settlements," where they could be "guarded from the influence of pestiferous whitemen." They should have comfortable houses, he added, schools, and instruction in farming and Christianity, and if they were not elevated, at least an honest effort would have been made to save "a fallen race."[17]

Palmer was given the responsibility for implementing the new policy in Oregon because of the election of Democrat Franklin Pierce of New Hampshire as president over the Whig nominee, Winfield Scott. The change in administrations meant a wholesale turnover of political power in the Oregon Territory after Pierce took office in March 1853. On April 30, an exultant Asahel Bush announced to the readers of the *Statesman* that the brig *Sophia* had arrived in the Columbia River from San Francisco five days before, carrying word that the new president had all but swept out the territory's appointed Whig officialdom. Bush predicted that the remainder would be ousted shortly. Replacing John Gaines as governor was Joseph Lane, but on the same page Bush trumpeted Lane as a candidate for reelection as territorial delegate in Congress.[18]

General Lane arrived in Oregon on May 16, resigned as governor on May 19, and actively entered the contest for delegate. His return to Washington and his chances for increasing his national reputation were at stake. His opponent was Alonzo Skinner. Bush bragged on June 4, two days before the election, that "wherever Skinner has *attempted* to make a speech he has lost votes" and that "Gen. Lane's *old hat* (and he wears a '*shocking bad*' one) could effect more for the Territory at Washington than Skinner could."[19] Frances Fuller Victor would call the election "a warm one, with all the chances in favor of Lane." The general "could easily gain the favor of even the whigs of southern Oregon by fighting Indians." Skinner, on the other hand, "was not a fighting man." Lane got more than three-fifths of the recorded votes.[20]

Safely elected, the general rode south to the Umpqua River valley, where he had taken up a land claim near the trail to California. He took the claim, he said many years later, because of the grass and water. "It just suited my taste. Instead of investing in Portland and making my fortune, I wanted to please my fancy."[21] Lane's new home would prove conveniently near the Rogue River valley, where he would soon take the lead in a fresh conflict.

During the summer of 1853, an excitement developed over the disappearance of seven miners who had been living at the west end of the valley on an island in the Rogue River. Indians had come in saying the miners had been drowned during the spring when high water washed over the island. They were not believed. Vigilantes hanged four Rogue River men. One of them, a headman called Taylor, was said to have confessed to the alleged massacre. Two more Rogue River men were shot after the vigilantes tied their hands behind their backs and ordered them to run.[22]

The next killing blamed on the Rogue River peoples was committed about two months later. A man named Edwards was killed at his cabin a few miles from Jacksonville, probably on August 4. T. McF. Patton, who described himself as orderly sergeant in the Jacksonville volunteers, reported that late on the night of August 4, the Jackson County coroner held an inquest, and a twelve-man jury determined that Edwards had been shot near the center of his spine, that his head had been nearly cut in two with an axe, and that an attempt had been made to cut his throat with a dull knife. The jury decided that Edwards had been killed by Indians. Patton did not explain what evidence supported that conclusion.

Patton said that volunteer troops "immediately started out and in a short time returned with a captive 'Siwash Tyee' [Indian leader], who was mustered to an oak tree and there 'strung up.' During the day, three others were hung beside the Tyee." Patton added that the whites were right to kill these men because their leaders, Apserkahar and Toquahear, had harbored "murdering and plundering" Indians.

The death of Edwards marked the beginning of a series of incidents that Patton blamed on the Rogue River peoples. He listed a yoke of cattle found dead, two burglaries, the wounding with arrows of two men—one the senior county commissioner of Jackson County—the wounding of a Jacksonville merchant with a firearm, and, the following day, the fatal shooting of a man named Rhodes Noland within a mile of town.[23]

The *Oregon Statesman* viewed the killing of Edwards as the signal of an "avowed determination to exterminate the whites, and regain possession of the country." The *Statesman* described the Rogue River peoples as well-armed and supplied with ammunition. "They have long been trading with the miners and emigrants for rifles, muskets, pistols, powder, lead, &c." Their leaders had gathered three hundred to four hundred men at Table Rock and had declared that "they will fight till the last Indian is dead, if they are not victorious."[24]

The *Statesman* reprinted two indicative paragraphs from the *Yreka Herald*:

> The present outbreak has justly led all to the conclusion that *extermination is the only way to secure peace.* We have "drawn the sword and thrown the scabbard away," and the tomahawk will no longer be buried, but in the skulls of the red foe.
> Let it be our last difficulty with Indians in this section of the country. They have commenced the work with their own accord and without just cause. Let our motto be *EXTERMINATION! and death to all opposition, white men or indians!*[25]

Three white men were arrested on Applegate Creek for providing arms and ammunition to the Indians, according to the *Statesman*, and three more white men "living with squaws" had been accused of providing not only arms but also instruction in their use.[26]

Capt. B. R. Alden of the regular army, stationed at Fort Jones in northern California, reported that his command became involved on August 7 when he received a petition from Jacksonville claiming that whites in the Rogue River valley "were threatened by a combination of several tribes of Indians, numbering about 250 warriors armed with rifles, and well supplied with ammunition." Half of Alden's twenty-two men were sick, he said, but nonetheless he packed twenty-five muskets, five carbines, and six hundred rounds of ammunition on mules and, with ten men (all who could be spared), marched to Yreka, where he enrolled eighty volunteers. Alden's command proceeded over the Siskiyous into Oregon, and on August 11 at Camp Stewart, about seven miles southeast of Jacksonville, he enrolled another 110 volunteers.

Alden planned to attack the Rogue River peoples, who were believed to be near Table Rock, only about ten miles from Camp Stewart. But the attack misfired when, at dusk, a rider came in announcing that Indians had appeared in force in the valley, killed two white men, and burned a house and several haystacks. The volunteers dispersed in panic.[27]

The rumor did not stop the fighting. A small party of volunteers was said by the *Statesman* to have been ambushed the following day on Applegate Creek by two hundred or three hundred Indians. More volunteers had been raised, and all the miners who could get arms and ammunition were reported to be "out hunting Indians." The newspaper reported that "Indians are shot down wherever they are found. Martin Angell, late of Oregon City, shot one from his door." One man said that he saw the bodies of ten or twelve Indians lying by the side of the road north of Jacksonville.[28]

Captain Alden finally gathered enough volunteers for a coordinated campaign on August 16. He was told that the Rogue River valley peoples had gone into the mountains. He organized a pack train and "made every preparation to pursue the Indians wherever they were to be found." On August 20, Alden turned his command over to Gen. Joseph Lane.[29]

Lane later reported that he had learned on August 17 that the Rogue River Indians, helped by Klamaths and Shastas, had united to attack the settlements in the Rogue River Valley. The general said he headed south with about fifteen men and reached Alden's camp on August 21. (The Klamaths in this case were not Klamaths in the modern sense—that is, members of the Klamath tribe of central southern Oregon, east of the Cascades—but Shasta people from the Klamath River country in northern California.[30])

Five companies of volunteers had been scouring the country and the allied Indians had fled into the mountains to the north, Lane said. On August 22, he ordered four companies of volunteers northward. Two companies under volunteer colonel John Ross went up Evans Creek, which flows down from the hills north of Table Rock and then turns west to meet the river about fifteen miles downstream. Lane and the other two companies climbed up into the hills north of Table Rock by another trail. About fifteen miles north of Table Rock, Lane found the trail the Indians had used. Early the next morning, he led his command through a country that "was exceedingly mountainous and almost impassable for animals, and as the Indians had fired the country behind them, the falling of the burning timber, and the heat delayed our progress."

On the morning of August 24, Lane's men crossed Evans Creek and then climbed a steep mountain, Lane said. He moved forward until he "could hear persons talking in their camp, about four hundred yards distant, in a dense forest, thick with underbrush which entirely obstructed the view." The men coming up behind him "were ordered in a low voice to dismount, tie their animals, and prepare for battle."

The general ordered Alden's regulars to attack the Indians in the front while a volunteer company hit their right flank. The men took cover behind the trees "and the fight became general." He found Alden badly wounded. He led a charge to within thirty yards of the defenders and was hit by a rifle ball that passed through his right arm and shoulder. Thinking his men were being attacked on their flank, Lane ordered them to extend their line and take cover in the trees. He himself went to the rear because he felt weak from loss of blood. While the general's wound was tended, the Rogue River valley people asked for a talk because, he said, "they were frightened and desired peace."

Two volunteers, James Bruce and Robert Metcalfe, went into their lines. When the Rogue River valley people learned Lane was there, "they expressed a great desire to see me," Lane said. He decided to go to them because it was clear that talking would be better than fighting, and he could at least examine their positions. He found that they had some two hundred men armed with rifles and muskets and well supplied with ammunition. He calculated that they could continue the fight as long as they wished and then retreat safely through difficult terrain, where his men would have difficulty following them.[31]

Lane met with Apserkahar, Toquahear, and another man, named in a later treaty as Anachaharah.[32] The general called them Joe, Sam, and Jim. He said they "told me that their hearts were sick of war, and that they would meet me at Table Rock in seven days, where they would give up their arms, making a treaty." While Lane was talking with the Rogue River valley people, Colonel Ross arrived with his two companies. Lane said that although this "gallant command" was anxious to fight, he declined to allow it because of the progress made in the negotiations.

The Americans lost three men during the battle August 24, Lane said. Another man was mortally wounded and four more, including Alden and himself, wounded seriously. Indian casualties included eight killed and twenty wounded, seven mortally, according to Lane. The *Statesman* reported that when the shooting stopped, the Indians took water to wounded whites "and furnished a party to assist in conveying the litters with our wounded for 25 miles, through the mountains. This appears to be a new feature in Indian warfare."[33]

A correspondent using the name Timon, in a letter to Bush dated September 7 from Camp Alden, said preliminaries of a treaty were concluded on September 3, when Apserkahar and his brother Toquahear came into camp "accompanied by the wise woman of their tribe" and held a council with Lane. Using Metcalfe as his interpreter, Lane asked them why they had gone to war. They said that they had been responding to reports that the whites were hanging or shooting every Indian they could find. They had gone to Alonzo Skinner and asked for protection, but Skinner told them he was no longer their agent.

The talks Lane was holding with the Rogue River valley leaders did not stop the killing. Companies of volunteers that had not been at Evans Creek were still roaming the valley. Asahel Bush reported that a certain Captain Owen and his company decoyed five Indians into a house on Grave Creek "under the pretence of having a talk" and then disarmed them, tied them up, and shot them. "This act, together with the killing of a defenseless Indian at the 'rancherea,' on Grave creek, are believed to be all accomplished by that company during the war," the *Statesman* reported.

Another volunteer captain, named Williams, got "the young chief of what is known as 'Taylor's Indians'" to come into his camp near Applegate Creek after Lane's treaty was made and then tied him to a tree and shot him, the *Statesman* noted, adding that the killing could have broken up the treaty talks. An Indian runner brought news of the killing to the council grounds and delivered it in the presence of the seven unarmed white men who had come to them to make the treaty. The Rogue River valley people complained that this showed bad faith "and said they might retaliate by butchering the seven white men then in their power but were too honorable to kill unarmed men who had come voluntarily into their camp." The *Statesman* writer observed that would-be "exterminators" could not count on further successes of this kind, "as the Indians will hereafter probably object to being disarmed or tied."

The making of the treaty was curiously complicated. Two treaties were made. A summary of the preliminary treaty made September 8 was printed in the *Statesman* under the headline "Treaty of Peace." Indian affairs superintendent Joel Palmer concluded "The Treaty for Sale of Lands" on September 10.[34] The making of the treaties involved two translations of everything said because no one, apparently, had an adequate understanding of both the language of the Rogue River people and English. What the negotiators said was translated first into Chinook Jargon and then into either English or the local language.[35]

The Indian negotiators seem to have been misled; Toquahear would complain four years later—in the presence of General Lane—that he been told in 1853 that the Table Rock Reservation would belong to his people permanently. "General Lane is now here," Toquahear said. "He knows what was told to us; that we would have to leave it for awhile; but we never sold it." No response on Lane's part was recorded.[36]

Five men signed the ratified September 10 treaty—Apserkahar (Jo), Toquahear (Sam), Anachaharah (Jim), John, and Lympe.[37] The man named as John apparently was the same person George Ambrose later called "Old Chief John," the principal leader in the final struggle against the whites two years later, also known as Tecumtum, that is, Elk Killer. He was one of the principal chiefs in 1853; the treaty called for houses to be built for the three principal chiefs, and the government was building a house for him on the Table Rock Reservation when the climactic phase of the Rogue River conflict broke out in 1855.[38]

By the terms of the 1853 treaty the Rogue River valley peoples gave up roughly two thousand square miles in return for $60,000, of which $15,000 was to be used to pay war claims by the whites. The remaining $45,000 would be paid out in installments in the form of "Blankets, Clothing, farming utensils, stock and such other articles as may be deemed most conducive to the interests of said tribes." Three houses were to be built, one for each of the three principal chiefs, for no more than five hundred dollars each. The Indians kept a parcel of about one hundred square miles north of the Rogue River with Table Rock at its southeastern corner. This land would be considered a reservation "until a suitable selection shall be made by the direction of the President of the United States, for their permanent residence and buildings erected thereon and provisions made for their removal."[39]

A correspondent called Socks informed readers of the *Statesman* in a letter dated September 13 from Jacksonville, printed next to the text of the treaty, that an attempt to get up "an indignation meeting" to protest the treaty "proved an entire failure." Bush argued soberly that extermination was easier to talk about than it was to do. The Rogue River valley peoples had killed about as many men as they had lost.[40] In a later issue, Bush informed his readers that extermination would be too expensive. The war had cost $250,000, or $7,000 a day, he said; supplies for the volunteers had necessarily been purchased at inflated rates. He added that experienced men estimated that it would take two years to exterminate the Rogue River valley peoples. "The enormous amount of money necessary for the work can be calculated, but the loss of valuable lives cannot be," he said.[41]

The treaty provision making the Table Rock Reservation temporary shows that Indian affairs superintendent Joel Palmer had decided that the Rogue River valley peoples would have to go. What he didn't know was where to send them. He was considering establishing a reservation on the central Oregon coast, but not for the Rogue River valley peoples.

The *Statesman* had reported on August 24 (the same day Jo Lane led two companies of volunteers against the people with Apserkahar and Toquahear) that Palmer was about to leave for the coast "for the purpose of thoroughly exploring the country along the same between the Tillamook and [Coos] rivers, and the valleys of those streams." Palmer wanted to know whether the country would make a suitable reservation for Willamette Valley and lower Columbia River Indian peoples. He said they were opposed to being sent east of the Cascades, where the country was not suited to their way of life.[42]

The exploration would have to wait; Palmer was distracted by the war in the south. A month after the treaties were made, he still was not certain where to send the Rogue River valley peoples, but he was sure they couldn't stay where they were. The miners "are of the most reckless and desperate character and affected with such feelings of hostility to the indians, that military restraint alone seems adequate to the preservation of peace," he told the commissioner of Indian affairs.[43]

By the time Palmer complained of the hostility of the miners in October, the army had established a presence in the Rogue River valley at a site between Jacksonville and the Table Rock Reservation. The new post, called Fort Lane, was home to three companies of infantry and one company of dragoons, but the companies were small, averaging only twenty-five members. Only a small detachment of dragoons was left on the coast at Port Orford,[44] where at least two serious conflicts would develop in early 1854.

Invasion in Force

The first reported violence of the new year took place on Deer Creek, east of the Illinois River between the coast and the valley. A committee of Illinois River miners complained to Indian service agent Samuel Culver that a party of whites from a camp called Sailor's Diggings had attacked people on Deer Creek on January 18. This, the committee complained, violated a private treaty they had made the previous fall. The willingness of the Illinois River miners to keep a private treaty with the local inhabitants demonstrates that there were communities of whites who rejected violence as a proper response to the presence of Indian people.

Captain A. J. Smith of the First Dragoons reported that the men from Sailor's Diggings, nineteen in all, had attacked a village containing only seven women and three children. They had killed a pregnant woman and two children and wounded three women and the other child before being chased away by three women and the wounded child.[45]

Before the month was out, a more deadly affair took place on the coast. Miners had been drawn to the coast in large numbers when gold was found in black sands on a beach at the mouth of Whiskey Run, north of the Coquille River, in 1852. During the summer of 1853, the mixed-blood proprietors of this beach mine sold out for twenty thousand dollars. A pan of black sand from this claim was said to be worth eight to ten dollars. A town called Randolph boomed into being, and by the fall of 1853, more than one thousand men were there, but only the one claim proved to be worth working.[46]

According to one of Joel Palmer's subagents, F. M. Smith, miners in the Coquille country had complained that the Indians behaved insolently to whites, rode their horses without permission, and stole such things as paddles. One Indian supposedly fired a gun at four white men. The miners said they had sent for the chief, that he had sent back word that he would kill them if they came to his house, and that he intended to kill all the white men he could.[47]

The miners held a meeting the following day and resolved "that the Indians in this vicinity are in a state of hostility toward the whites, from their own acknowledgement and declarations," and that as early as possible the following morning, the morning of January 28, they would attack the Coquilles. They elected one George H. Abbott as the captain of this expedition.[48] Abbott later reported that his company had surprised the Coquilles, even though "they have been making preparations for a stand for several days, and appeared to be very confident of their ability to fight the whites."

Fifteen Indians were killed, Abbott said, and the Coquilles' houses were destroyed. The miners "took all the women and children and old men prisoners, as far as possible." Abbott assured Smith that his men behaved with "the greatest regularity" and "avoided innocent bloodshed as much as possible." Abbott added, "I had almost forgot to say that our loss was none, in either killed, wounded, or prisoners. The Indians are in sight, hovering around the ashes of their homes."[49]

F. M. Smith was not pleased. "Why could they not have awaited my arrival?" he asked in his report, and then answered his own question: had they waited, peace would have been made, and they would have lost "the pleasure and opportunity of settling the alleged difficulty in their own peculiar way." He sarcastically called them "*Bold, brave, courageous men!* to attack a friendly and defenceless tribe of Indians; to *burn, roast, and shoot sixteen of their number*; and all on suspicion that they were about to rise and drive from their country *three hundred white men!*"

On the day following the miners' attack, Smith said, he went to the Coquille from Port Orford and early the next day sent for the Coquille chief, who came in immediately with about thirty of his people. He seemed "willing to accept any terms that I might dictate," Smith said.

The man also denied threatening whites at the ferry "but admitted that some of his people had." He confirmed that some of his people had stolen from whites and used their horses without permission, that his heart had been bad toward white men, and that he had hoped that they would leave. He denied anyone had shot at white people or their houses. The Coquilles had given up their arms to Smith and they "*amounted to just five pieces*, two of which *were wholly unserviceable*; as to powder and ball, I do not believe they *had even five rounds*."[50]

In February there was another deadly episode on the coast at the mouth of the Chetco River, the same episode about which Sam Van Pelt would write some eighty years later. Joel Palmer reported that A. F. Miller and his associates had come to the Chetco River in the fall of 1853 and built dwellings about a quarter of a mile up from the mouth of the river. The Indians had not objected. When newly discovered mines seemed likely to draw people to the area, however, the white men "projected a town speculation" and picked a site at the mouth of the river. There was an Indian town of about twenty houses on each bank of the river, and the would-be town site included one of the Chetco towns.

Over the protests of the Chetco people, the whites built a cabin, which Miller occupied. He then decided to take over the ferry business from the Chetcos, and the Chetcos who objected were threatened with arson. To protect himself, Miller brought in several men who had been recently fighting Indians in nearby northern California. After two weeks of inactivity, these intimidators were ready to leave, but Miller objected. He wanted them to take positive action to deal with his dissatisfied Chetco neighbors.

Palmer said he was told that "shortly before the massacre the Indians were induced to sell the whites their guns, under the pretext that friendly relations were firmly established." At daylight on February 15, 1854, the morning after Miller demanded action, a party of eight or nine well-armed men attacked the village. They shot men as they emerged from their houses. Three of the Chetco men stayed in their houses and returned fire with bows and arrows, Palmer said. To deal with them, Miller's men ordered two Indian women, whom Palmer described as "pets in the family of Miller," to set fire to the houses. Two of the Chetco men who were still fighting were killed by the fires. The third was shot dead while raising his head to catch a breath. In all, twenty-three men and several women were killed.

Miller was arrested, but a justice of the peace set him free on the mutually exclusive grounds that the evidence was insufficient and the attack had been justified. Palmer concluded that making arrests was useless because "no act of a white man against an Indian, however atrocious, can be followed by a conviction."[51]

In the valley, the terms of the treaty made September 10, 1853, were enforced early in the spring of 1854. Indian Service agent Samuel Culver gathered up the people whose leaders had made the treaty, and some others as well, and moved them to the Table Rock Reservation. Then came an epidemic. Culver called it "a bloody flux" with a fever. He could not keep the people on the reservation with the epidemic threatening them. He gave them leaves of absence for a limited period with the understanding that if a fresh conflict broke out, they would hurry to the reservation as soon as they got word from him.

The people also faced starvation. Culver said they could not hunt because a territorial law kept them from buying ammunition, and they could not gather the many types of roots that had once been used as food because "the whites have nearly destroyed this kind of food by ploughing the ground and crowding the Indians from localities where it could once be procured." Only the salmon were still available.[52] So Tecumtum's people had been permitted to return to their own country; they had given up only part of their land in the treaty of purchase in September 1853, and they still owned the land south of the Rogue River between Applegate Creek and the Illinois River.

Joel Palmer, who passed through the valley at the end of April 1854 on his way to investigate the Chetco River incident, reported that a conflict in the valley was likely to occur because of hunger, disease, and the recalcitrance of Tipsu Tyee. He said that the Indians there were "excited and unsettled." They had not been able to gather adequate food the previous summer because of the fighting, and they had lost their root grounds. The winter had been severe. Disease and starvation had killed about one-fifth of the people who stayed on the reservation. People were fleeing to the mountains to escape the sickness.

Palmer had also visited several bands of Umpquas who were "wretched, sickly, and almost starving. Their habits being exceedingly improvident, and the winter unusually severe, they had been kept from perishing by the limited assistance afforded by a few settlers."

Palmer's thinking on this subject suggests a curious blindness to the cause-and-effect relationship between the poverty of the Umpquas and the changes brought about by white colonization. He was aware that a new law prohibiting the sale of firearms and ammunition to the Indians meant that they could no longer hunt game, which in any case had become scarce and hard to hunt because of the white presence. He was also aware that white farmers and cattlemen had "greatly diminished the substance derived from native roots and seeds." But what he saw was improvidence rather than a struggle to survive in the straitened circumstances that had been created by the same people who were giving the Umpquas "limited assistance."

Palmer complained that Tipsu Tyee, who had belatedly agreed to the treaty made eight months before at Table Rock, had refused to bring his people to the reservation as promised and that his son had been involved in the murder of an unnamed settler. The Bearded Chief had also hatched a plan to kill Anachaharah, "who had been very active in discovering and arresting Indians committing depredations on the whites."

The plan, Palmer said, was to give the appearance that whites were responsible for the killing of Anachaharah, which would be the end of Indian confidence in whites and bring the Indian peoples together to exact revenge. Anachaharah "was shot from a house in Jacksonville, occupied by whites, who were then at home," Palmer said. The man who did the shooting was seen by friends of Anachaharah and identified as a member of Tipsu Tyee's band.

This account begs for an explanation of the presence of an armed assassin belonging to a notoriously hostile band in a house occupied by whites. But this curious circumstance made no impression on Palmer; he blamed Tipsu Tyee, despite his own report that there were whites who, "from revengeful or mercenary motives," were bent on provoking a war.[53]

According to the anonymous author of the 1884 book *History of Southern Oregon*, Tipsu Tyee was not the treacherous character his reputation would suggest. He was "less interesting and attractive" than other "barbarian aristocrats" of the valley, and his "occasional 'insolence' and mysterious character" irritated whites. Yet on one occasion, when a drunken miner hit him on the head with a stick, he declined to respond with violence:

The insulted savage, bow in hand, drew an arrow to the head and appeared about to pierce his assailant's heart; but shouting "*Hi yu lum; nika wake memeloose mika!*" lowered his bow. Experts in Chinook jargon translate the above as "You are very drunk or I would kill you!" This is certainly a case of forebearance [*sic*] on the Indian's part, as he had ample opportunity to escape to his brushy kingdom in the hills.[54]

After the supposed plot against Anachaharah was discovered, Palmer went out with forty dragoons to fetch Tipsu Tyee. Palmer rode with the dragoons for five days. The dragoons were still in pursuit when he returned to Fort Lane, near Table Rock. Tipsu Tyee eluded the troopers, but not death. He, his son, and his son-in-law were killed about May 18, 1854, by a band of Shastas who had hoped that by doing the killing they would avoid problems with whites. Nonetheless, the volunteer troops and Indians from central Oregon who had joined in the hunt made the Shastas prisoners and drove them to Fort Jones. Along the way, the Shasta headman was scalped and drowned by his captors, and several more Shastas were shot.[55]

Another party of Californians hunting the killer of a white man, this time among the Illinois River peoples, had crossed over into Oregon at about the same time that Tipsu Tyee was killed. George Ambrose, whose quarrel with Toquahear had promoted confrontation in 1853, informed Palmer of this expedition, adding that he had little doubt the Illinois River people were responsible. Ambrose considered them chronic malcontents because they complained that seven of their people had been killed in seven months, including one who was visiting the Chetcos when their village at the mouth of the Chetco River was burned. Ambrose's sympathies were clear. The dead had been "caught in bad company" and "treated accordingly."[56]

The Californians had decided to kill every Indian they could find, Ambrose said, and their first victim was the son of "Old Chief John" (presumably Tecumtum, whose home was on Deer Creek, a tributary of the Illinois[57]). Although wounded, he escaped and told his people what had happened. They fled into the mountains. Ambrose said he found them suffering without supplies and ready to go to the land assigned to them on the Table Rock Reservation.[58]

Among other indignities visited on the Rogue River valley peoples in 1854 was the rape of an Indian woman in Jacksonville in August. The circumstances suggest that the only remarkable thing about this rape was that it was mentioned in the newspapers. It was reported because it had political implications: a well-known Whig politician, David Logan, was accused of being the rapist. Matthew Deady, a Democrat who was a territorial supreme court judge, made the accusation in a letter written under a pseudonym to a Democratic newspaper in Portland.[59]

Deady later said that witnesses had told him Logan committed the rape "on open ground at the end of one of the Main Streets of the town in full view of a large number of persons male and female." Deady said, "After he was through and up, she having been screaming all the time, he gave her some money and went off to the creek nearby and washed himself."[60] The accusation did Logan no noticeable political damage; three years later he took part in writing the Oregon state constitution.[61]

In the major confrontations of 1852 and 1853, the successes of the hostile miners were less than convincing. The Rogue River peoples could fight. Had they been as bent on exterminating whites as the *Oregon Statesman* had claimed, they could have made more out of the strong position north of Table Rock that they held in 1853. Instead, their leaders agreed to a treaty giving up much of their land, and they provided stretcher bearers to take their wounded enemies home. They were willing to compromise. They were prepared to adapt.

Not all whites, moreover, were exponents of extermination, not even among the miners. The private treaty the Illinois River miners made and were eager to see kept in early 1854 demonstrates that. Joel Palmer, an influential official of the federal government, and his agent on the coast were bitter in their condemnations of attacks on Indian people. And some whites, like those arrested for providing arms and training to Indians in 1853, were willing to go much farther than just expressing disapproval.

Given that the Rogue River people showed no willingess to fight again, the next major confrontation, the devastating war of 1855–56, might have been avoided if all territorial officials had shared Palmer's attitude toward Indians and all miners in southwestern Oregon had shared the tolerance of the Illinois River miners. But the war did not grow out of intolerance. Nor could it be blamed on federal policy as such, ambitious army officers, or blundering bureaucrats. And land was not the issue, because Lane and Palmer had already taken most of the land in the 1853 and 1854 treaties.

The roots of the war would be a local political rivalry, a drought, Jo Lane's success as territorial delegate in Congress, and the widespread though ironic white belief in the ineradicable savagery of the Rogue River peoples. Joel Palmer's influence, energy, and sympathy would not be enough to make applied Indian policy in the Rogue River country conform to the humane ideals of the reservation policy that Commissioner Manypenny had enunciated in Washington.

4

Motivation for War

Notwithstanding the troubles of the summer of 1854, Joel Palmer, the territorial superintendent of Indian affairs, was in no hurry to remove the Rogue River valley peoples. His plan for a reservation on the coast, which seemed less attractive once he had seen the land, still did not include them when he explained it to the commissioner of Indian affairs in September.[1] When he went to the valley in November to revise the terms of the 1853 treaty and acquire more Indian land, the agreements he made implied that the Table Rock Reservation would remain the home of the Rogue River valley peoples indefinitely, if not forever.

On November 11, according to Palmer, he made an agreement with Apserkahar, Toquahear, Tecumtum, and Cholcultah that let the government set up individual farms for the people with the money owed for their lands.[2] On November 15, they and others agreed to share both the Table Rock Reservation and payments for their lands with any other people the government might send there. In return, Palmer agreed to give them "twelve horses, one beef, two yokes of oxen, with yokes and chains, one wagon, one hundred men's coats, fifty pair of pantaloons, and fifty hickory shirts." They would also get blacksmiths, farmers to teach agriculture, a hospital, and at least one school.[3]

Apserkahar was a sick man when he signed Palmer's amendments; the *Statesman* reported that he died about a week afterward of a "pulmonary complaint."[4] Joel Palmer apparently visited with Apserkahar not long before his death, and Apserkahar told him that many of his relatives were dead, his people had abandoned him, and he wanted to die.[5]

On November 18, Palmer got six representatives of bands with holdings on the upper Illinois River to sell their land for thirty thousand dollars.[6] The *Statesman* reported that Palmer had finished clearing Indian titles to all of inland southwestern Oregon at a cost of four to five cents an acre. The newspaper said the newly consolidated Rogue River tribes had agreed to move to other reservations when required,[7] but in the treaties themselves, the prospect of removal was reflected only in one vague statement: the different groups would continue to share payments for their lands "when at any time hereafter the Indians residing on this reserve shall be removed to another reserve."[8]

Meanwhile, Palmer's new subagent on the coast, Ben Wright, had taken over from J. L. Parrish.[9] Wright was an odd choice to keep the peace. As the captain of a company of Yreka volunteers in the autumn of 1852, he had directed the killing of about thirty-eight Modoc Indians after inviting them into his camp for negotiations. After this slaughter, the remorseless volunteers made a display of the scalps of the ill-reputed Modocs. Parrish later said that on one occasion, Wright stripped the clothes from his interpreter, who was called Chetco Jenny by the whites, and then whipped her through Port Orford.[10]

Palmer later described Wright as "quite a useful man" and said that he had "done much to restrain reckless persons and maintain peace."[11] Moreover, Palmer biographer Terence O'Donnell credited Wright with "one of the first instances of whites punished for mistreating Indians": the confinement of two men on bread and water for molesting Indian women.[12]

Although Wright sometimes seemed sympathetic to Indians in his letters to Palmer,[13] his response to A. F. Miller's attack on the Chetco people in early 1854 suggests that in practice he had not changed much since his Modoc-killing spree in 1852. Shortly after he became subagent at Port Orford, Wright reported that Miller had asked the Chetco people to return to the site of their burned-out village and had offered to assist and defend them. Wright quoted Miller as saying that the Chetco people had been "shamefully treated" but insisting that he was not responsible. Wright added that "every one speaks well of him, except for those who were against him before, which, in my opinion, was for private reasons to injure him." Wright added that he had talked the Chetco people into coming back to their burned-out village,[14] in effect putting them under the guardianship of their proven enemy Miller.

A little more than two months before Wright made this report, Joel Palmer, after his own visit to the mouth of the Chetco River, condemned Miller and expressed frustration at a thwarted attempt to convict Miller of the killings in court.[15] If Palmer was correct, then Wright was dissembling, but Palmer let it pass.

While Palmer was making treaties in the fall of 1854, a political rivalry was developing that would destroy the peace he hoped to ensure. The rivals were the dominant Democratic party and a new political grouping called the Know-Nothings. A few days after the Illinois River treaty was made, the *Oregon Statesman* launched an offensive of invective against the Know-Nothings. A product of the breakdown of the Whig party and a precursor of the Republicans, the Know-Nothings made opposition to foreigners and Catholics their political focus. In Oregon, the organization became a tool of opponents of the Democratic party. Its foundation was traditional Protestant Oregonian suspicion of Catholics and the Hudson's Bay Company, and it drew advocates of temperance and former Whigs.[16]

Asahel Bush complained in the *Statesman* that the Know-Nothings were engaged in "the most ridiculous piece of bigotry, intolerance, and (especially in this country) stupidity, *grown persons* were ever engaged in." Furthermore, he said, they were liars; some men "considered most credible" had solemnly stated that they were not members of the Supreme

Order of the Star-Spangled Banner, the secret society behind the Oregon Know-Nothing movement. Bush knew better because a spy within the order had supplied him with copious information about its rituals and membership.

Bush pronounced himself gratified that most of the names on the list of members belonged to Whigs, "and mostly of the *putty head* order at that. The most of them are *natural know-nothings*, and ought to have been admitted without initiation." He was displeased to find the names of a few Democrats, including "one or two who *are* democrats, naturally, and ought to be ashamed of, and renounce all connections with such an inquisitorial, illiberal, and anti-democratic order."[17]

In December, the Democratic legislative faction under Bush's influence would push through a plan to flush out Know-Nothings by abolishing the secret ballot. Historians have given the *viva voce* law credit for putting a stop to the Know-Nothing movement in Oregon. Priscilla Knuth said the movement was at an end after the June 1855 election, when Democrats who were Know-Nothing sympathizers had to stand with the Democrats to avoid political oblivion.[18] The Know-Nothings did not, however, disappear after the election, and their continued activity, especially in southwestern Oregon, is evidenced by the part Know-Nothings played in creating the final Rogue River War and the conspicuous fight they would make for control of the war's political potential.

The Know-Nothing movement may have influenced the conduct of Indian policy in Oregon in another way as well. Among the Democrats attracted to the movement was Joel Palmer, and rumors of that attraction were circulating among Democratic leaders by the beginning of 1855, sapping his influence in the party that had appointed him. The rumors were probably true, although Nat Lane, Joseph Lane's son and political agent in Oregon, rejected them. He told his father that the rumors were being spread by Orville C. Pratt, a rival of Lane within the Oregon Democracy, who was accusing Palmer and other Lane supporters of Know-Nothing sympathies to discredit Lane. Bush crony James W. Nesmith claimed in a letter to Lane that Palmer had joined the "Salem Wigwam" of the Know-Nothing lodge on October 8, 1854. Although

Motivation for War

Palmer denied his involvement in a letter to Lane, Nesmith told Judge Matthew Deady that Palmer had privately admitted joining the Know-Nothings to satisfy his curiosity and had said he regretted having done it.[19]

Palmer's critics were questioning not only his rumored membership in the Know-Nothings but also his dismissal of the agent in the Rogue River valley, Samuel Culver. The agent had been accused of making a personal profit from the sale of hay from the Table Rock Reservation. Culver had been the subject of complaints in 1853 that he had been unwilling to pursue the person responsible for the killing that set off the conflict in the fall of that year. He had reported to Palmer at that time that a petition was circulating to replace him with another Democratic worthy, Robert Metcalfe. This may have been a factional move by supporters of Joseph Lane to put one of their own into office in place of Culver, who was related to Lane's rival Orville C. Pratt.

Culver reacted to the new allegations by asking four men to investigate them and make their own report to Palmer. At the end of September, Culver's ad hoc committee called the allegations "a tissue of falsehoods, having no color of fact to sustain them."[20] According to Terence O'Donnell, Palmer nonetheless believed that Culver was guilty, suspended him, and then reinstated him because Palmer needed him to bring the Rogue River peoples to the reservation. Later, complaining that Culver was overbearing and served a scheming faction, Palmer finally dismissed him.[21]

The Culver affair and Palmer's flirtation with the Know-Nothings might be said to have affected his conduct of Indian affairs by reducing his political influence, but it is not clear whether the influence he lost would have been of much help as he struggled against the catastrophic failure of his administration a year later.

Many of the Rogue River people who had been allowed to leave the Table Rock Reservation in 1854 because of the sickness there were still away when the spring of 1855 arrived. Meanwhile, Palmer had replaced Culver with George Ambrose. Like his counterpart Ben Wright on the coast, Ambrose seems an odd choice for the job. He had provided one of the excuses for the main violent conflict of the summer of 1852 by arguing with Toquahear.[22] Later, he would write a letter showing an attitude substantially less humane than the policy he was supposed to implement. This letter, published over a pen name, justified the murders of Rogue River people by self-styled Jacksonville volunteers and called for Indian extermination.[23]

The new agent had been among the chosen supporters of Samuel Culver when he was accused of corruption.[24] By appointing him, Palmer may have been trying to make peace with Culver's friends.

Ambrose reported in April that he had kept busy responding to white complaints about the Rogue River valley people who were off the reservation. The headman Konechequot, called Bill, had been shot in the shoulder in a clash in the Applegate Creek valley, and so the Indian people there had agreed to go to the Illinois River valley. Ambrose said, "They cannot be induced to stay on the Reserve without being furnished food & in fact I believe at this season of the year if they were compelled to stay on the Reserve they would most certainly starve to death."[25]

Editor T. J. Dryer of the *Oregonian*, the Whig organ in Portland, took a six-week tour of southern Oregon in late spring and early summer of 1855. His description of the Umpqua canyon suggests how isolated the Rogue River valley was from the rest of the territory, and his description of the effects of that year's drought explains why many miners in the Rogue River valley would look with favor on an Indian war in the fall.

Dryer said that the road through the canyon was "the worst specimen of the name we have ever traveled over." Part of the road was unusually steep and the rest was "an unfathomable *mud hole*." Along the way he frequently saw "portions of broken wagons, broken ox-yokes and fragments of destruction to property."

In the Rogue River valley, he found many scattered farms. In Jacksonville, brick buildings were appearing, although it still appeared, "like all mining towns, to have grown up suddenly." Despite this evidence of development, the miners were having a poor season. Where there was water, they could make as much as five dollars a day, Dryer said, but he added that water was scarce and so most mining operations had been stopped.[26]

Mining was the heart of the region's economy, and miners without work needed money. Soon the exploitation of some other potential source of income would become necessary.

In June, there was yet another clash between Rogue River valley people and white Californians. The *Statesman* reported that two companies of California volunteers had ridden north to the mining village of Kerbyville, on the west fork of the Illinois, looking for revenge for the alleged killing of a miner in May. The new Indian Service agent, George Ambrose, got there first and persuaded several people to go to the reservation, but not all, and the Californians killed five men and one woman.[27]

In June and July, a federal paymaster was at work in southwestern Oregon and northern California paying the wages of the volunteers involved in the 1853 campaign. The paymaster disbursed a little less than $70,200 in hard money for wages. Businessmen who supplied the volunteers were paid with War Department funds funneled through the Democratic territorial governor, George Curry, and got about $151,400, making a total of about $221,600, or more than $4.4 million in 1990s dollars. Credit for getting the government to pay for the campaign went to another Democrat, delegate Joseph Lane.[28] The idea that fighting Indians for federal money might be a way compensate for the drought must have occurred to some miners. Even if they weren't paid quickly, they could at least eat on the government's credit.

At the same time, politicians of another stripe were having less success getting federal money for the suppliers of another foray by Jacksonville volunteers. Their situation suggested that making money on a campaign against Indians was essentially a problem of political tactics. The expedition, led by one Jesse Walker, had patrolled the immigrant road across northeastern California during the summer of 1854.[29]

Payment might not have become an issue but for a change in political faith undergone by two Jacksonville political figures, Benjamin F. Dowell and Charles S. Drew. Drew had been perceived as a good Democrat in the spring of 1854; he was named quartermaster-general of the territorial militia by then-governor John W. Davis,[30] an appointee of the Democratic administration of Franklin Pierce. During Joseph Lane's campaign in the

Charles S. Drew, shown in about 1865, defected from the Democratic Party in 1855 even though the Democratic governor had appointed him quartermaster general of the territorial volunteers. As a Know-Nothing, he promoted war with the Rouge River peoples. In later years he tried to get the federal government to pay more money to suppliers and soldiers involved in the war. (Oregon Historical Society, neg. CN 020573)

Benjamin F. Dowell, shown in about 1870, was linked with Charles S. Drew in Jackson County politics and was said to have written a series of letters signed "Clarendon," published in the *Oregonian*, which promoted the Rogue River War. Later, as a lawyer, Dowell solicited cases from people who claimed they were owed money by the government as a result of the Northwest wars of the 1850s. (Oregon Historical Society, neg. CN 006295)

spring of 1855 for reelection as territorial delegate, however, the Democrats discovered that Drew and his friend Dowell had gone over to the opposition.

In a letter to the *Statesman* in May, William J. Martin, the elected militia colonel in the Umpqua River valley[31] and a former Indian Service agent,[32] accused Drew and Dowell of supporting the Whig candidate for delegate even though they expected Lane to get a bill through Congress that would pay off their speculation in pack animals for the Walker expedition. Martin accused Dowell of bragging that he and Drew had concocted a report to convince Governor Davis that Indians planned to attack emigrants on the southern road. Dowell had also admitted that they expected to make twenty-eight thousand dollars on the scheme. Martin quoted Dowell as saying that Drew, then quartermaster-general, had "fixed all things right, and we have made a nice thing of it, and that is the way to do business."[33]

Dowell fired back through the columns of the *Oregonian* in a letter published June 30, saying that Martin's letter was "a tissue of falsehoods from beginning to end." He and Drew had consistently supported Lane's Whig opponent, he said, and Martin simply wanted to embarrass them "to make votes for Lane." If they had supported Lane, Dowell added, no one would have complained about their operations relative to the Walker expedition.[34]

The *Statesman*'s editorial position stated three weeks later was that the Walker expedition had been a "scheme to 'fight the emigrants' and plunder Uncle Sam." The expedition had cost about one hundred thousand dollars, which had not been paid, "and there is an opinion abroad, that, with the exception of the officers and men, *it never will be.*"[35]

The controversy over the Walker expedition didn't keep Dowell and Drew from beating the drum for a fresh campaign against the Indians. Alongside Dowell's letter in the June 30 *Oregonian* was another signed "Clarendon"—one of several that would be published over that signature during that summer that pushed for an Indian war in the Rogue River country. A *Statesman* correspondent calling himself Anti-Humbug (perhaps the Democratic stalwart Judge Matthew Deady[36]) would claim that

Clarendon's letters were written by Dowell to get revenge on Governor Curry for turning Drew out of office as quartermaster-general.[37]

Whoever Clarendon was, his sympathies were with the antiforeigner Know-Nothing movement, which at that moment was not easily distinguished from the Whig party—candidates listed in the *Oregonian* as "American," that is, Know-Nothing, were designated by Clarendon as "whig." Clarendon claimed the foreign vote had decided the election in Jackson County for the Democrats, who got the vote of "every uneducated man of foreign birth." As a result, three Democrats but only one Whig had been elected to represent the county in the territorial house of representatives. Nonetheless, Clarendon said, the end result was "a strong American feeling here, which forbodes [sic] a change in the political aspect of the county."[38]

In the contest for delegate, Lane rolled over his opponent 6,178 to 3,943.[39] Soon the *Statesman* was printing, under its second-page masthead, a banner reading, "Subject to the decision of the Democratic National Convention. For President in 1856, GEN. JOSEPH LANE."[40] Among the three Democrats elected to the territorial legislature from Jackson County—that is, the upper Rogue River country around Jacksonville—was James A. Lupton.[41] He was sometimes called Major Lupton, but the colonel of the Jackson County militia would later be quoted as saying that the title had not been earned.[42] Lupton would be the leading figure in the fall, when local Democrats tried to grab the credit for starting an Indian war from Clarendon and his Know-Nothing friends.

It may be that Clarendon, in his insistence on war, had at least one Indian counterpart during the summer of 1855. Federal investigator J. Ross Browne later claimed that a leader of the Nisqually Indians of the Puget Sound area, Leschi, had "traveled by day and night to speak for resistance to the whites" throughout the Northwest. Leschi, according to Browne, had told the Indian people about "*Polakly Illaha*—the land of Darkness,—where no ray from the Sun ever penetrated; where there was torture and death for all the races of Indians." If they did not go to war against the whites, he had said, the whites "would soon grow strong and

Motivation for War

many, and soon put all the Indians in their big ships and send them off to that terrible land."

Browne blamed Leschi for the three wars that broke out almost simultaneously in the Northwest—in northwestern Washington, in eastern Washington, and in southern Oregon.[43] If Leschi brought this message to the Rogue River valley peoples, however, they seem not to have acted on it, or at least not to have acted on it by the time their prospective enemies provoked a conflict for their own reasons. The immediate occasion for the provocation was familiar: an apparently unpremeditated brawl in northern California.

In late July, according to an anonymous *Statesman* correspondent whose writing style and concerns seem similar to those of George Ambrose, a band of Indians killed twelve white men in northern California without provocation. Mounted volunteers who had gone out to hunt down the killers had decided that the men they meant to catch had fled to the Rogue River valley. There were some among the Indians who would be "troublesome until they are exterminated," he said, but he also insisted that "the judicious and effective administration" of George Ambrose would soon improve the character and conditions of the Indian people generally. "There can be no Indian war here," he concluded.[44]

Another anonymous correspondent who may have been Colonel Martin, however, described the conflict as originating out of a drunken brawl. He argued that there was "no combination of tribes, or premeditated war," and said the incident began on July 24 when three Rogue River Indians went to the mining camp called Humbug on the Klamath River west of Yreka, got drunk, and bought a bottle of whiskey each. On their way home a miner saw the whiskey and demanded to know where they had gotten it.

The miner tried to take one man's bottle away. The Indian cursed the miner. The miner drew his revolver and shot the Indian, but not fatally. The Indian had his own gun, and he shot the miner, killing him instantly. Other miners killed two of the three Indians. Other Indians later killed ten white men in response. Five Rogue River Indians had been in the Klamath

River valley at the time, and "the whites about Yreka [had] no doubt of the guilt of these Rogue River Indians."[45]

An author using the name Truth, who sounds like Agent Ambrose, said in a later letter to the *Statesman* that the California volunteers who crossed into the Rogue River valley to hunt the killers demanded that Ambrose and Capt. Andrew Smith at Fort Lane deliver either six or seven men from the Table Rock Reservation.

Some of the accused men had undoubtedly been involved in the killing, Truth said, but Smith and Ambrose refused to give them up except to the authorities at Yreka. The volunteers were denied permission to go on the reservation to hunt them down. Had they been allowed on the reservation, the four hundred warriors there would not only have resisted them but also "found abundant cause to lay waste to the property of this valley again." Smith had two of the hunted Indians in irons. The correspondent proclaimed himself "satisfied that neither of the gentlemen I have mentioned [Ambrose and Smith] have any further respect for an Indian than that which is requisite to secure his friendly submission towards the whites."[46]

The man who called himself Clarendon did not accept the reassuring views of the *Statesman*'s correspondents. He complained that Indians responsible for killings were being protected by agents of the government on the Table Rock Reservation. The commander of Fort Lane had "utterly refused to accede to the reasonable request of an injured community" and give up the guilty men to the volunteers. Clarendon accused the Indian people in general of treachery and cruelty and of involvement in a "hostile confederacy" involving "every tribe for hundreds of miles around."[47]

In later letter to the *Oregonian*, Clarendon threatened that the volunteers would "prosecute the object of their mission to the bitter end" unless the Indians responsible for the killings were given up to them. He accused Governor Curry and the Democrats of having made "particular favorites" of the Indians by declining to sanction the volunteers. "The same line of policy should be adopted here with regard to the Indians that is pursued by our companions on the other side of the Siskiyou—viz: to commence a war of extermination," he said.[48]

Clarendon had pointed out in an earlier letter that such a war could bring economic benefits. He had taken note of the government's purchase of one hundred thousand pounds of flour in the Rogue River valley for the troops at Fort Lane. Government purchasing, he said, would "promote the interests of the farmer and grazier, and give an impetus to trade, generally, throughout this section of the country."[49]

The idea of making an Indian war as a pork-barrel project was not new. Californians had been fighting Indian wars for financial reasons for at least five years by 1855.[50] Just as the southwestern Oregon gold rush was an extension of the California gold rush, the Rogue River War would be an extension of the wars that accompanied the California gold rush.

As the pressure for war built up in the Rogue River valley, Indian affairs superintendent Joel Palmer was acquiring Indian land on the coast. He made a pact on August 17, 1855, with representatives of the peoples on the lower Umpqua River and on Coos Bay, and some of the Coquilles signed on August 23.[51] But Palmer ran into a temporary obstacle while he was holding talks near the mouth of the Rogue River on August 26 with representatives of the rest of the peoples of the southern Oregon coast: the Indian people fled when soldiers brought the corpses of two Indians and three whites to the council ground.[52]

They had been killed on the river while soldiers were taking one of the Indians, a young man, to Palmer by canoe. Ben Wright, the Indian Service agent on the south coast, had arrested the young man for wounding a miner in a scuffle. The wounded miner had not been hurt so badly that he was incapacitated; he and two other white men had followed the soldiers in another canoe, had come alongside them, and had opened fire, killing the accused man and another Indian. The soldiers had fired back, killing the three attackers.[53]

Rodney Glisan, an army surgeon who was with Palmer at the council grounds, anticipated that the local vigilance committee would attack Palmer's camp. But even though the miners who made up the committee were "much excited," they decided that the soldiers had only been doing their duty. The Rogue River peoples also put their excitement aside. After four days, some twelve hundred people came back to Palmer's camp, and their representatives concluded the agreement.[54]

On September 8, the last of the Coquilles signed, and the coastal treaty was complete. This document—at least in the written version, which none of the Indian signatories could have read—created a confederation of all the peoples of the coast. The confederation would be paid $90,000 over sixteen years for roughly 11,300 square miles of land—almost 5.9 million acres. Palmer had bought a timbered coast bigger than Massachusetts or New Hampshire for less than a penny and a half per acre.

The coastal people had promised to concentrate themselves on a reservation within one year after ratification of the treaty by Congress. Palmer had promised two sawmills, two flour mills, four schoolhouses, and the services of farmers, millers, teachers, and a doctor. He also wrote into the treaty the possibility of implementing the experimental idea of allotment—dividing land among individuals in the white fashion rather than leaving it in the communal possession of the tribes. The government could, at its discretion, parcel out reservation land among families, with a minimum of sixty acres per family. The confederation also acknowledged the right of Congress to make laws for its members and promised to be friendly to Americans.[55]

Tension was building in the Rogue River valley that autumn. In a letter dated September 28, Clarendon claimed that Indians had killed twenty-two whites. He added that "the extirpation of every Indian tribe infesting this section of country . . . is a sacrifice due to the glory of God and the security of the lives and property of our citizens."[56]

Indian Service agent George Ambrose complained two days later that September had seen "one continued series of aggressions." The aggressions were minor; complaints for one week included four minor burglaries, three cattle wounded by revolver bullets, and a ferryman claiming Indians were trying to burn him out. Ambrose could not get any Indian to admit guilt, but he blamed the problems on Tecumtum's people and their relatives, who, he said, were constantly going between the Table Rock Reservation, the Scoton camps in the Coast Range, and the villages on Galice Creek. If Tecumtum's people were not removed, Ambrose said,

Motivation for War

"I fear they will plunge the whole country in a war. . . . already the people talk of waging a war of extermination."[57]

Charles S. Drew later complained that Rogue River people were responsible for the ten killings of white men between June 1 and September 25 and added, "I believe in no instance were the Indians punished for any of these offenses, or any restraint whatever put upon them." Drew described the dispersion of the people who had left the reservation to escape sickness and starvation as preparation for carrying out a conspiracy hatched the previous summer.[58]

Meanwhile, the killing of an arrogant, aggressive Indian service agent in the arid country north of the Columbia River and east of the Cascades had set off the conflict that would be called the Yakima War. The killing provoked an expedition by a detachment of about eighty-five federal regulars. They marched north from a fort on the Columbia on October 3. Three days later, they got into a fight at Toppenish Creek. After two days of combat, their Indian opponents forced them to destroy their supplies and flee, leaving behind a buried howitzer.[59]

The Yakima War began at almost the same time the Rogue River War began, and both wars developed out of confrontations between native people and mainly white immigrants, but their roots were not the same. The Rogue River War was the epitome of a type of conflict that grew from gold rush conditions in California—the war to make money. The Yakima War, however, was perhaps the first example of a new kind of Indian war, a war made to enforce the new reservation policy. It grew out of the determination of federal officials, including the territorial governor of Washington, Isaac I. Stevens, and Joel Palmer,[60] to confine eastern Washington and Oregon Indian people to reservations, which required that they be brought into submission and forced to observe a dubious treaty.

Stevens, with Palmer's help, held stormy joint negotiations with leaders of several groups in late May and early June in the Walla Walla River valley. Three treaties were made. They involved sale of lands to the government and creation of three reservations.[61]

Kamiakin, perhaps the most prominent signatory, had tried to avoid making a treaty. Stevens decided for his own purposes to consider

Kamiakin, a leader with Yakima and Palouse affinities and head chief of the Yakimas. Kamiakin's reasons for signing are unclear. Stevens had threatened that Kamiakin would "walk in blood knee deep" if he did not sign, and relatives and friends probably asked him to sign as a gesture of peace and friendship. Kamiakin's later statement that Stevens forced the war on the Indian peoples by demanding that they go to reservations suggests that he signed to gain time to organize for a war that he saw was inevitable. Stevens chose to understand Kamiakin's reluctant agreement as binding on several groups Kamiakin by no means controlled.[62]

The Indian negotiators expected that they would not have to give up any land until the treaties were ratified by Congress. The final versions of the treaties, however, included provisions giving Americans the instant right to take over lands not actually occupied and cultivated by Indian people or included in reservations. And rumors of gold were circulating, encouraging Americans to do just that. The prelude to the killing of the Indian Service agent was a series of clashes with miners who had come into Indian country, leaving some eight miners dead. Indian people accused miners of rape and horse theft.[63]

Even as the regulars defeated at Toppenish Creek made their way back to safety, the beginnings of another war were being plotted in southern Oregon. On October 7, according to Charles S. Drew, Indian Service agent George Ambrose and James Lupton, the recently elected Democratic representative to the territorial legislature from Jackson County, went to the camp of the people Drew described as the Butte Creeks. Ambrose tried to get them to return to the reservation.

Their reply, Drew claimed, "was that they *would not return*; that they had decided on war, and were now prepared for it." When this was made known to the local volunteers, Drew said, they decided the time had come to take action. He claimed that Ambrose and Captain Smith condoned the organization of the volunteers because they had lost control over the Rogue River peoples and that the volunteers were needed to save the regular troops as well as the white settlements.[64]

Joel Palmer reported to the commissioner of Indian affairs on October 9 that peace and order could be secured only by "a peremptory order,

84   Motivation for War

requiring every Indian belonging thereto to remain constantly upon the reservation, and declaring every Indian found outside an outlaw." He added that whites were responsible for many aggressions blamed on Indians. He explained that white "murderers, robbers, horse-thieves, and vagabonds" lived among the Indian peoples and indulged in "the most unwarrantable excesses" against them. They also allied themselves with "the more reckless of the Indians" so that they could "carry out their plans of annoying the settlers."[65]

Four days later, Palmer ordered his agents to record the names of all male Indians over the age of twelve. A daily roll call would be taken, and "unless a satisfactory reason be rendered," any Indian man who was absent would "be regarded as a person dangerous to the peace of the country" and jailed. No man was permitted to leave his assigned camp without a written permit from an agent.[66]

Had Palmer been able to regulate white communities as he hoped to regulate Indian communities, his plan might have had some merit. He could not, however, and by that time no plan could have prevented a war in the south. It had already begun. John Beeson, a white resident of the Rogue River valley who sympathized with the Indian people, said that the war originated in public meetings called by James Lupton. The first meeting was held during the first week in October. The second meeting was held on Sunday, October 7, 1855, Beeson said, and was represented as a church meeting. Afterward, those who favored extermination formed themselves into war parties. At dawn, they began their attack.[67]

A newspaper report said seven parties were formed, composed of 115 men in all. Lupton himself led the largest group, made up of thirty-six men. Lupton was wounded by an arrow and died that night, and another man was also mortally wounded. Ten more of the whites were hurt. By this account, forty Indian people were killed.[68] John Beeson said that soldiers sent to bury the dead reported finding twenty-eight bodies of Indians, half of them women and children. Others were wounded and died afterward, and some bodies had been seen floating down the river.[69]

Charles S. Drew tried to explain the deaths of the women and children. He said that the volunteers attacked "while it was yet too dark to distinguish one Indian from another, and by this reason it so happened that several squaws and children were killed." While it was true that "the bodies of but few warriors were found on the ground after the action was over," that was because "the Indians observed their usual custom in such cases, and carried off their warriors as fast as they became disabled or killed."[70]

Beeson said some of the Indian people on the reservation went to Fort Lane for protection but others fled to the west, down the valley. As they went, they set fire to houses and killed white people.

When Captain Smith refused his support to the volunteers, according to Beeson, "a temporary check was given to their proceedings," so the volunteers confined themselves to hunting down the Indian people who had stayed behind in the valley. Beeson quoted one volunteer as telling him, "We found several sick and famished Indians, who begged hard for mercy and for food. It hurt my feelings; but the understanding was that all were to be killed. So we did the work." An Indian girl fetching water for her white employers was shot. An Indian boy "scarce in his teens" was hanged by miners, "with whom he was a great favorite."[71] A messenger from the Rogue River valley told Joel Palmer that the volunteers had "organized and commenced an indiscriminate slaughter of all Indians found on Table-rock reservation" and that they had killed 106 men, women, and children.[72]

Indian Service agent George Ambrose reported that most of the men belonging to the band that had been attacked by Lupton's party had come onto the reserve the day before the attack, leaving the old men and women behind to follow the next day. Ambrose went to the site of this massacre and identified the dead as members of a band led by the man he called Jake. He said the bodies of "eight men, four of whom were very aged, and fifteen women and children" had been found, and he supposed several more people had been killed whose bodies were not found. Ambrose also visited another camp, where the volunteers had killed a woman and wounded another woman and two boys.

Ambrose said that on the night of October 8, remaining members of the bands that had been attacked had joined Tecumtum, "who I suspect had been waiting some time for a pretext to commence hostilities, only desiring the assistance of some other Indians, which this unfortunate occurrence secured to him." They killed a young man employed on the reservation and left his body cut across the forehead and face with an axe. Ambrose also claimed that Tecumtum had killed the man who had been employed to build him a house, "declaring that he had 'wanted no house, but was going to fight till he died.'" The people who joined Tecumtum destroyed or carried away provisions and tools and marched down the Rogue River, attacking whites wherever they were found. "I do not believe more desperate or reckless men ever lived upon the earth," Ambrose said.[73]

Toquahear chose not to fight. Ambrose said that when the uprising began, Toquahear gathered his band and another and protected the white employees and agency property on their part of the reservation. "Neither he nor his people want war, nor do I believe they can be made to fight except in self-defence," the agent said. Ambrose said Toquahear told him that "Jake's people will fight till they are all killed off; John [Tecumtum] will doubtless do the same." Ambrose predicted that downriver bands led by the men he called George and Lympa (Lympe) would become involved. They did not want to fight, he said, but they were not on the reserve and "should either of them be caught sight of, he will most certainly be shot."[74]

Asahel Bush understood what had happened, and the *Statesman* criticized Lupton, not so much for the "indiscriminate slaughter" he had begun as for failing to recognize that "the project of exterminating the Southern Indians is chimerical and impossible." Moreover, the *Statesman* predicted that the survivors of Lupton's assaults would be "doubly exasperated" and would later "descend from their hiding places and devastate isolated settlements."

Governor Curry, however, called for volunteers for a territorial army because the Indian peoples had violated their treaty and were "menacing the southern settlements with all the atrocities of savage warfare." Curry was not alone in missing or ignoring the significance of Lupton's attack. The *Statesman* published a letter from one J. G. Woods, dated October 11 from Evans' Ferry on the Rogue River, which listed in detail the whites who were killed by the fleeing Rogue River valley people. Woods described Lupton's attack as if it had been a reaction to an attack by Indians, and so did Dr. A. G. Henry, on the same page.

Bush warned his readers that Henry "wrote under the influence of great mental excitement, and was too much excited for healthy judgement or counsel."[75] Bush had a political reason for this disclaimer; Henry had a history of Whig involvement. He had been appointed an Indian Service agent by the Whig government in 1850 and had been criticized by then congressional delegate Samuel Thurston, a Democrat, for having drawn $750 in pay without ever presenting himself for work.[76]

Henry said fifteen white men, women, and children had been killed by the Indians on October 9 between the Rogue River and Grave Creek. Only then did he mention that a "battle" had been fought the previous day by Jacksonville volunteers in which, he said, forty-one Indians were killed. He also said he had been involved in recruiting a company of thirty-five men on Cow Creek (a tributary of the Umpqua, between the Rogue River valley and the Umpqua canyon), for which he had been appointed quartermaster and commissary. Perhaps with the controversy over the Walker expedition in mind, he added that he would "conform to the army regulations, so that those who furnish supplies shall not be subjected to those long and vexatious delays that have heretofore resulted from want of form and regularity."

Notwithstanding his Whig background, Henry then invoked the name of Delegate Joseph Lane and, thus, the recent payments made to the suppliers and volunteers involved in the 1853 campaign. Henry said he felt certain that with the aid of Lane's influence in Washington, federal money for all the expenses of the projected war would be paid within six months.[77]

Bush clearly was less enthusiastic than Henry about the possibilities of the war, and a letter in the next issue of the *Statesman* that was signed "Sober-Sense" and purported to be from the war zone expressed that point of view. Sober-Sense said that Henry was "making a desperate attempt to get a seat on the Indian hobby; the result is now doubtful." The war could be waged by "two or three companies of mounted rangers, and we have got plenty of men here to compose them. . . . All we want is a moderate quality of arms, ammunition and supplies."

Sober-Sense lacked sympathy for both the white promoters of the war and their victims: "The sooner the poor red devils are put out of the way the better," he said, and when they were, "the worthless demagogues in this vicinity who ride the Indian hobby and can ride nothing else" would lose their occupation and would then have to "either steal, starve or work."

George Ambrose, even though he had seen the results of Lupton's work while the bodies were still fresh, was more sympathetic to Lupton than to the Indian people whose guardian he was supposed to be. In a letter written to the *Statesman* under the pen name Miner, Ambrose described the revenge exacted by the Rogue River people on October 9 as "savage barbarity," whereas the assaults that had provoked them had arisen, he said, from the reasonably exhausted patience of the whites. Lupton's men, he said, "were determined to teach them a lesson that they would not soon forget, and induce them to remain on the reserve." Any course other than extermination was "consummate folly," he added.[78]

In the *Oregonian*, the militant correspondent Clarendon informed his readers: "Since my last communication, this entire section of the country has been the scene of the most heart-rending massacres that has befallen the lot of man to witness." Clarendon recognized that the whites had attacked the Rogue River valley people first, but he offered an exculpating explanation. The volunteers, he said, had attacked three camps belonging to people "who had left the reserve with the obvious intention of committing depredations upon the settlers residing above the reserve." The Indian people killed had "suffered the penalty they have so long and so justly merited."[79] In addition to blaming the Rogue River peoples for starting the war, Clarendon blamed the Democrat superintendent of Indian affairs, Joel Palmer. "We are now reaping the bitter fruits of Indian philanthropy—the accursed results accruing from a corrupt administration of Indian affairs, particularly in southern Oregon," he said.[80] By putting the war into political perspective, Clarendon was foreshadowing the political struggle over the war that was already developing.

Although the war would give Palmer the opportunity to move the southwestern Oregon people to his long-planned reservation on the central coast, satisfying the initial demands of the new reservation policy, the men who started the war were not thinking in terms of any Indian policy but their own, and they had thus far implemented that policy with complete success.

The beginning of the war had divided the Indian peoples. The followers of Toquahear stayed on the path that the Rogue River peoples as a group had followed at least since the confrontations of 1851. Rather than going to war, most of the Rogue River peoples had chosen from that time on to tolerate the radical changes the gold rush had meant in their environment and thus their way of life. They even, for the most part, tolerated the chronic low-level violence that came with the gold rush.

Faced with a declared campaign of extermination in 1853, they banded together and fled into the hills north of Table Rock rather than make a war for revenge. Then they gave up territory for peace in the 1853 treaty. Now the people who stayed on the Table Rock Reservation accommodated even more. They chose to rely on the army and the Indian Service to protect them from the new campaign of extermination declared by the late Major Lupton. Presumably they did not know that their official guardian, George Ambrose, had called anonymously but publicly for their destruction.

The path taken by the people who followed Tecumtum off the reservation was, superficially, appropriate to the purposes of the whites characterized by Asahel Bush as worthless demagogues, riding the Indian hobby. Tecumtum and his followers gave them their excuse to try to tap the federal treasury. But this war would not be like the campaign of 1853.

5

The War
Within a War

The Rogue River people who chose to fight responded to the attacks by Lupton and his confederates by retreating, just as they had in 1853, but this retreat was different in two ways. This time they moved westward, down the Rogue River, perhaps planning to put themselves into a position where they could get support from the downriver and coastal peoples. And as they went, they killed the whites they encountered.

A group of fifteen to twenty volunteers rode out from Jacksonville on October 9 to try to save the white people along the route of the retreat. The volunteers soon fell in with fifty-five dragoons from Fort Lane. About twenty-five miles northeast of Jacksonville, the combined force found the house and outbuildings on J. B. Waggoner's farm burned to the ground. They also found the burned bodies of Waggoner's wife and child.

Some of the volunteers went into the chaparral behind the Waggoner house and were confronted by a rear guard of about thirty Rogue River men. The rest of the troops came up and charged at the Indians, killing six men. The survivors fled on horseback in the direction of the mountains. The whites pursued for about two miles, but the long ride they had already made had worn them out, and after two miles they quit the chase.[1]

As the Rogue River people retreated downriver, messengers went out to the Cow Creek band and probably to others. Americans living in the Cow Creek valley decided to talk with the Cow Creek native people. The whites adopted an approach that was in keeping with former local custom: they sent a woman to arrange matters. A white woman, Maximilla Riddle, volunteered to ride out to tell the Cow Creek people that the Americans wanted peace and to invite the Indians to talk with them. The woman's son, George Riddle, recalled that he was told that a young man he called Chief Tom, the son of one of the Cow Creek leaders, came to meet with the Americans. With him were about a dozen other men. They were prepared as if for war, again in keeping with former custom. But the discussion was not a customary discussion about how to make peace,[2] although the young spokesman expressed no animosity toward his white neighbors.

Riddle's father told the Cow Creek men the whites wanted peace, and he asked them to come and camp near his home and accept his protection. Chief Tom said that although Riddle's father had always been fair to the Cow Creek people, he might not be able to protect them. He recounted the many outrages visited on his people. He said Rogue River people had come to them and told them about the killings on Butte Creek four days before. The Cow Creek people believed the whites were trying to exterminate them, he added, and he and his friends meant to join the Rogue River people and die fighting.[3]

On October 13, when the Rogue River people fleeing westward into the Coast Range were about fifty miles downriver from Table Rock, they found their way blocked by a fortified miners' camp at Skull Bar, near the mouth of Galice Creek. According to Frances Fuller Victor, about thirty-five white men had taken refuge in the camp and constituted themselves a volunteer company. With them were nine Chinese miners. The volunteers were holding several captured Indian women and boys, so they must have been involved in the fighting before their position was attacked.

The War Within a War

Rogue River people were detected around the camp on the morning of October 17, setting off an exchange of fire that pinned down the miners until sunset. Victor said that the Rogue River people shot lighted arrows into the camp and burned down every building except the one held by the volunteers. A third of the miners had been killed or wounded. Having intimidated the miners, the Rogue River people resumed their journey down the river.[4]

Fifteen companies of volunteers were organized by October 20. Among the managers of this force was Charles S. Drew, who became the adjutant. His job was to handle the paperwork for the colonel of the Jackson County volunteers, Colonel John Ross.[5] Drew had already been identified as a Know-Nothing, and Ross would soon be put into the same category, in the columns of the *Statesman*.[6]

As the Know-Nothings mobilized their local army, the territorial government tried to get the mobilization under its control through a call issued October 15 by Governor George Curry. The governor asked for ten Oregon companies of volunteers to fight in the Indian war developing in western Washington Territory and nine companies to fight the Rogue River peoples. The nine companies to be organized for the south would include two battalions—a southern battalion of only four companies from Jackson County and a northern battalion of five companies from the counties to the north. Each company was to include sixty men and eleven elected officers, all with their own horses and weapons, who would serve until Curry discharged them.[7]

Curry and his Democratic colleagues moved five days later to use Curry's order to undercut the Know-Nothing military effort in Jackson County. The territorial adjutant general, E. M. Barnum, issued General Order No. 10, ordering the commanding officer of the southern Oregon battalion authorized by the governor five days before to "enforce the disbanding of all armed parties not duly enrolled into the service of the Territory." Barnum added, "A partisan warfare against any bands of Indians within our borders or on our frontiers is pregnant only with mischief, and will be viewed with distrust and disapprobation."[8] Although the concern Barnum expressed about the results of mob actions against Indians was reasonable, the context suggests he was less concerned with preventing warfare than with keeping Know-Nothings from taking over the war.

At about the same time that Barnum issued his order, an unenrolled armed party was marching northward through the Umpqua canyon. George Ambrose told Joel Palmer that these volunteers were "part of that same party of men who commenced the attack on Rogue river on the 8th ultimo"—that is, Lupton's group.

In the canyon, the unauthorized volunteers had "followed up their plan of extermination [by] waging an indiscriminate war upon every Indian whom they chanced to meet," Ambrose said. On the morning of October 24 on Lookingglass Prairie, a narrow, flat-bottomed valley about ten miles west of the village of Roseburg, they came upon the camp of a group of about thirty Indian people "who were friendly disposed, and had claimed protection of the citizens, and had moved down among them." The volunteers attacked the camp, killing eight. The rest, Ambrose said, escaped into the mountains. "I have not been able to learn that these Indians were charged with any crime," Ambrose said.[9]

A correspondent using the name Veritas wrote in the *Statesman* that twenty to twenty-five men had been involved in the daybreak attack. He said they had killed four "warriors" and wounded "a superannuated squaw." The Indians had possessed only three guns, and only one of the guns was working. "It was supposed some of the Rogue River tribe was among them, but there is no evidence of the fact," Veritas said.[10]

The day after the killings of Indian people on Lookingglass Prairie, Joel Palmer wrote to Commissioner Manypenny that he had settled on the idea of sending those Rogue River people who had not gone to war to the mouth of the Neachesna River, also known as the Salmon River, on the central coast. The reservation at Table Rock should be abandoned at once, the superintendent added, and the 344 people at Fort Lane, "in imminent danger of meeting the fate so boldly and recklessly threatened— that of annihilation," should be removed. He said he planned to put the remaining Willamette valley people on a reservation he proposed to establish on the upper Yamhill River, in a small valley that could be reached from the valley of the Willamette only by way of a narrow pass.

The War Within a War

Palmer told the commissioner that the peoples on the south coast had to be removed from their homes as well because they, like the inland Rogue River peoples, were surrounded by reckless men who considered the federal treasury "a legitimate subject of plunder" and wanted war "if for no other reason than the expenditure of large sums of money among them."[11]

Ben Wright, Joel Palmer's unlikely subagent on the south coast, went to see the Coquille River people after the beginning of the war to quiet fears aroused by a rumor that whites were coming from the Umpqua River valley to attack them. After he left the Coquilles, Wright met a white war party coming up the river, not from the Umpqua River valley but from Coos Bay. These volunteers told him they had come to protect whites from a rumored attack by the Coquilles. Wright's response was to take the volunteers back to the Coquille village from which he had just come and appoint one of them, a man named Hall, to watch over the Coquilles.[12] The Coos Bay volunteers subsequently killed eight Coquille River people.[13]

Palmer's friend R. W. Dunbar depicted the Indian people of the coast as pathetically dependent on Wright: "They beg of Ben not to suffer the whites to kill them; that they will do anything rather than have the whites come and kill them and drive them away from procuring food for the winter."[14] Was Wright energetically working to protect them, as Dunbar claimed, or was his objective to keep them under the surveillance of their enemies? He had helped Miller reestablish himself on the Chetco River the year before, and now he helped Hall, chosen from a white war party, as guardian of the Coquilles. The manner of Wright's death would be the decisive Indian commentary on his activities.

Meanwhile, the Willamette valley volunteers Governor Curry had called for were marching on the Rogue River valley. Harvey Robbins, a former Indiana resident, joined the company raised in his county because, he said in his journal, the Rogue River peoples had broken the treaty of 1853 and were "spreading death and desolation over the land."

Robbins's company camped near Eugene on the night of October 24. The volunteers held a parade the following day and heard "a very patriotic speech" from each of two exhorters. Then they resumed their march, rather slowly. Although they were mounted and responding to an emergency, on their best day they made only twenty-five miles, and they did not appear in Roseburg, in the Umpqua River valley, until October 29.[15]

Even as the Oregon volunteers were parading in Eugene, a few men calling themselves rangers escalated tensions between Indian and white people in the Puget Sound country toward the last of the three Northwest Indian-American wars that began in 1855.

According to Francis Fuller Victor, fears of an Indian uprising provoked many Americans with land claims in the White River valley to seek safety in Seattle, several miles to the north, as early as the beginning of October. A blockhouse was built at Seattle, and the navy sloop *Decatur* soon arrived, offering further protection.

On October 24, south of Puget Sound near Olympia, nineteen rangers went hunting for the Nisqually leader Leschi because, Victor said, he "was reported disaffected." The rangers did not find Leschi, but they found opposition "while reconnoitering," and two of them were killed. Four days after the rangers began their activities, Indian people descended on the White River valley, to the north, and killed nine whites. A series of deadly confrontations followed, promoting white panic and despair in western Washington.[16]

In southern Oregon, meanwhile, the Oregon volunteers were learning that they were not welcome in Roseburg. "The citizens of this place seem to treat the volunteers with but very little respect," Harvey Robbins said. "One man has even forbade us cutting wood on his claim." The following day, Robbins complained, "Rained all night. We have no tents yet. The citizens will not even let us sleep in their barns."[17]

Perhaps Robbins and his fellow volunteers in the northern battalion owed their cold reception to the men who had done the killings on Lookingglass Prairie on October 24. The presence of the volunteers might provoke the Indian peoples in the Umpqua River valley into a rage like that experienced by the whites in the path of the Rogue River peoples on October 9.

Another explanation for the cool treatment Robbins reported is suggested in the account of Cyrenius Mulkey. A volunteer in another company that passed through the Umpqua River valley at about the same time, Mulkey later recalled that the volunteers depended on the settlers along the road for food, and when the settlers had too little, "we killed anything we found from a chicken up to a steer."[18]

Harvey Robbins noted in his journal that on October 29, the volunteers elected a major to command their northern battalion, so called because it was raised to the north, that is, in the Willamette valley. William Martin was unopposed and became the unanimous choice. Having picked a leader, the volunteers began moving slowly southward once again. During the night of Wednesday, October 31, a messenger arrived at the northern battalion's camp with news that, farther south, a combined force of regulars and volunteers had attacked the Indians.[19]

The largest confrontation of the war, called the Battle of Hungry Hill, or the Battle of Grave Creek Hills, had begun. Accounts of this battle vary widely.

George Ambrose would report to Joel Palmer that on the morning of October 31, Capt. A. J. Smith and Colonel Ross, with about four hundred men between them, ordered an attack that began at about 9 A.M. "The fight lasted through the day without anything effective being done," Ambrose said. That night the troops were drawn back to get water and permit care for the wounded. When the sun rose again the Rogue River men attacked the camp of the volunteers but, according to Ambrose, were driven back after about two hours of fighting. The whites, however, were worn out and hungry. Their officers decided on retreat.

Ambrose minimized the retreat as a decision to go back for supplies but supposed that the Rogue River peoples were "flushed with success." Nine whites were killed and twenty-five wounded, the agent said, while Indian losses were unknown. The number of Indians in the fight was estimated as between 75 and 150, he said.[20]

Harvey Robbins's company had set out for the battlefield at dawn on November 1, the second day of the battle. The company rode twenty miles, arriving in the afternoon at a hostelry in the Grave Creek hills known as Six-Bit House, still about fifteen miles from the fighting. At 4 p.m., Robbins said, volunteers came in with the news that the whites were retreating with forty killed and wounded. They said that they had quit the field because they had been without provisions for two days.

Estimates of the number of Rogue River people who had fought the whites ranged from two hundred to five hundred, Robbins said. The Rogue River peoples had taken a position on a mountaintop surrounded by timber, chaparral, and manzanita. "The thickness of the brush would not admit of a charge and whenever attempted by the whites they were repulsed with a heavy loss," Robbins said. He helped carry out some of the wounded.[21]

Frances Fuller Victor ascribed the defeat to a sudden lack of discipline caused by enthusiasm. The attack was supposed to begin with howitzers firing on the Indian position, but before that plan could be executed, two volunteer companies and some other men charged into the thick brush, "all eager for the first shot." The Rogue River people fell back, Victor said, and then turned and formed a new defensive line where they fought off another charge. Sunset stopped the fight, and the whites fell back to their camp.

At sunrise on the second day, they were attacked on all sides, Victor said, and the fighting lasted until the middle of the day. Victor calculated that twenty-six volunteers had been killed or wounded, or were missing, and among the dragoons were four killed and seven wounded. "The number of Indians killed was variously estimated from eight to twenty," she added. "The number of Indians engaged in the battle was also conjectured to be from 100 to 300."[22]

Luther Hawley, a member of the only Willamette valley company that fought in the battle, sent a letter to the *Statesman* claiming victory, of a sort. Hawley said his company had rushed south from Deer Creek on the afternoon of October 28 after getting word of the impending fight. After making a rendezvous about four miles from the battlefield on the morning of October 31, Hawley said, the white forces included five companies of volunteers and 105 regulars.[23]

Cyrenius Mulkey, a member of the same company, later recalled that the American force numbered about four hundred, including 150 regulars, gathered about twenty miles from what was thought to be the camp of some five hundred Rogue River people. The troops made a two-day forced march only to find the Indians had left the camp. The men scattered to find their trail, and Mulkey, of course, claimed that he was the one who found it. Then he saw about forty young Rogue River men on a ridge who "danced a war dance" and then retreated as the volunteers advanced, tricking the volunteers into exposing themselves to fire from the Indian fortification.[24]

Luther Hawley said that the troops first saw the Rogue River men "marshalled upon a bald peak, awaiting our approach," about three-fourths of a mile away. In their eagerness to fight, the troops "threw their coats and blankets by the way-side, and the fleetest on foot were foremost in the charge." Their first charge drove the Rogue River valley men into the brush, but from the brush "they poured a deadly fire into our ranks."[25]

Mulkey said the charge, into a canyon, was disorderly. When it was driven back, the troops scattered, and in the confusion they could not be reorganized for another attempt on the Indian stronghold. "In many cases our men were shooting at each other," Mulkey said. Directing the Rogue River men, he added, was a woman he identified as Sally Lane, daughter of the late Apserkahar. Mulkey, whose recollections frequently seem somewhat overblown, claimed that he could see her clearly on a hill some six hundred to eight hundred feet above the battleground, mounted on a horse.[26]

Three regulars and four volunteers were left dead on the battlefield for eight days, Mulkey said, and there were twenty-three dead in camp and forty wounded, of whom five later died.[27]

At about sunrise on the next morning, Hawley said, the Rogue River valley people "surrounded our camp and made a general charge upon us, which was repelled in a manner which does credit to the officers and men under their commands." The fighting continued until about 10 A.M., when the Rogue River men withdrew.

According to Hawley, "We lost six killed on the ground, and thirty-one wounded—four mortally," but, he went on, "As to the report that we were *cleaned out*, I absolutely deny it." If there was any fault in what they had done, he said, "it lies in the superior officers of the day." Hawley complained that "the Indians chose their own ground, and we were obliged to fight them there or not at all."[28]

Which of these accounts comes nearest to explaining what took place at Hungry Hill cannot be known, but what is clear is that the Rogue River people had forced the retreat of a numerically superior command including regular troops.

On the day of the retreat, Palmer was addressing a letter to Bvt. Maj. Gen. John Ellis Wool, commander of the regular army's Department of the Pacific, asking for twenty men to accompany the people sheltered at Fort Lane, together with about three hundred Umpqua people, on their journey to the new reservation. Palmer said hostile meetings had been held in the Willamette valley towns along the route these people would take, and some citizens had expressed a determination to kill all Indians brought to the valley, as well as the whites who brought them.

Palmer repeated what he had told Manypenny: the war had been forced on the Indian people "by a set of reckless vagabonds, for pecuniary and political objects, and sanctioned by a numerous population who regard the treasury of the United States as a legitimate subject of plunder." The Indian people had been "driven to desperation by acts of cruelty against their people," acts "that would disgrace the most barbarous nations of the earth."[29]

In Major General Wool, Palmer had found a sympathetic audience. Wool was a 61-year-old New Yorker who had begun his military career as a captain of volunteers in the War of 1812. He was one of the many heroes of the Mexican-American War, getting part of the credit for winning the Battle of Buena Vista, the dubious victory that had also promoted the reputations of Joseph Lane and Jefferson Davis. In 1836, then a brevet brigadier general, Wool had been sent to the South to guard against an outbreak by the Cherokees, who were on the verge of forcible removal westward. He found the Cherokees more in need of protection than were the whites, but when he tried to protect them he was accused of usurping civil power and put in front of a court of inquiry.[30]

Two days after Palmer wrote to Wool, he found himself under fire in the *Oregon Statesman*. Asahel Bush claimed that Governor Curry "with ourself and other democrats . . . has complained of the employment of knownothing-whigs by the Superintendent of Indian Affairs." Palmer's flirtation with the Know-Nothings had been known to leaders of the Democratic Party for almost a year, but Bush's criticism seems to have been his first mention of it in print. When the *Statesman* called for the resignation of Know-Nothing officials on November 17, Palmer may have been the official Bush had in mind.[31] But Palmer neither admitted his involvement nor resigned.

Later in the month, a less equivocal figure in the political fight between the Democrats and the Know-Nothings, Charles Drew, was attacked in the *Statesman* by an unnamed correspondent who was either a warm supporter of William Martin, the elected major of the northern battalion, or the major himself. The correspondent said that Captain Smith and Colonel Ross had agreed to gather their men at the Grave Creek House inn on November 9 to begin a new pursuit, but that "at last accounts, the Jackson Co. battalion was not organized, nor likely to be" because "Charlie Drew was endeavoring to induce the companies who were engaged in the late battle in the Grave Creek hills, to disband, and not organize under the Governor's proclamation."

The correspondent said that John K. Lamerick, who had been appointed assistant territorial adjutant general to muster the troops in the south according to Curry's orders, had arrived in the south after the fight in the Grave Creek hills to find twelve or thirteen companies of twenty to eighty men asking for territorial recognition. Lamerick was willing to accept all who offered to serve, but he said they had to be organized into battalions of four companies apiece.

This proposal was unacceptable to Drew, the correspondent said, and Drew "declared that no company should be mustered in, unless all the companies that offered could be received into the same battalion, or rather regiment." Drew seemed to be concerned that his position in the local volunteer hierarchy would be threatened if Lamerick took his choice of the volunteers for the one battalion the governor had authorized, or even if Lamerick exceeded his authority and set up two or three battalions. If only four companies were mustered into one battalion according to Lamerick's plan, then James Bruce (one of the leaders of the Lupton expedition)[32] was expected to be elected major of the battalion over Drew or Ross, the correspondent added.[33]

The correspondent went on to say that Ross had shown his true political colors by sending the war enthusiast Dr. A. G. Henry to Major Martin's headquarters at Six-Bit House, the address given by the author of the letter. "While Martin was absent from headquarters, Henry arrived with an appointment from Ross, and took charge of Martin's hospital," he said.

Henry sent one of Martin's surgeons packing but told the other, Dr. Lucius Danforth, that he could stay on as an assistant. (Danforth had been appointed as a surgeon of the southern battalion by the governor, even though he had been accused of being a Know-Nothing.)[34] "Henry also posted up 'regulations' in the hospital, signed by himself as Chief Surgeon of the Volunteers." When Major Martin returned,

> a scene ensued—Martin went in and tearing down "them d——d regulations" he stuck them in Henry's face—told Henry that he would learn him not to insult a commander of a battalion by any interference with *his* hospital or *his* men. . . .
> There seems to have been strange work in making appointments all around. There was no necessity whatever for the appointment of any such trash.[35]

Meanwhile, Harvey Robbins and his fellow volunteers in the northern battalion had fallen back to the valley of Cow Creek, a tributary of the Umpqua River, where a party of Indians had been attacking farms. They found the fast-moving raiders were gone, so they occupied themselves with scouting and escort duty. On November 7, Robbins complained that most of them still had no tents and a cold rain was falling.

Snow fell on November 10, and they marched back to their camp-ground at Six-Bit House and set up winter quarters there. They went out to hunt down raiding parties later that month but had no success. Low on rations and complaining of soreness from having to make their way through the rough country on foot, they soon gave up.

Major Martin and about 150 volunteers arrived in the camp on November 23, together with Capt. H. M. Judah, the regular army commander of Fort Jones in California, who brought fifty troops and a twelve-pound howitzer. On November 24, according to Robbins, Martin gathered about four hundred men and "marched 15 miles over a mountain" looking for Indians.[36]

On the same day, Asahel Bush's subscribers were reading an editorial titled "The Knownothing Appointments." Bush complained that "full *two-thirds* of the *civil* places connected with the war," that is, in the medical, commissary and quartermaster departments, "are filled by members of a faction numbering less than *one*-third of the voters of the Territory, and far less than one-third of the men in the field"—the Know-Nothings.

Bush complained that William Martin had been called upon to submit to a second election for his position as major of the northern battalion. This arose from what one of his correspondents called "a secret attempt" by "knownothing emissaries" to replace Martin. They had failed, it was said, by two hundred votes. Governor Curry had informed Bush that the appointments Bush wanted overturned "were only temporary, and were made as a matter of necessity," and that the legislature, scheduled to meet shortly, would set the situation straight.[37]

In the mountains west of the Rogue River valley, meanwhile, Major Martin's troops encountered a foot of snow during their fifteen-mile march on November 24, but no Rogue River people. They camped in the Meadows, stretching along the Rogue River downriver from the mouth of Grave Creek. Early the following morning, according to Harvey Robbins, spies were sent out to look for the Indians. In the afternoon, Captain Judah and Major James Bruce (the Democrat who had been elected commander of the southern battalion two weeks earlier[38]) went to a high point with a spyglass. Robbins said they came back with the news that the Indians had burned their village.

Bruce's battalion arrived the next morning. A spy who had been sent out some thirty-six hours before came back saying that he had seen the Indians and they appeared to be preparing to fight. The southern battalion and Captain Jonathan Keeney's company, which included Harvey

Robbins, were ordered to cross the river. At about 1 P.M., while they were building rafts, about twenty-five Rogue River people began firing on them. When the shooting stopped some seven hours later, one volunteer was dead and twenty-one more were wounded. At about 8 P.M. the volunteers took their dead and wounded back to their camp, having realized, Robbins said, that "it was impossible to accomplish our objective or even do any good in any way."

On November 27, the volunteers buried the man who had been killed. The two volunteer majors, Martin and Bruce, sent for reinforcements and supplies. Two battalions of volunteers and Captain Judah's fifty regulars with their howitzer had been stopped only a few miles into the mountains by the opposition of about twenty-five men.

After three snowy days, Robbins said, the Indians still held their position. On the morning of Sunday, December 2, "Major Martin and Major Bruce seeing that we were in danger of being bound in here by snow, deeming it unwise to remain here longer, ordered their forces to march back for the settlement."[39]

A few months later, Martin got into a letter-writing match with a man called Greenwood over who should carry the blame for the retreat. Greenwood called Martin a traitor and accused him of personal responsibility for the failure. Martin reacted in the *Statesman* by saying that the decision to withdraw had been shared by nine officers and had been caused by lack of supplies.[40]

As the volunteers were withdrawing, Governor Curry and Adjutant General Barnum toured the war zone, where they were said to be looking into complaints that demobilization of unauthorized local volunteer companies had left white communities defenseless. Their chief concern, however, may have been to learn whether as many of Curry's appointees as Bush seemed to think were political liabilities. Curry and Barnum took only one action, and it had little to do with local defense: they ordered reorganization of the two battalions into one regiment.[41]

Meanwhile, volunteers still organized themselves at will, without the governor's permission. One such company was set up as the result of a scare in the Umpqua country. A correspondent using the pseudonym "Z" informed readers of the *Statesman* that one hundred Indians had descended on the valley of Lookingglass Creek on December 2. They had wounded a farmer named Rice and burned his outbuildings as well as a schoolhouse and eight other buildings in the vicinity. In retaliation, at daybreak the following day, fourteen volunteers descended on an Indian camp, supposedly the camp of the war party. But no more than thirty people were in the camp, not the one hundred men said to have made the attack.

"The Indians were completely surprised, but owing to thickness of the brush, they had time to seize their arms, and for a few moments fought with great desperation," said Z, adding that the Indians soon fled, leaving three dead. Several more were thought to have been mortally wounded and thrown themselves in the creek. The volunteers found twenty-three horses, three rifles, and what Z described as "a large amount of stolen property" in the camp. Only one volunteer was wounded, and only slightly.[42]

The severe early winter that almost immobilized the whites must also have strained the slender resources of the Rogue River peoples in their mountain refuges. The sufferings of the peace party among the Rogue River people camped at Fort Lane were recorded by George Ambrose on December 2 in a letter to Palmer. He told Palmer there were several inches of snow on the ground as he wrote and more was falling. The people under his questionable care had no winter clothing. Only a few had shoes and stockings. Many were sick. "Peace and plenty seem to be far more destructive to the Indian than war," Ambrose added, implying that in his estimation, "plenty" for Indians did not necessarily include the possession of adequate clothing.

Ambrose told Palmer that he could talk Toquahear's people into making the journey Palmer wanted them to make to the far-away reservation, but he warned the superintendent that the march to the Willamette valley "could not be accomplished without a vast deal of suffering among them."[43]

On the evening of the following day, December 3, the excitable Dr. Henry of Yamhill, whose services as quartermaster and surgeon had been spurned in the south, delivered a speech to the citizens of the territorial capital, Corvallis. The doctor complained that allegations made by Asahel Bush and Governor Curry that whites had started the war would stimulate "morbid sympathy" for the Indian people. If those allegations remained uncontradicted, Henry argued, Congress might "pass a law of outlawry against Southern Oregon" rather than appropriating money to pay the volunteers.[44]

In response, the *Statesman* crowed that Henry had "assured the benighted audience 'on honor' that Charley [Drew] & Co., were marvellously proper men" and challenged any man present to prove the accusation that the "knownothing, peculating faction had incited hostilities south," drawing comments from "two or three most prominent and respectable citizens south" who "rose and stated their belief that such was the fact—that hostilities had thus been deliberately incited was the candid belief of the southern community."

Not only that, but a certain Doctor Stone's recitation of "the *hospital scene* between Major Bill and Dr. H., 'brought down the house' in the most approved style," and Captain Tichenor, the founder of Port Orford, stated that "the war had been deliberately brought about by machinations of the above named faction," that is, the Know-Nothings. Bush's purpose at this point would not have been served, of course, if the Democratic leanings of James Lupton and his lieutenant Bruce had been noted. Tichenor went on to say that "we were in a war, and he [Tichenor] was for carrying it through—was for his country right or wrong." Bush echoed Tichenor: "Like Capt. Tichenor, whoever, or whatever brought on this southern war, we are for prosecution of it to the last."[45]

On December 5, Harvey Robbins noted that the candidates for colonel and lieutenant colonel of the new regiment Governor Curry had ordered organized "have been shouting here today, telling us their views and what they would do if elected. If they make their words good, woe unto the Indians."[46] Bob Williams, who had been captain of one of the companies of the southern battalion, was elected colonel, and Major Martin was elevated to lieutenant colonel.[47]

Williams, like James Bruce, was apparently involved in the Lupton killings. A California paper had reported that a "Captain Williams" commanded fourteen men under Lupton.[48] Another California paper had reported in the autumn of 1854 that Williams killed an Indian who declined to yield to his wife "to the reckless and wanton debauchery of a fiend clad in white man's skin."[49]

Despite the aggressive speech making of the candidates for regimental offices, the war was as good as over for Robbins and his comrades. On December 8, he noted, "Today we were ordered to march back into the Umpqua where we could obtain sustenance for ourselves and animals." They had been battered by rain and snow and were on short rations. Robbins had complained at one point that members of another company camped alongside "have provisions plenty, but take care to eat it themselves." The retreating men made Roseburg on December 28 and Eugene on December 31.[50]

Frances Fuller Victor explained that the men of the northern battalion had enlisted "to gratify an evanescent sympathy, or a love of adventure" and they "were becoming impatient of so arduous and unprofitable a service, and so demanded and received their discharge."[51]

As the Willamette valley volunteers in the south were being discharged, their counterparts on the Walla Walla River in eastern Washington were in action. They had captured the Walla Walla leader Peopeo Moxmox when he came into their camp under a flag of truce. Then, on December 7, they forced Palouse, Walla Walla, and Umatilla people into beginning an indecisive four-day battle. After the first clash, Peopeo Moxmox was beaten, shot to death, and mutilated. The Oregonians said that he and other prisoners, also killed, bolted when volunteers tried to tie them up. Parts of his body were sent to Oregon as souvenirs.[52]

The volunteers in southern Oregon were also in the field in December 1855. They were not, however, seeking combat with the main body of Rogue River people holding out in the mountains. Instead, they concerned themselves with people who may have been raiders or who may have been under the impression that they had opted out of the war.

A correspondent reported in the *Statesman* that on the night of December 24, one company attacked a camp east of the Table Rock Reservation, "completely routing them, killing eight bucks and capturing a considerable amount of stock and property heretofore stolen from the settlers." At about the same time, the correspondent said, another company attacked a camp on the north side of the Rogue River and killed or captured the last free members of Jake's band,[53] which the Lupton expedition had attacked in October.

On the following day, Gen. John Wool reported that the inflated costs of making war in Oregon Territory had prevented his organization of an expedition by regulars. Wool argued that the high costs of transportation and forage had been caused by "*the extraordinary course pursued by Gov. Curry, who is making war on the Indians on his own account*, and without the slightest reference to myself." If the government paid for the war, Wool said, "we shall have no peace, and war may be prolonged indefinitely, especially as it is generally asserted that the present war is a godsend to the people."[54]

After a visit to Oregon, General Wool reported that winter operations against the Indians would be impractical and unnecessary, and he repeated his belief that the war on the Rogue River had been caused by Lupton's massacres. Wool predicted again that the volunteers' war would go on indefinitely if the government paid for it. Commenting on Wool's report, a *New York Tribune* story (later reprinted in the *Statesman*) complained that the war could cost more than $4 million and hypothesized that "if Oregon were independent of the Atlantic States, her Indians would not be so shamelessly butchered, nor the Federal Treasury so atrociously plundered."[55]

On January 2, according to the *Statesman*, Delegate Joseph Lane wrote a letter promising that he would "endeavor to procure an appropriation with as little delay as possible for defraying the expenses of our Indian war."[56] As Lane was making his promise, volunteers were persistently running up the bill in southern Oregon. A correspondent signing himself Jim reported in the *Statesman* that one of the companies involved in the Christmas Eve attack had ridden out accompanied by twenty-five regular infantrymen and a howitzer after learning on New Year's Day of "a number of Indians fortified in cabins on Applegate." This party had scarcely left Jacksonville when one of the volunteers was shot down. The dead man was Martin Angell, who was said to have shot an Indian from his door during the excitement leading up to the 1853 treaty.[57]

The ill-fated expedition then lost all of its ammunition when a mule fell into the Applegate. Delayed by the wait for more ammunition, the troops didn't arrive at their objective until about 3 P.M. on Friday, January 4. They "planted their howitzer and let a shell through the roof of one of the houses, killing two Indians," Jim reported. The volunteers maintained a siege until about 2 A.M., when "the Indians broke by the guard" and got away.

The volunteers were said to be in pursuit, but their pursuit may have lacked sincerity; despite their possession of a howitzer, the whites had fought to a draw at best. Five whites were reported wounded and one killed. One man was shot through the leg at a range of about five hundred yards. "The whites all say the Indians can shoot well," the correspondent said.[58]

The political struggle of the Oregon Democracy to shake off Joel Palmer, meanwhile, was as noisy and ineffectual as the efforts of the volunteers on the Applegate. But Palmer's many opponents were now complaining about his implementation of the reservation policy as well as questioning his fidelity to the Democratic Party. On January 8, a caucus of Democratic members of the legislature discussed Palmer's behavior and forwarded a formal complaint to President Franklin Pierce. Palmer, the legislators complained, was trying to buy the land claims of whites "with the avowed intention of bringing thousand of Indians from remote parts of the country; and of colonizing them in the heart of this, the Willamette valley."

Furthermore, they told the president, Palmer had "bound himself with the perfidious oaths of that dark and hellish secret political order," the Know-Nothings, and had kept faith with them "by neglecting to vote for the nominees of the democratic party, and by appointing incompetent Know-Nothing Whigs to office, to the exclusion of sound, worthy, and competent Democrats."[59]

Joel Palmer informed Commissioner Manypenny in an angry letter written January 22 that he had dispensed with the services of his secretary,

Edward Geary, who had been suggested by the legislature as his replacement. Palmer said that Geary had agreed, in return for the legislature's recommendation, to abandon Palmer's reservation plan if he were appointed in Palmer's place.[60]

On the day Palmer wrote his angry letter, three companies of volunteers were making their way toward a reported hostile camp on Cow Creek, according to a letter in the *Statesman* signed by Edgar R. Stone, assistant surgeon of the Oregon Mounted Volunteers. They found the site of the camp on the following day, but the Indian people were gone, and they had left by way of a trail that was too rough for the pack mules carrying the volunteers' rations.

Some of the volunteers decided to turn back. About seventy men under a Captain Joseph Bailey stayed behind. But that night they were driven off, the doctor said, by ten Indians who started shooting into the camp when Bailey's men made a bonfire to provide light for a wrestling match.

Stone admitted that Bailey's retreat, involving ten Rogue River people against seventy volunteers who were well-armed and well-supplied, was hardly glorious, but he said that Bailey had acted wisely because he believed that the ten Indians were decoys and that a larger Indian force was nearby. Two whites were killed, the doctor added, and the attackers escaped injury. When Captain Bailey retreated, Stone said, "the Indians came into camp and fired off their guns, yelled, danced, and seemed to exult in victory."[61]

The Puget Sound War reached what historian Kent D. Richards called a psychological low point for the Americans when a combined force of Indians said to have been led by Leschi attacked Seattle on January 26. They apparently meant to capture the ammunition aboard the *Decatur*. The sloop had been beached for repairs and its guns removed, leaving vulnerable both the ship itself and the village it had been guarding.

By the time the attack was mounted, however, the *Decatur* was back in service. According to Frances Fuller Victor, the battle of Seattle began when the *Decatur* shelled a house where Indians were said to be hiding. In response, "the blood-curdling war-whoop burst from a stentorian thousand throats, accompanied by a crash of musketry from the entire

Indian line." The Indians occupied much of Seattle. But they seem to have been thwarted in their efforts to extinguish its defenders and were driven out when the captain of the *Decatur* had his gunners shell the ground and houses under their control.[62]

The Oregon territorial legislature decided on January 30 to send a memorial to President Pierce complaining about the conduct of General Wool. The memorial argued that almost all the Indians in large parts of Oregon and Washington territories had, "unprovoked on the part of the whites," engaged in "indiscriminate slaughter of all our citizens who fell into their hands." Volunteers had acted with "promptness and zeal," whereas Wool "remained inactive, and has refused to send the United States troops to the relief of the volunteers, or to supply them with arms and ammunition in their time of need." Worse yet, the general had shown "a disgraceful activity in his endeavors to persuade our merchants, and those of California, not to furnish ammunition and supplies for our volunteers." The legislators asked Pierce to recall Wool from his command.

The signers of this document were the President of the Council (the upper house) and the Speaker of the House of Representatives, Delazon Smith.[63] Speaker Smith had been among the critics of A. G. Henry's motives for supporting the war when Henry spoke December 3 in Corvallis.[64] Now, two months later, Smith was taking the very action Henry had recommended: informing the federal government that the war was not what Wool had represented it as being and arguing that the volunteers and their suppliers were worthy of payment.

Perhaps Smith's mind had been changed by Governor Curry's reorganization of the territorial army, which had put the war under Democratic auspices. The new commander of that army, picked by the legislature, was John Lamerick,[65] who quickly demonstrated his sympathies by picking Nat Lane, Jo Lane's son, as one of the enrollment officers who would recruit the new companies that would replace the old northern battalion.[66]

In Washington, D.C., on February 18, Joseph Lane wrote a letter to Governor Curry informing the governor that he had introduced a bill in Congress for the payment of the volunteers and their suppliers. "I am always in favor of any and all wars," Lane told Curry.[67]

The following day the *Statesman* crowed that, as predicted, Governor Curry had shorn the "brother know-nothings" of their war appointments, and complained that as a result, "the Oregonian is opposed to the war, and endeavoring to embarrass its prosecution, by throwing doubts upon the question of the payment of expenses, seeking to obstruct their payment by falsehoods and misrepresentations, and rendering 'aid and comfort' to Gen. Wool in his efforts to disparage the war and defeat the assumption of its cost."[68]

In fact, the *Oregonian* had rejected Wool's accusations point by point two weeks before. The paper had even denied Wool's claim that Governor Curry had failed to preserve vouchers for the expenses of the war.[69] No rational political reason for criticizing the war remained, even though the leaders of the *Oregonian*'s Know-Nothing constituency had cause for resentment, having been shouldered away from the choicest places at the public trough. Both Democrats and Know-Nothings stood to lose if their sniping at each other interfered with getting the federal government to pay their claims.

The men who had made the war took note of the evolving federal Indian policy of paternalistic apartness only in their complaints against the efforts of Joel Palmer to carry it out. Already vulnerable because of his flirtation with Know-Nothingism, Palmer made himself an easy target for his political enemies by criticizing the war and pushing stubbornly ahead with his plans to establish reservations.

6

Undefeated

On February 23, 1856, Indian Service agent George Ambrose sent word to Joel Palmer that Toquahear's people, the Rogue River people who had remained at peace, had begun their long, cold walk from Fort Lane to Grand Ronde,[1] the small valley on the Yamhill River where Palmer expected to set his Indian colonization plan into motion.[2]

In the south, meanwhile, the people who had gone into the mountains with Tecumtum remained undefeated, and the war had been renewed, not in the Rogue River valley but on the coast. Joel Palmer first learned of this new phase of the war when three letters from Port Orford arrived at his headquarters in Dayton on the morning of Tuesday, March 3. One had been sent by the collector of customs at Port Orford, the other two by Bvt. Maj. John Reynolds of the regular army Third Artillery, the commander at Fort Orford.[3] The attack had begun at daylight on February 22 near the big village three miles above the mouth of the Rogue River.[4]

R. W. Dunbar, the customs collector, had written that many well-armed Indians, strangers to him, had appeared on the coast. About three hundred men had attacked the camp of a volunteer company. All the dwellings between the Rogue River and Port Orford had been burned, and Ben Wright, the Indian Service subagent on the coast, was believed dead.[5]

Lucy Metcalf, an Indian woman who witnessed the war on the coast when she was about thirteen years old, told ethnographer Cora Du Bois that it started "because some Indians from way up the river came down and told the people to fight." It was "the Indians from the mountains," she told Du Bois, who "sneaked across the river" and killed Wright.[6]

Perhaps the attack on the whites on the coast was a way out of the dilemma that the Rogue River peoples faced as the spring of 1856 drew near. When winter ended they would have to begin their annual quest for food, which would scatter them and make them vulnerable just when the white expeditions against them would be getting under way. But the problem of whether to fight or eat might be solved if the whites could be expelled from the coast.

Palmer told Commissioner Manypenny that subagent Ben Wright had been confident that he could maintain peace up to his final communication. Was Wright a failed peacemaker, or was he essentially the same man who had displayed the scalps of murdered Modocs in Yreka in 1852? Perhaps he did strive for peace, but the manner of his death would be the decisive Indian commentary on his activities.[7]

According to Frances Fuller Victor, the whites had felt some insecurity before the attack; the men of Whaleshead or Gold Beach, near the mouth of the Rogue River on the south bank, had built "a rude fort" on the north bank. The local volunteer company that had been camped during the winter at Big Bend, about thirty miles upstream, had come back downriver and camped near the village called Tututunne near the mouth of the river.

Victor said some of the volunteers attended a "dancing-party" held on the night of February 22 in honor of Washington's birthday while fifteen men stayed in camp to guard it. The fifteen wallflowers were attacked so suddenly and furiously that only two got away. One of these was Charles Foster, who said he hid nearby and watched the massacre.

Meanwhile, other Indians had crossed from the village on the south side to a house on the north side where Ben Wright lived. They found him there with the captain of the volunteers, a man named Poland. They asked Wright to go back to the village with them and arrest "a certain half-breed named Enos, notoriously a bad man." Wright and Poland crossed the river and were killed, and their bodies were so mutilated, it was said, that they were unrecognizable. Thirty-one non-Indians died in the initial assault, and Chetco Jennie, the interpreter whose bare body Wright had once whipped in Port Orford, "betrayed him to his death and afterward ate a piece of his heart."[8]

When Alexander W. Chase of the Coast and Geodetic Survey visited the Siletz Reservation in 1868, he met a woman he called "Too-toot-na Jenny" who was said to have "headed the first outbreak" in 1856. Chase had been told that "after the murder of the Indian Agent [she] tore his heart from his quivering body, and to show her contempt and bravado, eat [sic] a portion of it." Chase added that "she strenuously denies the horrible deed of cannibalism." The daughter of the Tututunne chief Shell Drake, Jenny was said to have played a leading part in the war on the coast, "often leading the tribe into battle."[9]

In early March, a messenger slipped out of the fort at the mouth of the Rogue River where the white survivors were holding out and made his way to Port Orford. There was no help in Port Orford, so he plunged into the Coast Range to carry his plea to the inland settlements. By his account, at least one hundred whites were surrounded in the fort by three hundred to four hundred Indians. Captain Tichenor could not relieve the besieged fort by sea because of adverse winds. No other relief was in sight, and provisions were running out. Meanwhile, about eighty men, including thirty regular soldiers, were holding out at Port Orford in another make-shift fortification.[10]

While the Indian people on the southern Oregon coast were experiencing a kind of victory, however brief it might turn out to be, their counterparts in the Puget Sound country were coming to the end of their war. Regular troops commanded by Col. Silas Casey confronted them in the White River valley, and on March 1 took a blockhouse they had controlled. The regulars then declared the Indian threat at an end.

Territorial volunteers moving into the same area, however, reported that they were attacked on March 8 by a force of Indians, which they drove off. Afterward, according to Francis Fuller Victor, "the Indians did not attempt to make a stand." All that remained was to capture Leschi.[11]

The Oregon volunteers in the southwestern interior were beginning to stir as the weather improved. A correspondent writing from Deer Creek in the Umpqua country reported in the *Statesman* that the lately appointed General Lamerick seemed determined to fight the Indians at the Meadows, down the Rogue River from the mouth of Grave Creek. On March 4, an anonymous correspondent with an affinity for the style and concerns of Indian Service agent George Ambrose wrote that Lamerick was expected to begin the march to the Meadows the following day, that Bob Williams had resigned his commission, and that the Rogue River people who had been sheltered at Fort Lane—Toquahear's people—were thought to be coming north through the Umpqua canyon with George Ambrose and a military escort.

The following day the same correspondent claimed that Know-Nothings had tried to "stampede" the noncombatant Indians. Two men had entered Toquahear's camp and "deliberately shot down an old decrepid, worn out blind Indian." George Ambrose was quoted as having said that "had it been an Indian of influence or value in the tribe nothing could have prevented their breaking."

The correspondent said that Ambrose had learned from a disgusted former member of the Know-Nothings that they were "moving heaven and earth to break up the forces in the field and prolong the war." He claimed that the Know-Nothings had a plan to send two or three companies to join Lamerick's troops and "work his defeat" if there was a fight.[12]

Joel Palmer sent word to Indian Commissioner George Manypenny on March 8 that the war was not going well. "In every instance when a conflict has ensued between volunteers and hostile Indians in southern Oregon the latter have gained what they regard as a victory," he said. Moreover, he added, while volunteers had successfully attacked Indian camps, only Indian people "unprepared to make resistance and not expecting such attack" had been beaten.

Palmer said that "the avowed determination of the people to exterminate the Indian race" had pushed the coastal Indians into alliance with those from the valley. News of "the commission of outrages (of which there have been many) by our people" had spread quickly among the Indian people and was "used as evidence of the necessity for all to unite in war against us." Most of the Indian peoples south of Port Orford and west of Fort Lane, and probably the Coquilles as well, had become hostile, Palmer said, "and doubtless will remain so until they have positive demonstration of the folly of attempting to redress their own wrongs."[13]

General Wool, meanwhile, had taken steps to give the Indian peoples the positive demonstration of which Palmer spoke by sending regular troops to reclaim the south coast. The *Statesman* reported that the steamship *Columbia* arrived at Crescent City, California, at 9 A.M. on March 8 and debarked ninety-six men under Bvt. Lt. Col. Robert Buchanan. Early the next morning, the *Columbia* reached Port Orford and debarked another forty-two soldiers.[14]

One of Buchanan's officers, under the name "Sergeant Jones," wrote about his adventures for *Harper's New Monthly Magazine*. Jones, who has been identified as Capt. Edward O. C. Ord of the Third Artillery,[15] said the soldiers remained at Crescent City for a few days to drill fresh recruits and then marched north for the Rogue River. Most of the men were raw recruits, he said.[16]

Three days after Buchanan landed at Crescent City, a strident criticism of what the California papers were printing about the war was published in the *Statesman*. One San Francisco editor had questioned whether the Battle of Hungry Hill—"one of the most fatal engagements in the annals of savage warfare"—had ever happened. The *Statesman* said that "it is even contended that the war is prosecuted merely to afford a market for our surplus produce. Such statements seem too absurd for contradiction." The

Statesman predicted that neither the California papers nor the *Oregonian* could keep the volunteers from their work: "Savage atrocity will be punished and prevented, and a grateful Congress will appropriate to repay the patriotic citizens of Oregon the expenses incurred in the defence of their homes and families."[17]

Buchanan's regulars marched north from Crescent City on March 13 together with forty volunteers under George Abbott, the man who had organized the killings of Indian people on the Coquille two years before. On the same day, Captain Christopher C. Augur marched his troops south from Port Orford, planning to link up with Buchanan's command at the junction of the Illinois and Rogue Rivers.[18]

On the way to the Rogue River, Captain Ord said, Buchanan's men passed a burned-out farm and later, at a volunteer post, the graves of two Indian women who had come to talk to the volunteers. The volunteers, thinking the women might be spies, had shot them. Ord noted: "There is a fearful account in barbarity open between the settlers and the savages. Who can tell on which side the balance lies?" When the troops reached the Chetco, they found the ruins of a hut, apparently the former residence of A. F. Miller. Ord contended that Miller had brought the war to the coast through his bad treatment of the Chetco people.[19] Miller had apparently been driven away, but when Alexander W. Chase of the Coast and Geodetic Survey visited the Chetco River in the autumn of 1873, he found Miller still alive and in possession of his claim.[20]

At the mouth of the Rogue River, the soldiers found the ruins of the huts and flumes used by the miners, as well as many mangled, decomposing bodies, half eaten by birds. The attackers had shot some of them, crushed the heads of some with hatchets, and cut the throats of others after tying them up.[21]

Buchanan's command was late for its rendezvous with Augur's detachment from Port Orford, which was waiting at the junction of the Rogue and Illinois Rivers. Augur decided to march his men downriver. While they were still within sight of their camp, "some five or six Indians came into camp and throwed powder into the fire, discharged their rifles, and made several other demonstrations of victory," the *Statesman* reported.

The Indians then followed the troops down the river and the next morning "repeated the same proceedings as at the previous camp."[22]

In the Willamette valley, meanwhile, Joel Palmer's Indian colonization plan was provoking political opposition. Fred Waymire, speaker of the territorial House of Representatives at the last legislative session, complained that his efforts as enrolling officer for volunteers in Polk County in the Willamette valley were hampered by the fears Palmer was arousing by bringing Indians into the valley. Waymire contended that Palmer meant "to create a war where peace has so long prevailed." The Indians were said to have "arms and ammunition sufficient to commit a great slaughter of our citizens at their pleasure." Ammunition furnished to them, Waymire said, "is sent to the *war parties south*, wilst [sic] Palmer is feeding here the old, decrepit men, women and children."[23]

Unidentified Indian people attacked a company of volunteers commanded by a Captain Laban Buoy in the valley of Cow Creek on March 23. A correspondent for the *Statesman* who used the name Myrtle said that the Indians got away with about thirty horses. Buoy's men "followed them to the brush, but didn't go in, for fear they might get hurt." The following morning the raiders came back "and caught the volunteers napping, and came near burning their fort." In response, "the majority of the company evinced their contempt of the Indians, and their fearlessness of danger, by coming into Roseburg, and boarding at Rose's hotel." Myrtle added that he believed that although the volunteers claimed to have killed several Indians they killed only one, "and from that one they took *only eighteen scalps*, though some malicious persons persist in stating the number at nineteen."[24]

A detachment under Major Bruce was attacked on March 25 in the valley of the Illinois River while escorting a pack train, according to M. C. Barkwell, a surgeon for the volunteers. Barkwell said he was with a small party riding ahead of the main volunteer force when about one hundred Rogue River men confronted them. Barkwell's horse, carrying his instruments and medicines, was shot and captured by the Indians. When the main body of Bruce's volunteers came up, Barkwell said, the Indians retired from the field. By his count three volunteers were killed, but another report set the number at four and added that the volunteers lost about forty horses and saddles as well as twenty-eight mules and their cargoes, including ammunition. Barkwell was pessimistic. "The volunteers have had so little success that I am getting tired of it, would like to see the regulars take the field," he said.[25]

While the regulars in the interior seem to have stayed aloof from combat during the latter part of March 1856, the regulars on the coast did not. At 8 A.M. on March 26, Captain Ord marched his command of 113 men out of their camp at the mouth of the Rogue River toward the upriver village of the people Ord called the Mac-a-noo-te-nay. Ord's report to Buchanan said his guide led the company on a hard march through rough country "by circuitous Indian trails or bridle paths." They reached the village at about 2:30 P.M. They saw thirteen houses "in a pretty little river bottom," but the only Indians in view were watching the troops from a hill across the river.

Leaving their haversacks and the officers' riding mules behind, the company went into the village. Ord directed two of his men to set fire the houses. Then he decided that the Indian people across the river meant to cross upriver and then come down on his command "while my men might be busy burning houses or racing [sic] horses." He positioned some of his men to meet the expected attack. The Indian people crossed and skirmished with Ord's men over possession of the hills around the village. Ord claimed success. Eight Indians were killed and about as many more wounded, he said, adding disapprovingly that some Indian women were shot by his guide, who fired into groups of Indian people across the river. Only two soldiers were wounded, one of them Ord's first sergeant.[26]

Quoted in *Harper's New Monthly Magazine* as Sergeant Jones, Ord noted, "One old woman kept up a terrible screeching. The guides said it was because we had killed her baby." He spoke of the withdrawal of the troops as "a terrible night march" during which he had taken the wounded sergeant on his mule "and so carried him, in spite of cries entreaties, and fainting fits." He commented that "a few adventurers" who had chosen to "scatter themselves through the labyrinths of these mountain fastnesses" had no right to expect the government to send soldiers "to war against such an awful country and such well-wronged Indians." He suggested ending the war "by putting all the gold-hunters on a reservation, and paying them roundly to stay there, leaving this God-forsaken country to the Indians."[27]

Why Ord's company was sent to attack the Mikonotunne village is not clear. Nothing suggests that the people of this village were particularly responsible for what had taken place on the coast in February. Perhaps the village was cleared for some tactical purpose. Although it was scarcely a decisive victory, however, it was a demonstration of the vulnerability of the Rogue River peoples. If their homes and provisions were destroyed, they could not win. Unlike their enemies, they could not be reinforced and resupplied from outside the war zone.

On March 28, 1856, two days after Ord's men attacked the Mikono-tunne village, Joseph Lane of Oregon introduced a bill in Congress appropriating $300,000 for the Indian wars in Oregon and Washington territories. The *Democratic Standard* of Portland said Lane accompanied the bill "with an earnest appeal in behalf of his exposed and suffering constituency."[28] According to the Washington correspondent for the *New York Tribune*, Lane tried to rush his bill through the House but it was sent off to the committee on ways and means.[29]

In Oregon, meanwhile, the political heat directed at Joel Palmer was rising. On the same day that Lane asked for money for the war, attendees of a meeting in the town of Lafayette, only a few miles from Palmer's headquarters in Dayton, unanimously adopted a petition addressed to Palmer demanding answers to a series of questions about the Indian peoples he was settling on the Grand Ronde reservation. The petitioners expressed concern over "the numerous reports in circulation throughout the country, greatly agitating the public mind, rendering many fearful of their personal safety, and of the safety of their property." They wanted to know how many Indians were on the reservation, what sort of arms and ammunition they possessed, and "in what manner, and in what number Indians are permitted to leave the reservation."[30]

On the following day, Palmer's secretary sent a message to the committee appointed by the Lafayette meeting. The secretary said there were about one thousand Indian people at Grand Ronde and they were not allowed arms except under severe restrictions. Nor were they allowed to leave the reservation except to work as teamsters, accompanied by white men employed by the Indian service. Palmer himself sent a telegram from Oregon City promising that any arms in Indian hands would be taken away when he had returned to his post.

The committee was not satisfied. The following day, March 30, the protest meeting was reconvened at Lafayette and a series of resolutions was passed. Respected citizens had provided evidence, the protesters contended, that the Indian people had a large quantity of arms in their possession and that they constantly left the reservations in large groups. Furthermore, the protesters resolved "that the whole project of making an Indian Reservation upon our coast meets with our unqualified disapprobation; that our duty to ourselves and our country demands that we should use every means within our power to prevent the consummation of the same."[31]

In Washington, the ways and means committee reported out a substitute for Lane's bill on Monday, March 31.[32] This version, according to the *Democratic Standard*, called for $300,000 "for restoring and maintaining the peaceable disposition of the Indian tribes on the Pacific Coast, and $120,000 to purchase gunpowder," because "the Committee thought it would be better to report a measure looking to peace on the frontiers, as recommended by the Secretary of War."[33]

Representative John Allison of Pennsylvania opposed the bill, quoting General Wool in order "to prove that this war is an iniquitous fraud." A *Pittsburgh Gazette* correspondent said that Allison was concerned that Congress might set a precedent that could commit the government to spending as much as four million dollars and that he wanted the situation investigated.[34] In response, Lane made a speech in the House "to vindicate the character of the people of Oregon." Lane claimed that "when the time shall arrive that I can have a full opportunity to do so, I shall be able to satisfy every gentleman upon this floor that the people of Oregon Territory are in no way to blame for the war with the Indians."

He described the Indians of Oregon as "treacherous and ungrateful" and insisted that "they have commenced all the wars that have taken

122   Undefeated

place between them and the white settlers." He expressed regret that, "in defense of truth and justice," he was forced to oppose General Wool, "my old commander" and a "gallant man." But Wool's reports were not true, Lane said.[35] He accepted the replacement bill, however, and it was passed the following day, April 1. Unlike Lane's bill, the replacement did not commit the federal government to assuming the territorial war debt.[36]

On the same day, volunteers attacked a group of Rogue River people who had declared themselves at peace when the February outbreak of violence began on the coast. They had given up their weapons to Major Reynolds at Fort Orford and camped there under Reynold's protection until, a *Statesman* correspondent reported, two or three whites who apparently meant to keep the Indian service from protecting the Indians told them that they had been kept at Fort Orford so that they could be killed. The Indian people believed what they were told and fled northward. Volunteers caught them at the mouth of the Coquille River on April 1 and killed most of them.[37]

Gen. John E. Wool, at his post at Benecia on San Francisco Bay, could not have known what was transpiring in Washington, D.C., but on April 2 he wrote a letter to the editor of the *National Intelligencer* in Washington that was as good as a response to Lane's comments to the House two days before. The volunteers, said Wool, had given "little or no service" as protectors of the white inhabitants while carrying on a war "in the most signally barbarous and savage manner." He had done all in his power to defend localities assailed by the Indian people, he said, and he was certain that "but for the indiscriminate warfare carried on against them, and the massacre of several parties of friendly Indians by the troops of Gov. Curry, the war would have long since been brought to a close in Oregon."

The general argued that "the determination of the Oregonians to exterminate the Indians . . . may prolong the war almost indefinitely. Another Florida war may be had in Rogue River Valley, owing to the mountainous character of the country." He estimated that exterminating the Indians "would cost from fifty to one hundred millions of dollars, besides thousands of innocent and valuable lives."

The conduct of the Oregonians toward the Rogue River people who had been gathered during the winter at Fort Lane demonstrated their attitude, Wool said. Captain Smith had reported that it took most of his two companies of regulars to keep the citizens from murdering the Indians at the fort. On their way north to the new reservation, "although escorted by over 100 soldiers, they were followed by a citizen, who shot one of the Indians, declaring at the same time that he intended to follow them and kill all he could."[38]

On April 8, the *Statesman* reprinted, with an oddly restrained commentary, a story taken from the *Missouri Republican* of St. Louis. The Missouri newspaper's account said news had come by way of California of "a battle between four hundred regulars and volunteers and some three hundred Indians, in which the former, after nine hours hard fighting, were compelled to retreat." The *Republican* editorialist had been incredulous; the claim that an American force had been forced to retreat by a smaller force of Indians "ought to have made the California people a little wary about believing such foolish gossip, but they were not, and the story has had a run all over the country."

The St. Louis paper added that the family of Capt. A. J. Smith in St. Louis had received letters from him dated as late as November 6 "in which he does not even allude to any battle with the Indians." Thus, said the *Republican*, "we look upon the account of the battle as an unadulterated hoax, gotten up to force the Government to send additional troops to that region."

Appended to this was a comment from the *Ohio State Journal*, which had reprinted the St. Louis story "in order that our readers may know something of the tricks practiced upon the Government for the purpose of getting the Government troops sent to the Territories." Reports of Indian depredations and murders were "either totally false or gross exaggerations," the Ohio paper insisted.

Asahel Bush of the *Statesman* said he did not know why Smith had not mentioned "the fight at Hungry Hill (called so because the troops were in the engagement for forty-eight hours with nothing to eat), . . . but we know that he was in it, and a disastrous contest it proved to be."³⁹ The editors in Missouri and Ohio were, of course, mistaken, but their comments demonstrated that there was a growing suspicion in the States that the wars against the Indians in Oregon and Washington territories were being misrepresented.

In the same issue, the *Statesman* carried a letter from former Lt. Col. William Martin in which he complained of being blamed for the difficulties of the volunteer army at the Meadows and on Cow Creek while he had been "subservient to a Col. prejudiced and persuaded by a clique of uncompromising knownothings" (presumably John Ross). To an earlier correspondent's claim that "two-thirds of the people in the south and nearly the whole army are against him," Martin responded that "if two-thirds are knownothings of the *Drew*ed order, I don't doubt it, nor would I desire it otherwise."⁴⁰

On April 13, Captain Smith rode out of Fort Lane with eighty dragoons en route to Port Orford to meet Buchanan's command. An unidentified dragoon said later that Smith's men had to "take to the mountains on foot, as we had to climb most of the way where our horses could not go." They fought a group of Indians and burned their village. They wandered seven days in a thick fog and their provisions ran out.⁴¹

The three hundred men of the southern battalion of the second regiment of Oregon Mounted Volunteers under Lt. Col. W. W. Chapman would follow Smith into the mountains, but their goal was the Meadows, where they expected to find a large force under Tecumtum. Chapman said that he had been told by coastal Indians coming upstream that people had come up from the Klamath River country to join Tecumtum and guessed that he had as many as six hundred people with him.

Chapman was worried over the pending expiration in about thirty days of the terms of service of his volunteers. He assumed that the volunteers would simply leave when that happened and said that "unless recruits can be had, what will become of us, God only knows!" Only if Congress appropriated enough money "so that men may live"—perhaps two or three million dollars—could the territorial army in the south stay in service.[42] Poor conditions and financial uncertainties notwithstanding, the volunteers of the southern battalion began advancing down the valley on the south side of the Rogue River on April 15, according to the *Statesman*.

While the volunteer companies were making their way into the mountains, Joel Palmer's friends in the lower Willamette valley were responding to the accusations made against him at the Lafayette protest meeting at the beginning of the month, and further accusations made in the *Statesman* by a correspondent who had signed himself W and had, among other things, called Palmer "an unprincipled coward."[43]

Among those present at a meeting in Palmer's support held in Dayton on Friday, April 18, was A. G. Henry, former surgeon of the volunteers, war enthusiast, and reputed Know-Nothing. Also present was Courtney M. Walker, a special Indian agent. A few days later, Robert Metcalfe identified Walker as a Know-Nothing in a letter to Joseph Lane. Palmer had given an Indian Service job to Metcalfe, one of Lane's emissaries in the 1853 peace negotiations and the proposed replacement for Samuel Culver. Metcalfe's loyalty, however, was to Lane, and he informed Lane that four of the five main employees on the Grand Ronde Reservation where Walker was employed were Know-Nothings.[44]

Henry's support for Palmer and the apparent prevalence of reputed Know-Nothings among Palmer's employees might seem to suggest that Palmer had decided to accept Know-Nothing support. Palmer, however, could never have won the support of Know-Nothings who agreed with the pro-war line featured in the *Oregonian*. Moreover, he would have inevitably lost the support he had to have to hold on to his office—the support of Joseph Lane—if he had openly acknowledged his Know-Nothing involvement.[45] Perhaps Palmer never invited Henry's support and his hiring practices had more to do with availability and affinity than with politics.

Henry, Walker, and three more Dayton men had been chosen to draft resolutions "expressive of the sentiments" of Palmer's friends. They were careful; they "would not be understood as either *endorsing* or *disapproving* the policy of the present national administration" that Palmer was putting into effect. The "odium" of the policy of colonizing the Indians on the

Coast Reservation, they said, "should be made to fall upon the administration at Washington City" and not upon Palmer; they expressed "entire confidence in his honesty, integrity and frank sincerity."

On the same day, twenty-three men signed a letter from Dayton refuting the W letter item by item and arguing that if Palmer's plans for the Indian people were carried through, "within a few years we will see this unfortunate race rise (in almost full uniform) in the ranks of civilization."[46]

The next day, according to a writer calling himself Percussion in a letter to the *Oregonian*, the northern battalion, numbering a few more than two hundred men, left its winter quarters for the Meadows. The ride took two days, and the volunteers had hardly stationed their pickets when Rogue River people fired on them. On the following day, Tuesday, April 22, Colonel Kelsay probed the difficult terrain with fifty men and ran into enough Indians that he was compelled to retreat to his camp. The southern battalion came up the next day.[47]

Two days later, Joel Palmer sent two small bands of Willamette valley Indians to the reservation at Grand Ronde with Courtney Walker and a small detachment of dragoons commanded by Lt. Phil Sheridan. The next day, April 25, Palmer went to Oregon City aboard the steamship *Franklin* "to obtain coin and have an interview with Gen'l. Wool," who was visiting the Vancouver barracks near Portland. Wool told Palmer it was time to begin negotiations with the Indian peoples on the south coast.[48]

While Palmer was talking with Wool, readers of the *Oregonian* were treated to a curious, anonymous work of satire. Editor T. J. Dryer frequently sought to get a laugh from his readers. For example, he printed several letters on political subjects written in Irish dialect, supposedly by one Paddy O'Bush-Whacker, the name being a not especially subtle reference to his rival in the territorial capital.

Alongside the thoughts of Paddy O'Bush-Whacker in the *Oregonian* for April 26 was a collection of dispatches ostensibly drawn from "the *Wasco Root-Gatherer*" and purporting to report the doings of Kamiakan, the best known among the leaders of the Indian resistance east of the Cascades in Washington Territory. "His Excellency Kamiakin," according to the first item, had "adopted the policy of Gov. Curry" in his appointments "by selecting Know-Nothings exclusively." Kamiakin was himself a Know-Nothing and intended "to drive every 'furriner' out of the country unless they will submit to be ruled by himself and his people—that they are the only true Americans, and that '*Americans shall rule America or bust!*' "

In a proclamation addressed to "the Whites and Missourians now resident in Oregon and Washington Territories," Kamiakin expressed concern that "young and delicate youths" in Portland had to stand guard in the rain, "thereby not only subjecting them to an attack of the influenza, but actually taking the starch out of their *standing shirt collars.*" Kamiakin proposed "to immediately visit that portion of my domains, with a sufficient force to protect the above mentioned citizens."

He commanded that friendly whites "proceed to some suitable point on the Willamette, as may be designated by Agent Geo. L. Curry" and stay there until he could "make permanent arrangements for placing them upon a reserve; they will, therefore, be expected to immediately give up their arms and ammunition, when they receive provisions and blankets."

Making reference to events in Kansas, where abolitionists and advocates of slavery had begun to fight out the implications of the Kansas-Nebraska Act of 1854, the *Oregonian*'s Kamiakin pronounced himself "deeply pained to learn that the Missourians have gone to war with the Americans on the other side of the mountains." He had hoped to make a treaty with the Missourians "for a reserve upon which to place the Oregonians as that was the 'Home of their fathers.'" Kamiakin also announced his intention to run for the Senate should Oregon become a state.

In the final item, "Gen. Kamiakin" was reported to have "entered the Willamette Valley with 100,000 warriors," and to have "issued a proclamation which appears in his organ, the *Oregonian*," stating his intention to form "a corps of friendly whites" headed by Curry that would attack California and capture General Wool, "who so grossly insulted both Kamiakin and Gov. Curry by thinking them small potatoes."[49]

The unnamed author, writing for a newspaper that had nailed the name of Know-Nothing presidential candidate Millard Fillmore to its masthead, could nonetheless see the irony inherent in the white nativism of the Know-Nothings. But the writer's recognition of that irony was only skin deep, and the implied equivalence of stature between Kamiakin and Curry was not meant to be to the credit of Kamiakin.

The political punch line of this elaborate joke was that Kamiakin would pay territorial war expenses sooner than George Curry would get the money from the federal government. Kamiakin was willing to pay the war debt, "providing the whites will settle upon a reservation in Missouri," and so scrip (notes issued by the territory to pay for supplies) had risen to one and one-half cents on the dollar.[50]

7

The War Ends

Although the Rogue River peoples remained undefeated as the spring of 1856 arrived, any hope that the coast could be kept clear of whites was gone. No more large forces would gather to successfully oppose the regular troops occupying the coast or the volunteers moving downriver from the valley. The people had to choose between starvation and vulnerability, and the course of events suggests that most decided against starvation, even if that meant surrender.

The politicians who created and sustained the war ruined Joel Palmer's efforts to keep the peace and demonstrated the impotence of federal Indian policy in Oregon. But they also created the conditions necessary for the quick implementation of the new reservation policy. The war allowed Palmer to gather up noncombatant Indians without much need for persuasion, and as it lurched toward its climax, he could collect the remaining Indian people and remove them to the reservation as prisoners of war.

The volunteers mounted the second phase of their spring offensive on Sunday, April 27. Colonel Kelsay led some one hundred men of the northern battalion out of their camp at the Meadows before dawn. They moved downstream on the north side of the river to take possession of a canyon downstream from a camp on the south side occupied by Lympe's band. The idea was to distract any Rogue River men guarding the opposite bank and block a downriver retreat while a detachment from the northern battalion came down on the south side to attack the camp itself.

Kelsay's men didn't get into position as quickly as planned and would have been seen by the Rogue River people were it not for a dense fog. They found no opposition in the canyon, so they doubled back and went over a ridge to a position opposite Lympe's camp. The volunteers were within what Kelsay estimated was about two hundred yards of the river before the people on the other side saw them. Then the volunteers rushed down into the rocks and trees on the bank of the river and opened fire on them, "throwing them into the greatest confusion," Kelsay reported. The women and children fled into the forest.

About 150 men of the southern battalion under Major Bruce who had followed Kelsay's detachment downriver from the Meadows came up at this point, but on the north side of the river, not the south side as planned. They took a position alongside Kelsay's men. Kelsay said the volunteers kept up their long-distance attack on the camp for the rest of the day,[1] but one of his men said that after the volunteers had been shooting into the camp "in good earnest" for about an hour, they returned to their camp "very much fatigued and hungry." The fire that was returned, he said, "was quite feeble."[2]

Kelsay reported that the Indian people had been taken completely by surprise and calculated their losses as no less than twenty or thirty killed and wounded. The volunteers lost only one man.[3] They returned the following day and fired into the camp from about 9 A.M. until 3 P.M. An *Oregonian* correspondent said if the original plan had been followed and the southern battalion had come up on the south side of the river, "a decisive blow could and would have been struck." For some reason, he said, the troops had refused to cross over. The volunteers apparently preferred to do their fighting at a distance. The entire force finally did cross the river on the third day and found the camp abandoned. Lympe's people had retreated down the river.

The plan to block the downstream canyon had been forgotten, and rather than press on in pursuit the volunteers decided to go back to the valley. According to the correspondent, "The weather was cold and rainy, and the provision getting very scarce." Lamerick left four companies behind at the Meadows—202 men under Major Bruce—to build a fort. That was the end of "the long expected expedition to the Meadows."[4]

Even as the volunteers pressed their attack, the political argument over the war continued in the East. On April 26, the day before the volunteers began their assault on Lympe's camp, the *Chicago Daily Tribune* had published a commentary quoting Joel Palmer's statement that the war had been "forced upon these Indians against their will, and that too by a set of reckless vagabonds for pecuniary and political objects." The commentator viewed "the doom of the Red man" as inevitable, given "the conquering superiority of the Saxons," but added that the Indians in Oregon were being subjected to a "bloody scheme" by "murderers" and, not for the first time, "the manhood of America has been disgraced by barbarities designed to hatch a war out of which money could be made."[5]

On April 30 the *National Intelligencer* republished a commentary from the *New Hampshire Democrat* suggesting, in view of the recent appropriation to maintain "the peaceable disposition" of the Indians in Oregon and Washington territories, that the war was too expensive a proposition. The commentator suggested "no more wars with the Indians after we get out of these." Rather than buying powder and shot, he said, "let us adopt prompt and liberal measures to spread among them the arts of civilised life."[6] Two days later the *Intelligencer* published the lengthy and argumentative defense of his views on the war that Gen. John E. Wool had written a month before in California.[7]

In Oregon, T. J. Dryer complained in the May 3 *Oregonian* that the "long *humane articles*" he had been reading in the eastern papers "exhibit not only a total ignorance of the history of this war, its cause and progress, but an entire want of knowledge of the Indian character, as well as the manner in which the war has been conducted." Dryer proposed to "enlighten these 'humane and pious writers'" by laying out his own badly twisted version of the history of relations between whites and Indians, beginning with the "*christian enterprise*" twenty-five years before that had brought missionaries to Oregon. The missionaries had "done all that could be done" to improve and convert the Indians. "They clothed, fed, and restored them, and in return, their benefactors were murdered or driven out of the country," Dryer said.

When "the Anglo-Saxon race began to flock to this coast in large numbers," Dryer added, the Indians made treaties that were broken "just as often as the Indians wanted a new supply of blankets, guns and ammunition." And they went "prowling about the country begging, stealing and committing all sorts of outrages upon the whites." Millions of dollars of the public money had been spent in Oregon for presents and annuities for the Indians, he complained. Not for the *Oregonian*'s editor was the basic premise behind Joel Palmer's Indian colonization plan, that is, Indian survival: "The Indians will either be wiped out, or the whites will leave for that 'country from whose bourn no traveler ever returns,'" Dryer said.[8]

On May 7, in Washington, Delegate Joseph Lane rose in the House of Representatives to respond to remarks made by Representative Stanton of Ohio during a debate on War Department funds. Stanton had read a letter written by General Wool arguing that the governors of the Oregon and Washington territories had made an unnecessary war. Lane argued that the colonizers of Oregon were "honest, industrious people." Accusing them of fighting the war "for the sake of plunder," he said, was "a slander upon chivalrous, high-spirited, and gallant men who have periled their lives and bared their bosoms to the weapons of a skulking and treacherous foe."

Lane called General Wool "a tactician after the fashion of the military fogies of Europe" who was incapable of fighting Indians. Lane even insisted that the Rogue River valley people killed by the Lupton party had been "murderers, and deserved the fate that befell them."[9]

In southern Oregon the volunteers not left behind in the Meadows were making their way out of the mountains. A correspondent calling himself

Percussion claimed in the *Oregonian* that the volunteers had intended to pursue the Indian people down the river, "but upon sending out spies it was discovered to be impossible to proceed with pack animals on their trail." He described the troops as "very much fatigued" and said many of them were suffering from sickness "caused by the hard marches they have had to perform. We had a good deal of snow, rain, and cold winds." Besides, they were irritated by the lack of sugar and coffee. "The men declare that they will not go into the mountains 'without their coffee,'" he said. One of the withdrawing volunteers reported in the *Oregonian* that as of May 9 they were about sixty miles north of the Meadows en route to Roseburg. He and his companions were "almost bare-footed" and "worn out with the fatigue of the journey, and the disagreeable weather which we have had since we started on the expedition."[10]

Events on the coast soon demonstrated that Joseph Lane's critique of General Wool in the House of Representatives was mistaken, although the general's successful tactic amounted to nothing more than directing Bvt. Lt. Col. Robert C. Buchanan to accept surrenders. Buchanan arrived at the mouth of the Rogue River on May 7. The following night, he reported, he sent out two Indian women with a message to the Rogue River people who were still at war. By that time, five companies of regulars had gathered at Buchanan's camp, including Capt. A. J. Smith's men from the valley. When the morning of May 9 came, Buchanan started up the south side of the river with three companies and sent Smith with two companies up the north side. Smith reached the junction of the Rogue and Illinois Rivers on May 12. Buchanan's column, delayed by the lack of a trail, arrived at Oak Flat, a few miles up the Illinois from Smith's camp, on May 13.

Four Rogue River men sent by Smith were waiting for Buchanan. They told him that many Indian people had come into Smith's camp at the mouth of the Illinois. Rather than going down the Illinois to join Smith, however, Buchanan decided to set up camp at Oak Flat.[11]

Superintendent Joel Palmer reached Port Orford on the steamship *Columbia* at 10:30 A.M. on Friday, May 16. He had brought six tons of flour for the Rogue River people. Indian service agent Nathan Olney, appointed by Palmer to take the place of the deceased Ben Wright, told

The War Ends

him 365 people had come in to the temporary reserve at Port Orford. Nonetheless, the superintendent was apprehensive. He noted in his diary, "Nothing has been heard from Col. Buchanan for several days. All persons have abandoned the country from this place to Smith's River,"[12] that is, to a few miles south of the California border.

Buchanan reported that on May 16, "Old Joshua, Chief of the tribe at the mouth of the Rogue River; the Chetcoe Chief; and several others came in to have a talk." He told them they would have to surrender unconditionally, "and to this they finally agreed." Capt. E. O. C. Ord, escorting a supply train on May 18, found what Buchanan called "almost the entire force of the upper Indians" (that is, from the upper Rogue River) at the mouth of the Illinois. They had come down from the Meadows, Buchanan said, "in consequence of an invitation sent them by Capt. Smith a few days before." Buchanan sent word to Smith that he wanted a talk with their leaders.

Cholcultah, the upper Rogue River leader called George by the whites, wanted Buchanan to come to him. Buchanan insisted that Cholcultah come to his camp instead, "for I felt assured in my own mind, that *his coming to me* would be the first great step towards bringing him under my control." Cholcultah and Lympe arrived at Oak Flat at about noon on May 19. Buchanan got them to gather the leaders of the upper river peoples, including Tecumtum, as well as the leaders of the coastal and lower river peoples who had already agreed to give up. The meeting was set for the morning of May 20. He said that when he told them they would have to go to the Coast Reservation, "they unanimously demurred." They were willing to stop fighting, but they wanted "to remain on their own country, where the whites might dig gold if they wished."[13]

Frances Fuller Victor quoted Tecumtum as having told Buchanan, "You are a great chief; so am I. This is my country; I was in it when these large trees were very small, not [taller] than my head. My heart is sick with fighting, but I want to live in my country. If the white people are willing, I will go back to Deer Creek and live among them as I used to do; they can visit my camp, and I will visit theirs; but I will not lay down my arms and go with you on the reserve. I will fight. Good-by."[14]

At some point in the negotiations Buchanan apparently made a seeming concession, though it was not mentioned in his reports. Eight years later at the Siletz agency on the Coast Reservation, a man identified as Old Bill of the Rogue Rivers, probably Konechequot,[15] told the superintendent of Indian affairs, "We were promised by Major Buchanan that we should return after four years, and we want to go now or have better treatment."[16] This promise seems to have allowed the leaders of the Rogue River peoples to give up on the war without accepting the permanent loss of their homes. Tecumtum, however, would remain unwilling to submit, and the last major action of the war would arise from his stubborn resistance.

Cholcultah came back on May 21 and said, according to Buchanan, that he and the others "did not want to fight, nor did they want to go to the Reservation." Buchanan reported that he told Cholcultah that the Indians would have "peace and kind treatment if they should yield, or, war and all its evils should they refuse." Although they could get no further concessions from Buchanan, at least by Buchanan's account, Cholcultah and Lympe came back with a promise that no later than May 26 they would be at Big Bend, between the Meadows upstream and the mouth of the Illinois downstream, ready to depart for the Coast Reservation to join Toquahear. (Big Bend is a meadow along the right bank of the river that is almost a mile long and as much as a quarter of a mile wide.[17])

"George expects, *also* to bring with him *the Galice Creeks and Applegates*, who have hitherto been with Old John," Buchanan reported. "This will leave Old John with only his own band and the Klamaths, amounting to 29 warriors, which will compose the entire remaining hostile force in the field."[18]

Captain Smith, commanding his own company of dragoons and a detachment of infantry, arrived at Big Bend at about sundown on May 24 to receive the people led by Cholcultah and Lympe as well as any others who might come in and surrender. The following day was rainy and disagreeable, and when the people he was awaiting did not arrive, Smith assumed the bad weather had kept them from traveling. Early the next morning, on May 26, several Indians came into his camp and told him that Cholcultah was about nine miles upriver trying to make his way down with his people and the Applegate, Galice Creek, and Cow Creek bands.

If they were not stopped by Tecumtum, they were expected to reach Big Bend that day, Smith said. That afternoon, "some Indian boys that had been in my camp for several days" told Smith "that it was the talk among the Indians that Old John was to attack us early next morning." The captain believed them; after dark, he moved his camp to a hill overlooking the meadow, "having to transport my howitzer ammunition, stores, etc., on the backs of my men."[19]

Buchanan had abandoned his camp at Oak Flat that day and gone down to the mouth of the Illinois. Buchanan did not demand a hard march. He went only about three miles on May 26, and on the following day he intended, by his account, to travel about seven miles and make camp at the point where the trail from the mouth of the Illinois branched north to Port Orford on the left and west to Big Bend on the right.[20]

At Big Bend, early on the morning of the following day, May 27, "several Indians came in camp, some of them George's people, and told me the Indians were coming in," Captain Smith reported. He said he "soon saw a number of canoes land and small parties moving up the hill, all apparently friendly, though being armed I would not permit them to enter camp." They kept coming in until about 10 A.M. Smith said that "as soon as I ascertained that many of John's people were among them I placed my whole command under arms, not suspecting up to this time their treachery."

During the hour that followed, the Rogue River men surrounded Smith's camp. "The Indians fired the first gun about eleven o'clock," he reported. Firing canister from their howitzer, the regulars drove back simultaneous attacks on three sides, Smith said, and then the Rogue River men occupied "a ridge to our left, on the slope leading up to our camp from which they procured a cross fire on the men in position on that flank." The soldiers were forced back from the crest of the hill, but they kept up a continuous fire, and periodic dashes out of their positions forced the Rogue River men to retreat.[21]

While the battle continued, Joel Palmer reached Buchanan's old camp at Oak Flat on the Illinois that morning and found it deserted. He and his escort, three whites and three Port Orford people, went down the Illinois to the point where it flows into the Rogue, where Buchanan had camped the night before, and there Palmer found part of Buchanan's command. The superintendent learned that Buchanan had induced most of the Rogue River and coastal peoples to assemble either at Big Bend or near the Mikonotunne village, six miles below the mouth of Illinois River.[22]

Palmer said the message reached Buchanan in the evening and that the lieutenant colonel was four miles north of the mouth of the Illinois at the time, not in his camp,[23] which would have put him only three miles from Smith's threatened command. By that time, presumably unknown to Buchanan, Smith and his troops had been under attack for several hours.

Rather than sending more men to Big Bend, Buchanan pulled back. He decided to concentrate his forces back at the mouth of the Illinois. At that point, he explained, he could keep Indians from going upriver to the Big Bend to help the people who were threatening Smith. He could still reinforce Smith if necessary (although from four miles farther away), and he would be in a better position to reinforce a pack train then coming up the south side of the river if it were attacked. He went back to the camp opposite the mouth of the Illinois with Augur's infantry company and sent messages to Smith and Major Reynolds, who was on the trail to Port Orford, to join him there in the morning. He directed Smith to send word immediately if he was attacked.[24]

Palmer said that in the evening "quite a number of canoes filled with Indians came up the river" past the camp at the mouth of the Illinois. Some of these people seemed anxious to get to Big Bend. Others said they wanted to fish. Yet others said they wanted to go upriver to inform the people there that Palmer had arrived. The troops kept them from continuing upriver, Palmer added, and "quite a number remained with us through the night."[25]

At Big Bend that night, Captain Smith counted his casualties and learned that four soldiers had been killed and fifteen wounded, "besides my guide, and an Indian boy [servant] to Lt. Sweitzer." The Rogue

River men surrounding the hill "kept up their fire until after dark, and occasionally through the night."

Smith said that at about 11 P.M., all the men who could be spared started building "a breastwork on the southern part of the hill composed of blankets, saddles, tents, provisions, etc." In front of this makeshift fortification, Smith had his men dig several rifle pits that could each hold as many as five men. When the Rogue River people discovered what he was doing, Smith said, "they raised a signal fire and by four o'clock in the morning of the 28th renewed their attack which they kept up by brisk fire until 4 P.M. & making several attempts during the day to charge us."[26]

Buchanan said that the messenger he had sent to Big Bend had returned on the morning of May 28 with the news that Smith had been fighting all night and was still fighting, although the messenger had been able to get no closer than "good hearing distance." Buchanan sent Augur's company to reinforce Smith.[27] Joel Palmer, Nathan Olney, and W. H. Wright went with Augur. Wright, who had come with Palmer from Portland as a messenger, was the late Ben Wright's brother. They reached the Big Bend at about 4 P.M. Palmer said they "found the Indians assembled to the number of, perhaps, 200, and the camp entirely surrounded."[28]

The hill where Smith's troops were trapped, Palmer said, "was sparsely covered with timber, and the Indians would crawl up within a few yards of the camp and fire, unseen, upon such of the troops as were uncovered." Several times they charged to within thirty yards of the breastwork. "They generally showed a determination to conquer at all hazards." Smith's men had been under attack for thirty-six hours and without food for twelve hours. Seven were dead and seventeen wounded, Palmer added.[29]

Captain Augur reported that the hills around Smith's position were covered with Indians. The women and children ran for the river when Augur's men arrived. Although Smith's command was still under fire, Augur drove his company forward "in double quick time" hoping to intercept the women and children, but they got to the river and crossed in canoes before he could stop them. Augur then wheeled his company around and charged up the nearest hill, but the Rogue River men only dropped back about fifty yards to the next hill.

"Many of my men had been marching all day in a very hot sun, and had come the last mile at a run, and were nearly exhausted," Augur said. "I therefore rested them here about ten minutes." Augur then sent part of his company to charge the Rogue River men on the next hill while another detachment moved into position to intercept them if they tried to get away.

The Rogue River men "retreated down a precipitious [sic] and almost impassable ravine, and were seen ascending the mountain on the other side, and soon after disappeared."[30] Palmer said that while Augur's soldiers were pushing the Rogue River men back, "Capt. Smith and those with him charged those in the rear of his camp and the rout became general, and a junction formed of the commands." When the fighting finally ended, Palmer added, "the men proceeded to cook a meal, a luxury which they had been denied for nearly 36 hours. No Indians were seen during the night, and the camp rested quiet."[31]

Palmer and his companions apparently took part in the fight. A correspondent calling himself Orford told readers of the *Statesman* that "Gen. Palmer used his pistol with good effect, till he obtained a musket as it fell from the hand of a dying soldier." His companions Olney and Wright also took a hand, the latter "in a manner becoming a man who seeks to avenge the murder of his kindred." Buchanan's report mentioned that Palmer, Olney, and Wright volunteered to go with Augur "and rendered valuable service." J. S. Rinearson, who had been captain of a volunteer company earlier in the war, sent a letter to Palmer saying Charles Foster had told him that Palmer was "compeled to *pitch intoum*. Well I congratulate you that you still wair your *hair* whair the 'Hair ought to grow.'"[32]

Buchanan said his command had lost eleven killed and eighteen wounded. The losses of the Rogue River peoples were unknown, he said, but had to be considerable because of their "frequent and most daring" attacks on Smith's position.[33] The *San Francisco Herald* would report that the number of Indian dead "could not be ascertained for they were fighting in such a position that the bodies of those falling could be dragged into the thicket by the squaws and hidden." But they must have suffered many losses, by this account, to judge from "the howlings of the Indians with tar and ashes on their heads, as they mourned in camp some nights after this fight."[34]

The last major engagement of the Rogue River War had been fought, but upriver the volunteers were once again on the march. According to Major William Latshaw of the Oregon Mounted Volunteers, he left Fort Lamerick (the post built by the men left at the Meadows after the fighting at the end of April) on May 27 with 212 men.[35] On the first day, the correspondent Volunteer told readers of the *Statesman*, he and his comrades marched ten miles downriver and made camp near the Big Bend. (They were not near enough, however, to hear the sounds of the fighting going on around A. J. Smith's position. If they had marched ten miles, they were still at least five miles from Big Bend.[36])

"Soon after we camped," Volunteer said, "Capt. Barnes' Spy Company went out and discovered the enemy in considerable force."[37] The people the volunteers had found were not those who had elected to fight, who had gone to Big Bend. They apparently were the people led by Cholcultah and Lympe, who had submitted to Buchanan but had not yet gone downriver because Tecumtum had threatened to shoot them if they went in.[38]

Latshaw reported that during the early hours of the morning of May 28, two officers, Massey and Blakely, crept with their companies to within 150 yards of the Indian camp with thirty-two men. They were across the river from the camp. Latshaw, meanwhile, went with the main body of volunteers over the high ridge that separated his camp from the Indians' camp. He expected to take a position looking down on the camp and drive the people there down the river. The men with Massey and Blakely were supposed to cut off the retreat.

The results were disappointing. Latshaw's men saw a few Rogue River men, killed one, and mortally wounded another, Latshaw said, adding that, "At the same time Capt. Blakely exchanged several shots with them on the right, with what effect is not ascertained." The volunteers then "moved down the river in pursuit of the enemy, who fled before us or took to the mountains. We took 7 women and 5 children prisoners, and killed one warrior and wounded another, who was taken prisoner."[39]

A volunteer using the name Pacificus said in a letter to the *Statesman* that when the main body of Latshaw's men got into position, "a brisk firing commenced from our men, the Indians retreating without firing a gun." When the volunteers took up the pursuit, he said, they "overtook and killed one squaw, taking the other two, with one papoose, prisoners."[40]

The accomplishments of Latshaw's men on the following day amounted, by his own account, to finding "several lodges that had been abandoned, and two old women who had been left" and killing two more men. The volunteers also suffered one of the only two casualties recorded by Latshaw during his expedition, the wounding of a sergeant whose company was preparing to cross the river.[41]

On the morning of the same day, May 29, Joel Palmer sent out two Rogue River women who had been in A. J. Smith's camp during the siege with instructions to go to Cholcultah and Lympe "to advise them to come in and comply with the demand made by Col. Buchanan."[42] Palmer noted in his diary that he had told the women to say that he "had been told they were not in this fight. I hoped this was true. That all hostile Indians were great fools to suppose they could conquer the whites."[43]

Palmer said that the two women and a boy on horseback came into camp at about noon saying that "the Volunteers had attackt George's band at or near the Meadows, killing George, Jo Lane, and the Galeose [Galice] Creek chief, and a good many women and children, and taken prisoners all their families" (the Jo Lane mentioned here obviously was not the long-dead Apserkahar, who had acquired the name from the white Jo Lane in 1851, but his identity was not explained). Lympe sent back word that he had taken no part in the fight at Big Bend and wanted Palmer "to come up and stop the Volunteers from killing their people, and they would quit."

Palmer sent back a message ordering the people upriver to come to his camp and deliver their arms to him. If they did, he said, they would be fed and protected and would be sent to the reservation at the end of the war. That evening, Palmer said, "Jo Lane and Tom returned, informing us that George and Jo Lane and Galeose Creek chief were not killed as supposed, but they were attacked and the latter taken prisoner, together with 8 women and 2 children."[44]

The War Ends

On Friday, May 30, Palmer noted that he had again sent messengers out to Cholcultah's people telling them "if they did not come in today, I should return and there would be no more talk with them." They came in that evening. Palmer said that when they were asked to give up their arms, "They cheerfully complied and brought forward 14 rifles and 6 revolvers." Both Cholcultah and Lympe came in. They denied that they had fought at Big Bend and said they would have come to Palmer sooner had not Tecumtum threatened to shoot them if they tried.

On the following day, 150 volunteers led by Major Latshaw reached Big Bend. Palmer clashed with Latshaw over the women and children the volunteers were holding as prisoners. "I requested that they might be turned over to me, as the men to whom the women and children belonged were prisoners in my camp," Palmer reported. Latshaw insisted that he hold his prisoners for his superior officer "and declared if they attempted to make their escape, or if they [his company] were attacked by other Indians, he would put them all to death."

Latshaw also said, according to Palmer, that the Rogue River peoples would have surrendered to the volunteers three months before on the same conditions they were getting from Palmer. The volunteers would not make peace. Latshaw said their orders were to take no prisoners. Latshaw's superior Lamerick eventually turned the women and children over to Robert Metcalfe, who turned them over to Buchanan.[45]

The *Statesman* correspondent called Volunteer said that Buchanan "treated our officers and men very coolly" and "did not like to acknowledge that we had any business there, or, that the volunteers had accomplished anything during the war." A. J. Smith "was more affable."[46]

Two companies of regulars and a company of volunteers that had come up from the coast were sent back downriver to attack any people who refused to surrender and be removed. Palmer said Indian people in his camp had admitted that many of the downriver people had been involved in the fight with Captain Smith's detachment at Big Bend. Augur's troops killed three men and one woman at the Shasta Costa village five miles below Big Bend on June 2. Palmer said they were seen on an island in the river and "upon being called to, attempted to flee, when they were fired upon."[47]

The following day, Augur's men attacked a camp when a few people in canoes tried to get away when the soldiers hailed them. The volunteers accompanying Augur's company closed in on them as they tried to cross the river. "Fourteen Indians were killed in this attack, and a number—men, women, and children—were supposed to be drowned in their attempt to escape," Palmer said. "Very little resistance was made by the Indians, no one in the companies receiving the least wound from them."[48]

On June 4, the volunteers who had marched to Big Bend started back for Fort Lamerick in the Meadows. "The health of the battalion is not good—considerable diarrhoea," the correspondent called Pacificus reported. Two of their prisoners, a man and a woman, escaped on the trail. On the morning of June 5, "Gen. Lamerick gave us a speech, and read Gen. Lane's speech in Congress to the volunteers. Three hearty cheers went up for Lamerick, and three still louder for old Jo."

Lamerick reported to Governor Curry the following day from the Meadows that he was going out again to hunt down Tecumtum "or any other hostile Indians we may fall in with." If the regulars helped, he promised a quick end to the war. If Buchanan refused to help, then he would do his best with his own troops and Buchanan would have to "reconcile his acts to his country."[49]

Joel Palmer reported that he went to Captain Augur's camp at the downriver assembly point on June 10 while Buchanan left Big Bend for Port Orford with the 277 Indians in his camp. On June 11 two sons of Tecumtum came to him asking the conditions for surrender. Palmer repeated the terms already offered by Buchanan. They said they would use their influence to get their father's followers to come in. Palmer sent a Rogue River man who had been to the reservation at Grand Ronde, a man well known to Tecumtum, to talk to him. The impression left on this messenger by his visit was that Tecumtum and his entire band would come in.

By the morning of June 12, Palmer counted 421 Indian people in Augur's camp, and when Augur took his prisoners to Buchanan's camp they had control of more than seven hundred prisoners. On Saturday, June 14, Palmer and his party reached Port Orford.

The whites in this village and the Indian people camped nearby were profoundly suspicious of each other, Palmer said. Indian women "claimed by white men" were said to have accused the Indians at Port Orford of entertaining spies from the Rogue River at night. According to these rumors, "a plot had been matured by which they were to attack and destroy first the town and next the garrison." Indian agent Nathan Olney had accepted the rumors as truth and sent a messenger to report the situation to Palmer.

The mutual fears had subsided by the time he arrived, Palmer noted, but then at 4 P.M. on Sunday, June 15, Buchanan and his captives reached the fort at Port Orford, and "lovers of excitement" passed around a new rumor that "a plan had been arranged among these tribes to cut off the garrison and town and cooperate with those still in the field." Palmer said he was "satisfied the whole thing was concocted by evil-disposed persons to cause a stampede among the Indians."

Many of the Indians held prisoner "were unable from old age or sickness, to travel by land," Palmer said; further, he had no means of transport for the provisions they would need. He decided to send them to Portland by steamboat and then by riverboats to Dayton. From there they could be sent to their new home on the coast.[50]

With the war virtually concluded, the volunteers made one more foray. General Lamerick ordered Major Latshaw on June 13 to take seventy-five men down the north side of the river and meet his own command, going down the south side, at the river's mouth. Lamerick reported that all Indian villages and supplies in the path of his volunteers were destroyed and forty canoes were captured.

He then sent Major Bruce south toward Pistol River. Bruce claimed that an Indian messenger he sent ahead came back saying that the people on the Pistol River refused to surrender and threatened to kill any whites who came into their country. Lamerick said he sent reinforcements to Bruce, whose expedition subsequently straggled into Lamerick's camp over two days, June 20 and 21, with thirty-one prisoners. Bruce claimed to have killed three more of the prisoners.[51] The claim that the Pistol River people refused to give up was contradicted by the correspondent Volunteer, who said, "The Indians did not retaliate, but laid down their arms and surrendered in every instance."[52]

The steamer *Columbia* arrived at Port Orford late on the night of June 20, and by 9 A.M. the following day the first group of Indian people had been put aboard. Palmer said they had come from most of the tribes of southwestern Oregon, but they were mainly friendly people who had been camped at Port Orford during the war. Many of them were sick. "They were very much crowded on the forward deck," said Palmer, who embarked with them. Among them were "199 men, 226 women, 127 boys and 118 girls; 95 of the boys and girls were infants," he reported. The fare was a bargain: "$10 per head (usual steerage fee $20)." The *Columbia* did not ordinarily carry so many passengers; eight months later, for example, the *Columbia* would arrive in Portland from San Francisco carrying just fifty-seven passengers.[53]

Aboard the *Columbia*, Palmer noted in his diary, the Indians suffered "on account of sea sickness and being crowded up, and for want of proper covering and diet." The steamer entered the Columbia River at about 6 P.M. June 22 and reached Portland at about 11 A.M. the following morning. At 3 P.M. he sent the people on to Oregon City.[54]

One last detail remained—the surrender of Tecumtum. The correspondent Volunteer said that on June 20 five members of Tecumtum's band had come into Buchanan's camp at Port Orford to say that he would come in if he were received on the same terms as Lympe and Cholcultah. He also asked for an escort to protect him from the volunteers and said he would start for Port Orford on June 23 from his camp in the vicinity of Oak Flat on the Illinois River. On June 24, Buchanan sent out 110 men under Major Reynolds to escort Tecumtum to Port Orford. He and his followers got to Port Orford on July 2.[55]

Joel Palmer suggested the following day in a letter to the commissioner of Indian affairs that the arrest and trial of the leaders of the attack on Captain Smith's command would "undoubtedly have a salutary influence."[56] There would be no such prosecutions.

A detachment of the Fourth Infantry escorted the lower Rogue River people and the bands of Cholcultah and Lympe to the new reservation on the steamer *Columbia* on its next voyage north. Major Reynolds of the Third Artillery was detailed to march Tecumtum's followers, together with the Pistol River and Chetco people, north to the reservation by land beginning July 9.[57] The war was over.

8

Unsatisfactory Results

The results of the Rogue River War were not quite what anyone had hoped. Much of the money asked of the federal government to pay for service and supplies was never appropriated. Joseph Lane's inability to squeeze the money out of Congress would contribute to his political ruin in Oregon. Frances Fuller Victor said his difficulties were created by "the allegations made by the highest military authority on the Pacific coast that the people of Oregon were an organized army of Indian-murderers and government robbers, in support of which assertion was the enormous account against the nation, of nearly six million dollars, the payment of which was opposed by almost the entire press of the union. It is doubtful if any man could have successfully contended against the suspicion thus created."[1]

The original inhabitants of southwestern Oregon lost not only their homes and roughly eight thousand square miles of land but also about 80 percent of their population. Ethnohistorian Stephen Dow Beckham has

148

estimated conservatively that the peoples involved in the war had numbered about 9,500 in 1851.[2] By the middle of 1857, Indian Service agents counted only 1,943 survivors on the Coast Reservation.[3] Even given the fact that some people avoided being sent to the reservation, this was a catastrophic loss.

The steamship *Columbia* carried the second shipment of about seven hundred Rogue River people to Portland en route to the Coast Reservation in early July 1856. Tecumtum's people and the peoples from the Pistol and Chetco Rivers would have to walk to the reservation with an escort commanded by Major Reynolds.[4] But they were not the last to leave. In the middle of January 1857, whites in the Rogue River valley came across about seventy-five Rogue River people who had refused to surrender for transportation. An Indian service agent reported that "a party of settlers, believing the Indians still hostile, went out and killed all the men, about ten in number." The rest were sent to the reservation.[5]

William Tichenor became a special agent for the Indian service for the purpose of collecting the people who had stayed behind. On August 3, 1857, he reported that twenty-four people on Pistol River had declared that they would not go to the reservation. At Gold Beach there were two men, with twelve women and children, who were a danger to travelers. On the upper Chetco River, he said, there were seven men and some forty women and children "who have been hostile always."[6]

These people were collected by November 1 and moved north to the mouth of the Umpqua River. They would not stay long. The subagent there, E. P. Drew, reported that "some dissatisfaction was manifested by the chiefs, and there being no troops present to guard them they all left for the mountains."

Tichenor and a detachment of regulars collected them again on the Chetco River—"about one hundred and fifty, consisting of children and old and decrepit men and women." While Tichenor was taking this group to the reservation, Drew said, about twenty men, "the most desperate warriors," had stayed in the mountains with their families and, after the troops left, had attacked white settlements on the Rogue River, burning several houses and killing two or three whites.[7]

Unsatisfactory Results 149

Tichenor returned in the spring of 1858 and, by May 21, had brought seventy people into submission. They were moving north on the morning of May 27 when the lieutenant commanding Tichenor's escort sent his pack train back south for supplies. Not far from camp, relatives of the people who were being taken away fired on the pack train and killed one man and ten animals.

On the morning of May 28, the captives tried to escape. Tichenor had already sent to the Rogue River for volunteers and was waiting for them when the men ran in one direction and the women and children in another. "They believed we would pursue them, when their women and children could run and hide," Tichenor said. Fifteen of them were killed.

"I am perfectly satisfied that no other course could be pursued to settle the difficulties of the country," Tichenor said. He claimed that the people who were killed had told him how they had recently drowned two boys belonging to a band they had exterminated. "They were the most desperate and murderous of all the Indians on the coast," Tichenor insisted.[8]

The original inhabitants would never be entirely removed. In the winter of 1947, an *Oregonian* reporter visited the middle reaches of the Rogue River to write about a doctor who went monthly to the village of Agness to hold a clinic for the Indian people who lived in the area. Agness was on the north bank of the Rogue River opposite the mouth of the Illinois, about where Major Buchanan had camped after deciding not to reinforce A. J. Smith, and near where the plank house villages of Tleatti'ntun, Tcetci'wut, and Setla'tun, the three parts of Cistakwusta, had once stood.[9]

The reporter described most of the people as "descendants of the Rogue River Indian tribes and the soldiers, miners and fortune hunters who fought against the Rogues." The removal of the Indian people who were sent to Siletz Reservation was "a near thing," he said, in the memory of one woman, Edna Fry. Her maternal grandfather was Charles Foster, who had been a volunteer in 1856 and had watched from hiding as his company's camp on the lower Rogue River was assaulted on the night of Washington's Birthday. Her grandmother was sent to the reservation and died there, never again to see her white husband or her daughter, Edna Fry's mother.[10]

Tecumtum did not escape removal, but his spirit was not entirely damp-
ened by reservation life. He would be among the principal men brought
to the commissary storehouse at the Siletz agency on September 21, 1857,
for a council with a visiting special investigator for the Indian Office, J.
Ross Browne. Lympe and Cholcultah were also there. Tecumtum said
many of his people had died since coming to the Siletz Reservation, that
they had no game, and that they were sick at heart. He also said that Joel
Palmer had told them that the Table Rock Reservation belonged to them
"but for the sake of peace, as the white settlers were bad, we should leave
it for a while. When we signed the paper that was our understanding; we
now want to go back to that country."

Cholcultah said that they had sold Palmer everything but "two small
tracts, one on Evans' Creek and one on Table Rock." He had told Palmer
"we would never consent to sell him those lands; we wanted them to live
upon; we could always fish and hunt there; we only wanted the mountains, which were of no use to the whites."

Browne gave them a tongue-lashing for their ingratitude. They were
given beans, flour, shelter, shirts, and blankets. "Were they better than
white men, that they should live without working?" They had the reservation, where they would be protected, and if they went back to their
homeland they would all be killed.[11]

Toward the end of the following month, according to army surgeon
Rodney Glisan, two "medicine men or doctors" on the Coast Reservation
were attacked by Tecumtum's son, Cultus Jim. They were accused of
causing a sickness by means of "witchcraft." Cultus Jim ("cultus" means
"bad" in the sense of "useless" in Chinook Jargon) killed one of the doctors
and wounded the other. Cultus Jim was killed by the agent, Robert
Metcalfe, and an army lieutenant.[12]

Tecumtum was arrested on April 22, 1858, with his son Adam and
sent to San Francisco under guard.[13] Glisan said they were arrested for
threatening Metcalfe's life.[14] They were put aboard the steamer *Columbia*
and at first, according to a San Francisco newspaper account, "appeared
to take matters in a very phlegmatic and resigned manner." But early
in the morning, while the steamer was anchored off Humboldt Bay,

Tecumtum blew out the lights in steerage and attacked the sergeant guarding them.

According to the newspaper report, John gave an "ear-piercing warwhoop," which produced a "galvanic effect on the passengers, who incontinently quitted their berths and ran as fast as their legs could carry them up the hatchways and into the cabin," shouting that the Indians had taken the ship and were killing the passengers. The captain of the steamer, two ship's officers and five passengers went into steerage to subdue Tecumtum and Adam. When the first mate slashed at Tecumtum with a saber, Tecumtum caught the blade in his hand.

Finally subdued, the two men were landed in San Francisco and sent to imprisonment at the Presidio.[15] Rodney Glisan said he had been told that Tecumtum was shot through the nose and his son was shot in the leg, which was amputated when they reached San Francisco.[16]

They were returned to Oregon in 1862. Indian affairs superintendent William H. Rector explained that Tecumtum's daughters, who were on the Grand Ronde Reservation, had made a strong appeal for their return to their families, which he had relayed to the military authorities.[17] Tecumtum soon got the privilege of making visits to his old home. A soldier stationed at Fort Yamhill, at the Grand Ronde Reservation, wrote in his diary that on May 13, 1862, "'Ty John' and 16 other Rogue Rivers passed here enroute for the old hunting grounds." On May 23 he wrote, "Nothing of interest to-day except 'Tyee John,' the famous warring chief of the Rogue Rivers, had returned. Has filled up a house in a sumptious [sic] style."[18]

On June 15, 1864, the *Oregonian* reported, "John, the War-Chief of the Klamath and Rogue river Indians, known and dreaded for several years on account of his desperate hate of the whites, died of old age at Fort Yamhill on the 6th inst.," that is, on June 6.[19]

Leschi, the Nisqually leader said to have preached war throughout the Northwest in the summer of 1855,[20] who had been pursued by white antagonists ever since, was arrested in November 1856 for murdering a prominent white man killed during the Puget Sound War. The jury in Leschi's first trial failed to agree on a verdict, but the jury in the second trial found him guilty, and he was sentenced to be hanged. Army officers who were sympathetic to Leschi deliberately delayed the hanging by arresting the local sheriff for selling liquor to Indians, keeping him from delivering the death warrant, but Leschi finally went to the gallows on February 19, 1858.[21]

While General Wool included the Puget Sound and Yakima Wars with the Rogue River War in his denunciations of attempts to steal from the federal treasury, the main objective of the two northern wars was not making money but asserting control. The Yakima War was begun and ended by regulars, not volunteers. Control was achieved.

Kamiakin, blamed for the Yakima War, outlived Leschi, Tecumtum, and his antagonist Isaac I. Stevens, who was killed by a bullet in the head while leading his troops as a Union general near Chantilly, Virginia, on September 1, 1862.[22]

The Yakima War continued on until the late summer of 1858, long after the Oregon volunteers had lost interest and the burden had been passed to the regulars. The end came after two battles near the Spokane River. The Indian allies faced an expedition of some 570 regular troops armed with six howitzers and new types of rifles. On August 31, an awe-inspiring cavalry charge on the regulars was broken by the howitzers and unexpectedly long-range rifle fire, and then dragoons drove off or rode down the disorganized Indians.

On September 5, after setting a fire to pin down the advancing regulars, the Indian people were driven into a stand of trees by dragoons. Kamiakin, accompanied by his youngest wife, was knocked off his horse when a howitzer shell tore away a tree limb. Foot soldiers pursued the Indian people into the trees. They were dispersed, never again to organize themselves into such a force as they had been.

Kamiakin and some Palouse followers fled to Montana by way of Canada, but they came back to live in the Palouse country in 1860 when assured by friends that the government wanted peace. He died of an illness in 1877 after a last-minute baptism by a Catholic missionary.[23]

Joel Palmer, accused of political infidelity, slandering the citizens of Oregon territory, and making reservations where Oregonians didn't want them, saw his political career blighted by the Rogue River War.

Even as he was supervising the final operations of the war, Palmer was condemned at a public meeting in Roseburg at which Joseph Lane's friend William Martin played an important part. The level of outrage in the statement produced by this assemblage suggests how untenable Palmer's position had become. Martin and his friends accused Palmer of "erroneous and false statements which have gone abroad officially and otherwise, in regard to the people of Oregon, and the war now in our midst." They resented the characterization of many of "our best citizens" who had taken part in Lupton's expedition as "a band of unprincipled vagabonds." They even accused Palmer of responsibility for General Wool's opposition to the war, because Palmer's official report "was well calculated to deceive the old General." The report itself, they declared, "was false in conception, false in fact, and without the shadow of foundation in truth."[24]

On July 1, the *Statesman* reported without comment that Palmer had been removed and would be replaced by a steamboat captain, Absalom Hedges.[25] On the same day, Palmer's friend R. W. Dunbar sent him a letter saying that Hedges had told Captain Tichenor that he (Hedges) had a commission to take Palmer's place and that "the Indians should never go on that [Coast] Reservation." Palmer would record that he handed the job of territorial Indian superintendent over to Hedges on July 16.[26] Curiously, two months later Hedges contracted with Palmer and his brother to build a farm at what would become the agency on the upper Siletz River,[27] as if Palmer were being given a sop in return for leaving the superintendency quietly.

Palmer's principal success as superintendent was the making of the Coast and Grand Ronde Reservations, but he could not have accomplished it as quickly as he did but for the war, which was his principal failure. The reservation-making process had gone too far by the middle of 1856 to be stopped by anyone. Most of the surviving Indian peoples of southwestern Oregon had been uprooted, whether they were directly involved in the war or not, and so Palmer did not have to convince them to leave their homes. He began sending them to the reservations as soon as possible, quieting the potential for further conflict, but also making

Unsatisfactory Results

reversal of the reservation policy in Oregon prohibitively expensive, complicated, and embarrassing.

Palmer would make a political comeback. He would win the Republican nomination for governor without opposition in April 1870. The *Oregonian*, which had become a Republican paper, said Palmer was "identified with the growth and progress of the State" more than any other man and possessed a spotless reputation for "integrity and for honest duty."[28] During the campaign, Palmer's position on the Rogue River War fourteen years before was used against him, and he was also accused of having cheated Phil Sheridan in a business deal in 1861. He lost the election in June, but by only 631 out of 22,821 votes.[29]

The following year, with a recommendation from the Methodist Church, Palmer would return to the Indian Service as the agent at Siletz.[30] His actions as agent are discussed in chapter 10.

As for Joseph Lane, he would rise to prominence as an exponent of slavery, and apparently he came close to getting a presidential nomination in 1860, but his downfall would be soon in coming and altogether final.

While the Rogue River War was being concluded, he made himself noticeable in the city of Washington in the controversy around a beating administered May 22, 1856, by Rep. Preston Brooks of South Carolina to Sen. Charles Sumner of Massachusetts. The beating was in retribution for a speech about the slavery conflict in Kansas in which Sumner had supposedly insulted both South Carolina and Brooks's uncle, one of that state's senators.

On May 29, according to the *Richmond Enquirer*, Lane carried a challenge to a duel from Brooks to Sen. Henry Wilson of Massachusetts, a challenge which Wilson declined.[31] According to Lane biographer James E. Hendrickson, the general also served during the summer as Brooks's second in an abortive duel with Rep. Anson W. Burlingame of Massachusetts. William Martin, the former volunteer officer, described by Hendrickson as "Lane's devotee and neighbor," wrote from Oregon to tell Lane, "Thare is afiew of us out heare having a cane made to Send to the Hon. Brooks of South Carolina to replace the one he broke over Sumner."[32]

Joseph Lane and Delazon Smith became Oregon's first two senators on July 5, 1858, chosen by the first legislature to meet under the new state constitution. That constitution would not go into force until Oregon was admitted as a state on February 12, 1859. It specified truncated terms for the first senators. Lane and Smith were sworn in two days later and drew lots for the longer term, which would expire in 1861. Lane won the drawing, and so Smith served less than a month.[33]

Lane hit his political height in the spring of 1860 when he was nominated for the vice presidency by the pro-slavery faction of the Democratic Party. Perhaps he could have reached higher. A member of his political entourage claimed many years later that before the Democrats divided into factions, Lane had been close to gaining the nomination. James O'Meara claimed that when it became apparent that neither John Breckinridge nor Stephen A. Douglas could be nominated, "a movement was broached to harmonize the two factions by nominating General Lane."

All was going well until what O'Meara described as "a leak in the telegraph office" alerted friends of Douglas that Lane had sent a message in support of following the lead of delegates from the lower South who had walked out over the slavery question. The Douglas faction backed away from Lane, and thus he was, by O'Meara's reckoning, prevented from saving the country. His nomination would have kept the party together, and he would have been elected. "There would have been no secession of States; no colossal internecine civil war."[34]

With the presidential election lost and his truncated term in the Senate expired, Lane went back to Oregon. Before he arrived, the *Statesman* printed an elaborate allegation linking Lane with Sen. William Gwin of California in a fantastic scheme to establish a slave-holding republic patterned after the Renaissance republic of Venice, if the southern states carried out their secession.[35]

Politics had changed in Oregon. The state had turned in a narrow vote in favor of Abraham Lincoln in the 1860 election.[36] Southern sympathies were not extinct in the state, but Lane's prominence as a member of the breakaway pro-slavery wing of the Democratic party did him no good. Moreover, he had made no discernable effort in 1858 to either urge the admission of Oregon as a state or get the war claims paid. According to Frances Fuller Victor, "it began to be said that he was purposely delaying the admission of Oregon until the next session in order to draw mileage as both delegate and senator."[37]

Two months before Lane returned to Oregon, the *Oregonian* complained that since the election of a Republican administration, "all the little Lane-shriekers" had been demanding that the Republicans get the war claims paid even though "the disunion Treasury-thieves" were still in power until Lincoln took office. "Gen. Lane has had a chance to procure the payment of the War Debt any time in the last four years," the newspaper argued.[38]

When Lane reached Portland on April 30, 1861, he was aboard the same steamer that brought news that the war had begun, according to Victor. She said that "hatred and insult greeted him from the moment he came in sight of these Pacific shores." Some of his friends in Portland wanted to hold a public welcome in his honor, but "they were assured that such a demonstration would not be permitted in that town. Even the owner of a cart refused to transport his luggage to the house of his son-in-law."

While Lane was crossing over into the Umpqua valley on his way home, he sustained an accidental pistol wound. While he was convalescing, he supposedly confessed the Pacific republic scheme to the old settler Jesse Applegate, who talked him out of it.[39] Whether or not he ever seriously considered leading a secession of the Pacific coast from the union, Lane's political career was over, though he would live on for another twenty years.[40]

The projected war-claims bonanza was delayed and then radically reduced. A three-member commission reported in 1857 that the expenses of the war, not counting claims for damage done by Indians, had amounted to $4,449,949 in Oregon.[41] The final figure approved by the commission for both the Oregon and Washington campaigns was $6,011,457. But when the third auditor of the Treasury examined the accounts, he disallowed more than half that amount. Even allowing the "incredible" amount of $11.15 per day for keeping a man in the field, the auditor said, the government should pay only $2,714,809.

Aaron Rose, proprietor of the Roseburg Hotel, had claimed payment for 4,336 meals at one dollar apiece. The auditor allowed less than one-third of that amount—$1,239. Asahel Bush of the *Statesman* had claimed $3,447 for printing and advertising. The auditor allowed $1,092.25. Many claims were made for forage and stabling of horses at two dollars a day. The auditor reduced them all by two-thirds. An Umpqua River ferryman claimed $1,990.32 for his services. The auditor allowed $434.

The auditor allowed claims for the purchase of 1,697 horses, 746 mules, and 1,015 oxen for the use of Oregon volunteers although he found it "difficult to imagine for what purposes they could all have been needed." Most of the mounted volunteers had claimed pay for the use of their own horses, he noted, and on top of that about $300,000 had been claimed for the rental of animals. Although the auditor was satisfied that these claims could be reduced, he said he had no data to determine what the reduction would be and no evidence of fabricated claims.

Even making allowance for high prices in southern Oregon, the auditor said, extravagance and "the irregular and irresponsible manner in which the war was carried on," especially in Oregon, had resulted in an excessively costly war.[42]

A bill to pay the claims based on the report of the third auditor was finally passed on March 2, 1861. Congress appropriated $2.8 million, including $400,000 for pay and $2.4 million for supplies (a total of about $56 million in 1990s dollars). According to an 1872 report, the War Department had by then paid out $2,436,610.

The lieutenant who wrote the report questioned the efforts of Charles S. Drew and Benjamin F. Dowell to collect claims dating from the Walker expedition in 1854, and their activities raised questions about Rogue River War claims in which they were also involved. The lieutenant recommended that "nothing short of a judicial procedure should now induce the head of this Department to issue requisitions to pay claims of the class known as 1855–'56."[43]

Speaking to a meeting of Indian war veterans in Portland in the spring of 1888, thirty-two years after the Rogue River War ended, Dowell argued that the government still owed at least $3,296,659 for the wars of 1855 and 1856.[44]

Although the Rogue River War was not a bonanza for the Oregon economy, it was proof that politicians could create an otherwise pointless Indian war for local political and economic purposes, ignoring the humane spirit of the stated Indian policy of the federal government. On the other hand, the war stimulated the development of the western Oregon reservation system and forced Indian acceptance, just as later wars would be needed to force other Indian peoples to accept reservation life.

Joel Palmer's need for a war to set up the circumstances in which he could implement a policy meant to be humane is not the only contradiction the case of western Oregon suggests between applied policy and ideal policy. When Joel Palmer chose the site of the Coast Reservation partly because it seemed undesirable to whites, he made a politically obvious and perhaps inevitable choice. But putting Indian people on land so poor and isolated that white people didn't want it meant forcing Indian people into poverty and dependence as long as they were confined there. In addition, Palmer's dismissal, which in large part occurred because he insisted on implementing federal policy, showed not only the influence of local political interests on Indian Service appointments but also that Indian Service officials had more reason to concern themselves with the comfort of their local political allies than with the welfare of the Indian people, who had no influence over appointments.

These early indications from Oregon should have suggested that the reservation policy could not produce the self-sustaining Indian communities living in peace and mutual respect with their white neighbors that George Manypenny had envisioned.

The adaptation of the southwestern Oregon Indian peoples to white expansion was not a product of the reservation policy; it was already under way when the Rogue River War began. Removal influenced adaptation more than it promoted adaptation. On the Coast Reservation, people willingly learned farming and the English language, and some learned to read, write, and figure. But white teachers could not teach them how to live decently in a country where Indians were looked upon as childlike or even somewhat less than human. Integrating spiritual survival with physical survival was necessarily an Indian task, commonly undertaken in the face of official incomprehension, indifference, or even hostility.

9

The Coast Reservation

On November 9, 1855, a few weeks after the beginning of the Rogue River War, President Franklin Pierce signed the executive order that established the Coast Reservation. It included almost 1.4 million acres—about the area of the state of Delaware. It stretched along the Pacific coast for more than one hundred miles from Cape Lookout on the north to an obscure stream between the Siuslaw and Umpqua Rivers on the south, and it took in all the land to the eighth range of townships west of the Willamette meridian, as much as twenty-two miles inland.[1]

Most of the southwestern Oregon Indian people who survived the war would be moved to the Coast Reservation, which was among the first few established under the new western reservation policy. Their experience would be, among other things, a test of whether the humane intentions of that policy could be put into practice. Commissioner George Manypenny, who began implementation of the new policy, explained in 1853 that it was intended to save Indians from the bad effects of white expansion

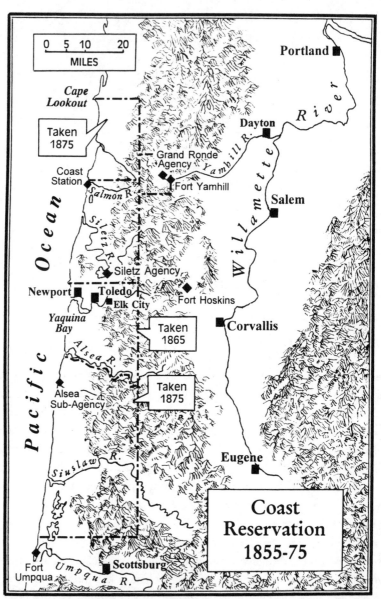

Coast, Siletz, and Alsea Reservations, 1855–75. Established by Joel Palmer on land depopulated by epidemics, in 1856 the Coast Reservation became the new home of most of the survivors of the Rogue River War. The federal government unilaterally cancelled the reserved status of its middle section in 1865, leaving the Siletz Reservation in the north and the Alsea Reservation in the south. Ten years later, after a token effort to win Indian ratification, the government closed the Alsea Reservation and also took the northern part of the Siletz Reservation.

by concentrating them in isolated places, limiting their contact and thus conflict with whites, and training them to become self-supporting farmers, similar in their habits to whites. Manypenny knew that the policy would be expensive at first but expected costs to diminish as Indians learned to sustain themselves.[2] Manypenny predicted in 1855 that the policy would lead to mutual acceptance between whites and Indians once both parties understood that Indian removal to some distant place (like the removal of the Cherokees from Georgia to Indian Territory in 1838) was no longer an option.[3]

Manypenny's intentions were ignored on the Coast Reservation. Politically appointed agents and superintendents treated their jobs as opportunities to become bigger men, politically and financially. The reservation included too little good land to become self-supporting through farming, and the government diminished what there was in response to special-interest lobbying. Indian people learned to integrate themselves into the new white world around them, but they were motivated more by the failures of the reservation than by its dubious successes.

The Coast Reservation's main agency—the headquarters compound—would be built inland in the northern part of the reservation on a hill overlooking a broad expanse of meadow on the Siletz River. Joel Palmer had designated the meadow a temporary Indian reserve on May 18, 1854, for three families who were farming there.[4] Three forts were set up along the borders of the reservation. Fort Yamhill, east of Grand Ronde, came into being in March 1856. Capt. Christopher Augur established Fort Hoskins in July across the Coast Range from the site of the Siletz agency. Fort Umpqua was established later that month in the sand on the north shore of the mouth of the Umpqua River, near the southern boundary of the reservation.[5]

Indian agent Robert Metcalfe, who took charge of the coastal district on August 20, described it as extending about twenty miles inland and including all the land from the mouth of the Salmon River to the mouth of the Alsea, or about one thousand square miles, of which eight hundred were "so mountainous and destitute of vegetation . . . that even mountain goats would perish with hunger." In the northern part of the district the mountains were covered with timber and elk and deer were abundant, but the rest of the reservation presented "a most gloomy prospect" of sharp mountains and deep canyons "covered with immense forests of dead timber." Another observer would report seeing "continued deserts of burnt trees" between Fort Hoskins and the Siletz agency. Metcalfe said the prairies along the Siletz, including about five thousand acres, made up about all the arable land in his district.[6]

The first survivors of the war to arrive on the Coast Reservation were sent by boat to Portland aboard the steamer *Columbia* and then to Joel Palmer's headquarters at Dayton in the Willamette valley. They were marched out of Dayton on Monday, July 7, 1856, to their next stop, the agency Palmer had set up on the Yamhill River at the edge of the Willamette valley at the Grand Ronde. Finally they were moved to the mouth of the Salmon River on the coast.[7]

Federal investigator J. Ross Browne would argue that only Robert Metcalfe's "extraordinary firmness and energy" kept the people sent to the Coast Reservation from abandoning it. Regarding complaints that Metcalfe was verbally abusive, Browne agreed that he had "a way of his own of talking to Indians" but claimed that they liked him anyway and he understood their character thoroughly.[8]

Metcalfe would be called corrupt. Frances Fuller Victor said that Metcalfe took $40,000 away with him after serving as agent.[9] A later Oregon Indian Service superintendent claimed that Metcalfe "received about all the benefits that could be derived" from appropriations for the Coast Reservation and had $60,000 (or $1.2 million in 1990s dollars) when he left Oregon in 1861 to join the Confederate army in Texas.[10]

Metcalfe was one among many Indian Office employees accused of cashing in on their jobs. T. W. Davenport, who would become agent at Umatilla in eastern Oregon in the 1860s, said agents commonly took kickbacks from merchants. He had questioned one merchant's complaints of corruption by saying, "It is easy to say that all the agents pilfer in this way, but what do you know about it?" The merchant answered, "I say all because all I know are guilty. The agent at Warm Springs, at the Grande Ronde, at Umatilla, at the Siletz does, and I presume that the rest of them do the same."[11] Corruption and incompetence in the Indian Service should not have been unexpected given that superintendents and agents were political appointees who enjoyed considerable independence in a context in which, as the dismissal of Joel Palmer had shown, conscientious competence could become a political liability.

Superintendent Hedges experimented with supplying the reservation by sea with mixed results. After a contracted schooner got into Yaquina Bay with most of its cargo intact, Hedges described the bay as "perfectly safe, or at least, sufficiently so for our purposes—perfectly safe in good weather."[12] But a supply schooner was wrecked in December while trying to get into Siletz Bay.[13] As a result, the people at the nearby mouth of the Salmon River were moved to Yaquina Bay, where the flour the earlier supply schooner successfully delivered was quickly used up. Metcalfe contracted with a mill in King's Valley for more flour. Snow was two to four feet deep in the mountains, and neither wagons nor pack mules could get through. J. Ross Browne said Metcalfe induced "the strongest and most reliable of the Indians" to pack in the flour on their backs—twenty thousand pounds in all.[14]

Hedges, complaining of poor health, announced in December that he wanted to resign as soon as a replacement could be found.[15] Metcalfe, meanwhile, seems to have been absent. Lt. Phil Sheridan reported on February 4, 1857, that "a very bad state of affairs" existed at the agency because "there has been no agent here for months and not a man about the agency that could speak Chenook, so that the Indians have had things their own way and have been very Saucy."[16]

A little more than a week later, Captain Augur reported general dissatisfaction on the reservation because of the incompetence of Hedges, whose plan to bring in supplies by sea had proven to be a failure. About fifteen hundred people "are now and have been for over a month without a pound of flour and are now without meat," Augur said. Many were saying that they would return to southern Oregon in the spring, "quietly if they are not opposed, but prepared to fight if they are."[17]

In April, Sheridan talked the recalcitrant leaders of some eleven hundred people at Yaquina Bay into moving to the valley of the Siletz. He reported telling them "that they would have to regard the Siletz as their future home, and that they must not only abandon all intentions of leaving, but would have to stop talking about it." Sheridan blamed the unrest partly on hunger and partly on "the determined hostility of the *agents* placed over these Indians." Metcalfe, he said, had "surrounded himself with employés who were engaged in hostilities with them in the lower country, and who do not hesitate to express the most improper and hostile language towards them." Sheridan got into an argument with Metcalfe because the agent wanted his help in disarming the Indians.

While negotiating the move to the Siletz, Sheridan had told the Indian people that they could keep their guns.[18] Metcalfe argued that his employees wouldn't stay "whilst the Indians have the means within their possession of taking their lives."[19] Sheridan said he was satisfied that the Indians had "the best intentions" of remaining peaceful.[20] Metcalfe complained to Captain Augur at Fort Hoskins, saying he had armed some of his employees and called a council at which he demanded the Indians' arms. All "except for a few desperadoes" were complying. Nonetheless Metcalfe threatened to "abandon the public works" if Augur refused to cooperate.[21]

Sheridan reported to Augur that Metcalfe's conduct had been "impolitic and excitable" and he "had used the most violent language" with the Indians. The lieutenant said Metcalfe decided he would issue no rations until the last of the holdouts had given up their guns. He had told Sheridan that "hunger would compel them to take things by force, and that he would pitch into them and kill as many as he could." The confrontation never came, but Sheridan complained that Metcalfe had, "to a great extent, destroyed the good feelings with which the Indians had moved to Siletz."[22]

Metcalfe described the people under his supervision as both promising and threatening. He reported from the Siletz in July 1857 that there were 554 "Shasta, or Upper Rogue River Indians" in his district together with 1,390 members of the Athapascan-speaking groups and 105 members of local bands. He said they were "wretchedly poor, and destitute of all the necessaries and comforts of life, except what is supplied them by the government." But they were also "generally industrious, and manifest a disposition to imitate the whites," he added, and the children "learn very readily." Nonetheless, they regarded whites as their enemies and "express a strong desire to return to their native country, and appear to have a superstitious awe of having their bodies [buried] in a foreign land."

Metcalfe said many of the Indians wanted to take up farming and he had about 280 acres under cultivation, but the wheat on 150 of those acres had been planted too late. Food would have to be supplied, he said: "Should the government withhold its aid, the condition of these people would be truly distressing; hunger would drive them to desperation, and war would be the inevitable result."[23]

While Metcalfe detected some potential for civilization among the Indian peoples, in the form of an interest in farming, the new superintendent of Indian affairs did not. He was James W. Nesmith,[24] and in his first annual report in 1857, he said that the Rogue River peoples were a continuing threat; he claimed that they were "ready to take up arms and resume hostilities" if the government failed to feed them, that they had never been "chastised for outrages committed on our people," and that they had "suffered little by the war." Nesmith did not agree with the fundamental idea behind the reservation policy; "So far as their ultimate civilization or Christianization is concerned, I am convinced that all such ideas are utopian and impracticable," he said, adding that "starvation, disease, and bad whiskey combined is rapidly decimating their numbers, and will soon relieve the government of their charge."[25]

The reservation regime itself promoted starvation and disease. The Indian Service provided neither adequate food nor adequate housing. When J. Ross Browne visited the Siletz agency in late 1857, he saw "twenty-seven Indian board houses; and timber and boards ready for thirty more, which will probably be completed in a month." So there were at most fifty-seven houses that winter for all the Indian people in the Siletz district, not counting "a few shanties for fishermen at the mouth of Yaquina Bay."[26] Metcalfe had reported in July that there were 2,049 Indian people in the district,[27] or almost 36 for each prospective house.

Although the people were willing to farm, the land was not promising. In the summer of 1858, Metcalfe reported that he had five hundred acres under cultivation but he had learned "that neither corn, beans, nor vines of any kind will grow here, and many other garden vegetables are killed by the cold night." Nor was the land of much use for grazing stock, "there being little or no grass, except on the small prairies which will be required for cultivation." Game, "tolerably abundant" the year before, had been "driven back to the high mountains, and as the spring salmon do not run up any of these streams it leaves us entirely destitute of food during the spring and summer, except as it has been supplied by the government."[28]

What Metcalfe called "the upper Rogue River Indians" were, he said, "diminishing very rapidly" in numbers; of the 590 counted twelve months before, 205 had died. "They die with disease of the lungs contracted by exposure during the war," he theorized. "A few more years will put an end to the most fierce and warlike race of people west of the Rocky mountains."[29]

In a letter in August, Nesmith reported that "the supplies raised at the Reservation, together with the appropriations made for subsisting the Indians during the present fiscal year, will be exhausted by the first of December next." As he would be compelled to stop issuing rations, Nesmith said, he respectfully suggested that the War Department be informed of the need to reinforce Forts Yamhill, Hoskins, and Umpqua "for the purpose of holding four thousand starving Indians in check, and preventing them from depredating the settlements."[30]

What the Indian people thought of their treatment was suggested when C. H. Mott, an inspector sent by the Department of the Interior, went to the Siletz agency in late 1858 for a council with the leaders of the coastal tribes about their unratified treaties. One man from the Port Orford country, Ty-gon-ee-shee, told Mott that he was tired of talking. J. Ross Browne had "promised to carry our hearts to the President, and send us his in return. He has not done so, and how do we know you wont [sic] lie to us, as he did?" His people had spilled no white blood and had been promised that "if we would sell our lands, and come here we should have houses and live like white people. We come and have been very poor ever since." His people were ashamed that they had lost their lands, and he wanted to leave the reservation.[31]

In Washington, the reservation was still regarded as a tentative arrangement. George Manypenny's successor as commissioner, Charles E. Mix, described the new reservation system as still tentative in his 1858 report and said that Indians would be supported on reservations only "for a limited period." Mix said that five reservations had been established in California, two in Oregon, and two in Texas, adding, "The operations thus far, in carrying out the reservation system, can properly be regarded as only experimental."[32]

Nesmith was soon on his way out as Indian superintendent, probably because he clashed with Joseph Lane and used his power to hand out federal jobs to support the anti-Lane Democratic faction led by Asahel Bush.[33] On April 2, 1859, the Indian Office sent Edward R. Geary his commission as superintendent.[34] Geary was the man Joel Palmer had dismissed as his secretary three years before after Geary promised to give up the reservation idea if legislators supported his bid for Palmer's job.[35]

On the Siletz, Metcalfe resigned as agent effective September 30. Geary recommended Daniel Newcomb as Metcalfe's replacement and Joshua B. Sykes as subagent to move the lower Umpqua and Coos Indians onto the reservation.[36]

Like Metcalfe, Newcomb, who was a Virginian, had involvements in southwestern Oregon where the Rogue River War had been fought and with the Democratic party. He had represented Jackson County in the 1857 state constitutional convention as a regular Democrat. He had also been a member from Jackson County of the 1858 legislature that elected Joseph Lane a U.S. senator. That same legislature elected him state brigadier general.[37] Newcomb may also have been one of Major Lupton's lieutenants; a "Mr. Newcome" was said to have led fourteen members of Lupton's party.[38]

Newcomb reported that Metcalfe had made "considerable improvement of permanent character," but he also said in his first annual report that Metcalfe had left far too little food on hand for the winter. The wheat and oats at the agency had to be saved for seed. Twenty-five thousand bushels of potatoes, together with fish caught by the Indians, got them through the winter, but "most of them were in an enfeebled and half-starved condition in the spring from the want of a sufficiency of proper food," Newcomb said.[39]

He claimed he had built a sawmill and was building a flour mill, and that a school had been kept from March till August of 1860. Attendance had been poor because children were often with their parents trying to get food. Those who attended showed "much sprightliness of mind." He suggested that the children be removed from the influence of their parents "at an early age and taught the arts of civilized life."[40]

In the summer of 1860, the subagent for the southern part of the Coast Reservation, Joshua B. Sykes, reported that he had built two buildings and planted about twenty-five acres of potatoes and vegetables at the site he had chosen for the subagency buildings, six miles south of the Alsea River. The Indians had gotten through the winter without Indian Service help, he said, because the army had given them a large quantity of "condemned clothing."[41]

Edward Geary was replaced as superintendent by William H. Rector not long after the Civil War began in 1861,[42] presumably because he was a Democrat. Daniel Newcomb, the agent at Siletz, was also replaced,[43] and he was soon accused of having shown strong Southern sympathies. B. R. Biddle, who took over the agency on October 1, reported that he had found it "in the utmost confusion" and that the "savages" had been "tampered with by bad, designing men" who told them "the government was already destroyed."[44]

A citizen of the inland town of Corvallis complained that Indians had left the reservation because "they were told the Government was *broke up*" and that the former agent, presumably Newcomb, had given them twenty muskets and twenty revolvers. "We claim this *aid* afforded them by Secessionists in the way of arms is dangerous and that they should be taken from them," he said.[45]

A more sensible explanation for people leaving the reservation was provided by Capt. Frederick Dent of the Ninth Infantry, brother-in-law of a little-known former army officer named Ulysses Grant. Dent, in command at Fort Hoskins, told Rector the Indians said they left because "they have not food or clothing, nor can they get either if they remain on the Reserve."[46]

Superintendent Rector went to the Siletz in May 1862 and was told by a man identified as Sixes George that the people had to eat frozen, rotten potatoes and the carcasses of dead horses. Er-ches-sa, chief of the Sixes, said he had no confidence in Biddle and wanted "another agent that will give us what you send here for us and not sell it."[47]

By August 1862, Biddle reported that no more than half of the people were on the reservation. They had been away for two months, "scattered up and down the coast to their former country. Passes have been given to a large number to go into the Willamette valley, to assist the farmers in harvesting, and more have gone without passes."[48] Daniel Newcomb, the agent before Biddle, had expressed a more rigid attitude, saying in his 1860 report that he had done all he could, with the help of Captain Augur, to maintain isolation from whites. "The Indians under my charge have had little opportunity for acquiring habits of dissipation," he boasted.[49]

Allowing people to leave the reservation on passes was a necessary innovation that legalized what they were already doing in order to survive. It may also have been a way for Rector to apply pressure to get more money from the government. Rector said in his annual report for 1862 that the lack of the funds he had requested for the tribes with unratified treaties had forced him to use the pass system. "To compel even Indians to remain on a reservation without food or clothes, or even the means of obtaining them, is unjust and inhuman," he said.[50]

Leaving the reservation, with or without a pass, would become an ordinary aspect of reservation life. There is an obvious parallel between this migratory labor and the annual cycle of travel to food sources that had been an important part of life only a decade before. Instead of gathering the products of nature, however, the people now ensured their survival by collecting wages from farmers involved in a market economy.

In contrast to this informal adaptation undertaken by the Indian peoples themselves, Biddle's slender effort to provide a formal education on the reservation went wrong. Biddle said at the end of June that the problems were lack of funds and the immorality of former teachers, which had led the Indians "to believe that the whites were only here to gratify their lusts . . . hence their reluctance to send their children, especially the older girls, to school."[51]

By that time, Superintendent Rector was questioning Biddle's fiscal morality. On June 7, Rector sent a letter to the commissioner of Indian affairs saying, in effect, that Biddle was neither honest nor competent.[52] Biddle described himself as the target of a conspiracy of disappointed job seekers and dismissed employees. One of these, it developed, was Biddle's private employee, Frank Cooper, a packer. Biddle admitted that he had bought some mules and horses and hired Cooper. He had no funds to pay an outside contractor to pack in agency supplies, he said. Cooper had been listed as the contractor in Biddle's accounts, Biddle said ingenuously, "for mere formality, and to save my own name from appearing." Biddle was willing to admit that it was "irregular" for him to have contracted with himself.[53]

Agent Biddle was finally relieved in October 1862. He complained that Rector had given no reason.[54] Rector, in turn, complained about his agents generally, saying that "frauds, peculations, and even direct robbery have been the distinguishing characteristics of Indian Agents in Oregon."[55] On December 24, James W. Nesmith—who had become U.S. senator in 1861—joined with another member of the Oregon congressional delegation to inform the commissioner of Indian affairs that, in their opinion, both Biddle and Rector should be dismissed immediately.[56] The politically inimical *Oregon Statesman* claimed that Rector had sold a government draft for $73,000 in gold coin, bought greenbacks with the gold at a premium of 5 to 7 percent, paid off creditors of the Indian Office with the greenbacks, and kept the difference.[57]

The chief clerk of the Department of the Interior forwarded commissions for a new superintendent and a new agent at Siletz to the Indian Office in January 1861.[58] Rector turned the superintendent's job over to J. W. Perit Huntington,[59] a Connecticut-born former schoolteacher and surveyor in his early thirties who had been a member of the state legislature in 1860.[60] The new agent at Siletz was Ben Simpson,[61] who

William Hipple Mitchell, a Republican senator from Oregon, had been a lawyer for the disreputable transportation magnate Ben Holladay. Mitchell conspired with Benjamin Simpson to push through closure of the Alsea Reservation as an economy measure, but put forward the legislation only after he had failed to remove some territory containing valuable timber from reservation jurisdiction. (Oregon Historical Society, neg. Or Hi 80888)

Benjamin Simpson was agent at Siletz for eight years and was said to have been brusque and brutal with the people there. He became federal surveyor general and worked with Mitchell to allow white exploitation of stands of cedar along the Alsea River. As a special commissioner in 1875, Simpson falsely certified that the Indian peoples on the Alsea Reservation were willing to be removed. (Oregon Historical Society, neg. Or Hi 54771)

had come to Oregon from Missouri some seventeen years before and had been a member of both state and territorial Oregon legislatures.[62]

One of Simpson's successors said that when Simpson was agent, "The whipping-post and the buck and gag were in constant requisition."[63] When Alexander W. Chase of the Coast and Geodetic Survey visited the reservation during Simpson's tenure, several people were confined "for breaking their passes," that is, for staying off the reservation to work for whites or hunt and fish longer than the time Simpson had allowed them. In "bad cases," Chase said, they were whipped.

Simpson told Chase that at the beginning of his term he told the people that anyone who left the reservation without permission would get forty lashes. The following day "four or five of the most desperate ran away." When they were brought back, Simpson told them that "his heart was very sick" because he had promised to whip them and would now be forced to carry out that promise. "Yet he would leave it to them," Chase said. The prospective victims discussed the question and decided that "they had better be whipped, as they would rather bear it than have a Ty-ee lie to them."[64]

Chase apparently meant this story to show Simpson's control over the reservation people—"the wonderful influence that he exerts over the savage natures around him." Simpson, he said, had "one of the few faces met with that have 'power of command' stamped plainly." The Indian people "are taught to obey promptly, and it is strictly impressed on their facile minds that punishment is sure to follow infraction of the rules."[65]

Simpson had tried an experiment with four Indian children, two girls who "were domesticated in his own family" and two boys who were apprenticed, "one to a carpenter, the other to a blacksmith." As they were "isolated and removed from their relatives [they] grew up under good influences," and in time they became couples who wanted to marry "after the fashion of the whites." This was done with considerable ceremony, with Simpson presiding over an Episcopal-style service. Soon many couples were asking to be married as white people were. But even the intimidating Simpson could not keep a hold on all the details of the lives of the Indian people indefinitely. After a while they "concluded that the Indian laws were best" and went back to their former custom of buying wives.[66]

A Tututunne woman named See-nee-nis Baker would relate, many years later, another experience with Simpson that suggests that he did not always exercise the command attributed to him by Alexander W. Chase. Baker told a reporter in 1937 that she had been one of several girls who "rebelled from Simpson's regime and ran away to Portland." They had no difficulty fitting into white society: "In Portland they applied for domestic work and all were quickly placed." One day Baker and a cousin, by then "attired in the prevailing styles" of the city, met Simpson on the streets of Portland. They "accosted Simpson and kidded him. Simpson failed to recognize them and the incident was a subject of fun for the twain for some time."[67]

Alexander W. Chase himself provided another example of a situation involving Simpson that may have provoked some merriment among his Indian subjects. Simpson, "desiring to gratify some friends who were visiting him, sent for the head chiefs and asked them to get up a dance." They did as they were asked, coming back "in full costume, with all the young squaws and men of the tribes." But then a chief told Simpson that "dancing was very hard work, and they had been to considerable trouble and expense." They wanted fifty dollars, which "staggered him a little," but with everyone assembled and Simpson not wanting to disappoint his friends, he paid them the fifty dollars.[68]

Simpson presumably was not accustomed to coming out on the short end of bargains with reservation people. Corp. Royal A. Bensell, a young soldier stationed at the Siletz agency, wrote in his journal that Simpson kept a store where the goods that were supposed to have been distributed were sold—"bolts of Calico, Needles, Thred, Buttons, Shoes, Blankets, Hats, ribbon, &c. . . . Indians go there and buy what U. Sam payed for." Simpson allowed the Indians a dollar a day when he gave them work, Bensell added, but rather than paying them in cash, he gave them orders on his store. "Thus, in reality, he sells goods for three times their value, and Uncle Sam pays the Bill. In a few words, Indian Agencies are a curse to the Indians and likewise the country."

Bensell added that every Monday, the head of each family could receive "a few 'Spuds' and a little Wheat. . . . Just now, and for some time to come, the Agent will answer a supplication for 'Muck-a-muck' [food] after this style, 'Nika halo Muck-a-muck' [I have no food]. Poor Indians, this is your reward for trusting the 'Boston man' [American]."

The reservation's two mills were useless, Bensell said. The sawmill could not even furnish the lumber to keep the agency buildings repaired, and the flour mill was "unkeept, molding and moss-covered."[69]

Simpson would be involved in two reductions of the Coast Reservation that would, within thirteen years, leave it about one-fifth its original size. The first involved Yaquina Bay. In his annual report for 1863, Simpson described the mouth of the bay as a good harbor "with an entrance easy of access, and safe." He added that "it might at some future time become very valuable." If the government committed itself to keeping the Indian people where they were, he said, then the bay and the navigable part of the Yaquina River should not be part of the reservation.[70]

This was the first official suggestion of a reduction of the reservation set aside eight years before by a presidential order. Simpson's idea that the bay might have commercial value contradicted previous estimates. Absalom Hedges, a sailor before he was Indian Service superintendent, had been equivocal; the bay, he had said in 1856, was "perfectly safe in good weather."[71] Two years later, Superintendent James Nesmith had said the bay had "only a tolerably safe entrance for small vessels during the summer months," adding that it was "rendered exceedingly dangerous by reason of storms usually prevalent during the winter."[72]

Although Yaquina Bay was not the fine harbor its exponents claimed, it had another attraction for a particular class of sailors: oyster pirates. A San Francisco oysterman named Richard Hillyer, captain of the schooner *Cornelia Terry*, visited Yaquina Bay as early as December 1862 and had been ordered away, but he soon returned, built a store, and tacked up notices claiming the land around the store for himself and his partners.[73] Superintendent Huntington ordered outsiders to leave the bay, and Simpson served the order on Hillyer, who ignored it.[74]

Another San Francisco company acquired the exclusive right to take oysters from the bay in December 1863,[75] and about two months later, Corp. R. A. Bensell took a detachment down to the bay from the Siletz to arrest Hillyer. At the oyster beds there was now a small town. The shore was lined with Indian women collecting oysters. Bensell arrested Hillyer when he tried to take oysters aboard his schooner but released him pending trial.[76] Hillyer went to Corvallis and filed suit against Simpson and Bensell, arguing that tidelands could not be included in reservations. Huntington said that the Coast Reservation might as well be abandoned if Hillyer prevailed because that would be "practically the same as if the whole district were opened to settlement."[77] The court ruled against Hillyer.[78]

Huntington's argument that control of Yaquina Bay was essential to the integrity of the reservation was hollow, as his recommendation for removing the bay from the reservation would demonstrate before the Hillyer case had even been decided. What was being protected in the Hillyer case was the right of Indian service officials to control reservation resources.

Simpson repeated his suggestion for taking the bay out of the reservation in his annual report for 1864,[79] and Superintendent Huntington agreed in his, calling the bay "safe and navigable" and arguing that a wagon road from the Willamette valley to the head of navigation was already partly open, promising farmers in the valley a short route to ocean shipping. He added that land on the bay could be given up for white use without doing harm to the interests of either the government or the Indian peoples.[80] The Office of Indian Affairs in Washington inquired further of Huntington, who responded on December 12, 1864, that he would not object to opening the entire southern half of the reservation to white occupation if the Indian people living there gave their consent and agreed to be moved north of Yaquina Bay.[81]

The road Huntington mentioned was the project of the Corvallis and Yaquina Bay Wagon Road Company, which had been incorporated in the previous year (1863) by the former Indian agent B. R. Biddle, who was mayor of Corvallis in 1864,[82] together with James R. Bayley, who was government physician at the Siletz agency in 1863,[83] and T. B. Odeneal, editor of the *Corvallis Gazette*.[84] The incorporators had promised a road that would terminate near the mouth of Elk Creek, a tributary of the

Yaquina River,[85] that is, at a point about ten miles inside of the eastern boundary of the reservation. What Huntington and Simpson proposed would, in effect, reward the road company for proposing to penetrate Indian country.

Former superintendent James W. Nesmith, who had described the bay in 1858 as dangerous during winter, was a U.S. senator in 1865,[86] and thus a member of the Oregon congressional delegation that advocated opening the reservation. On December 21, 1865, one day after receiving a report on the subject from Interior Secretary James Harlan, President Andrew Johnson signed an order opening Yaquina Bay to white settlement.

Harlan had told Johnson that Oregon's delegation in Congress considered the reservation too large and wanted access to the bay for "the numerous settlers in the fertile and productive valley of the Willamette." Only "a small and rugged portion of the reservation in the vicinity of Aquina Bay, not occupied or desired by the Indians," was involved, he said, and he suggested that all the land between the Alsea River and a line drawn two miles south of the Siletz agency should be opened—almost 212,000 acres. Johnson accepted the suggestion.[87] Huntington was surprised by the "great influx of settlers" that followed and feared their presence would lead to trouble.[88] He had never suggested that the bay was a desirable location for white settlement, only that it might be a useful port for the Williamette valley.

On January 16, Huntington sent a telegram to the commissioner saying, "Whites are seizing farms & houses of Indians on relieved Part of Coast Reservation what shall be done."[89] The superintendent later complained that the Indians on Yaquina Bay should have been removed before the land was opened as he had suggested beforehand. Some of the Indians "had been encouraged to open farms, erect dwellings, and establish themselves permanently." Suddenly the agent was powerless to protect them, "and whites occupied the lands as they pleased."

Huntington was also concerned that the new southern boundary of the Siletz portion of the reservation was so close to the agency that "any vagabond white or half-breed who desired to do so" could "establish a whisky shop within two miles of the largest settlement of Indians on the

Pacific coast." He had counseled his superiors that the entire southern part of the reservation could be handed over to white settlers without doing any harm to the Indian peoples. Now he complained, "The whole treatment of the government toward these Indians has been full of bad faith."[90]

R. A. Bensell and two other men, one of them another former member of Bensell's company of California volunteers, became the first whites to file a claim on the newly opened land. They took over a site on Depot Slough, a stream that flows into Yaquina Bay from the north at the point where the mill town of Toledo now stands. Bensell and his partners later built a steam sawmill on their claim.[91]

The Corvallis and Yaquina Bay Wagon Road Company got its reward on the Fourth of July, 1866. Congress granted the company an estimated 76,800 acres along the new road, with the title to pass when the completion of the road had been certified.

At the hotel that James R. Bayley and his partner Samuel Case had built on the north shore of the bay near its mouth, Independence Day was celebrated by some four hundred white people, according to newspaper correspondent David Newsom, and "near 300 of the red people of this region were also assembled to witness the new and strange procedure of the 'Boston men.'" Bayley and Biddle made speeches, and Biddle presented a flag "on behalf of the noble ladies of Corvallis." Samuel Case read the Declaration of Independence; at noon, "dinner was announced and about three hundred and fifty whites partook of a most excellent dinner, after which some two hundred and fifty Indians satisfied their apetites [sic] with the abundance left."

That afternoon the owners of claims in the vicinity organized a town they named Newport. "Here is the germ of the San Francisco of Oregon," David Newsom said.[92] But the bay was no better a harbor than it had been ten years before, and no rival for either San Francisco Bay or the proven Columbia River route to Portland.

Oregon historian Leslie M. Scott called a later Yaquina Bay railroad scheme the product "of rosiest optimism"; the idea that a route through the Coast Range to a harbor with a channel depth of only fifteen feet at high tide could take the place of the old route to the sea by way of the

Willamette River was obviously mistaken.[93] But that does not mean that schemes promoting Yaquina Bay as a harbor were ill-considered from a strictly financial point of view. The Corvallis and Yaquina Bay Wagon Road Company would get the land granted by Congress no matter what became of Yaquina Bay.

Again, as in the case of the Rogue River War, local interests supported by Oregon's congressional delegation prevailed over the ideals of federal Indian policy. In this case, however, federal authorities gave their consent and encouragement, although J. W. Perit Huntington repented when he saw the unexpected effects of what he had done. The goal of a self-sustaining Indian community, isolated from white vices, had been forgotten in the throes of the real estate deal being pushed to a successful climax by the organizers and friends of the wagon road company.

Given the political nature of appointments to the Indian Service, this was predictable. The administrators of federal policy in Oregon were only remotely responsible to the commissioner of Indian affairs in Washington and not responsible at all to the Indian people whose lives they were supposed to manage. It was not their concern that the Indians got only the leftovers from the Fourth of July banquet.

Their chronic inattention simplified the task facing the peoples on the Coast Reservation as they learned to survive under the irresponsible control of the government. By turning themselves into migratory workers for white farmers, meshing their old pattern of seasonal migration with the demand for labor in white society, they won survival and a measure of control over their own lives. This adaptation was not what federal policy called for, ideally; the pass system broke down the isolation between Indian people and whites. But, again, local needs and conditions were more significant than the ideals of policy.

When Indian Service inspector John W. Wells came to the Siletz agency in January 1867, he found the people there "all decently clad in the garments of civilized life;—their decorous deportment and manner excited my admiration." Only their color "indicated the assemblage to be other than that of a meeting of farmers and their households," he said.[94] Among the many lessons the inhabitants of the reservation had learned since being marched there under guard was how to appear to John W. Wells to be a comforting example of the success of the reservation policy. But they were not what they seemed.

Although the people farmed, their agent-guided agricultural enterprise was not self-sustaining, and they had to rely on their earnings as migratory workers to feed and clothe themselves. Their homes were not on their own parcels of land, like the homes of white farmers, but were grouped on the reservation farms in villages. And their land—if it could even be considered their land—was being loudly coveted by whites.

Joel Palmer described the people on the Siletz Reservation in 1871 as "huddled together in small villages of from ten to fifteen families."[95] These villages were similar in size to the villages where the people had lived before the war, described in chapter 1, and were presumably similar in other ways. They could not have been precise reflections of the villages the people had left behind in southwestern Oregon, if only because there were fewer people to populate them. But the old village structure retained power. According to ethnologist J. Owen Dorsey, most of the old villages had their own burial grounds on the reservation when he was there in 1884, and he implied that the old restrictions against marriage within a village group were still in force.[96] The traditions retained their force even though the villages themselves were broken up between the visit of Wells in 1867 and the visit of Dorsey in 1884.

The villages usually went unnoted by Indian Service employees, who understood Indian social and political organization in terms of tribes occupying areas. The Rogue Rivers, for example, were on Upper Farm, up the Siletz River from the agency. The Shastas were on Shasta or Klamath Farm, between Upper Farm and the agency. And six southwest coastal tribes were on Lower Farm, downriver from the agency.[97] These tribes were led by chiefs. When the agent wanted confirmation of a grazing lease in 1874, for example, his clerk prepared a document bearing the names of nine men who were described as chiefs of tribes.[98]

John W. Wells was made acutely aware of white pressure on Indian land during his 1867 visit. Wells said the people on the Alsea Reservation were living in a state of "constant dread" because nearby whites were trying to have them removed. Wells said they were "in no man's way," and even if Yaquina Bay were developed, creating a demand for Alsea land, "it would still be injust to remove this peaceful and otherwise contented people from their homes."[99]

A clash on the Alsea Reservation in October 1867 provided an argument for removal. An agency employee was reported to have shot and killed an unnamed Indian in a fight over digging potatoes. Ben Simpson sent a messenger to Yaquina Bay to tell the whites there that the shooting had enraged the Indian people. The editor of the *Corvallis Gazette* warned that the "wily and treacherous" Indians were well armed.[100] Former corporal R. A. Bensell remarked that "some sensible comments" had been made in the newspapers about "removing these Indians to some place where their proximity will not endanger lives and property." All problems would be resolved, he said, if the government bought the reservation from the Indian peoples and moved them elsewhere.[101]

Agent Simpson, however, saw no advantage in removal. What would become of his job and the patronage power that went with it if the reservation were abolished? In late January 1868, he stopped at the *Gazette* offices in Corvallis while on his way from Salem to Siletz and visited with the editor, who called him "an intelligent, affable, and kind-hearted gentleman." Simpson said that the Indian people were "in a very quiet state of subordination." He also said that he had just received $87,000 for disbursements, and the editor commented that "a much larger sum of money is annually put into circulation in Benton county, through this means, than we supposed." Simpson said the reservation would support no more than 150 white settlers and, on the whole, was "more profitable as it now stands than if thrown open for settlement."[102]

Reservation statistics for 1869 suggest relative prosperity. About 2,300 people were reported to be living on the Siletz portion of the reservation, where they had 102 frame houses and 140 log houses (or about one for every 9.5 people). More than sixteen hundred acres were under cultivation, and the reservation produced 6,670 bushels of potatoes (about 2.9 per person), 3,170 bushels of turnips (about 1.4 per person), 140 tons of hay, and a little wheat and corn.[103] Simpson reported in the fall of 1870 that farming was going well, the reservation was quiet, and he had begun picking leaders for the Indian peoples from among the young men who were "more industrious and energetic than the majority."

Progress toward meeting the goals of the reservation policy was meaningless, however, to the whites who continually pushed for further land takeovers or even the closure of the reservation. In the spring of 1870, whites had circulated a petition demanding the closure of Siletz Reservation so that whites could have the land. Simpson said in his report that local whites had told the reservation people that "it was useless for them to plant their crops, as they would be removed before they could harvest them." Some people, discouraged by this campaign, had left the reservation, Simpson said, but others would be killed before they would be removed. He argued that removal was impractical because there was no better place in Oregon for the reservation, which could house 8,000 or 9,000 Indian people but "would not furnish comfortable homes for fifty white families."[104]

One week after Simpson wrote this report, the Oregon legislature sent a memorial to Congress asking for removal of the Indians from the Siletz Reservation. The legislators pointed out that a wagon road had been built and a lighthouse and railroad were planned for the bay. They claimed that as many as 40,000 acres of good farmland were bottled up for the sake of no more than 800 Indians.[105] (Indian office statistics showed 2,300 people in the Siletz district and another 500 people in the Alsea district.[106]) The memorial was ignored in Washington.

Under the Grant administration's so-called peace policy, the government gave churches much control over reservations. The Methodist Episcopal Church received jurisdiction over the Siletz Reservation. Church leaders recommended one-time superintendent Joel Palmer as agent for Siletz in January 1871.[107] Simpson turned over the agency to Palmer on May 1.[108] The change was no defeat for Simpson, who was soon appointed federal surveyor general for Oregon.[109] Nor had the Indian people seen the last of him. Simpson's involvement in the next reduction

reduction of the reservation would be a direct link between the period of political management and the period of Methodist management, as well as a suggestion of how little difference there was between the two.

10

Dancers, Dissenters, Refugees, and Methodists

The Grant administration, which came to power in 1869, invited churches to take part in making Indian policy and managing reservations, which historian Francis Paul Prucha called "an admission by the government that it was unable to carry out its obligations by ordinary procedures." One of the functions of the churches under this aspect of Grant's "peace policy" was nominating agents. Reformers expected church-approved agents to be more honest and competent than politically appointed agents. Prucha said this expectation grew out of public confidence in churches and the "obvious conclusion that if evils were caused because bad men were appointed agents, then the evils could be corrected by appointing good men."[1]

In an extensive study of the involvement of churches in Indian policy during this period, historian Robert H. Keller, Jr., argued that Indian reservations in the nineteenth century, like the Congo and Vietnam in the twentieth century, "were places that destroyed good men of

185

good intentions." Church-nominated agents were essentially better men than their party-nominated predecessors, but they were poorly funded, underpaid, badly housed, threatened with violence, closely watched, and weighed down with paperwork. The policy supplied a "surprising number" of "excellent agents," but they were unable to "save Indian tribes" because the roots of the failure of the country's Indian policy went too deep.[2]

Most of the five church-nominated agents on the Siletz seem to have begun with good intentions, but none of them could be described as excellent. They were less likely to be blatantly corrupt than were the agents who came before them, but they were not noticeably more effective. Their church connection was a burden. One resigned because, among other reasons, he was criticized in the church by a self-seeking rival. Another complained that Methodists expected to get all the jobs and contracts the reservation could offer, regardless of merit, and church officials later asked for his removal.

Joel Palmer held out some promise, as the first Methodist agent on the Siletz, that the denominational connection would produce a more humane administration. The manner of his leaving, however, suggests that under the new plan, local denominational politics had more influence than did denominational ideals.

Palmer abolished whippings[3] and set up a rudimentary court. He would report in the autumn of 1871 that the people had "elected three jurymen to hear & determine differences among themselves" and that this court, with himself "acting in the capacity of Judge," was meeting every Saturday.[4]

Palmer was not pleased with conditions on the reservation. He complained soon after his arrival that no moral improvement had been made since the people had been brought to the reservation. Children were raised to steal. Women were "bought and sold like cattle," a reference to the traditional custom of the bride price,[5] but Palmer equated the results with prostitution, saying that "daughters are loaned, hired, or sold at from twelve to sixteen years of age, as inducements are offered, sometimes for one night, one month, a year, or a bona fide sale."

The buildings were dilapidated and the work animals worn out, he said. He argued that the Indian people should have become herders of cattle and sheep because they were more likely to accept that sort of life than farming, but only one man, George Harney, a young Rogue River leader, had any cattle. Palmer added that if the land had been divided among the Indians "as originally contemplated," they would not have become "the roving, thriftless people they now are."[6]

Palmer's criticisms of the Simpson regime may have been deliberately overblown to make Palmer's prospective accomplishments seem larger by comparison. Could the immoral, shiftless Indians described by Palmer have been the same people who excited the admiration of John W. Wells four years before? But even if Palmer was in some sense accurate in describing what would seem to be Simpson's failure to implement the ideals of the reservation policy, he saw only what was on the surface, just as he saw only the surface of traditional marriage and interpreted it as prostitution.

Many inhabitants of the reservation could have been described as "roving" during the periods when they were migratory farmworkers, or, in other words, when they were off the reservation making money to buy necessities reservation life could not provide. Perhaps Simpson had been satisfied to maintain the reservation as a base for migratory workers instead of demanding self-sufficiency, recognizing that self-sufficiency through farming was an unrealistic goal and that trying too hard to achieve it would only deny white farmers the labor of the Indian people.

Palmer tried to divide the reservation's farmland into twenty-acre parcels to distribute to Indian families. In his first annual report, he said that before he could implement this allotment plan, he would have to build a sawmill to make lumber for the new houses the people would need on their new tracts of land to replace the houses in their villages. Implicitly, Palmer's plan involved breaking up the villages and disturbing traditional, extended-family-based social and political structures.

Lack of lumber was not the only problem with his allotment plan that Palmer reported; the surveyors hired to divide the land were hampered by the difficult terrain, according to Palmer, and wildfires had destroyed some of the survey markers.[7] This survey, in 1871, seems to have failed; former Indian agent T. W. Davenport contracted to make a new allotment survey in the summer of 1872.[8] Davenport said his friend Palmer, although an old man, worked with the survey party and insisted that the lots should have as much frontage as possible on the Siletz River, "thus changing the previous method of subdivision."

Palmer's generosity was not enough to make his plan a success. The Indian peoples, Davenport recalled, "were at that time opposed to any system of allotment and secretly destroyed the land-marks of the survey."[9] Superintendent Alfred B. Meacham ordered Palmer to suspend his allotment plan for reasons not explained in Indian Service documents. Palmer claimed that the failure to make allotments had "been a source of uneasiness to the Indians" and had weakened their confidence in the government. Similar anxiety was reported by Palmer's successor.[10]

A minority, at least, favored allotment. Five men who spoke at a council with an Indian Service inspector in 1873, including three men identified as chiefs, asked for division of the land. One chief said, "Divide the land, and I will no longer be afraid of them driving us from our country." Another said, "We want the land divided; then when we die our children will get it; that is the way the whites do." But eight men, including seven identified as chiefs in 1873 or 1874, defended their right to the reservation without mentioning allotment. Another six men, five of them identified as chiefs, mentioned neither land nor allotment specifically.[11]

Although none of the men who spoke at the 1873 council was recorded as having opposed allotment, some person or persons had already proven the existence of opposition by destroying survey markers. Perhaps those who objected to allotment understood what Palmer's successor recognized when he argued that once allotments were made, the Indian peoples could be kept on about 5 percent of the land taken up by the reservation, releasing the rest for white use.[12] Such a loss of land would not necessarily have hurt the already anemic agricultural potential of the reservation; Palmer's plan would probably have allotted practically all the genuinely useful farming and grazing land for Indian use. But it would have trapped the Indian people forever on small parcels of land, surrounded by white-owned properties, perhaps cut off from hunting and fishing sites. Moreover, as already noted, it would have disturbed the social and political arrangements implicit in the continued existence of their villages.

Allotment was certainly not rejected on grounds that the people rejected agriculture or individual responsibility—they already had both. Palmer found a system of land allocation in place when he arrived, involving "large fields, bordered on one side by the river, and these fields cultivated by from ten to fifteen different families, each having their separate tracts designated by stakes or strips of uncultivated land." The cultivators of these tracts understood the white economy; they sometimes produced surpluses, which they sold "to whomsoever will pay the most," Palmer said with some irritation.[13]

Under pressure from dissatisfied clergymen and would-be landowners wanting Indian land, and discouraged by lack of money to carry out his plans and possibly by his own financial difficulties, Palmer submitted his resignation in November 1872. His resignation was submitted after a controversy among the Methodist leadership over his treatment of John Howard, a minister working on the reservation. Howard seems to have accused Palmer of lacking interest in converting Indians. Palmer, who said that Howard wanted to take his job, dismissed him. A Methodist paper supported the minister, thundering, "Let no one suppose the church is either careless or powerless in this matter." Palmer later told one-time Indian agent J. L. Parrish that "envy in the church" had left him open to critics of his policies, and that his enemies had "flattered and hoodwinked" some of the Indian people, causing "a constant turmoil and excitement."[14]

Palmer made no mention of Indian opposition to his plans, and he may have been genuinely unaware of it, just as he seems to have been unaware of the significance of the Ghost Dance, which promoted the Indian identity Palmer hoped to extinguish. The Ghost Dance was one of many revitalization movements that seem to have been provoked by European and Euro-American colonialism. One scholar has said that although such movements are primarily religious, they also seek "salvation from the possibility of having the traditional culture destroyed and the native society wiped out as a historical entity."[15]

The Ghost Dance began among the Paviotsos of northeastern California and northwestern Nevada after the prophet Wodziwob had a revelation in 1869. It would spread throughout the West. Wodziwob was said to have seen a vision of a railroad train carrying the Indian peoples' ancestors, who would return to life after a great explosion. The earth would swallow everyone, but believers would be resurrected and live in happy immortality.[16]

Anthropologist Cora Du Bois gathered information about the Ghost Dance from Indian informants in the early 1930s. She reported that people from the Grand Ronde Reservation learned the Ghost Dance in northern California in 1871 and taught it to a man named Sixes George, who lived at Lower Farm on the Siletz Reservation. Sixes George was a prominent man on the reservation, and at least one other prominent man was involved in promoting the Ghost Dance: Depot Charlie, later known as Charles Depoe.[17] Depoe took the dance to the Tolowa people in northern California.

One Siletz man who was involved in the Ghost Dance, Coquille Thompson, told DuBois that people began "dreaming and getting excited. About a hundred old ladies danced like young girls. It was so crowded in the dance house that you could hardly walk in." People "dreamed the dead were coming back" and that "the whites were to be driven back across the ocean where they came from and no one but Indians would be here." "The dream dance they used was old, but it started up strong when this new message came," Thompson said. "Everywhere there were Indians dancing."[18]

Fearful local whites complained to Indian Service superintendent Thomas Benton Odeneal that Indian people had burned a house, and they demanded troops for their protection. Odeneal said it was clear the Indian people "entertained not the slightest intention of harming any one." As for the house, he said there was no evidence it had been burned by Indians, and he noted that it "was insured for its full value, and I could hear of no other house in that part of the country upon which there was any insurance."[19]

Joel Palmer, who had remained at Siletz awaiting his replacement, reported in February 1873 that the dancing was still going on. Like Odeneal, he expressed confidence that the people had no warlike intentions. In a letter to the *Gazette* published February 8, Palmer pointed out that "even children and old blind women" took part, and he denied that it was a war dance. They danced, he said, for "the spirits of their departed relatives, with a hope that they may be restored to them on this earth." Although he had urged them to stop dancing because the dances alarmed whites, Palmer said, he considered the dances "less harmful than gambling."[20]

A variation of the Ghost Dance, the Warm House Dance, seems to have arrived on the Siletz Reservation during the summer of 1873. Coquille Thompson told Cora DuBois that three Shastas named Bogus Tom, Peter, and Mollie brought the dance from California. He said they had done the dance in Corvallis, where they put up a canvas fence and charged a dollar for admission. People from Siletz who were doing farmwork in the Willamette valley saw them there, and later Bogus Tom went to Upper Farm on the reservation.

Tom had told the people that white people "put things down in books, anything they want. We Indians see what is right. We have to give these dances. They are right for us." Three dance houses were built on the reservation. One dance began on Monday morning and continued through the week. "They danced all night and slept during the day," Thompson said. But the dance did not appeal to everyone: "The old people danced hard, but the young ones didn't join in much because they didn't believe. The dance was kept up maybe twenty years, then the old people died off. The dance houses just rotted away."[21]

If the dancers died out during the 1890s, they were probably born in the 1830s and 1840s, and so they were members of the last generation that came to maturity before the war and removal to the reservation. The dances seem to have comforted them with the hope that the world they had known could somehow be reconstructed. More significantly, the dances gave form to their insistence on defining their own identity, and defining it as distinctly Indian, even as their authorized white protectors were working, usually incompetently and often without conviction, at making them into deliberately inferior copies of white people.

The white protectors did better at promoting reduction of the Indian land base than at promoting cultural change. Superintendent T. B. Odeneal recommended in the spring of 1873 that the government move the people off the land to the north of the Salmon River in Tillamook

County and also off the entire southern or Alsea portion of the reservation. He wanted to put them all at the mouth of the Salmon River. Odeneal said removal had been requested in a petition from Tillamook County whites and by "settlers residing in the vicinity of the Alsea subagency."[22] Anyone living south of the Alsea River, six miles north of the subagency, was squatting on reservation land. Odeneal should have been concerned with evicting them, not satisfying their demands.

Palmer's successor, J. H. Fairchild, opposed reductions of the reservation, in the beginning. Fairchild complained at the end of September 1873 that "one or two unprincipled persons" planned to circulate petitions at the elections in October to ask for Indian removal. Proponents of removal had left nothing untried, short of violence, in their efforts "to produce some outbreak on the part of the Indians or at least such conduct as would give color to the petitions for their removal." Curiously, Fairchild blamed whites for the enthusiasm for the Warm House Dance, which he had tried to prohibit. He said local whites were encouraging the people to keep up "their dances for the dead" and had claimed to "have seen and talked with their dead friends, returned to life."[23]

Fairchild reported in October that both candidates for U.S. representative in the forthcoming election had declared that they favored removal of the Indian people.[24] Two days later he said the people had come to him and told him that they didn't want to leave the graves of their people who had died there, that they thought it bad policy for the government to abandon its improvements, and that in any case "they would all die before they would go elsewhere."[25]

An Indian Service inspector named Edward C. Kemble went to the Siletz to look into the situation. On a stormy Monday, December 15, 1873, he held a council at which George Harney, now head chief of the confederated tribes, spoke first, saying he wanted the whites to stop troubling the Indians about removal. "We were driven here, and now this is our home, and we want to stay," he added.

Tututni chief William Strong said he would stay put even if soldiers were sent. "If they want to hang me they can do so, but I will not leave," he said. Charles Depoe said, "I don't want them to take this land from us; want you to keep this in your heart." He added, "God sees you. I am talking to my brother; that is what I call you; I think I have talked straight to you."²⁶

Kemble calculated that only about twenty-four hundred acres on the reservation could be used for farming and said no one could give him any reason for removal except that the presence of the Indians "was an impediment to the growth of the country and prejudicial to the interests of white men in that section." He concluded that talk of removal was the product of "a handful of speculators."²⁷

In January 1874, John Hipple Mitchell, a young first-term U.S. senator from Oregon, endorsed reduction of the reservation. Mitchell was a man of dubious integrity. He had absconded from his wife and law partnership in Pennsylvania before coming to Oregon, where he associated himself with the ill-reputed transportation magnate Ben Holladay. He would be convicted in 1905 of involvement in land fraud. Nonetheless, he managed to be elected to the Senate four times and developed a reputation for his advocacy of direct democracy and women's rights and for his ability to get federal funding for Oregon projects.²⁸

Mitchell's plan was similar to what Odeneal had proposed, except that at first he was willing to let the people on the Alsea Reservation stay on a twenty-square-mile block around the subagency, separated by a five-mile buffer from the Alsea River.²⁹ He seems to have worked out this plan with Ben Simpson, who had become federal surveyor general for Oregon.³⁰ Although Mitchell and Simpson tried to avoid complete removal, their plan would have forced Indian people on the Alsea River to leave their homes in what was later described as a large village of comfortable "lumber houses" at the mouth of the Alsea.³¹

J. H. Fairchild reported at the end of January that three men from the Alsea Reservation had told him that "some people were telling them they would have to remove and their hearts were sorry." They said their country "was nearly worthless to the whites" and they wanted to stay there. Fairchild said this was a "reasonable and just" request.³²

George P. Litchfield, who was about to take over as subagent on the Alsea Reservation,³³ argued that genuine settlers were not interested in the poor land on the reservation and that the Alsea and Siuslaw peoples were "on their own original Soil and they do not want to give it up." Litchfield added that the Alsea people should retain some river frontage. "The Lumber Men have not expected near five miles," he said.[34]

Access to timber was the point of Mitchell's plan. Simpson told Mitchell in June that taking the land for five miles south of the mouth of the Alsea would not hurt the Indians, as he saw it, "but will greatly accomodate [sic] the whites as they can use the timber which the Indians have no use for."[35] R. A. Bensell would later describe the hills along the Alsea River and its numerous tributaries as "covered with a dense growth of pine or fur [sic], spruce and cedar." He said the millions of board feet of valuable timber could be floated down to Alsea Bay, milled into lumber, and shipped to San Francisco.[36]

Young head chief George Harney, who would play a part in the plans of Mitchell and Simpson, went to Washington, D.C., in late 1874 with former superintendent A. B. Meacham, who was making a lecture tour in the East.[37] Harney would later write to the commissioner of Indian affairs recalling their discussions.[38] Fairchild got a letter about Harney from the commissioner in March 1875 and responded that Harney was "a remarkable young man," although he added, without further explanation, that "in some respects he is hardly what I could wish." Fairchild said he had told Harney that if the reservation was self-supporting when he departed, "no white man would be required as Agent" and Harney would naturally be put "at the head of affairs."[39] George Harney would never get the job of agent that Fairchild all but promised him, but he would be heard from again.

By the end of 1874, Fairchild had come around to Senator Mitchell's way of thinking about removal, which he now claimed to view as necessary to the civilization of the people involved. Some of them would object, he said, "but I think there would be no difficulty in overcoming their objections."[40]

Mitchell made his first attempt at removal with a bill introduced on January 26, 1875, which went into the Senate Indian Affairs Committee and never came out.[41] He tried again on February 20 with an amendment

Dancers, Dissenters, Refugees, and Methodists

to an appropriations bill, but now he proposed it as an economic measure that would save the expense of maintaining the Alsea subagency by closing the entire Alsea Reservation. Mitchell said the secretary of the interior and the commissioner of Indian affairs wanted the removal and that the Appropriations and Indian Affairs Committees had given their consent. Senator William B. Allison of Iowa, chair of the Indian Affairs Committee, disagreed. He pointed out that his committee had objected to Mitchell's original bill because it included an appropriation of $25,000 to pay removal expenses.

Sen. John Sherman of Ohio expressed suspicion of Mitchell's willingness to do without the appropriation in order "to get a mandatory clause in the law for removal of the Indians." The amendment had not been reported by the Indian Affairs Committee, he added, and the money for removal would come from "an appropriation made nominally for some other purpose, perhaps made for the education and support of these very Indians, which will be used in removing them forcibly against their will." Allison amended Mitchell's amendment to require the consent of the Indian peoples, and it passed.[42]

Actual removal would not be as easy as passing an amendment. Fairchild reported in the spring of 1875 that the Alsea Indians had finished planting and thus could not be removed until fall. Many had "good comfortable houses, which it would hardly be just to require them to abandon, till they can be provided with others to replace them." Without a sawmill he could not hope to do that before fall, he said.[43]

As for the people living north of Salmon River, Fairchild tried to tell them their country was already open for white settlement when he and Joel Palmer met with them on June 1. He said bad whites would debauch their women and bring in diseases unless they moved. Palmer said whites would cheat them out of their land. Joseph Duncan, described as chief of the Tillamooks, rejected their arguments. He said, "We all want to stay in our own country and take up land like the whites—Our people all think alike on this subject."[44]

Fairchild reported that the leader of one of the northern bands, the Nestuccas, had declined to come to the council but had sent word that he had been told by the agent at Grand Ronde that no one had the right to remove him.[45] After a later conversation with this man, Fairchild said he and his friends "seemed to be well-acquainted with the provision of the law, that they could not be removed without their consent previously had." They also said that they would take their own land under the homestead laws.[46]

Fairchild got about the same results when he met with the leaders of the Alsea Reservation on June 17. Albert, leader of the Alseas, said, "We have houses which we built ourselves—have little farms and places, and we do not want to give them up even if our land is not all fenced." Another Alsea leader, William, said the people had livestock and houses built of milled lumber and they had never done wrong to the whites. "Why do the Whites have sick hearts for our land[?]," he asked. A man called Siuslaw George said, "How can the Whites believe in a just God and try to drive the Indians off their land[?]."[47]

Someone in Washington apparently decided a firmer hand was required, and in July the commissioner of Indian affairs appointed none other than Surveyor General Ben Simpson as special commissioner to negotiate a way around Senator Allison's consent provision.[48] Simpson went to the mouth of the Alsea River on August 24. He would claim that he had sent ahead of him three men from the Siletz agency—George Harney, Charles Depoe, and William Strong—to talk to the people on the Alsea Reservation and "prepare their minds for the coming council."[49] Curiously, Fairchild's clerk, M. N. Chapman, who was present at the council and wrote a detailed description, did not even mention that Harney, Depoe, and Strong were there.[50]

Simpson said that George Harney gave a talk at the council, emphasizing "the great importance of obeying the wishes of the Department and the benefits that would result to them if they accepted the proposition." When the Coos and Umpqua leaders objected to removal, Simpson adjourned the council until the next afternoon and handed out beef and tobacco. When the council resumed, Simpson said, the three men from the Siletz gave talks insisting on removal, and Fairchild's clerk, M. N. Chapman, told the people that Fairchild was preparing mills for their benefit. When Chapman was through, the leaders of the reservation people again objected to removal, Simpson said, "though in a milder form than before."

Like the Tillamooks, they said they would stay on their own land by taking homesteads. Simpson told them that they could only take homesteads on surveyed lands and their lands were not surveyed.[51] Chapman said that several Indians then spoke, "all mildly declining to make the proposed change and stating that they preferred to remain where they were."[52]

Three days after this council, Litchfield sent a confidential letter to the commissioner. He called attention to Simpson's relationship with Mitchell and accused the two of them of undermining the Republican Party in Oregon. He described Simpson as an enemy of the Peace Policy and a demagogue. He said he could not complain openly "owing to the dangerous opponents we have to the Indians in Oregon." If an agent tried to explain the true situation, Litchfield said, "his life would be almost in jeopardy."[53]

Fairchild blamed Litchfield for the resistance to Simpson. He claimed that Harney, Depoe, and Strong had told him that the leading men on the Alsea Reservation had told them privately that "they expected to remove to Siletz, but only wanted time to prepare themselves for the change." The men he had sent to the Alsea, "being of the same race, and speaking the same language, their opportunities for forming correct conclusions, are far greater than any white man could possibly have," Fairchild misleadingly surmised.[54] This claim was the only suggestion that any form of consent had been obtained.

Simpson was supposed to have finished his work by negotiating a treaty in September with the people north of the Salmon River.[55] He certified on October 28 that the consent required by Allison's addition to the Mitchell amendment had been obtained.[56] Fairchild provided a clearer concept of what had happened when he informed the commissioner two days later that if forcible means proved necessary to move the people from the Alsea agency to Siletz, it would be better to wait until February or March because there still was no lumber at Siletz to build them houses.[57]

Ben Simpson, predictably, had simply pushed his way through the paper wall that Senator Allison had erected to protect the Indian people, and proved again what the Cherokee removal had proved almost forty years before: adaptation to white practices and values offered no protection against whites with "sick hearts" who coveted Indian land and possessed the political influence to get it.

The pious J. H. Fairchild, who had proven susceptible to the dubious influence of Ben Simpson and Senator Mitchell on the Alsea removal question, submitted his resignation in September 1875, pleading illness and private business problems.[58] At the end of October, he left the agency in charge of William Bagley,[59] the agency farmer.

Five months later, Bagley was appointed agent.[60] English lawyer Wallis Nash, who later visited Siletz while viewing possible investments in the Yaquina Bay area, said Bagley reminded him "of that class of man to be chosen for the head of a reformatory, or an industrial school, or a training ship, and therefore the most suitable for the post."[61]

Bagley's impending promotion had not been well received by George Harney. On November 1, Fairchild wrote to the commissioner from Portland that Harney (who may have supposed that he had a chance to take over, based on what Fairchild had told him) was trying to keep Bagley from becoming agent. He accused Harney of treachery and drunkenness and said he was being influenced by Joseph Howard, his brother-in-law, "a half breed keeper of a low liquor saloon at Newport."[62]

Notwithstanding Harney's fall from Fairchild's grace, Fairchild sent a letter to Ben Simpson on November 11 in which Harney was once again described as a witness to the consent of the Alsea Reservation people to their removal.[63]

Harney sent a letter to the commissioner in December complaining that the people on the Siletz did not want Bagley. As agency farmer, Bagley had "never seemed interested in our struggles to become tillers of the soil," Harney said, and the crops had failed. The people wanted to select their own agent.[64] Indian Office statistics support Harney's evaluation of Bagley's farming skills. Before Fairchild and Bagley arrived, in 1872, Joel Palmer reported 4,305 acres under cultivation, with a yield of 6,670 bushels of potatoes, 7,785 bushels of oats, and 1,425 bushels of wheat.[65] Two years later, with Bagley as farmer, Fairchild reported only 1,128 acres under cultivation. Production of oats, used mainly as feed for livestock, more than quadrupled, according to Fairchild's figures, but production of potatoes dropped to less than a seventh of what it had been two years before.[66]

By the fourth year of Bagley's management, 1876, only 360 acres were cultivated, according to his own report, and the yield was 1,000 bushels of wheat and 1,450 bushels of oats. The yield of potatoes was not reported but apparently was included with vegetables, of which only 300 bushels were raised.[67]

In addition to being a poor farmer, Bagley was a doggedly obedient administrator. This bureaucratic virtue weighed heavily on the people who accepted removal to the reservation under the Mitchell plan. The Tilla-mooks were the first to go to what was supposed to become the new home of the people being removed—the narrow, broken, seven-mile stretch of sand and brush between the south bank of the Salmon River and the north shore of Siletz Bay where Lincoln City now stands. Bagley had gone ahead with the plan even though he could do nothing to provide the Tillamooks with what they needed to survive. The day before Christmas, in 1875, Bagley himself reported that they "were without shelter of any kind and destitute of food and clothing [and] suffering from the heavy rain and wind storms." Without funds to help them, he said, "the plan of moving the Alsea Indians in the Spring, if not altogether thwarted, will be very much delayed, on account of the discouragement of the Indians, at the non-compliance of the Department with the promises."[68]

Nevertheless, the secretary of the interior told the commissioner of Indian affairs in March 1876 to remove the Alsea Reservation people to Siletz as soon as it could practically be done.[69] According to an Oregon newspaper correspondent's report from Washington, D.C., Mitchell and Simpson had gone to the capital to get the order issued.[70]

The winter of 1874–75 was hard not only on the Salmon River but also on the Siletz. Bagley reported at the beginning of June that extreme hunger among the people on the Siletz had forced him to give passes to more than three hundred people so that they could look for work off the reservation. Many others had left without his permission.[71] When Bagley compiled his statistics the following year, the population had dropped to eleven hundred.[72]

Bagley went to the Alsea agency on September 9, 1876, to claim the government's property from Litchfield. At the Alsea River he saw "a large village with comfortable Lumber houses but not an Indian to be found." At the agency he saw "quite a number of very comfortable houses but the former occupants were gone," presumably avoiding him because they thought he had come to remove them. There was another deserted village at the mouth of the Yachats.[73] At the beginning of October, Litchfield told a reporter in Salem that the reservation had been officially vacated on September 16 and that a number of squatters had already moved in.[74]

The Alseas finally agreed at a council with Bagley on August 2, 1877, to move to the Siletz Reservation. Bagley said they were willing to move because of "the excited state of feeling among white settlers on account of the alleged understanding among all the tribes of the West, concerning a general uprising." (The Nez Perce War was in progress at the time, and the defeat of George A. Custer had taken place barely a year before.) Only the Alsea band proper seems to have accepted removal, not the Siuslaws, Umpquas, or Cooses.[75] A census of "Indians belonging to the Siletz Agency," which was sent to the Indian Office on August 20, reported 108 Alseas. According to a note at the end of the census, the Cooses, Umpquas, and Siuslaws were not counted because they were not on the Siletz Reservation. They were estimated to number two hundred.[76]

Although the Alseas were supposed to settle with the Tillamooks south of the Salmon River, most of them got no farther than the north shore of Yaquina Bay near Newport, apparently because Bagley had no money to finish moving them. George Harney signed a letter in the September 7 *Gazette* saying the Alseas were "now actually dying off fast, from starvation." Most had only mussels and the remains of a whale that had washed ashore. Harney said Bagley had no funds to help these people "or he would cheerfully do so."[77] Bagley responded that no Indians had died of starvation, that he had "furnished considerable provision," and that the ocean supplied adequate food. "Could they be given all the food in Oregon, they would eat whale blubber as a luxury," he said.[78]

J. J. Winant, a sea captain, wrote a letter published on the front page of the *San Francisco Chronicle* in October saying that he had seen "seventy to eighty poor Indians in a starving condition" at Yaquina Bay, most of them people removed from the Alsea Reservation. He blamed the problem on the removal plan, on federal policy for neglecting the stomach in favor of the soul, and on Fairchild, who "had prayers early and late. He prayed long and often; but hunger and poverty were preying too, and the Indians continued to grow thinner and weaker, and new-made graves became plentiful."

Winant put a different spin on Bagley's comment about whale blubber when he described the arrival of a dead whale that drifted into the bay. "It was not only dead, but very dead, judging from the smell of it, and it would naturally be supposed that the Indians would be welcome to this contribution of Providence," he said. After they had waited two days for the whale to come ashore, however, "a white man rushed in and laid claim to it, and they were not permitted to enjoy a mouthful of this delectation until they paid the enterprising white man for it."[79]

On November 9, the *Corvallis Gazette* printed a letter from the Alsea valley reporting, "About 25 of the Alsea Indians have returned to their old homes on the Alsea Bay. They say they had nothing to eat on the reservation, and are very destitute at present."[80] Bagley reported on November 26 that he had been forced to let the Alseas go home.[81]

George Harney's dissent against Bagley's handling of the Alsea situation may have played a part in the tone of Bagley's report in November describing what he called "something near a war between tribes." This conflict, as he explained it, developed out of the beating the previous summer in the Willamette Valley of the chief of the Klamaths or Shastas by members of the Rogue Rivers. The Rogue Rivers, Bagley said, were tried for their crime at the agency and required to pay damages.[82]

Some Klamaths were still dissatisfied, according to Bagley, and they caught two Rogue Rivers in their neighborhood and "endeavored to return to them just the same amount of blows as had been given their Chief in the summer." Bagley's rival Harney, a Rogue River, supposedly tried to stop the beating by shooting the Klamath chief, but his pistol misfired. Then Harney went to the agency and got Bagley and his clerk to ride out to the Klamath village. Bagley said he found the two Rogue Rivers on the road, beaten but alive, and got the Klamaths responsible for beating them to go to the agency with him.

Near the agency, Bagley said, "we were surprised to see the Head hief and his two friends armed with a shotgun and knives attempt to renew the fight." They would have killed the Klamath chief, among others, Bagley claimed, "had it not been for the timely assistance of Employes who wrested the gun from their hands and overpowering them held them in check." The bad feeling between the Klamaths and Rogue Rivers was talked out the following day, he said. Harney—whose name, significantly, never appears in this account—was suspended from office as head chief until the beginning of the year. He was told that the people of the reservation might reelect him then if they wished.[83]

Bagley may have expected that suspending Harney would silence him, but Harney put his name on an anti-Bagley petition in early 1878 as chief of the Rogue Rivers and government interpreter. Eighty-one men signed the petition, which asked the Methodist committee responsible for overseeing the Siletz agency to replace Bagley. The petitioners complained that Bagley was inefficient and "slow in the management of the business of the reservation." Moreover, his inattention to a conflict between white newcomers and Indians on the Salmon River had led to the deaths of two men, an Indian and a white man.[84] The petitioners also complained, "We have no confidence in his word, he will promise us one thing to-day and tomorrow forget it." Finally, they accused Bagley and some of his employees of raising livestock on the reservation and selling it to the government for less than the Indians could afford to accept.

The petitioners listed themselves as members of eight tribes—Nestuccas, Tututunnes, Sixes, Rogue Rivers, Galice Creeks, Shasta Costas, Coquilles, and Joshuas. Signers included all the chiefs of those tribes, among them prominent men such as William Strong and Sixes George, the Ghost

Dancer. Charles Depoe, another Ghost Dancer who was not a chief but was credited with considerable influence, also signed.[85]

If the names genuinely reflected agreement with the petition, then Bagley was opposed by a significant majority of the chiefs of tribes, although less than one-third of the men over twenty signed the petition. Six tribes listed in an 1877 census were not represented among the signers. Among them, predictably, were the Klamaths,[86] who had clashed with the Rogue Rivers and specifically with Harney, and who had received Bagley's support in the form of his suspension of Harney as head chief.

Bagley responded that the petition had been gotten up by former agency physician F. M. Carter, whom Bagley said he had dismissed. The agent also blamed his problems on a disappointed applicant for the post of farmer and a defeated candidate for head chief,[87] presumably George Harney.

Whether the petition influenced the course of Bagley's career is unclear, but a Methodist official mentioned it in a September 1878 letter to the secretary of the interior as an argument for dismissing Bagley. J. S. McCain, who described himself as the presiding elder or superintendent of church work on the Siletz Reservation, said that all the leading men on the Siletz Reservation were dissatisfied with Bagley and his clerk. Only the promise of a speedy change kept them from taking unspecified action against Bagley, who, McCain said, "is not a bad man but lacks decission [sic] and energy." He added that Bagley had been asked to resign "but seems inclined to hold on. I am thoroughly convinced that a change ought to be made, and fear that serious trouble will result from a failure to make it."[88]

An Indian Service inspector, apparently motivated by a letter from F. M. Carter, recommended Bagley's dismissal in December. E. C. Watkins told the commissioner of Indian affairs that during his visit to Siletz agency fifteen months before, "the agency was in a dilapidated condition and there was much to criticise in the management of Agent Bagley." If the reservation was to be continued, he said, "it would be well to send a new man and relieve Agent Bagley."[89]

As the opposition mounted, Bagley planned a clumsy attempt to entice people missing from the reservation to return. In November 1878, Bagley reported that he planned to send two trustworthy Christians to southern Oregon to use an Indian "religious dance festival" to preach return to the reservation.[90] Despite his clashes with George Harney in the past, he sent Harney and another member of the Rogue River tribe, John Adams. There are two accounts of what happened, allowing us a rare chance to compare Indian and white perceptions—specifically, the perceptions of Bagley and the perceptions of Coquille Thompson as recorded by Cora Du Bois.

According to Thompson, the dance Harney and Adams went to southern Oregon to see was a product of what Du Bois called the "Big Head cult," a movement related to the Warm House Dance that seems to have developed in Round Valley in California. The men who had brought the Warm House Dance to the people in Oregon had promised that this dance would be given to them as well. Harney and Adams went to investigate the dance. "Before they left," Thompson told Du Bois, "Depot Charlie told them to be on their guard, not to be fooled. He said they should find out the truth. He said, 'I dance all the time for this. I sweat hard and I want to know if it is true.'"[91]

Bagley described the people responsible for the dance as renegades and expected Harney and Adams to find many people there who were absent from the reservation without permission. He had arrived at this expectation, he explained, because many people had asked him for passes so that they could go. The renegades had proposed to "show the Reservation Indians some marvelous and mysterious things in connection with their religion." The dance was held, judging from Bagley's statements, on about the seventeenth of January 1879.[92]

According to Thompson, the dance was held in a canvas enclosure, and the man in charge was "one big fellow, called Humbug John, who wore a stovepipe hat." Another leader of the Big Head Dance, a man called Frank, was also there. The dancing began about noon. Du Bois paraphrased Thompson, saying that when Humbug John began to circle the fire, "everyone was quiet, even the whites who had paid a dollar to come in and see the dance." Four dancers came out, Thompson said, and the dance was much like the Warm House Dance done at Siletz.

That afternoon, Harney and Adams met with the leaders of the dance to discuss "if the dance was good and true." Du Bois said, "Humbug John hurled defiance at them for trying to stop the dance. He called them slaves of the whites. . . . There were recriminations about the Rogue River War and general hostility was current." But when the council was over, "George Harney and John Adams took Humbug John into town and bought provisions enough to feed all the Shasta."

That night, they saw the Big Head regalia for the first time. The man wearing it, said Thompson, "had on a great big feather headdress with feathers standing out all the way around. It was awful. Everyone blew on him as he went by." Afterward, John Adams spoke. According to Du Bois's paraphrase, "He said that the Siletz Indians were trying to become civilized and become law-abiding citizens. He tried to calm the Shasta. He said they didn't want to stop the dance." They also did not want to buy the regalia, however, and the next morning, although Humbug John had said they would dance for three days, the Shastas went home to California.[93]

Bagley said that his picked men had met a number of Indians who wanted to go to the Siletz Reservation. He also said that Adams and Harney "were so much the superiors of their *Prophets* in point of intellect and a general knowledge of the world that their religious dance was a total failure so far as obtaining proselytes was concerned." Bagley added that he had paid out two hundred dollars for traveling expenses and hoped to be reimbursed by the government.[94] Some of the money Bagley advanced presumably went to pay for the feed Harney and Adams put on for the Shastas.

Bagley finally resigned in the spring of 1879.[95] His successor was Edmund A. Swan,[96] who came from western New York State[97] and got the job on the recommendation of the Methodist Board of Missions in New York.[98] Bagley turned over the agency to Swan on July 15. Swan said Bagley gave him a warm welcome.[99]

Like Fairchild, Swan felt the pressure of whites interested in acquiring Indian lands, but unlike Fairchild, Swan kept up his resistance. He informed the commissioner of Indian affairs in November 1879 that a representative of "an English company having large landed interests adjacent to

John Adams (*lower left*), shown with his family in about 1873, was an ordained Methodist minister, but Charles Depoe asked him and George Harney to judge whether a Ghost Dance–related ceremony should be brought to Siletz. They rejected the ceremony but used agency funds to pay for a conciliatory dinner. Adams was on the committee and negotiated the sale of "surplus" lands after allotment. With Adams, *in the front row, from left*, are Sarah Adams, Martha Adams, and Adeline Karnoswky, *and, in the back row*, Russel Adams, Mae Adams, and Dick Adams. (Oregon Historical Society, neg. Or Hi 48491)

Charles Depoe was involved in the 1870 Ghost Dance and took it to the Tolowa people in northern California. Agent J. H. Fairchild alleged that Depoe, with William Strong and George Harney, verified Indian "consent" to closure of the Alsea Reservation. Depoe became an outspoken member of the surplus-lands negotiation committee. (Lincoln Councy Historical Society)

this Reservation" had asked him to supply Indian help to build a shorter wagon road to the Siletz agency. Swan turned them down because he did not want a shorter road: "the fewer Avenues for exit the better," he said. Also, a shorter road would mean only more settlers, and "the white settlers adjacent to this Reserve are aggressive, and already have caused me much trouble."[100]

Swan later complained that a removal plan put forward by Sen. James H. Slater of Oregon was supported by the English company.[101] Slater had introduced a bill in March calling on the secretary of the interior to negotiate with the tribes on four Oregon reservations, including Siletz, for their removal out of Oregon.[102] Senator Slater decided at Christmas that his removal bill could be modified to let two of the four reservations alone, but he still wanted the Siletz Reservation vacated. He was, however, willing to see the Siletz peoples moved to the adjacent Grand Ronde reservation if no place could be found for them outside the state.[103]

By the beginning of 1880, Swan was convinced that Slater and the English company were planning "a secret move" to get an appropriation to open a new road and "scatter these poor Indians from this their long promised home."[104] If this conspiracy existed, it had no effect. Slater's bill was never passed. Perhaps that was because it had come at the wrong time, just when policymakers had decided that removals were not working well.[105]

Swan's approach to the Alsea problem was benign neglect. In September 1879, a correspondent in the *Gazette* complained that Swan had avoided giving whites on Alsea Bay a definite answer concerning his plans for the "straggling Indians," several of whom were "holding valuable land claims, which they are not entitled to."[106] Swan reported in August 1880, that a letter had come from one of the Alsea people "saying that they would all come here in four or five weeks, as soon as their early vegetables are suitable to be gathered." Swan asked, in what seems in context to be a mildly sarcastic tone, whether he should use force if the Alsea people still refused to come "at the expiration of their own time."[107] He claimed that they finally submitted in April 1881.[108]

He reported in 1882 that sixty-seven Alsea people had been located six miles downriver from the agency and fifteen houses were being built for them "in charge of our Indian carpenter, who designs to have them ready for occupancy before the fall rains set in."[109]

During Swan's administration, crop production improved dramatically. He had estimated that Bagley's last crop would amount to about 1,500 bushels of wheat, 3,000 bushels of oats, 2,500 bushels of potatoes, and

3,000 bushels of turnips.[110] In 1881, two years later, Swan reported that Indian farmers had produced 3,150 bushels of wheat, 12,780 bushels of oats, and 23,700 bushels of vegetables, including about 16,000 bushels of potatoes.[111] They also grew about 425 tons of hay.[112] The figures reported the following year were better in every category except wheat, and Swan reported almost twice as many bushels of oats harvested.[113] (Oats and hay were the main cash crops on the reservation, according to a later agent.[114])

Swan tried to allot land, and he seems to have had more success than Joel Palmer. (Fairchild and Bagley had spoken well of the concept,[115] but neither claimed to have put it into practice.) In August 1881, Swan reported that he had promised the Indian peoples 160 acres per household and that they were even then locating land, building houses, and putting in crops. He claimed his program was drawing many "roving and way-ward" people to return to the reservation, and 121 allotments had been made.[116] A year later, in 1882, Swan said Indians had "continued to come in from far and near, taking lands, building houses, so far as materials were furnished them."[117]

The allotments Swan made were unlike the allotments that would be made a decade later under the 1887 General Allotment Act in that he was not concerned with giving people legal titles to their allotments. But his plan was not entirely informal; it was approved by the commissioner of Indian affairs, who told Swan that he should parcel out forty to eighty acres of farmland and about the same amount of timberland per family.[118]

Swan's enthusiasm for allotment and the commissioner's encouragement may have grown out of the interest contemporary reformers were showing in the concept. The Senate debated a general allotment bill for several days in January and February of 1881. It was not enacted, although it was supported by Carl Schurz, the secretary of the interior, among others.[119]

Indian Service population counts don't support Swan's enthusiastic reports of people returning to the reservation to take up land. In 1879, the year he arrived, there were officially 1,089 people under the jurisdiction of the Siletz agency.[120] Reported population declined in 1880 and 1881, stayed the same in 1882, and declined by one, to 997, in 1883,[121] the year Swan left.

But Swan's allotment project was a success in the sense that it was the beginning of the process that concluded a decade later, when titles for allotments made under the General Allotment Act of 1887 were handed over to their Indian owners. Swan's system of allotments had been revised by that time, but it was continued and expanded by his successor, who claimed in 1886 that the entire population of the reservation was living on allotted land.[122]

Edmund A. Swan might be described as the most successful of the Methodist agents on the Siletz, given the results of his allotment plan and the great increase in crop production under his administration. But these successes can be attributed to factors beyond Swan's devotion to Indian progress.

Swan's willingness to make allotments of as much as 160 acres made his allotment plan more attractive than the twenty-acre plan Joel Palmer tried to impose. And one possible reason for resistance to allotment during Palmer's term—that it would change the social and political arrangements inherent in the village pattern of housing—had quietly become moot by the time Swan became agent. The villages Palmer had seen on his arrival were gone by 1879, replaced by solitary houses. An observer who visited Upper Farm in that year commented, "Here and there stand the houses of the Indians, each with its grain- and hay-fields," and at the agency, he said, the houses were "dotted around."[123]

The increase in crop production was probably stimulated by what Swan described as "the liberality of the department in furnishing our Indians with such implements as are requisite to a successful tilling of the soil."[124] But no improvement could have been made without the willing efforts of the Indian peoples.

Swan's experience with the Methodists suggests that the policy of church involvement, rather than replacing political corruption with churchly uprightness, gave scope to the corrupt impulses within the churches. Swan objected in June 1880 to "the idea so prevalent here" that all of the employees had to be Methodists "regardless of fitness in other important things." Soon after he arrived, he said, he had been forced to dismiss a man who had shown himself to be "an improper person for

Government service from the fact of his dishonesty, though an active member of our church."[125]

About two months later, the Oregon Methodist Episcopal Conference met and, according to Swan, approved "a petition secretly circulated in the Willamette valley" recommending that a man named Wadsworth be put in Swan's place. Swan said he was being opposed because he would not give in to church control of appointments or to the demand "that all the patronage of this Reserve was to be given exclusively to Methodist tradesmen, as such, regardless of economy."[126] Swan was replaced in 1883, not, apparently, because he had irritated the English land company or whites on the Alsea River, but because he had resisted local Methodist influence; his successor was one F. M. Wadsworth.[127]

Wadsworth was appointed after the end of the period of church involvement—that is, after Henry M. Teller, secretary of the interior, informed a Methodist official in a widely circulated letter in 1882 that the government would no longer turn over its duties to churches.[128] But Wadsworth had been recommended in a church petition, and for a time he paid lip service, at least, to the Methodist connection. The agency teacher in 1883 was a minister who also took responsibility for promoting church membership, which Wadsworth called "this branch of the work."[129] Wadsworth said in his 1884 annual report that J. S. McCain (the Methodist minister who had criticized William Bagley) was supervising church work but implied that it had not gone well. "Where thistles and brambles now grow we hope and expect to see roses blooming," he said.[130]

Given the policy change, however, Wadsworth was not subject to the denominational pressures that had troubled Palmer and Swan. In his 1885 report, he made no mention of religion, Methodist or otherwise,[131] and in his last report, in 1886, he said that he gave encouragement to a Catholic priest who visited once a year and noted that a United Brethren minister came to Siletz occasionally. He made no mention of the old Methodist connection.[132]

Farming was not as successful during Wadsworth's term as it had been under Swan, but the decline was not substantial.[133] Swan's other success, his allotment program, also continued under Wadsworth.[134] The population continued to decline, dropping from 997 according to the 1883 report to 907 in the 1884 report and to 612 in the 1886 report.[135] Wadsworth said in 1883 that, in fact, there were only 637 Indians on the reservation. The missing people were Siuslaws, Cooses, and Umpquas, he explained, and they were "scattered along down the coast all the way between here and the California line."[136] The sudden drop in reported population in 1886 probably reflects a decision by Wadsworth or the Indian Office to stop including people missing from the reservation in the census.

The church policy on the Siletz does not seem to have lasted much longer than it did elsewhere, even though Wadsworth, the last church-approved agent, held onto his job until the beginning of June 1887. J. B. Lane, who took over from Wadsworth, said the Methodists had been inactive on the reservation for some time, "for reasons of which I am not apprised." Moreover, Wadsworth was nothing like the kind of agent the church policy was supposed to produce, at least as Lane depicted him.

Lane began his regime by dismissing several of Wadsworth's school employees because they were "wholly unfit for their positions, and morality was at a low condition."[137] He soon complained that Wadsworth, who remained on the reservation for a time, was a bigot, an egotist, and morally corrupt, and that he "had allowed the grocest [sic] immorality to exist under his sight and permitted and upheld his own sons to practise the same with the Indian School Girls." Lane also called Wadsworth "a petty tyrant by nature" who was "loud in his denunciation of democrats and the Indian department in general and against religion and moral teaching." Lane was confident, moreover, that "a thorough overhauling of his accounts would find crookedness."[138]

The more-effective Methodist agents, Swan and Wadsworth, were no more than facilitators. The worst, Fairchild and Bagley, made their marks by taking part in the cruel and unnecessary removal of the people on the Alsea Reservation.

Despite their difficulties with their agents, the Siletz peoples worked their way to relative prosperity during the years of Methodist involvement, and their community increasingly looked and functioned like a white farming community. They even adopted a white political tactic. When they found their way blocked by an incompetent agent, they got up a petition against him, much as whites who wanted their land got up petitions against them. But even though their communities became more like white communities during the Methodist years, the Siletz peoples did not surrender control over their own identities, and in the Ghost Dance they found a way to articulate and protect those identities.

11

Achievements of Allotment

The General Allotment Act of 1887, or the Dawes Act—the basic tool the government used to privatize Indian land for more than forty years—became law on February 8, 1887. The act gave the president authority to impose individual land ownership on Indian communities. Reservations chosen would be divided into private 160-acre tracts, which the government was expected to hold in trust for the new Indian owners, who received citizenship along with their land. Surplus land—that is, land not allotted or needed for administrative purposes—could be purchased by the government.[1]

Only seven months later, a special Indian Service agent began work on the allotment of the Siletz Reservation. Effects of allotment on the Siletz would include a drop in crop production and a radical reduction in the size of the reservation, followed by the loss of much of the land that had been allotted. But allotment would not completely destroy the reservation community, and in 1935 that community would decide that the pattern of ownership that developed out of allotment was worth defending against the Indian New Deal.

Despite the fact that allotment led to reduction of the reservation, Oregon's congressional delegation took no coherent position on the Dawes Act. For the first time since Joel Palmer had brought the Coast Reservation into being, local influences played no conspicuous part in the development of a significant government initiative affecting western Oregon Indian peoples.

This disinterest in allotment suggests that local concerns had lost their previous significance in the application of Indian policy. Perhaps this reflects the declining significance of Indian people themselves both as the occupants of land—because of the shrinkage in their land base over the previous three decades—and as a part of the total population of the state, which grew from 174,768 in the 1880 census to 317,704 in 1890 and 413,536 in 1900.

Historian Frederick E. Hoxie has argued that between 1880 and 1920, which is to say during the period when the Dawes Act was being applied, politicians and intellectuals gave up thinking about how to incorporate Indian people into American society. They "moved away from a faith in universal citizenship and general equality, and towards a more hierarchical view."[2]

As we shall see, this change was reflected in the attitude of the Indian Service administrators on the Siletz Reservation, who did not even give lip service to older ideas of assimilation and had no obvious difficulty reconciling their old role as supposed guardians of the Indian community with their new role as real estate agents selling off the land base of that community.

Allotment was not a new idea in 1887; according to the 1886 report of the commissioner of Indian affairs, 7,673 allotments had been made by the year before the Dawes Act became law.[3] The allotment process mandated by the Dawes Act differed from earlier approaches in being compulsory, at the discretion of the president, and in providing a process for reduction of Indian lands through negotiations for government acquisition of so-called surplus land remaining after allotment.

As we have seen, the central idea of allotment, the division of land, had been put into practice on the Siletz in a limited way no later than 1871 and more thoroughly under Edmund A. Swan in 1881. But Swan's program did not provide people with legal title to their allotments. Under the Dawes Act, people did get title, although the government was supposed to keep their properties in trust for twenty-five years.

The philosophy behind the Dawes Act was a near-mystical belief in the efficacy of private property ownership, which was expected by some to erase the differences between white and Indian people and to lead, at last, to the assimilation of Indians into American society.[4] Neither the act nor the discussions of the reformers who advocated it provides any specifics concerning what the Indian people would do with their individually owned land, beyond a vague assumption that they would take up farming.

During the period when allotment was becoming federal policy for all Indians, prominent whites interested in Indian policy gathered annually at the Lake Mohonk resort in New York. The proceedings of these meetings were printed as part of the reports of the commissioner of Indian affairs. Sen. Henry Dawes, the sponsor of the Dawes Act, explained at the 1886 conference that his objective was simply absorption of the Indian people into "this body politic" as self-supporting citizens.[5] The only specific mention of agriculture at this conference came when Dawes was asked whether Indians given allotments would be provided seed and implements. Dawes responded, "Whether Congress will be liberal enough to set him up, I don't know."[6]

At the 1887 conference, Dawes said he wanted the government to "put [the Indian] on his own land, furnish him with a little habitation, with a plow, and a rake, and show him how to go to work to use them. . . . The only way is to lead him out into the sunshine, and tell him what the sunshine is for, and what the rain comes for, and when to put his seed in the ground."[7]

Not only was Dawes patronizingly innocent of any knowledge of either indigenous or government-sponsored agriculture, but what he professed to desire for the Indian people was absent from the Dawes Act, which did nothing to provide homes, tools, or training. Moreover, it removed whatever incentive agents had to promote agriculture by making farming the individual responsibility of people who got allotments.

Historians have long argued that allotment failed because Indian people would not or could not make cultural adjustments. Francis Paul Prucha, for example, wrote that the government's effort to make Indians into independent farmers and ranchers "did not take sufficiently into consideration the nature of traditional Indian ways or the geographical conditions of the area in which the allotted Indians were supposed to work out their destiny." Prucha understood that factors aside from culture were at work, but he still saw culture as the most significant.[8]

More recently, Janet A. McDonnell blamed the assumed failure of allotment on lack of capital and lack of good farmland but also, again, on Indian resistance to cultural change. McDonnell understood that noncultural barriers were involved and was aware of the diversity of Indian cultures. Nonetheless, she said that many Indians considered farming women's work, that the government's expectation of a rapid transition from a hunting to a farming economy was "sociologically unsound," but also that "Native Americans often had neither the aptitude nor the desire to replace a diversified subsistence farming system with more materialistic commercial farming."[9]

McDonnell even placed the failures of the federal government in the context of its presumed responsibility to break down cultural barriers. The government "did little to educate the Indians in the use of the land," failed to provide financial support, and "forced the responsibilities of individual land ownership and citizenship on [the Indian people] without preparing them to meet these responsibilities."[10]

Largely through allotment, the government shrank the national Indian land base from 138 million acres in 1887 to 52 million acres in 1934.[11] But its potential as a tool for prying land away from Indians seemed insufficient to Sen. James H. Slater of Oregon (who in 1879 had wanted Indians exiled from the state). During an 1881 debate on a general allotment bill, Slater complained that "One of the gravest and most serious objections to the bill is that it gives too much land to the Indians."[12]

Another Oregon senator, Joseph N. Dolph, had a different reason for opposing allotment. In the debate on the Dawes bill in 1887, Dolph said he feared that after the twenty-five years in which the government would hold allotted lands in trust, the Indian owners would sell off their lands. By then, he said, the money to be paid under the bill for unallotted or surplus reservation land would be gone. He predicted that the Indian people "will not have been prepared by the policy of the government to be self-supporting; and the result will be that we shall have a quarter of a million paupers, or more, on the hands of the government."[13]

The process that provoked the opposition of Slater and Dolph began on the Siletz Reservation in September 1887, when a special allotting agent arrived. Agent J. B. Lane said this agent, M. C. Connelly, worked until December and made about seventy allotments, but then the work had stopped. "As there is no opposition by the Indians to continuing this work, I am at a loss to know why the field has been abandoned," Lane said.[14]

While the allotment process was left hanging, Lane was accused of an implied moral failing in his relationship with a teacher at the agency school. The commissioner of Indian affairs asked Lane in January 1888 to explain a report that the teacher was disinterested in her duties and did not stay at the school as expected but, rather, at the agent's house.[15] Lane, a bachelor, said he lodged employees in his house because it was "the only house fit for decent occupancy by white persons," and the teacher directed his Indian maid and cooked in return for room and board.[16]

The commissioner seemingly accepted Lane's explanation,[17] but the teacher left the agency school in April.[18] In May, Beal Gaither, Lane's clerk, stepped in to replace Lane[19] until a new agent, T. Jay Buford, arrived in October.[20]

The allotment process began again in May 1891 with the arrival of a new special agent, but it was a bad start. Buford complained that the special agent had set up "a little administration of his own" and "caused more dissatisfaction, dissensions, and trouble among the Indians in the short space of three months than has been known for years before."[21] A new agent sent in February 1892 restored order.[22]

The Dawes Act did not require the sale of the reservation land that was not allotted or otherwise reserved for Indian or agency use, but negotiations for the sale of this land were built into the allotment process. A three-man commission was sent in 1892 to negotiate with the Siletz peoples. The commissioner of Indian affairs told the negotiators that they should not exert "undue pressure" but said that the people should be told that if they kept their remaining lands as reservation lands they could not expect much of a return, but the money the government would pay for their lands would bring in a considerable income if it were invested at 5 percent interest.[23]

The commissioners held a general council on October 17. The leaders of the Siletz peoples demanded "cash in hand" and wanted $1.25 per acre.[24] George Harney told the commissioners that many promises had been made in the past without being kept. He said the people would sell the land but had to be paid first, "so before we die we will see the money with our face and will get the benefit of the money."[25]

The commissioners said the government did not pay cash. One of them, W. H. Odell, insisted that no whites, including the commissioners, would benefit from the agreement they proposed. If they could not agree, he said, the commissioners would "go home and leave you just as you are." Harney responded, "I don't believe anybody speaks bad of you gentlemen," and said again that all the people wanted was to have the money "before they die."[26]

A second session of the general council met with the commissioners on October 29. Charles Depoe was worried over the fact that any agreement would have to be submitted to Congress. "We understand that when Congress meets back there and settles it nobody can move it again," he said. "May be we make a bargain here to-day and may be it won't stay." Commissioner H. H. Harding suggested that the Indian people pick a committee to do the negotiating. According to a transcript of the proceedings, the council selected seven men by unanimous vote. Among them were Charles Depoe and George Harney.[27]

Precisely what happened next was not recorded in the transcripts of the proceedings. A journal written on behalf of the commissioners covered this most critical part of the discussion in two short paragraphs, reporting a "long discussion" but not its content. The negotiators met in the Indian court room at the agency. The members of the committee demanded $175,000, from which at least $100 per person would be paid in cash. The final agreement called for a payment of $142,600 and a $75 payment per person.[28]

The Siletz agreement was signed by the committee and another 112 men. Four of the seven members of the committee wrote out their names, and so did 55 of the 112 men whose names were included at the bottom of the agreement. It called for the Siletz people to receive $142,600 for "their claim, right, title, and interest in and to all the unallotted lands within the limits of said reservation," excepting five sections of timberland. Those five sections would be managed under the direction of the secretary of the interior "so as to secure an equality of benefits to the Indians, employment for them, and judicious aid to them in becoming self-supporting."

The payment was to be divided into two portions. The government would set up a $100,000 fund. The interest on the fund, set at 5 percent, would be divided among the members of the Siletz tribes and paid on the first of March each year. The other $42,600 was to be paid out on the same date each year in installments of $75 per person, presumably until the whole amount had been paid. Individuals judged "competent and capable" by the secretary of the interior could get their share of the money in a lump sum.

The commissioners also forwarded to the secretary of the interior a petition said to have been signed by 118 men who wanted Congress to grant them full title to their properties in no more than five years, rather than the twenty-five years specified by law. They described themselves as "civilized Indians, living in houses, and dressing like white men," and said most of them could read, write, and manage their own business affairs.[29] The three commissioners endorsed this proposal, saying that they had found the Siletz people "exceptionally intelligent, living and dressing, and, mostly, using the same language as white people, citizens of the United States, and mostly fully capable of taking care of themselves and their property."[30]

Why did they sell the surplus land? Aside from the likelihood that they needed the money, they knew that during the past thirty years the government had taken most of the original reservation without paying them a penny for the land. Now the government was willing to pay for what it had never clearly conceded to them in the past.

Some seventeen months after the negotiations, the House Indian Affairs Committee reported favorably on the Siletz agreement, noting that the government had agreed to pay $142,600 for more than over 175,000 acres, which would be offered to the public at $1.50 per acre. At that rate, the committee said, the government would turn a profit of $120,000.[31]

Most of the allotment certificates on file with the Lincoln County clerk in Newport are dated July 26, 1894, and most show allotments of approximately eighty acres.[32] According to a 1953 Bureau of Indian Affairs report, 44,459 acres were distributed to 551 people.[33] Not even the most optimistic of the agents who managed the reservation had ever claimed that it contained such a quantity of farmland. The application of the Dawes Act on the Siletz obviously had little, if anything, to do with the idea that allotment would encourage farming.

This was only one of several cases in which the government gave out more land in allotments than there was supposed to be tillable land on a given reservation. (The land in question was tillable only in the opinion of the Indian Service employees who collected the data.) Between 1887 and 1904, the government allotted forty-one reservations for which published statistics in 1887 showed some quantity of tillable land. On twenty-eight of those reservations, the amount of land allotted exceeded the amount of land reported tillable in 1887. Altogether there were 3.02 million acres in allotments on those reservations in 1904, although only 1.05 million had been reported tillable in 1887.[34]

Congress approved the agreement to buy the Siletz surplus land on August 15, 1894,[35] and it was scheduled to be opened to claimants at noon on Thursday, July 25, 1895. On July 14, the *Lincoln County Leader* in Toledo published an extensive description of the land that was about to become available, calling attention to river bottoms containing "hundreds of acres of the richest land that an Oregon mist ever fell upon or the sun ever warmed with its genial rays." The newspaper estimated that about 38,000 acres of good grazing and crop land would be opened. At 160 acres per settler, that would allow "240 homes for actual settlers, homes where they may live and prosper."[36] This estimate of crop land was, of course, fabulously in excess of any figure ever offered in the past.

A writer for the *Oregonian*, George L. Curry, Jr., found the opening boring in comparison with the openings of reservation lands in Oklahoma a few months before. He said that "not over half a dozen people crossed the line when the conventional gun was fired." Curry was at the southern edge of the reservation and had been told that perhaps two hundred would-be settlers were expected to enter from the northern boundary, but he said, "Be this as it may, it has the aspect of a very tame opening."

Curry said the Indian people had selected "the better class of lands" for their allotments, not only farming and grazing land but land on the coast, "where nature is grand, and fishing and hunting and camping out is desirable." The remaining land, Curry noted, included about fifty thousand acres of the choicest timber, and the salmon-canning industry could take advantage of Siletz Bay and the lower Siletz River, where a large quantity of fish had in the past been "monopolized by the Indians." All that was holding up immediate development was the twenty-five-year trust in which Indian lands were held. "Should the government ameliorate this serious restriction and permit the Indian to sell out to the whites, one of the richest agricultural communities in the country would rapidly develop itself," he said.

He claimed that Indian people had told him that they did not want to keep the allotted land. It brought them no money, they didn't want to work it, and they expected to be extinct in another twenty-five years. "They want their money now, together with the privilege of selling out to the whites their holdings of realty," he said.[37]

Another reason for the lack of a land rush was later suggested by a professional land-fraud organizer named Stephen A. D. Puter in a confessional titled *Looters of the Public Domain*. Puter said that when the former reservation land was thrown open for settlement, everyone understood that it was not farmland. Much of it was impenetrable forest that would have cost three hundred dollars per acre to clear. Puter claimed that opening the former reservation land for homesteading "was merely a ruse to cloak the real motives of those interested, who figured wisely that few honest claimants would attempt to comply with the prohibitive conditions of the law, and go there with the idea of making a home."[38]

Farming on what remained of the reservation declined after allotment. Vegetable crops, including the important harvest of potatoes, also declined. Agent Beal Gaither said in his 1894 annual report that potatoes, turnips, and carrots grew well on the Siletz and almost all the people were growing enough for home consumption. Some grew them for sale.[39] The peak potato production during this period was 17,000 bushels reached in 1897.[40] Two years later the yield had fallen to 9,736 bushels,[41] and in 1904 it was only 6,225 bushels.[42]

Oats, an important cash crop, did well in 1892, when 15,920 bushels were reported grown,[43] and in the following year, when the yield was said to have been 18,160 bushels.[44] In 1899, however, the crop of oats was only 8,460 bushels,[45] and in 1904 the yield had declined to only 3,500 bushels.[46]

Agent T. Jay Buford reported in 1899 that oats were doing well but far fewer acres had been planted than in the past. Planting was down, he explained, because spring had come late and because the two threshing machines owned by the Siletz people were worn out. In addition, people were anxious to work in the hop fields in the Willamette valley in the fall, so the agent had a hard time keeping enough men on the reservation to finish the threshing.[47] In 1900, Buford said the production of oats had declined because oats had been selling for a low price for several years and also because the fall rains had come early two years running and ruined the crops.[48] In 1901, Buford said that although the reservation might appear "unkept," the people had more money than when they had relied on the crop of oats for their income. In addition to picking hops, the people were doing well fishing for a cannery that had been established at the mouth of the Siletz River and gathering medicinal cascara bark.[49]

Buford's successor, Duncan D. McArthur (who was a superintendent rather than an agent, in line with new government nomenclature), saw the situation differently. He argued that the Indian people had become less industrious and that the cause was "traceable to the sale of surplus lands whereby a tribal fund was created, from which payments began to be made." Young men relying on this income were "but little disposed to use the ax, the spade, the hoe, the plow, and other implements of toil." During November and December, 1901, much of the $100,000 held back when surplus lands were sold to the government was paid out. McArthur observed, "The effect of the distribution of this fund on the Indians will eventually be very beneficial, in that when the money has all been spent they will resume industrial work."[50]

Siletz Reservation was typical of an entire class of reservations, however, in its decline in crop production. As we have seen, on twenty-eight reservations, including Siletz, the amount of land allotted by 1904 was considerably more than Indian Service estimates of tillable land. In total, about three times as much land was allotted on these reservations as had been considered usable farmland. The amount of land under cultivation on these reservations declined by more than one-sixth, and grain production dropped by almost one-half. The number of cattle increased by about half, however, which suggests that people who acquired allotments that were not suitable for farming made the best of the situation by turning to stock raising.

Agriculture was much more successful on reservations that were not allotted. At least forty-seven reservations were still unallotted in 1904, and on these reservations there were modest increases in the amount of land farmed and in grain production, and the number of cattle more than quadrupled.[51]

But agriculture was even more successful on reservations where the estimated amount of tillable land exceeded the amount of land that was allotted. At least thirteen reservations allotted by 1904 fit into this category, and on these reservations, Indian farmers doubled the amount of land being farmed, more than tripled their grain production, and more than doubled their number of cattle.

A little more than a decade after allotment, the privatized Siletz land base began to go the way of the money for the surplus land. The immediate reason was Indian Service handling of inheritances. When holders of allotments died, the Indian service at first divided the land among the heirs. Only three years after allotment, the agent at Siletz complained of having to cope with the contending would-be heirs to 166 such allotments amounting to more than nine thousand acres.[52]

The so-called Dead Indian Act of 1902 simplified the problem by allowing the Indian Service to convert the land into cash.[53] Properties of Siletz allottees who had died were advertised in legal notices printed on the front page of the *Lincoln County Leader*. On July 29, 1904, for example, twenty-eight such allotments were advertised, among them the allotments that had belonged to Charles Depoe and Alsea Albert.[54] A new superintendent, Knott Egbert, said in his 1905 annual report that about 256 allottees—nearly half—had died.[55]

In only two years, between the autumn of 1904 and the autumn of 1906, about a fifth of the allotted land was sold off and about a tenth was leased. Forty-four Siletz allotments or parts of allotments were sold during that period, or a little more than thirty-three hundred acres. The average price was about $7.12 per acre. When Egbert made his annual report on August 6, 1906, another eight allotment transactions were awaiting approval. Egbert also reported that twenty-six leases had been granted.[56]

Several members of the Siletz tribes wanted to sell the five sections of timberland left after the surplus land sale. They argued that they needed the money more than they needed the land. In a letter to President Roosevelt in late 1907 that was signed by seventy-seven men, they said, "We all have land and need tools, implements and stock and the money derived from the sale of this Reservation would be of vast help to us."[57] A bill was introduced in Congress in 1908 to allow sale of the last five sections of Siletz tribal land at the discretion of the secretary of the interior.[58]

In a letter supporting the bill, acting interior secretary Frank Pierce said that the bill, if passed, would mean that "it will be possible in a short time to dispense with practically all governmental supervision" and that the sale would "enable the Indians to become integral parts of society." Pierce was satisfied that the people were ready and it would not be long before they would be given titles to their allotments.[59] The Siletz land sale act presented to Congress in 1908 was finally approved May 13, 1910,[60] though less than one section was finally sold.[61]

Although the Siletz peoples were low on funds and the government closed the Siletz boarding school in 1908, the report of the commissioner of Indian affairs for that year was optimistic. Few people on the Siletz were getting "gratuitous support" from the government. The people were "perhaps, above the average [in] civilization." Most of them lived in good houses, a number of which were "neat and sanitary." Nearly all of them spoke English and wore "citizens' clothes." They supported themselves by farming their allotments, he said, and by working for nearby farmers who had bought inherited allotments.[62]

Notwithstanding these evidences of progress, Superintendent Egbert looked upon the people under his nominal control as being in need of supervision. Asked in 1909 to name eminent Indians on the reservation, Egbert responded, "Judged by ordinary standards I have never met an eminent Indian, particularly an eminent full blood." John Adams, he said, was "a genuine Christian, almost or quite the only member of the tribe who has any adequate conception of what constitutes a Christian." But even Adams, he said, "has to have a jolt once in awhile to keep him in line."[63]

Old ways, Egbert reported in the late summer of 1909, sometimes led to neglect of livestock. The feather dances that older people organized once or twice a year were not a problem, but the stock sometimes suffered "on account of the old fashioned three days gambles sometimes indulged in."[64] In a later report, he complained that even though eggs were selling for forty cents a dozen and "all the Indians know how to raise eggs," there were those who would not own chickens because that would keep them from leaving home in the summer to pick hops or camp by the ocean.[65]

Old ways and supposed Indian restlessness did not entirely account for Indian reluctance to fully undertake a settled farming life, even by Egbert's account. "Bad roads interfere with marketing bulky products like oats and perishable products such as fruit," he said in 1910. The road from Siletz to Toledo was "all hills" and not always passable, and the railroad trip from Toledo to Portland took about eleven hours and required a transfer.

Achievements of Allotment

He hoped that better transportation would solve "one of the chief problems in the matter of inducing Indians to take up agricultural pursuits."[66] In addition, he recognized that the land itself was difficult. The Siletz country, Egbert said, was "seven-eighths hills, which hills are steep and often sparsely covered with soil."[67]

Egbert also admitted that white people on the coast were, in his eyes, only marginally better than Indian people at living his idea of the industrious life. In 1909, he described the people on the reservation as "fairly industrious as the inhabitants of this coast region go," although this industriousness was "most apparent in a limited number of individuals."[68] In his 1910 report, he noted that several Indians worked in sawmills, in logging camps, and at the salmon cannery at the mouth of the Siletz River and said that the Indian people compared "fairly well with the white citizens of this locality in the matter of industry. Strenuous living is not participated in, in this country to any dangerous degree."[69]

Congress never responded to the request the Siletz people had made when their surplus land was sold that they be allowed to sell their allotments before the twenty-five-year trust period expired. But in 1906, Congress passed the Burke Act, which modified the allotment process in two important ways: citizenship was to be granted to allotment holders only when their properties were no longer held in trust by the government, and, more significantly, the fixed trust period was tossed out and the secretary of the interior was authorized to give ordinary titles to allotment holders when they were deemed competent.[70] So Siletz allotments became available for sale long before the trust period would have run out in 1919. According to Egbert's 1910 report, "perhaps ninety-five percent of the land patented in fee is sold sooner or later, although there is not always great haste in this matter." The people were "pretty good at getting fair market value for their land when they sell it themselves," he said, adding that "the Indians have made just as good sales on an average by themselves as have been made by the government."[71]

Superintendent Egbert made a point of denying responsibility for agriculture. In his 1910 report, he said, "We visit Indians at their homes sometimes and talk with them about farming, not trying to tell them too much." Necessity, he said, was "the chief force that will produce permanent results," so the Indian people were "thrown on their own resources."[72]

Farming continued to decline on the reservation during this period. Indian Service statistics for 1911 showed there were supposedly 28,000 acres of allotted agricultural land on the Siletz reservation but only 420 acres under cultivation. No income at all was reported derived from the sale of crops. The principal source of income, making up $10,323.46 out of a total of $16,935.46 listed under "incomes of Indians," was from the sale of lands.[73]

A previously uncounted Indian population of some 3,000 people was revealed in southern Oregon when an agency was opened in 1910 in Roseburg.[74] These were people who had taken or hoped to take allotments in the public domain. Their numbers suggest the magnitude of the drift of population away from the Siletz, Alsea, and Grand Ronde Reservations. These people and about 5,000 people in northern California who were also under the jurisdiction of the Roseburg agency were reported to be holding 108,000 acres of allotted lands, including 83,000 acres of timber lands.[75]

Many of these allotments seem to have been cancelled for reasons that are not clear. George Wasson, a member of the Coos tribe, told a 1931 hearing that in about 1911, an agent came through southwestern Oregon and made the cancellations. Another man, James Buchanan, speaking through an interpreter, complained that his allotment was cancelled "just because there were a few trees on Indian land." C. E. Larsen, the chief clerk for the Indian Office in Salem, told the hearing that records did not show any cancellations. He added, however, that he could look into the question "as far as the records go, but I am afraid they do not go far enough."[76]

The response of the Siletz people in World War I suggests how far they had gone toward an accommodation with the majority society since their war with the United States only sixty-one years before. Superintendent Edwin Chalcraft reported in 1919 that "The Indians responded freely in the war with both men and money as far as they were able." Two men had died in battle and another had died on his way back to the reservation,

School buildings on Government Hill at Siletz, circa 1910. The Indian Service effort to educate Siletz children began no later than 1860. On-reservation schooling fell out of favor among policymakers toward the end of the nineteenth century. The government closed the agency boarding school in 1908 and the day school in 1918. Seven years later the agency was closed as well. (Lincoln County Historical Society)

the superintendent noted.[77] Seventeen Siletz men were in the armed forces in World War I, according to a later count.[78]

In June 1918 the Indian Office closed down the Siletz Reservation day school, which, according to the *Oregonian* newspaper, had been under the direction of "Professor Robert DePoe, an educated Indian." Robert DePoe was the son of Charles Depoe. Henceforth all Indian children would attend public schools.[79]

The 1918 population statistics showed 446 people on the Siletz Reservation and 3,000 people scattered on public lands who had been under the jurisdiction of the Roseburg agency, which had recently been shut down. Those on the Siletz Reservation were all citizens of the United States. Among them were 250 voters, 260 churchgoers, 240 who were literate, and 370 who spoke English. There were still 210 people with allotments, and 96 had received titles to all or part of their allotments.[80]

Income from farming was up considerably in 1918. It was reported to be $21,975, although only 720 acres were being farmed by Indian people. The sale of land was still the leading source of income, however, but at $23,600 it was less than half of the $54,611 total. Most of the rest of the reservation's income came from "native industries" and wages, and very little—only $248—was in the form of rations and "miscellaneous issues" by the government. The people were not living on welfare, but they were still in the process of selling off much of their capital in the form of land. Forty-two allotments were leased for farming, providing an income of $2,240.[81]

In the following year, the relatively slow loss of Indian land on the coast was accelerated by persistent grants of land titles under the Burke Act. Indian affairs commissioner Robert Valentine had set this process in motion more than a decade earlier, after deciding that Indians were using the trust status of their lands to avoid paying taxes. Valentine had called for a competency commission to root out Indians who should be given fee-simple patents—that is, ordinary titles—for their land. His plan was incorporated into the Omnibus Act of 1910. Over the next two years more than two hundred thousand acres of trust lands were cut loose nationally. One result was than about 30 percent of the people handed patents "failed to make good," as Valentine put it.[82]

The first wave of competency investigations missed the people on the Siletz, but fresh inquiries would be launched by the commissioner of Indian affairs chosen by the Democratic administration of Woodrow Wilson, which took over from the Taft administration in 1913. The commissioner was Cato Sells, formerly a Texas banker, who in 1917 linked competency to race and education by ordering immediate patents for graduates of government schools and people who were less than one-half Indian. In 1919, Sells reported that 10,956 patents had been given out since 1916, more than during the previous decade.[83]

Three Indian Service officials, one of them Siletz Reservation superintendent Edwin L. Chalcraft, were chosen to issue patents to people on the Siletz Reservation. They were appointed in April 1919 and made their report the following month. White expectations were suggested by the *Oregonian* newspaper's headline for its story about the patent process: "Indians May Sell Lands."

General opinion on the coast, the newspaper reported, was that "a large number of Indians will receive patents," that "many of the Indians will dispose of their farms when they receive patent rights," and that the government would sell the allotments of aged and infirm Indians and then give them "a living allowance in the form of a pension." As much as eighteen thousand acres of "very rich" land might be available.[84]

Perhaps the outcome assumed by the *Oregonian* was not quite what Sells had in mind when he insisted that "The Indian's rich agricultural lands, his vast acres of grass land, his great forests should be so utilized as to become powerful instruments for his civilization." According to policy historian Francis Paul Prucha, however, Sells and Wilson's secretary of the interior, Franklin K. Lane, "were obsessed with the idea that land and other natural resources should be fully utilized." Moreover, even though it was soon obvious that "a very high percentage of the patentees quickly sold or mortgaged their land and wasted the proceeds," Sells was not deterred.[85]

A somewhat more subtle idea of what was involved in the quick sale or mortgaging of land is suggested by the experience of Hoxie Simmons, a Siletz Indian who had asked for a patent on his own allotment and later was pushed into a patent on another 160 acres of allotted land that he had inherited and would subsequently lose. Simmons said he applied for a patent on his allotment in about 1911 "because I thought I wanted to help my white brethren to pay taxes, build roads, and I believe good schools, good roads, and good bridges." The Siletz area had bad roads and no bridges, and he was concerned with the schools because he had small children, most of whom went to public schools.

E. A. Towner (*above*), shown in 1950, was a lawyer who spoke approvingly of proposed Indian New Deal legislation when it was presented to an Indian congress in Salem in 1934. But he soon became a critic of the Indian New Deal, and he was blamed for the rejection of the Indian Reorganization Act by the Siletz people. (Oregon Historical Society, neg. CN 014887)

Hoxie Simmons (*right*) is shown in 1945 carrying a load of ferns gathered to be sold to florists. Simmons was a member of the Siletz business committee in the 1920s. At a hearing in 1931 he asked that the government allow the Siletz Indians to sell their timberland so that elders could be cared for. (Oregon Historical Society, neg. CN 014160)

When the competency commission came to his case, Simmons said he did not want a patent for the 160 inherited acres. He did not want to pay taxes on this land. The commissioners asked him how old he was and whether he had been in school. They talked it over and told him, as he recalled, "We have decided you are capable to manage your own affairs. We have decided to let you have the patent. You can not dodge around the bush any longer. You will get your fee simple patent."

Simmons was the kind of person Sells wanted removed from federal protection. He was obviously competent. But the inherited land was of little use to him as a farm; "It was hilly land, no cultivated land at all," Simmons said, "so I mortgaged it." He spent the mortgage loan on livestock and a building on his only slightly more promising eighty-acre allotment. He had been a young man when allotments were made, and "we young people, you might say, we took the back sites." Only about fifteen acres could be farmed, he said.[86]

Despite his competence, Simmons's cattle and farming enterprise did not pay off, and he lost the inherited land to foreclosure when he could not make payments on the five hundred dollar loan. He also had a loan on his own allotment that needed to be paid.[87]

Simmons's problems were common among American farmers during this period. After a boom during World War I, American agriculture went into a depression in 1920, and by 1921 the ratio of prices received by farmers to prices paid for their needs (parity) had slipped to 67 percent of its 1918 level. The value of the average American farm had declined by 1930 to less than 54 percent of what it had been in 1920, and the number of farms fully owned by their operators slipped 13.5 percent.[88] The people who were given patents by Sells's commissions were obliged to sink or swim in a strong riptide, and unpromising land like the Simmons farm could only make the situation even less hopeful for its undercapitalized owners than it was for the average farmer.

J. E. Cooter, who came to Lincoln County in 1918 as county agricultural agent, would recall that before people began to get patents for their land, the Indians on the Siletz Reservation "appeared to be in pretty satisfactory condition." Cooter said that Indian people had many of the best farms on the Siletz, but when patents were issued people lost their land either because they failed to pay their taxes or because they had taken loans against it. Cooter said that "a great deal of land was mortgaged and the mortgage sold, either foreclosed or directly sold. So from that time to the present time the better lands on the Siletz have passed out of the hands of the Indians."[89]

Superintendent Chalcraft reported in May 1921 that his office was still coping with a number of heirship cases—that is, sales of the allotments of people who had died. That work, he said, was an obstacle to issuing land patents. Nonetheless, he added, "We have issued many fee patents and have a large number of land sales under way which we want to finish up as soon as possible."[90] According to the Indian Service statistics, 209 patents had been issued for original allotments by the middle of 1920 and sixty-six more for inherited allotments. These patented allotments amounted to 26,920 acres, or more than 60 percent of all allotted land. Ninety of the patents had been issued during the 1919–20 fiscal year.[91]

The Indian Shaker religion, which had begun on Puget Sound in about 1881, arrived at Siletz in the early 1920s. The teachings of the Shaker prophet, John Slocum, were much the same as Christian teachings. Anthropologist Lee Sackett has argued that the Ghost Dance and the Warm House Dance prepared the way for the advent of Shakerism at Siletz. Sackett, who interviewed what he called the last three Siletz Shakers in 1970, reported that the church first came to the central Oregon coast when a few Indian converts were made in what is now Lincoln City, where they met in members' homes or barns. The first services were held in Siletz in about 1925, and in 1926, Shakers there put up a church building.[92]

Just as the Ghost Dance had spread from Siletz to the Tolowas in coastal northern California,[93] so the Shaker church spread to a northern California group from Siletz, in this case to the Yuroks at what is now Klamath, California, and later to others. Shakerism would decline after 1933 at Siletz, mainly, it appears, because members divided over whether they should use the Bible. A congregation of some seventy people declined to only about fifteen members by the early 1940s.[94] But as long as the

234   Achievements of Allotment

Shaker church was active, it seems to have provided what the Ghost Dance had provided some fifty years before: a way of asserting Indian identity at a time when the community was under great stress, in this case because of allotment.

The process of breaking up the Siletz Reservation had come so far by 1925 that the Indian Service determined that no resident superintendent need be kept there. In the November 12, 1925, issue of the *Yaquina Bay News* of Newport was a brief item announcing after seventy-five years (actually it had been sixty-nine years), the agency was being closed down that same day. "Many of the Indians have gone to the happy hunting grounds and others have been scattered," the newspaper reported. "The land has been sold and more whites than Indians live on the one-time reservation."[95]

The closing of the agency did not mark any great change in the way the Siletz people lived. For almost as long as the reservation existed, they had been adapting themselves to white society by going out to work for white people. This adaptation was not a deliberate result of any federal Indian policy either ideally or in application. It was a result of the failure of the government to make the reservation work as policy implied it should.

What allotment had achieved, aside from dismembering what remained of the reservation's land base, was a withdrawal of federal management as much as was possible, a withdrawal that had begun long before the agency was shut down. Allotment and its permutations had turned the resident superintendent into a real estate agent and done away with his responsibility for promoting agriculture and other aspects of assimilation. The competency commission had done away with much of the trust responsibility of the Indian Service. The closure of the Indian school had ended the government's responsibility for reservation education.

But withdrawal of management did not mean withdrawal of control, and so the government became an obstacle when Siletz community leaders made an effort to use remaining tribal resources to cope with poverty. Hoxie Simmons was chair of the reservation business committee late in 1925, when a fresh effort was made to induce the government to sell the remaining four sections of tribal timberland. "The timber is getting overripe and the Indians are in need of money for expenses," the business committee informed the secretary of the interior.[96]

In 1929, the business committee would again petition the commissioner of Indian affairs for permission to sell the timberland. The committee pleaded that the timber was decaying and noted that logging companies already were operating nearby.[97] There was no response, and sale of the remaining tribal land was an issue when a Senate Indian Affairs Subcommittee held a hearing at the Chemawa Indian School near Salem on May 30, 1931, on the condition of Indians. Sen. Lynn Frazier of North Dakota was on hand, together with Burton Wheeler of Montana. (Wheeler would be a major sponsor of the Indian Reorganization Act, also known as the Wheeler-Howard Act of 1934.) Also on hand was J. Henry Scattergood, assistant commissioner of Indian affairs, who has been described as one-half of what amounted to a joint commissionership with Charles Rhoads.[98]

One of the witnesses was C. E. Larsen, who described himself as agency clerk at Chemawa and said he had been the clerk at the Siletz agency before it was abolished. Larsen said about 250 people were living on the Siletz Reservation and there were 459 people on the census roll. He said he was not sure what the Siletz people did for a living, but he mentioned roadwork and work in the woods. He added that the Indian people also did some fishing, but not commercial fishing, and did very little farming because "they have lost practically all the good farmland." What had not been taken for nonpayment of taxes and loans had been sold.[99]

Asked by Frazier what might be done to improve the situation on the Siletz Reservation, Larsen asked for "a better appropriation for the care of the aged Indians." Lincoln County had asked the government to pay thirteen hundred dollars for support of the Indians during 1930. The county court (that is, board of commissioners) had complained that many of the recipients had inherited Indian lands, so having to give them welfare was an imposition on the county. Larsen said the Indian Service had spent only about two hundred dollars in 1930 to care for elderly Siletz people.[100]

J. E. Cooter, who was secretary of the Lincoln County Chamber of Commerce and was representing the county government at the hearing, explained the county's theory that the elderly Indians for whom the

Achievements of Allotment

county was providing were landowners. Cooter said the four sections of remaining tribal land were, in effect, "an estate for the Indians which could be used to take care of them." Asked by assistant commissioner Scattergood how the land might be used, Cooter suggested it could be sold or used as collateral for a loan.

Scattergood said, "In that way you are recommending that the Indian use up his principal to take care of him for a little while longer, and at the end of that time he would have less than he has now?" Larsen responded that he "would say that the Government still owes the Indians of the Siletz Reservation a sufficient amount, when the thing was analyzed, to take good care of them."

Cooter tried to use an illustration. He said that about a month before, an Indian woman named Jane Butler had died. She had been getting about twelve or fifteen dollars a month from the county. "She leaves three or four little children. They are not wards of the Government, and they are heirs to part of this timber. Their mother is gone. Who should take care of the children?"

Senator Frazier said they were wards of the government, but Scattergood claimed there was a "conflict of authority" and that "the comptroller has ruled that no Federal funds can be spent for that kind of case." He added that there were "scores of thousands of Indians in many states in exactly the same situation."

After Scattergood rambled through a monologue on the themes of intergovernmental cooperation and the difficulties of assimilation, a special assistant to the Indian Affairs Committee said there was in fact no conflict in authority and "the commissioner has been reminded of it almost every day for the past two weeks." The courts had decided Indian people clearly were wards of the government, he said.

Scattergood then complained, "They do not give us any funds at all." The assistant responded, "That is not the question."[101]

Hoxie Simmons from Siletz said the tribes were ready to sell the four sections, as J. E. Cooter had suggested, but the secretary of the interior had refused to allow it because the price of timber was down. Perhaps, he suggested, a government loan could be arranged. The situation demanded a response: "We have been through the depression for two years and we have had a hard time. The Indians are all just the same, young or old. There is no work around the country, except one logging camp running in the county now. There are a few men employed. We are asking the Secretary of the Interior or Congress to act on that, because we will have a share and share alike in that."

Although young people were having a hard time, Simmons said, he was especially concerned for the old people. "You turn an old horse loose in a poor pasture to die," he said. "That is the condition of the old Indians today." Simmons was willing to let the land go to resolve the deep crisis of that moment; what was more important, what was critical to his sense of community, was for the money to be divided "share and share alike."[102]

Another Siletz Indian witness, Frank Carson, owner of a garage in Toledo, echoed Simmons's concern for the old people. If the other Indian people could do enough for them, he said, "we would not ask anybody else. You know the nature of the Indians generally, they do not let each other go hungry."[103]

Although allotment devastated the Siletz community, the people had come to accept its results by 1935, as they showed when they were forced to decide whether to accept the Indian Reorganization Act of 1934, or Wheeler-Howard Act. This legislation, the centerpiece of the Indian New Deal, was developed by John Collier, who became commissioner of Indian affairs on April 21, 1933, shortly after Franklin D. Roosevelt became president. Collier came into office with a reputation as a reforming spokesperson for Indian causes. He rejected the old policy of assimilation in the rigid form that it had taken under his predecessors, and he proposed radical changes in the land tenure system that had grown out of previous policies.[104]

In early 1934, Collier suggested that members of tribes should pool their lands under tribal corporations and thus "return" to an autonomous communal way of life. The bill that evolved into the Indian Reorganization Act, as it was introduced in February, 1934, allowed for the creation of specially chartered tribal corporations for self-government and resource management, training of Indians to take over Indian Service jobs, study of

Achievements of Allotment

Indian culture, repeal of the General Allotment Act, and return of the surplus lands bought by the government during the allotment process.

Collier also wanted tribal governments to take over the trust allotments of people who died and to have a form of condemnation power over trust allotments so that they could consolidate communally owned lands.[105] At committee hearings, some Indian spokespersons expressed misgivings about this aspect of the bill; landless people might get together to take property away from the people who had managed to keep it.[106]

This concern over the effects of tribal autonomy on private property could be interpreted as a sign that allotment, as Dawes had hoped, had infused Indian people with a white concept of private property. That interpretation, however, assumes that some general Indian tradition of tribal ownership had been lost.

The Siletz peoples, among others, had never had a tradition of tribal ownership because the basic unit of government among their ancestors was the village, not the tribe, a concept that would have had little meaning for them. The temporary alliances of earlier times, organized for particular purposes, had been welded into a permanent unit by the war and the reservation experience. The idea of communal ownership had no meaning on the reservation because common resources had been owned by the government and managed by its agents.

Thus the concept of a tribe, which was implied in the Indian Reorganization Act, was not necessarily traditional. For many people, it was a cultural development rooted in the collision of traditional societies with the organizational demands of the federal government. If they turned their backs on the program John Collier proposed, they were not necessarily rejecting their own traditions. When people who had stayed in their Indian communities during the lean years since allotment sought to protect their property, they were trying to protect family and community resources as tradition demanded, not reacting selfishly because they had absorbed white values.[107]

The new tribal powers Collier proposed amounted, in any case, to something less than genuine autonomy. As historian Graham D. Taylor has pointed out, the Collier bill proposed that the secretary of the interior retain ultimate control over Indian lands. Reformers feared that Indian people would be tempted, especially considering the economic problems of the time, to sell off their remaining resources and distribute the proceeds and remaining tribal funds through per capita payments to members.[108]

To counter Indian suspicions about what was known by then as the Wheeler-Howard bill, Collier held a series of ten Indian congresses around the country. The second one was held March 8–9, 1934, at the Chemawa Indian School, near Salem.[109] The *Oregonian* described the people who attended the congress as "more than 300 colorful redskins."[110]

Newspaper reporters perceived a divide at this congress between backward elders who opposed the bill and young progressives who supported it. The *Oregonian* said of the latter that "their faces had paled and bleached from generations of the white man's influence." The progressives said they wanted "the freedom to organize for purposes of local self-government and economic enterprise," whereas "the old men thought of their land security and muttered 'No.'"[111] The *Oregon Statesman* said, "Chiefs of the tribes and veterans in earlier war councils were virtually wholeheartedly opposed to any change, but the younger braves favored the proposal."[112] Later responses to the Indian Reorganization Act in western Oregon suggest that the reporters misinterpreted what they saw; the division was not between the old and the young, or the backward and the progressive, but rather between Indians who had left their communities and those who had stayed.

The *Statesman* reported that much of the criticism of the act at the Chemawa conference "centered around the fact that while it would give Indians so-called self-government, they would still be controlled by department of interior officials." The critics also complained that the Indian congress itself was controlled by white men and that the bill failed to address local issues.[113]

General suspicion of anything the government might propose was in evidence. One man was quoted as saying Indians were suspicious of whites by nature. "If you should stack $20 bills on the table and say they were for the Indians, many in the audience would not go after them," he said.[114]

Hoxie Simmons went to this congress and served as interpreter for aged Abe Logan, who on the second day gave a quick, jaundiced sketch of Siletz

Achievements of Allotment

history and then added, "What I have heard from you gentlemen seems to please me. I am going home now to my mother who is over 90 years old and the younger people and tell them what you have said."[115]

George Wasson, who had been involved in a long effort to get the federal government to pay for land taken from the Cooses, Lower Umpquas, and Siuslaws, was more skeptical. The "great White Father" had frequently sent men to explain matters to the Indian people, he said. They had come at the time of allotment, which the public had considered "the greatest act that Congress ever passed for the Indian." The people had been allotted land and suffered by it, he said, "and now these great men come out from the Seat of the government to tell us that this is a failure." Wasson asked whether another commissioner might not come to their grandchildren one day "and tell them this community system is a failure."[116]

Elwood Towner, a lawyer and a member of the Rogue River tribe, also took part in the congress, speaking in favor of John Collier and his policies. Towner said, "we do owe a moral obligation to those who do not own land," and added that if the bill were passed, "we will be practically helping those that are practically destitute."[117]

When the congress was over, the consensus among reporters was that those in attendance narrowly favored the Wheeler-Howard bill. The *Oregonian* said that if a vote had been taken it would have passed, by a narrow margin, "owing to the large number of young and progressive delegates present." The *Oregon Statesman* said the congress had constituted a "tempered" endorsement for the bill.[118]

As it was later passed by Congress, the Indian Reorganization Act of 1934 retained many of Collier's ideas, but mandatory transfer of allotted lands from individual to tribal ownership was omitted. That, however, does not seem to have quieted fears about Collier's intentions. Groups that did not want the act applied to them were offered a way out, but by means of a process that handed an automatic disadvantage to opponents: a majority of all adult members had to vote against accepting the act in a referendum called by the secretary of the interior. In effect, people who did not vote were counted as favoring acceptance. This loaded system prevailed during most of the process, until Congress mandated ordinary majority rule in a 1935 amendment extending the one-year deadline for referenda to be held.[119]

The results of these referenda amounted to a victory for Collier, but there was significant opposition, and that opposition, particularly, has yet to be convincingly explained. Some might question the statement that the referenda were a victory for John Collier. Also, one has to be suspicious of Collier's unnecessarily contrived method of implying the amount of support for the act by adding up the number of members of tribes voting in favor. The commissioner's annual report for 1940, for example, explained the results in terms of a positive vote by 189 tribes with 129,750 members and a negative vote by 77 tribes with 86,365 members,[120] which implies that about 60 percent of Indian people were in favor of the act.

But Collier's method actually understated the support Indian voters gave the act. When that support is calculated in the usual fashion in which elections are calculated, then we can see that about 38,000 of the 62,000 people who voted were in favor of the act—a little more than 61 percent. About 97,000 people were eligible to vote, so the turnout was slightly less than 64 percent.[121]

The depth of this support was not always great; historian Lawrence C. Kelly calculated that seventy-two tribes that accepted the act subsequently failed to adopt the constitutions that they needed in order to take advantage of it.[122] But that does not mean that we can discard the results of the referenda as a positive Indian statement about the hopes of John Collier for basic changes in Indian relations with the government.

Vine Deloria, Jr., and Clifford Lytle have attributed much of the success of the act in tribal referenda to what they called John Collier's "bandwagon strategy," which involved putting the proposition to tribes that were likely to accept the act before going on to the less-likely tribes. Deloria and Lytle made the Navajos their main example of a tribe that rejected the act, and they explained that rejection as a result of resentment growing out of a stock-reduction program and pressure from Christian missionaries and white businesses.[123] But Navajo rejection of the act says little about why other Indian peoples rejected it; although the Navajos were the largest tribe in the country, their case was hardly typical.

The case of the Siletz and Grand Ronde referenda may be more useful in understanding Indian attitudes in general. On the surface, most members of both the Siletz and Grand Ronde tribes seemed essentially "progressive"—long since allotted, with many members living outside their communities. But when the act was put before the Siletz peoples in 1935, it got only 54 votes out of the 177 people who voted, and it was rejected. Nonresidents provided the majority of the support for the act: 29 of the votes in favor were cast by absentees. And an overwhelming majority of nonresidents voted in favor: 29 out of 47. In contrast, only 25 of the 135 resident voters were in favor of accepting the act. Even though 55 nonvoters were counted in favor, the act failed by 109 to 123.[124]

At Grand Ronde, a majority of voting residents voted against the act, but it was only a bare majority of 49 out of 92. The absentees, who made up a little less than 46 percent of the voters, compared with a little more than 26 percent at Siletz, were even more likely to vote for the act than the Siletz absentees. Fifty-nine voted in favor, 19 against—or a little less than 77 percent in favor, compared with about 61 percent of the Siletz absentees. Even if the forty-three people not voting had not been counted in favor, the act would have passed overwhelmingly at Grand Ronde. The official result was 145 to 68.[125]

Clearly, absentees were far more likely to favor the act than were residents; just as clearly, residency was not the only factor, because both residents and nonresidents voting in the Grand Ronde referendum were more likely to favor the act than were their counterparts in the Siletz referendum. Beyond the greater proportion of nonresident voters at Grand Ronde, the difference between the two reservations that seems most likely to explain the results of the referendums is the substantially greater amount of allotments still in trust at Siletz.

The 1934 statistical report of the superintendent for both reservations shows that 7,046 acres of land remained in trust at Siletz, made up of ten allotments totaling 828 acres held in trust for living persons and ninety-two allotments totaling 6,218 acres held in trust for persons deceased. By contrast, at Grand Ronde only fourteen allotments totaling 830 acres were held in trust, all for persons deceased.[126]

Superintendent James T. Ryan blamed the Rogue River lawyer Elwood Towner, who had seemed to support the act at the Chemawa conference, for its defeat at Siletz. Ryan said Towner had held a meeting against the act and that many people were swayed by his arguments.[127] Towner himself was an absentee; his ballot was sent to him at the Portland YMCA.[128] His subsequent career suggests that he saw an opportunity to leap to prominence by opposing John Collier.[129] Less than a week after supporting the Wheeler-Howard Bill at Chemawa, Towner wrote a letter to Collier rejecting most of the thinking behind the bill. Towner said Indian people felt that the self-government provisions of the bill were "too communistic and will not develop initiative, ambition and independence." Expanding on his remarks at Chemawa, he added that the Indian people felt "that it is good to provide lands for Indians that are landless and homeless, but they do not want to revert to becoming wards of the Government. They want the government to purchase lands for the landless."[130]

Towner was expressing, somewhat obliquely, what seems to be the essential reason for the later rejection of the act at Siletz: the fear that it would lead to a redistribution of land, a process that would have been much more disruptive at Siletz than at Grand Ronde.[131] So the vote against the Indian Reorganization Act at Siletz was a vote to hold on to the pattern of property ownership that had developed out of allotment. In a sense, it might even be said to have been a manifestation of the acculturation of allotment.

12

Claims, Termination, Salmon, and Restoration

Much of western Oregon, including the entire coast, had been seized from its original inhabitants with no hint of payment. By 1919, the descendants of those original inhabitants were taking their first steps toward going to court to get the federal government to pay for their lands.

Their legal struggle would be long and complex, their first effort would fail, and they would have to settle for less than expected. But even though their success was measured, it led to a new government effort to finish the process of federal withdrawal that had begun with allotment. Even before the claims cases were completely settled, the area director of the federal Bureau of Indian Affairs (BIA) began working toward what would be known as the "termination" of the western Oregon Indians.

The Coos, Lower Umpqua, and Siuslaw Indians, who had been left landless by the Mitchell removal, comprised the first western Oregon group to go to court trying to get payment for their lost lands. To sue the government, they had to have the consent of Congress. They managed as early as 1919 to have a bill introduced to grant them that consent. Their case would not be decided, however, until 1938.[1]

At the end of October 1925, a group of western Oregon Indian people met in Roseburg with Sen. Robert N. Stanfield to discuss payment for five million acres of land taken through unratified treaties. An *Oregonian* correspondent said the Indians involved were asking for $12.5 million, based on the premise that they should be paid $2.50 an acre. According to the *Oregonian*, Stanfield cajoled the tribes into submitting the claim to Congress rather than going to court. Stanfield, it was said, was "arranging to introduce a bill at the next session appropriating the sum to which the Indians are believed to be equitably entitled."[2] Stanfield's plan went nowhere.

On the verge of the Great Depression, on February 23, 1929, Congress passed an act allowing the Coos, Lower Umpqua, and Siuslaw Indians to sue the federal government.[3] According to a House report issued before the bill was passed, the three tribes had agreed to give up as much as 1.2 million acres, and the government had promised in return that it would create a reservation for their exclusive use and make cash payments for the land. "No part of the agreement was carried out by the United States," the report said.[4]

The act was passed despite objections by Calvin Coolidge's interior secretary, Hubert Work. The secretary noted in a letter to the chair of the House Committee on Indian Affairs that a similar bill that had included the Coos, Lower Umpqua, and Siuslaw tribes among a number of western Oregon tribes had been given an unfavorable report in early 1928.

Work's fundamental argument was that the government's records were bad. He said that "the records are indefinite as to just which were parties to treaties with the United States or where they reside at the present time." The records also failed to show what land was claimed by the tribes and what they might recover if the bill should pass.[5]

Only one treaty was involved, made by Joel Palmer in 1855, and it had been printed in a Senate document only thirty-five years before. The peoples involved had agreed to give up the entire coast of Oregon. The treaty did not specify which lands had belonged to which tribes, but it not only listed the Coos, Lower Umpqua, and Siuslaw tribes as parties but also included the names of all the men who had agreed to it. The treaty had never been ratified because, according to the acting commissioner of Indian affairs at the time the treaty was published, it was not submitted for ratification until 1857 "because of the hostile condition of our Indian relations in that quarter," and then it was "accidentally overlooked."[6]

Although the act allowing the Coos, Lower Umpqua, and Siuslaw tribes to go to court was passed, almost a decade would go by before the claim would be decided in court. Meanwhile, the rest of the tribes of western Oregon did as the Coos, Lower Umpqua, and Siuslaw tribes had done and asked Congress for permission to sue. A bill to allow a suit reached the desk of Charles Rhoads, Herbert Hoover's commissioner of Indian affairs, in 1930. Rhoads, a banker from Philadelphia, was a Quaker who had once been president of the reformist Indian Rights Association.[7]

Rhoads has been described by Francis Paul Prucha as a believer in the old ideal of assimilationism who nonetheless made proposals that "offered a far-sighted and statesmanlike approach."[8] Rhoads even suggested that Congress create an Indian claims commission, which would "hear all causes, those that are human and moral as well as those that are legal and equitable."[9]

When the bill to allow the western Oregon Indians to go to court came to Rhoads, however, he made no reference to human and moral causes. His response was a cold-eyed rejection suggesting that no action on the cases involving unratified treaties should be taken until the case brought by the Coos, Lower Umpqua, and Siuslaw tribes had been resolved. As for the ratified treaties, Rhoads argued that everything promised under those treaties had been appropriated by Congress and paid.[10]

Rhoads repeated this argument when a fresh bill on the same subject was submitted to him two years later and added, "The claims of many of the bands of Indians mentioned in the bill have never been definitely formulated, and we are therefore unable to recommend that S. 826 be enacted." A bill that would have given the Tututunne people the right to sue the government as a separate group failed to get Rhoads's recommendation because of the government's lack of information about them.[11] The western Oregon tribes other than the Coos, Lower Umpquas, and Siuslaws would not get permission to sue for their claims until 1935.[12]

The Coos, Lower Umpqua, and Siuslaw claims finally came to judgment before the Court of Claims on May 2, 1938, and the government prevailed. A BIA official later attributed the loss of the case to faulty presentation of evidence. The following year, the three tribes appealed the case to the U.S. Supreme Court, which decided against them.[13]

A ten-year plan compiled by the Grand Ronde–Siletz agency in 1944 implied a limited economic future for the Siletz peoples and that relocation away from the reservation community was their best hope. The author of the plan also anticipated later developments in federal policy by suggesting termination of government assistance.

The plan recommended taking advantage of the effects of World War II in raising the price of timber,[14] and its author also considered how, once the war was over, Indian people would replace the wartime employment that had allowed them to work their way out of general poverty.[15]

The author declined to estimate the value of Indian-owned timber because of a lack of recent data. The plan called for hiring a senior ranger, getting a "cruise"—that is, an expert estimate of the quantity, character, and quality of the timber—and selling the timber while prices remained high. The plan implied that conditions did not favor setting up a government-managed sustained-yield unit.[16]

According to the plan, Indian people were working at sawmills, were "quite proficient and readily engaged" in fruit picking and other farm work, and were working in shipyards and other defense plants. Most of the Siletz people appeared to be self-supporting, the author said, but they were "enjoying earnings never before received" because of the war. Forty-one of seventy-seven resident families were what the plan characterized as defense workers. The author was concerned that after the war, depression conditions would return.[17]

The principal remedy suggested for postwar unemployment was vague, and the plan implied that the most promising solution was getting Indian people out of the reservation community. People "who have secured good positions, wherever the location, should remain if possible after the war," the author recommended, "although the values of community life and associations . . . should not be entirely disregarded." Many families had "already solved many of their own problems by settling in communities away from the reservation." The plan's author predicted that "the number in a permanent outside work status will be increased materially by their war-time experiences."[18]

On the author's list of goals for "any future program for these people," the concluding item was "Decreasing Government assistance during the next ten years and final termination of such help at the end of that time."[19]

Forty-nine Siletz men and women served in the armed forces during World War II, according to an Indian Service estimate.[20] Many years after the war ended in August 1945, Pauline Ricks recalled that many men who had left Siletz as "happy young boys" had returned "broken bitter men, some crippled, . . . some brought home silver stars, some purple hearts." Some did not come back at all. "How happy our people were with our boys coming home again," said Ricks, later a Siletz tribal council member. But they had come home to a community that would soon be "under duress from the government."[21]

A few months before the end of the war, the Court of Claims decided that some western Oregon tribes and bands without ratified treaties who were involved what was called the "Alcea" case were entitled to recover the value of their original lands. On February 4, 1946, the court made a similar decision in the "Rogue River" case, which involved western Oregon tribes claiming that the government had failed to meet obligations in ratified treaties. The value of lands ceded in the treaties was not considered in this case, only the value of reservation lands taken without payment.[22]

The Alcea land-claim case was carried to the Supreme Court, which ruled on November 26, 1946, that the coastal tribes were entitled to be paid for 2.77 million acres. E. L. Crawford, lawyer for the tribes, was quoted in the *Oregonian* as expecting a payoff ranging between $10 million and $15 million. E. Morgan Pryse, western regional director for the Bureau of Indian Affairs, predicted the settlement would be "a great thing for those Indians." He said they had been "the worst off of all the tribes in the United States."[23] But success in the claims cases would come to be linked with plans of the ambitious area administrator of the Bureau of Indian Affairs to carry out what the 1944 plan for Siletz called "termination" of government involvement.

The court victory in the Alcea case inspired an *Oregonian* editorial writer to ask, "Couldn't the Indians, by right of prior residence, claim all of the United States?" Readers were warned to check their property deeds. The tone of the editorial was not friendly; the writer approvingly quoted Marcus Whitman, the missionary killed by Cayuse Indians in 1847, as having written that "when a people refuse or neglect to fill the designs of Providence" Christians did not have "to be anxious on their account." The Indians had failed to "multiply and replenish the earth" and thus had no right to complain about being displaced.[24]

On October 20, 1947, the coastal tribes involved in the Alcea case asked a commissioner of the Court of Claims for $65 million, including interest. The government's lawyer opened his case by claiming that the tribes did not actually exist, because of intermarriage, but the claims commissioner turned down the argument saying it should have been raised earlier; his function was simply to determine how much was owed.[25]

The government took the case to the Supreme Court, which ruled the following year that the government owed the Indians for the land. But the amount of the payment was still to be decided. After the Supreme Court ruling, a reporter went to the coast and found "the large majority" of the claimants "in shacks on hillsides" from Grand Ronde down to Gold Beach. He found 74-year-old Hoxie Simmons, who said with "deep feeling" that "the worst thing that ever happened to the Indian was when the government ruled that he could sell his individual allotment of trust lands." Simmons had, since 1931, lost his own allotment for nonpayment of a loan. "The only hope for the young people is to put them back on farms where they are able to make a modest living," Simmons added.[26]

The Court of Claims ruled on July 3, 1950, that the government owed a little more than $16.5 million to the coastal tribes involved in the Alcea case. Then the Supreme Court ruled on April 9, 1951, that the government did not have to pay interest. E. Morgan Pryse estimated that something more than $3 million would be paid and said about 1,100 people would get amounts varying from about $700 to about $6,000. Congress eventually appropriated a little less than $2.26 million to pay off the claims, however.[27]

In the "Rogue River" case, only three groups—the Molalla tribe, the Umpqua band, and the Calapooia band of Umpqua Valley—got judgments. They were awarded somewhat more than $347,000 in 1950, and Congress passed an appropriation for that amount the following year. The Confederated Tribes of Siletz, dropped as plaintiffs from the Alcea case, took their case to the Indian Claims Commission, which eventually awarded somewhat less than $434,000.[28]

Significant victories had been won, but they were somewhat like the victories won during the Rogue River War; whatever temporary satisfactions they provided, they did not change the long-term prospects of the Indian people. Even the minority of people whose government checks ran to four figures got scant compensation for the century of compulsory adaptation and poverty on the margins of white society that had resulted from American control over their ancestors and their lands. Nor was it enough money to turn poor communities into significantly less poor communities for more than a short time.

Steady employment in the timber industry was more important to the economic health of the Siletz peoples in the postwar period than were land claims settlements; logging had become the basic source of employment for Siletz men. "During World War II and the Korean conflict, jobs were plentiful for the Indians," according to Robert Rilatos, later vice-chair of the tribal council. "The Siletz Indian men were recognized as the best loggers ever known," he said. He himself worked in the woods for nineteen years, beginning at the age of fourteen.

The timber industry, however, can be unstable, depending on competition and local conditions, and in the middle 1950s the industry went into a slump in western Oregon.[29] When the area director of the BIA proposed withdrawal of federal recognition, or termination, it looked like a solution to the problems of hard times. Holding onto federal recognition certainly would not have helped the Siletz people to counteract the effects of the slump, given that such BIA services as there were had long since ceased to be available locally.

The movement toward termination was, among other things, a release for the pent-up energies of assimilationists after their nemesis, John Collier, gave up his job as commissioner of Indian affairs. Collier resigned in early 1945 when a senator threatened to force deep cuts in the 1946 BIA budget if he stayed.[30] Collier's successor, William Brophy, believed many Indians were assimilated enough to do without their traditional relationship with the federal government, and he shared that perspective with the man who appointed him, Harry Truman.[31]

Among the groups the Bureau of Indian Affairs would classify as adequately assimilated for termination were the Siletz Indians; by getting along without a government school since 1918 and a resident superintendent since 1925, they had demonstrated that they did not need federal services or supervision. But by cutting its last ties with them, the federal government would also be destroying the tribal government and thus any chance for effective representation of the interests of the members of the tribes.

William Brophy's immediate successor, acting commissioner William Zimmerman, began fleshing out the concept of termination in 1947 when he suggested that BIA expenses could be reduced by denying federal services to some tribes and, by implication, to all tribes at some point.[32]

The movement picked up considerable momentum during the term of Truman's last appointee as commissioner of Indian affairs, Dillon S. Myer, who took over May 5, 1950. According to historian Francis Paul Prucha, Myer was efficient but insensitive and poorly informed about Indians. He was a career government administrator who had headed the Federal Housing Administration. He had served from 1942 to 1946 as director of the War Relocation Authority, the agency that managed the evacuation of Japanese and Japanese-Americans from the West Coast and their internment in camps. When he was named commissioner of Indian affairs, Myer replaced leftover Indian New Dealers with friends from his relocation authority days.[33]

Myer promoted legislation that looked toward termination, and he warned BIA officials that Congress was not interested in funding activities not aimed at termination. He said the BIA would prepare for termination even if Indian leaders opposed it. Congress didn't formally adopt the new policy, however, until after Myer had left office in the transition from the Truman administration to the Eisenhower administration. The new policy was stated in House Concurrent Resolution 108, adopted August 1, 1953, which called for an end to federal supervision as soon as possible.[34]

The idea of terminating the Siletz and Grand Ronde tribes, however, predated not only House Concurrent Resolution 108 but even the administration of Dillon S. Myer. A form of termination had been suggested in the 1944 Siletz plan. And E. Morgan Pryse, the area director in the Portland office of the BIA, had started holding meetings on termination with western Oregon groups in 1948. He said that for three years he spent his weekends meeting with Indian people to develop a resource management program "looking eventually to withdrawal of the Government supervision over their affairs and property."[35]

Pryse would later file an extensive report including letters of support from the governor and the Lincoln County government and a number of termination-related tribal resolutions that suggest the leaders of the tribes were somewhat uncertain about what was happening.

A resolution passed July 29 asked Pryse to cancel three obsolete special-purpose accounts and put the funds into a new account that could be used for "communal undertakings." This is the only Siletz resolution in Pryse's report that includes the number of people who voted on it. At the general council meeting that adopted it, a meeting open to all members, only 23 people voted, all in favor. The Siletz rolls included 731 people as of June 1, 1950, so the vote cannot represent more than about 5 percent of the eligible members.[36]

This resolution implies a continuing tribal organization with a relationship to the BIA. Curiously, a resolution that was passed the same day at the same place, presumably by some of the same people, unquestionably looks toward termination. This resolution was passed by an unspecified majority of a general council of the Chetco tribe.

It dealt with the money due the Chetco tribe as a result of the Alcea case. A connection between the money and termination of the tribe is implied throughout. The tribe asked that payments be made before federal supervision was withdrawn so that any tax exemptions based on tribal status would be effective and the BIA area office could still distribute the money. The area office was made the headquarters for the final tribal enrollment. The resolution firmly opposed "any use of claims money in performing tribal, communal, or collective enterprise."[37]

Later, the Siletz Confederated Tribes passed a resolution requesting termination. An unspecified majority of a general council asked for withdrawal of all existing restrictions and services as soon as possible, and also asked for titles to tribal and individual trust lands, with the understanding that members "shall thereafter be accorded full citizenship."[38]

E. Morgan Pryse made the connection between termination and the payment of claims clear in an interview with a reporter on January 16, 1952. The resulting story, headlined "43 Coast Indian Tribes May Win Independence," told of Pryse's preliminary work toward the termination of the tribes that had won awards in the Court of Claims. Only those tribes were included in his planning. Pryse said, "Ever since the award was made more than a year ago, representatives of my regional office have been interviewing the Indians and acquainting them with the withdrawal proposition."[39]

The linkage came up again during a 1954 congressional hearing on western Oregon termination. When the question of consent arose, Pryse said 1951 resolutions passed by the Siletz and Grand Ronde people that asked for termination were still in force. Only two or three people had objected to termination, he said, and that was because they feared that afterward, claims pending before the Indian Claims Commission "would not be handled or paid out expeditiously."

Pryse was asked whether the Indian people had been told that they had to accept termination to get their claims paid. He tried to sidestep the question by saying, "It was explained that the money had to be appropriated and the rolls made up first." The question was restated and Pryse said, "Oh no." The questioner asked, "At no time?" Pryse said, "No. The point I want to be sure to bring out is that the tribes have never withdrawn their resolutions and they are still asking for this type of legislation."[40]

Among the resolutions mentioned in the Pryse termination report was one made April 15, 1951, which gave Pryse authority to sell the timberland the Siletz tribes still owned—somewhat more than four sections. Another resolution, passed by an unspecified majority of the Siletz tribal council on June 3, accepted Pryse's estimate that an acceptable price for the land would come to $237,000 (or about $88 per acre).[41]

There was reason to question how well his office could handle this aspect of termination. Even as Pryse pressed ahead with steps toward termination in 1952, the *Oregonian* was revealing a scheme involving officials in the BIA area office that had resulted in the sale of eight hundred acres of southern Oregon trust allotment land for a fraction of its value.

Reporter Wallace Turner learned that the land had been sold without having been advertised. A sawmill had been willing to buy the land for $416,000, but it was sold for $135,000. Turner explained that a BIA regulation allowed the sale of the property of incompetent Indians to other Indians without bidding. The initial purchaser was an Indian woman from Portland who got Pryse to remove trust restrictions and immediately resold the land for $160,000. The new owners then granted an option to two couples to buy the land for $300,000.[42]

Eventually, three men were convicted in federal court of a conspiracy to defraud. A BIA realty officer was fined $5,000 and sentenced to serve six months in prison. A logger who bankrolled the scheme was fined $25,000, and he and a man who had worked for him drew one-year prison sentences. Another BIA employee was dismissed for his involvement.[43]

Pryse told a reporter that his knowledge of the transactions involved in the land-fraud case was sketchy, but he had given his approval to all the aspects of the transactions that involved the BIA. He implied that he had relied on his staff's recommendation. At an earlier point in the scandal, the reporter noted, Pryse had "stoutly defended" the fraudulent purchase price, saying timber in the same area had been sold for less.[44]

Did the resolution for termination that E. Morgan Pryse included in his report represent the opinion of the members of the Confederated Tribes of Siletz Indians? The evidence suggests that it did, but the evidence also suggests that much of what they were told to expect from termination did not come to pass.

Pauline Ricks would remember more than two decades afterward what had led up to termination: "Talk of big money, giving us deeds to our lands, living like a first class citizen, they were going to train us for jobs. They were going to give us training and prepare us to go down all walks of life, side by side with our white brothers. A beautiful picture was being painted right before our eyes. This looked good to our people who survived the depression and war years, for our people have never been out of depression."[45]

The tribal council would make a joint statement in 1976, when termination had long since lost its attractions, blaming "the system of the 1950s" for termination. The loss of BIA services did not mean much at the time because they were "a shambles." People did not understand that their children would lose the right to go to Chemawa Indian School near Salem and get loans for education. Indian veterans of World War II who had come home unwilling to accept racial discrimination believed what they were told about termination meaning equality.[46]

Hardy Simmons, a World War II Air Corps veteran[47] who had come back to Siletz and worked as a logger, said people had not seen the purpose of the meetings that had been held about termination and he didn't think "more than a handful of people" had known what termination meant: "Most people only knew about Termination through rumors, and there were a lot of different rumors."[48]

Lindsay John said, "The BIA painted a pretty picture of Termination" in which people were told they would get training and jobs and that termination would end discrimination against them. He said that his brother, a member of the tribal council at the time of termination, "felt that there was no way you can beat the Federal Government; they'll Terminate us no matter what we say."[49]

When joint congressional hearings on western Oregon termination were held on February 17, 1954, no Indian people were heard. Only E. Morgan Pryse and two other BIA officials spoke in person, and the Indian people were represented only by the protermination resolutions Pryse had collected about three years before.[50]

The termination act, Public Law 588, became law August 13, 1954, terminating BIA supervision of trust lands and BIA provision of services for all the Indian people of western Oregon. Tribal properties could be preserved as such, but the process for doing that was somewhat involved. The usual procedure contemplated by the act was the transfer of tribal properties to trustees chosen by the secretary of the interior who would liquidate them and distribute the proceeds, normally within three years.

The act said that before a termination proclamation was published by the secretary of the interior, the secretary was authorized (not directed) to provide training to help the Indian people (soon to be no longer recognized as Indian people) to cope with non-Indian life, including "orientation in non-Indian community customs and living standards."[51]

There is no evidence of a job training program for the Siletz people, and their tribal property would not be preserved. Interior Secretary Fred Seaton issued the termination proclamation two years and one day after the act became law. The *Oregonian* reported that about 2,100 people were members of the terminated groups. Tribal properties, the newspaper said, had been sold and the proceeds distributed.[52]

Pauline Ricks said that at the time termination went into effect, timberland in the area was almost all logged off. Men who had worked in the woods and mills were without jobs. "We began to make our exit out of Siletz, seeking a new home," she said. The community was breaking down.[53] Lindsay John said, "Our land had all been logged off and there were no jobs. There was no such thing as an Indian getting a job unless you walked across a picket line in the logging camps."[54] Robert Rilatos said changes in the lumber industry, including automation, pulp mills, and plywood, eliminated jobs for Indian people. Many people moved to Willamette valley cities to find work.[55]

Why did termination became the new goal of Indian policy after the Collier years? Francis Paul Prucha suggested that in addition to matching the philosophical assimilationism of its supporters, termination was in line with the postwar budget-cutting mentality and the economic and political needs of the moment. "The period was a time of economic growth, and the tying up of Indian lands and other resources in tribal enclaves went against the prevailing mood," he said, and "national unity and conformity" were demanded by Cold War politics.[56]

When applied to the termination of the western Oregon bands, however, this explanation will not work. The resources involved were minuscule, and to the extent that they were not tied into the overall economy, the cause was administrative inertia in the BIA. The people involved already conformed as much as anyone could have been expected to conform to the needs and expectations of the larger society that surrounded them, which was, of course, why they were considered good prospects for termination.[57]

If resources and assimilation were, in this case at least, not especially significant motives for termination, what remains would seem to be a desire to close out the relationship between Indian people and the government and, at long last, relegate the problems and failures of that relationship to history. It was the logical end of the claims process; with the blood money paid, any remaining guilt or fear rooted in the existence of Indian groups could be banished by declaring those entities nonexistent.

Behind the hopes and sentiments of the policymakers, however, were unyielding realities, particularly the continuing poverty of Indian communities. A number of western liberals in Congress began criticizing the effects of termination in 1956, and the Senate passed a resolution in 1957 that demanded that the BIA provide services to recognized tribes without pushing for termination in return. Among these western liberals was Sen. Richard Neuberger of Oregon.[58]

Perhaps their regional and political affinity is no coincidence; termination represented a transfer of responsibility from the federal government to state and local governments in their states and thus a financial loss for those governments. As liberals they supported government-managed social services. As westerners they supported paying for those services with federal rather than local funds.

Indian people also began to criticize termination. Leaders of the Mesquakie Indians in Iowa, for example, told a federal official in 1960 that termination would mean tribal "extermination." Robert Yellowtail, former superintendent of the Crow Reservation, called termination a "policy of liquidation."[59]

Congress passed twelve termination acts, six of them—including the western Oregon act—in 1954, but the last act, for the Poncas in Nebraska, was not passed until 1962, with an effective date of 1966. When termination was finally over, few Indian people had been affected directly. According to Francis Paul Prucha, only about 3 percent of federally recognized Indians lost that status—13,263 people. And only about 3 percent of Indian lands no longer were held in trust—1,365,801 acres.[60] Donald L. Fixico provided a slightly different set of numbers—"a minimum of 1,362,155 acres and 11,466 individuals."[61]

For the Siletz Indians, however, termination was a total loss; all members of the Confederated Tribes lost their Indian status, and all their tribal lands were lost. Measuring the other effects of termination is difficult because there seems to be little comparative data, but an extensive study published in 1976 suggested that whatever the effects of termination on the Siletz people were, they were not positive.[62]

The study was done for the federal American Indian Policy Review Commission. A survey taken for the study showed that a substantial majority of western Oregon Indian people believed that termination had promoted unemployment, damaged family ties, pushed up the school drop-out rate and the Indian crime rate, increased drug and alcohol abuse, damaged cultural identity, and generally reduced "the ability to meet life's basic needs." Not even one western Oregon Indian surveyed believed the effects of termination were positive.

According to this study, 44 percent of Indian people between the ages of 17 and 25 in Siletz had not finished high school as of 1974. In addition, Indian unemployment in Lincoln County in 1976 was estimated at 43.8 percent, and the average family income of Indians in Siletz was estimated at 45 percent of the average income of all families.[63]

Joe Lane, a member of the Chetco tribe who was a state revenue agent living in a Portland suburb, was among the leaders of the movement in the early 1970s to put the Siletz tribes back together as a recognized group. Lane said that the problems caused by termination led to a series of meetings over a period of several years. Indian organizations, BIA officials, and former members of the Confederated Tribes were involved.

The meetings finally led to a general meeting of former members at Siletz toward the end of September 1973 that drew fifty-four people. They unanimously endorsed reorganization and elected a tribal council. Lane became chair and Robert Rilatos became vice-chair.[64] They organized themselves as a nonprofit corporation. The Native American Rights Fund and Portland lawyer John Volkman helped prepare a bill for restoration of federal recognition. An average of more than two hundred people attended monthly meetings.[65]

People began to hope, Joe Lane said, that soon they would be eligible for BIA programs that would give them a chance to improve their lives. Moreover, they were enjoying the rebirth of their Indian identity. They were no longer in "a state of limbo, unrecognized as equals by members of the white community, and looked down upon by other Indian people as well."[66]

The drive toward restoration attracted support from members of the Oregon congressional delegation. Rep. Wendell Wyatt introduced an unsuccessful restoration bill in June 1974.[67] Sen. Mark Hatfield introduced a restoration bill, S. 2801, on December 17, 1975.[68] Rep. Les AuCoin introduced a similar bill in the House.[69] For the first time in a century, the Oregon congressional delegation was seriously interested in legislation affecting western Oregon Indian peoples, and for the first time in history that delegation backed legislation originated by those peoples.

In introducing his bill, Senator Hatfield claimed that the Siletz people had been "ill-prepared to cope with the realities of American society" at the time of termination and that they had been "tossed abruptly from a state of almost total dependency to a state of total independence" and told "to leave the only way of life they had known." Hatfield apparently did not know that they had received few BIA services for many years before termination, and his argument implied that the roots of their problems were in themselves, not in their lack of resources.

The heart of the matter was getting federally funded social services. Hatfield quoted statistics establishing that unemployment, poor education, and inadequate health care were serious problems. "The basic thrust of the bill is to formally recognize the Siletz as a tribe, and make this group eligible for the Federal services to which other federally recognized Indians are entitled," he said.[70]

Hatfield entered into the record a letter from the Lincoln County Board of Commissioners in favor of restoration. The commissioners took note of the significance of tribal identity. But they seemed more interested in benefits. Restoration would "correct some of the loss of Federal benefits received in Health, Education, and Welfare that these individuals have not had the benefits from," they said. And recognition would bring in federal money to increase employment, improve education, and provide jobs under the Comprehensive Education and Training Act, they observed.[71]

Their reasoning was somewhat similar to the argument C. E. Larsen and J. E. Cooter had made in 1931 on behalf of the county government, which had wanted to stop paying welfare benefits to Indian people.[72] Hatfield and the county commissioners were saying, in effect, that the problems of the Indian peoples should be the responsibility of the federal government, not the state or the county. Restoration was, from this perspective, a matter of getting federal money to pay for certain social services to be delivered in Oregon.

Despite this, it was a unit of the state government that put up the most determined resistance to restoration. The problem was fishing rights, which had been at the center of a long and sometimes violent series of clashes between Indian and non-Indian fishermen in the neighboring state of Washington.

Five years before, in 1970, several tribes in Washington had gone to federal court to get a determination of their fair share, under their treaties, of the catch of fish in the state. In a ruling that brought down some of the bitterness of the fishing controversy on himself, District Judge George Boldt had decided in 1974 that the members of the tribes had the right to fish in any traditional location, on or off a reservation, and that they had a right to as much as 50 percent of the total of all the fish catch.[73]

Hatfield and AuCoin did not want to be responsible for creating a situation in which the Washington fishing rights quarrel could spill over into Oregon. In a letter to the governor of Oregon, they agreed that "the issuance of additional rights to the Indians would be undesirable." They pointed out that the restoration bill specifically avoided granting any such rights.[74] But their assurances did not calm the opposition.

Hearings were held on Hatfield's restoration bill on March 30 and March 31, 1976. Fishing and hunting rights were the principal issue. Beverly B. Hall, assistant state attorney general, speaking for the Oregon Fish and Wildlife Commission, argued that restoration would raise questions about rights lost at the time of termination. Tribal members had kept the right to hunt and fish on trust lands without state regulation until termination eliminated trust lands. Undoing termination could mean restoring those rights,[75] even though the restoration bill included a paragraph saying that it would not give or return "any hunting, fishing, or trapping rights of any nature to the Tribe or its members."[76]

If federal recognition were restored, Hall argued, members of the tribes would have "the entire weight of the U.S. Department of Justice" on their side if they chose to go to court and ask for confirmation of their rights. The state fish and wildlife department was certain, moreover, that individual members of the tribes would go to court for fishing and hunting rights if recognition were restored.[77]

Hatfield contended that this objection was based on a misinterpretation of the Boldt decision. If the Siletz peoples had any fishing or hunting rights, they had them whether or not recognition was restored. They might go to court to get a determination of those rights in any case, he argued, but his bill was neutral on the issue.[78] He also pointed out that the Klamaths in south central Oregon had filed a fishing and hunting rights suit after their termination and had been supported by the Justice Department even though their tribe had been terminated. The Siletz peoples had exactly the same rights and expectations of federal support before restoration that they would have if restored.[79]

Art Bensell, a retired BIA school administrator who had become Siletz tribal chair, was among the witnesses at Hatfield's hearing. When Hatfield raised the issue of fishing and hunting rights, Bensell said that the tribes were not concerned about the fishing and hunting issues. Both former chair Joe Lane and council member Robert Paul Tom also testified that the tribes were not seeking fishing and hunting rights.[80]

Beverly Hall asked for amendments that would confirm both the authority of the state to regulate fishing and hunting by members of the tribes and the right of the tribes to file a claim for compensation for loss of their fishing and hunting rights. The latter amendment, she explained, would convert "Oregon fish into Federal dollars in terms of compensation which they may expect." Giving up unregulated hunting and fishing rights, she said, was a "reasonable exchange for the special benefits resulting from reactivating the Siletz."[81]

Hatfield said the commission's amendments would create a federal liability, and so putting them into the bill would bring the federal Office of Management and Budget into the argument against restoration. "We might as well kiss the bill goodbye if we are going to follow that procedure," he said. Moreover, Suzan Harjo of the National Congress of American Indians said at the hearing that if "restoration becomes an exchange of social programs for Federal Indian rights, every tribe in this country will be threatened." Harjo added, "All Indian tribes would be forced to actively oppose the bill."[82]

In the end, Senator Hatfield's 1975 bill to restore recognition of the Confederated Tribes was unsuccessful, but he and Sen. Bob Packwood introduced a new bill, S. 1560, in May 1977. Rep. Les AuCoin introduced a companion bill in the House, H.R. 7259. The Oregon Fish and Wildlife Commission again went into opposition.[83]

The new bill, like the old one, did not propose to grant or restore fishing and hunting rights. Unlike the old bill, however, it directed the secretary of the interior to negotiate with the tribes about creation of a reservation and to develop a reservation plan within two years.[84]

In a commentary published by the *Oregonian* on July 12, the day before a Senate subcommittee hearing on restoration was held in Washington,

AuCoin made the familiar argument that the restoration bill was neutral on fishing and hunting rights.[85] On the same page, a member of the state Fish and Wildlife Commission insisted that restoration would affect potential Siletz claims for water, mineral, and timber rights as well as fishing, hunting, and trapping rights, which he claimed "almost certainly would be assured" if the Siletz people got a reservation.[86]

In Washington the following day, Jack Donaldson, director of the fish and wildlife department, suggested an alternative bill. The commission, he said, wanted to let the Siletz people have health, education and welfare benefits without endangering "the things we hold so dear; that is, the State's rights to manage hunting and fishing relative to Indian reservations."[87]

The alternative had no reservation plan and included a paragraph giving the state specific authority to regulate fishing and hunting.[88] The Fish and Wildlife Commission's version was not accepted, however, and the bill went out of committee without substantial changes.[89]

The restoration bill was passed by the Senate on August 5 and the House on November 1. It was sent to President Jimmy Carter on November 3 and approved November 18.[90] A year and a half later, on June 2, 1979, members of the tribes voted to adopt a constitution.[91] Five months after that, on November 1, voters in the town of Siletz (no longer an Indian enclave) expressed a willingness to give back about thirty-six acres of former tribal land on Government Hill, the old agency site, but by a narrow margin of 148 to 134. The Confederated Tribes had turned the land over to the city government at termination.[92]

As a means of bringing federal money into Oregon, restoration was an obvious and rapid success. The tribes soon had twenty employees and an annual budget of $1.2 million. They also had a plan calling for a reservation of about 3,630 acres, not counting the land on Government Hill. The land, picked from land under the jurisdiction of the federal Bureau of Land Management, was expected to provide $600,000 in timber revenues every year. Mark Hatfield introduced a Senate bill to give the land back to the tribes. But fishing and hunting rights were still a problem; Les AuCoin, who had grown more cautious since 1977, declined to introduce a bill in the House until an agreement on the issue was reached between the tribes and the state.[93]

The Siletz leadership would settle for a narrow definition of fishing and hunting rights in order to get a reservation. On December 14, 1979, Art Bensell and Charles Wilkinson, a law professor serving as an attorney for the tribes, made a proposal to the Fish and Wildlife Commission. They told the commission the tribes did not intend to go to court to get any fishing and hunting rights to which they might be entitled.

Instead, they asked for an agreement with the commission that would leave management with the fish and wildlife department while setting up quotas for fish and game and restricting the taking of fish and game under those quotas to the proposed reservation. No commercial fishing would be involved. Wilkinson proposed a "friendly lawsuit" in federal district court that would result in a consent decree defining tribal hunting and fishing rights.[94]

Senator Hatfield's reservation bill was approved in the Senate on March 19. The consent decree Wilkinson had proposed was still to be approved, but Hatfield maintained that his bill was neutral (just as his restoration bill had been). A spokesperson for AuCoin told a reporter that he was still waiting for a conclusion to the negotiations between the tribes and the Fish and Wildlife Commission.[95]

Both the commission and the tribal council approved the proposed consent decree on April 21, and it was signed by U.S. District Judge James Burns in Portland on May 2. It allowed members of the tribes to take as many as 375 deer and 25 elk annually plus a maximum of 200 salmon. The salmon had to be taken at designated sites on three tributaries of the Siletz River and could not be taken from the river itself. About fifteen members and potential members of the tribes registered their objections, among them Darrelle Dean Butler, a member of the American Indian Movement, who argued that the tribal membership (by that time about eleven hundred people) had not had a fair chance to respond.[96]

When the hearing was over, Les AuCoin held a courthouse press conference to announce that he would introduce a reservation bill the following week. He said passage was certain. AuCoin would set the terms of the fishing and hunting rights agreement in concrete by writing them into his bill. A bargain had been struck—land for rights.[97] The House approved AuCoin's bill on August 18, 1980, and President Carter signed it on September 5.[98]

In 1985, the Siletz tribal government asked the federal government to return 12,480 acres under Bureau of Land Management jurisdiction.[99] The original reservation grant had not fulfilled its promise because of a new collapse in the timber market.[100] Rep. Les AuCoin declined to take a position on the issue, saying it was controversial and the tribes would have to have a good explanation for needing more land.[101]

When the tribes held a celebration in 1986 marking the anniversary of restoration, one of AuCoin's field staffers said a few words on his behalf. None of those words concerned the pending land plan, or even the general statement of Dee Pigsley, the tribal chair, that "The goal of the tribe is to survive, and to survive we have to have a solid economic base." AuCoin's staffer conveyed nothing more than the thought that cultural diversity is good thing for America.[102]

Perhaps the main value of Indian people to politicians has arisen from the idea that Indians are outsiders with whom someone must deal, as the Siletz peoples had to be dealt with in 1980 because of the Northwest fishing rights controversy. Joseph Lane, James Lupton, John H. Mitchell, Mark Hatfield, and Les AuCoin all sought to gain political capital by dealing with them. To the extent that they cease to be outsiders who must be dealt with, they cease to have political meaning.

When they have had political meaning, that meaning has become the foundation of the policy applied to them, whatever the official policy of the moment may have been. When they have lacked any strong political meaning, as they did during most of the reservation period, then the character of applied policy seems to have depended on a haphazard combination of two main factors.

One of those factors, although it lost meaning after termination, has been the character of their overseers (the brutal Simpson, the incompetent Bagley, the humanitarian Swan, the ambitious Pryse). The other factor has been the degree of intensity the federal government has brought to enforcing official policies (the reformist demand for allotment, the progressive demand for determination of competency, the assimilationist demand for termination).

This history suggests that policy, whether official or applied, has had little relation to the interests of Indian people, except that which Indian people themselves have created. Policymakers and their operatives were so blind to Indian concerns that they failed to notice the adaptations taking place in clear view. They acted as if Indian people were inherently backward even as the Indian people worked, in effect, toward meeting the stated objectives of policy.

The Siletz people and their ancestors constantly demonstrated their realistic willingness and their ability to adapt to the white world. That willingness was always the most fundamental demand of ostensible policy. But it didn't save their homes on the Rogue River, or Yaquina Bay, or the Alsea Reservation.

Even when there was some congruence between policy as made and policy as applied, and when the Indian people appeared to agree with the policy, as in the cases of allotment and termination, the people who applied the policy worked with abstractions that did not take local needs and conditions into account.

Restoration of federal recognition and a land base constitute the one clearly positive accomplishment of the government in this history, but it was not the same accomplishment for the Siletz people that it was for the men who put it through Congress. For the Siletz people, it was a matter of community survival. For Mark Hatfield and Les AuCoin, it was a matter of getting federal funds for Oregon and resolving the fishing problem.

This conflict of motivations is a thread running through the history of the Siletz peoples and their ancestors since the beginning of intense contact in the middle of the nineteenth century. They struggled for survival and, in better times, for improved living conditions. They had some success.

With only a few exceptions, however, those responsible for the government's side of its dominating relationship with the Siletz people—the agents, superintendents, politicians, and makers of policy—were too occupied with their own ambitions and their own ideals to take much note of what Indian people thought, wanted, or worked for.

Like Ben Simpson encountering his former servant See-nee-nis Baker on the streets of Portland, even when they were looking at the Indian people, they didn't really see them.

Notes

Preface

1. This interpretation supports the argument of historian Frederick E. Hoxie in *A Final Promise* that the optimism that motivated supporters of the Dawes Act soon turned sour. Indians came to be popularly understood as a vanishing aspect of the past. Intellectuals questioned whether they could ever be successfully assimilated. Makers of policy accepted partial Indian accommodation to non-Indian society as a more reasonable goal. The federal government rushed to integrate Indian resources into the American economy by opening them to white farmers and businesses, and Indians who could not swim in the economic mainstream were left to drown for the sake of progress. See Frederick E. Hoxie, *A Final Promise: The Campaign to Assimilate the Indians, 1880–1920*, 145, 187.

2. Probably the most eminent and influential of the works focused on the making of policy is Francis Paul Prucha's indispensable two-volume study *The Great Father: The United States Government and the American Indians*. Nowhere in this work of more than 1,200 pages is the Coast Reservation, the Alsea

Reservation, or the Siletz Reservation mentioned. Frederick E. Hoxie noted in a 1984 bibliographical essay that anthropologists, social historians, and tribal historians had recently shown that federal policy was only one aspect of relations between Indians and non-Indians, but he argued that their works had tended nonetheless to be built on a perceptual framework that implicitly accepted the role of government action as the underlying determinant. Moreover, of the six case studies he mentioned, only two provided a comprehensive account of the impact of policy on tribal cultures. See Frederick E. Hoxie, "Indian-White Relations: 1790–1900," in W. R. Swagerty, ed., *Scholars and the Indian Experience*, 106–107, 112.

1. Original Inhabitants

1. Stephen Dow Beckham has identified Tipsu Tyee as a Shasta as well, but his tribal background seems difficult to determine (Stephen Dow Beckham, *Requiem for a People: The Rogue Indians and the Frontiersmen*, 74).

2. Dennis J. Gray, *The Takelma and Their Athapascan Neighbors: A New Ethnographic Synthesis for the Upper Rogue River Area of Southwestern Oregon*, University of Oregon Anthropological Papers, no. 37 (1987), 40, 58.

3. James A. Cardwell, "Emigrant Company," ms. P-A 15, Bancroft Library, Qniversity of California at Berkeley, quoted in Beckham, *Requiem*, 74.

4. Gray, *Takelma*, 34–35.

5. Philip Drucker found that ethnographic informants gave varying descriptions of the significance of slavery on the coast and hypothesized that "few slaves were held at one time, and most of these for debt." See Philip Drucker, "The Tolowa and Their Southwest Oregon Kin," *University of California Publications in American Archeology and Ethnology* 36 (1943): 274.

6. Catharine Holt, "Shasta Ethnography," in *University of California Publications in Anthropological Records* 3, No. 4: 313.

7. Joseph Lane "Autobiography." Ms. P-A 43, Bancroft Library, University of California at Berkeley, 91.

8. Kearny to Hooker, 20 June 1851, in War Department. Records of the Office of the Secretary of War, RG 393, Box 3, National Archives.

9. Holt, "Shasta," 313–14. When Shastas went out as warriors in their traditional way they wore armor made from sticks or elk hide. The elk-hide armor was shaped from a whole hide by wetting it down and stretching it over a large basketry platter, where it dried into a hard covering arranged to leave the right

arm free. (Holt, 313.) Their neighbors to the north, the Takelmas and the Latgawas, tied their hair back when going into combat, painted their faces white, and put on decorated elkskin armor and elkskin helmets. Their main weapon was the bow. (Gray, "Takelma," 34–35.)

10. Joel Palmer, *Journal of Travels over the Rocky Mountains*, 102–3.

11. Gray, *Takelma*, 2.

12. This description of southwestern Oregon geography is based on personal observations and an ordinary road map. See Oregon, State Highway Division, "Official Highway Map of Oregon," 1985.

13. William G. Loy, ed., *Atlas of Oregon*, 6.

14. Loy, *Atlas*, 144–46.

15. J. Owen Dorsey, "The Gentile System of the Siletz Tribes," *Journal of American Folk-Lore* 3 (January–March 1890): 232. Dorsey described this collective term as "destitute of any sociologic meaning."

16. John R. Swanton, *Indian Tribes of North America*, 456–57.

17. Swanton, *Indian Tribes*, 472–73.

18. Swanton, *Indian Tribes*, 455–56.

19. Swanton, *Indian Tribes*, 463.

20. Robert T. Boyd, "Demographic History, 1774–1874," in Wayne Suttles, ed., *Handbook of North American Indians*, 7:136. As a result of the work of demographer Henry F. Dobyns and others, all older estimates of Indian populations before contact are now in question. See Russell Thornton, *American Indian Holocaust and Survival*.

21. Swanton, *Indian Tribes*, 459.

22. Swanton, *Indian Tribes*, 470, 474.

23. Stephen Dow Beckham, *Land of the Umpqua: A History of Douglas County, Oregon*, 35–36.

24. Swanton, *Indian Tribes*, 468, 514.

25. See Betty L. Hall, "Faces of the Shasta People: Who We Were and Who We Are, the Shasta Nation," in Nan Hannon and Richard K. Olmo, eds., *Living With the Land: The Indians of Southwest Oregon*, 138–39.

26. Steele to Office of Indian Affairs, 27 May 1873, in United States, Office of Indian Affairs, *Letters Received by the Office of Indian Affairs, 1851–1880*, National Archives Microcopy (hereafter NAM) 234, Roll 617, 1–2, 4; George Minot, ed., *Statutes at Large and Treaties of the United States of America*, (1855), 10: 1018–21, 1119–21.

27. Holt, "Shasta," 301, 317.

28. Dennis J. Gray has found evidence of a third subdivision of the Takelmas living in the upper Rogue River country whom he calls the Northern Takelmas (Gray, *Takelma*, 24–25).

29. Swanton, *Indian Tribes*, 514; Jeff LaLande, "The Indians of Southwestern Oregon: An Ethnohistorical Review," 107. Nonetheless, modern Shastas claim a leader of the Umpquas was the father-in-law of the Rogue River valley leader Apserkahar, whom they identify as a Shasta. See Hall, "Faces," 137.

30. Swanton, *Indian Tribes*, 469–70.

31. Boyd, "Demographic History," 135.

32. Leslie M. Scott "Indian Diseases as Aids to Pacific Northwest Settlement," *Oregon Historical Quarterly* 26 (June 1925): 144, 161.

33. Boyd, "Demographic History," 146–47.

34. Parrish blamed "their mode of treatment" for what he perceived as the destructiveness of the epidemics, saying, "They also, like all the other tribes along the coast and in the interior, practice sweating in houses built expressly for that purpose, and invariably when they sweat themselves by this process they immediately plunge into cold water and in consequence of treating smallpox and measles in this manner it proved fatal to most of them, so that many of their once populous villages are now left without a representative" (Parrish to Palmer, 10 July 1854, in United States, Senate, *Letter from the Secretary of the Interior*, 53rd Cong., 1st sess., 1893, S. Ex. Doc. 25, Serial 3144, 31).

35. Gray, *Takelma*, 57.

36. Gray, *Takelma*, 39.

37. Gray, *Takelma*, 64, 56, 37.

38. Sam Van Pelt, "Before the White Man: An Indian's Story," *Oregonian* (Sunday magazine), 5 February 1939, 8.

39. Gray, *Takelma*, 36–37.

40. Drucker, "Tolowa," 271–80.

41. Drucker, "Tolowa," 272, 279; Gray, *Takelma*, 37, 55.

42. Philip Drucker, *Cultures of the North Pacific Coast*, 85.

43. Holt, "Shasta," 316.

44. Gray, *Takelma*, 30–31; Van Pelt, "Before the White Man."

45. Drucker, "Tolowa," 232–33; Van Pelt, "Before the White Man."

46. Van Pelt, "Before the White Man."

47. Drucker, "Tolowa," 232–33.

48. Holt, "Shasta," 314–15.

49. Gray, *Takelma*, 53, 36; Holt, "Shasta," 315. This game is often called "shinny," the name of an Irish version of field hockey. Lower Rogue River men are said to have used the terminology of the game as a code while on sea-borne hunting expeditions to avoid using direct language that might draw unwanted spirit attention. (Drucker, "Tolowa," 277).

50. J. Owen Dorsey, "Indians of Siletz Reservation, Oregon," *American Anthropologist* 2 (January 1889): 56–57.

51. Holt, "Shasta," 313–14.

52. Holt, "Shasta," 320; Gray, *Takelma*, 41, 59.

53. Gray, *Takelma*, 60, 44; Drucker, "Tolowa," 258.

54. Gray, *Takelma*, 60, 44–45.

55. Dorsey, "Indians," 58–60.

56. Van Pelt, "Before the White Man." The elder Van Pelt was not, it appears, always as forthcoming with his Chetco relatives as his son's account implies. Alexander W. Chase of the U.S. Coast and Geodetic Survey noted after an 1873 visit that "T. Van Pelt, an American married or living with an Indian woman at the mouth of the Chetco, once found on an old grave a very perfect spear head of obsidian." Knowing they would not have even touched the spear-head had they known it had come from a grave, Van Pelt "informed the Chetko Tribe that he had procured the implement from the far North," and they paid almost fifty dollars (almost $1,000 in 1990s dollars) to buy it from him. (Alexander W. Chase, "Shell Mounds of Lat. 42° 02', 42° 05', & " 42° 15', Coast of Oregon; Description of Stone and Other Implements Found in Them, with Some Notes on Existing Tribes of That Section of the Coast," Bureau of American Ethnology Manuscript 3230, National Anthropological Archives, Smithsonian Institution, Washington, D.C., 81; quoted in R. Lee Lyman, "Alexander W. Chase and the 19th Century Archeology and Ethnography of the Southern Oregon and Northern California Coast," tms., University of Missouri-Columbia Anthropology Department, undated, 38–39.)

57. Van Pelt, "Before the White Man."

2. Expeditions

1. Nathan Douthit, "The Hudson's Bay Company and the Indians of Southern Oregon," *Oregon Historical Quarterly* 93 (Summer 1992): 48.

2. Douthit, "Hudson's Bay Company," 48–49.

3. Applegate to Dart, 19 August 1851, in NAM 234, Roll 607.

4. Douthit, "Hudson's Bay Company," 48–49.

5. T. C. Elliott, ed., "The Oregon Coast As Seen by Vancouver in 1792," *Oregon Historical Quarterly* 30 (March 1929): 35–38.

6. Douthit, "Hudson's Bay Company," 34.

7. Robert T. Boyd, "Demographic History, 1774–1874," in Wayne Suttles, ed., *Handbook of North American Indians*, 7: 146–47.

8. K. G. Davies, ed., *Peter Skene Ogden's Snake Country Journal, 1826–27*, 76–77, 79, 82; quoted in Douthit, "Hudson's Bay Company," 28–29.

9. Douthit, "Hudson's Bay Company," 31.

10. See Gray, *Takelma*, 30–35, 48–51; Catharine Holt, "Shasta Ethnography," *University of California Publications in Anthropological Records*, Vol. 3, No. 4: 308–12.

11. Douthit, "Hudson's Bay Company," 29–31.

12. Gray, *Takelma*, 35; Douthit, "Hudson's Bay Company," 29.

13. Boyd, "Demographic History," 146–47.

14. Douthit, "Hudson's Bay Company," 28, 45–47, 49.

15. Douthit, "Hudson's Bay Company," 49.

16. Douthit, "Hudson's Bay Company," 47–48.

17. Douthit, "Hudson's Bay Company," 49.

18. Charles Henry Carey, historical note for W. Lansford Hastings, *Emigrants' Guide to Oregon and California*, x–xi; Hastings, 65.

19. Overton Johnson and William H. Winter, "Route Across the Rocky Mountains with Description of Oregon and California, Etc., 1843," *Quarterly of the Oregon Historical Society* 7 (June 1906): 163, 205. (Johnson and Winter took part in the 1843 overland emigration to Oregon but did not travel from Oregon to California until 1844.)

20. Johnson and Winter, "Route Across," 170.

21. Hubert Howe Bancroft (Frances Fuller Victor), *The Works of Hubert Howe Bancroft*, Vol. 30: 42–43. Bancroft was the editor of the histories of Oregon published under his name, while Victor was the actual author. See Hazel Emery Mills, "The Emergence of Frances Fuller Victor—Historian," *Oregon Historical Quarterly* 62 (December 1961): 309–36, and Henry L. Oak, *"Literary Industries" in a New Light*, 37–38.

22. Cyrenius Mulkey, "Eighty-One Years of Frontier Life," Ms. 981, Oregon Historical Society, Portland, 13–17.

23. Mulkey, perhaps improving somewhat on the reality of his youth, painted a colorful picture of these pursuers. He claimed that they were carrying flags made from fabric taken from a Hudson's Bay Company schooner that had been wrecked recently at the mouth of the Rogue River. "Each Indian had a flag of five or six yards on a pole about ten feet long, and they were running just fast enough to straighten the flags to full size." See Mulkey, "Eighty-One Years," 33–34.

24. Joseph Lane, "Autobiography," Ms. P-A 43, Bancroft Library, University of California at Berkeley, 89.

25. James E. Hendrickson, *Joe Lane of Oregon: Machine Politics and the Sectional Crisis, 1849–1861*, 1–2.

26. *Oregon Statesman* (Salem), 27 September 1853.

27. Charles H. Carey, *History of Oregon*, 142, 95.

28. Bancroft, 30:97.

29. Hendrickson, *Joe Lane*, 20.

30. Bancroft, 30:97, 99.

31. Lane, "Autobiography," 89.

32. Howard McKinley Corning, *Dictionary of Oregon History*, 36.

33. Lane, "Autobiography," 89.

34. This was the name later recorded for him in the ratified treaty of 1853, with the translation added to the signatures on an 1854 amendment. See George Minot, ed., *Statutes at Large and Treaties of the United States of America*, (1855), 10:1020–21. He was a Takelma or Latgawa if the conventional division of groups or correct. See William G. Loy, ed., *Atlas of Oregon*, 607. A modern Shasta account lists Apserkahar as the son of the "chief of all the Shastas," whose name is given as "Look Up Into the Sky" or "Sky," and also as "John." See Betty L. Hall, "Faces of the Shasta People: Who We Were and Who We Are," 137.

35. Lane, "Autobiography," 91.

36. Lane, "Autobiography," 92.

37. See Skinner to Dart, 6 August 1852, in United States, House, *Message from the President of the United States*, 32nd Cong., 2nd sess., 1852, H. Ex. Doc. 1, Serial 673, 454.

Double translations were necessary three years later when Lane held further talks with Rogue River leaders. See James W. Nesmith, "A Reminiscence of the Indian War, 1853," *Quarterly of the Oregon Historical Society* 7 (June 1906): 217–18.

38. Lane, "Autobiography," 93–94.

39. Cyrenius Mulkey said that when he got to the California mining country, Indians there had discovered that gold was valuable and had been successful in finding it so that they could use it in trade. Mulkey said he made between $600 and $700 in a few days, that is, as much as $14,000 in current dollars, trading blankets and salt with Indians for gold. See Mulkey, "Eighty-One Years," 27–28.

40. Lane, "Autobiography," 95–96.

41. Howard C. Brooks and Len Ramp, *Gold and Silver in Oregon*, 167.

42. Thomas Smith, "Rogue River Indian Wars of 1853 and 1856," ms., Bancroft Library, University of California at Berkeley, 3–4.

43. Smith, "Rogue River," 6–7.

44. Smith, "Rogue River," 53.

45. Bancroft, 30:154; Corning, *Dictionary*, 39.

46. *Oregon Statesman* (Oregon City), 20 June 1851.

47. *Oregon Statesman*, 20 June 1851.

48. *Oregon Statesman*, 20 June 1851.

49. Bancroft, 30:223.

50. *Alta California* (San Francisco), 3 July 1851.

51. Bancroft, 30:192–93.

52. Corning, *Dictionary*, 250.

53. J. M. Kirkpatrick, *Heroes of Battle Rock, or the Miners' Reward*, ed. Orvil Dodge, 24.

54. *Oregon Statesman*, 15 July 1851.

55. See Kirkpatrick, *Heroes*, 15.

56. *Oregon Statesman*, 15 July 1851.

57. Gaines to Lea, 18 November 1850, in United States, Office of Indian Affairs, *Letters Received by the Office of Indian Affairs, 1824–81*, NAM 234, Roll 607.

58. *San Francisco Chronicle*, 18 May 1873.

59. Kirkpatrick, "Heroes," 33–34.

60. Kirkpatrick, "Heroes," 34–35.

61. *Oregon Statesman*, 4 July 1851.

62. Allen Johnson and Dumas Malone, eds., *Dictionary of American Biography*, 5:271–72.

63. Kearny to Hooker, 20 June 1851, in United States, War Department, Records of the Office of the Secretary of War, RG 393, Box 3, National Archives.

64. *Oregon Statesman*, 22 July 1851.

65. Dart to Spalding, 1 March 1851, NAM 234, Roll 607.

66. Dart to Lea, 22 July 1851, NAM 234, Roll 607.

67. Gaines to Dart. 8 July 1851, NAM 234, Roll 607.

68. Corning, *Dictionary*, 225.

69. Minot, *Statutes*, 1020–21.

70. Skinner to Dart, 25 November 1851, in United States, House, *Message from the President of the United States*, 32nd Cong., 2nd sess., 1852, H. Ex. Doc. 1, Serial 673, 452–53.

71. Kirkpatrick, *Heroes*, 15.

72. *Alta California*, 1 August 1851.

73. Bancroft, 30:231–32.

74. *Oregon Statesman*, 16 September 1851.

75. *Alta California*, 26 August 1851; Lorin L. Williams, "First Settlements in Southwestern Oregon. T'Vault's Expedition," Ms. P-A 77, Bancroft Library, University of California at Berkeley.

76. Williams, "First Settlements."

77. *Alta California*, 18 September 1851.

78. "Treaty . . . between Anson Dart . . . and the Chiefs and Headmen of the . . . Yo-yo-tan, You-quee-chee, and Qua-ton-wah," 20 September 1851, in United States, Senate, *Letter from the Secretary of the Interior*, 53rd Cong., 1st sess., 1893, S. Ex. Doc. 25, Serial 3144, 4–6.

79. "Treaty . . . between Anson Dart . . . [and] the Undersigned Chiefs and Headmen of the 'Ya-su-chah' Band of Indians . . . ," 20 September 1851, in Senate, *Letter*, 1893, Serial 3144, 6–7.

80. Hitchcock to Conrad, 25 October 1851, in United States, House, *Message from the President of the United States*, 32nd Cong., 1st sess., 1851, H. Ex. Doc. 2, Serial 634, 148–50.

81. *Oregon Statesman*, 20 December 1851.

82. *Oregon Statesman*, 30 December 1851.

83. *Alta California*, 14 December 1851, quoted in Beckham, *Requiem*, 67.

3. Invasion in Force

1. Kevin Starr, *Americans and the California Dream, 1850–1915*, 50–51. The population of this westward extension of young America was atypical at least in that it was predominantly masculine; during the typical month of May 1850, the emigrants registering at Fort Laramie (who were going to Oregon and Utah as well as the California goldfields) included 30,062 men and 8,344 women.

The invaders of the gold rush years were also far thicker on the ground than were previous emigrants. Only about 2,735 overland emigrants went to California in the years 1840 through 1848. Then in only two years, 1849 and 1850, some 89,000 emigrants went overland to California. See John D. Unruh, Jr., *The Plains Across: The Overland Emigrants and the Trans-Mississippi West, 1840–60*, 122, 119–20.

2. McKee to Bigler, 5 April 1852, in United States, Senate, *Report of the Secretary of the Interior*, 32nd Cong., spec. sess., 1853, S. Ex. Doc. 4, Serial 688, 311.

3. McKee to Bigler, 12 April 1852, in Senate, *Report*, 316–17.

4. Bigler to McKee, 15 April 1852, in Senate, *Report*, 319.

5. See Edward D. Castillo, "Impact of Euro-American Exploration and Settlement," in Robert F. Heizer, ed., *Handbook of American Indians: California*, 8:107–108; and Albert O. Hurtado, *Indian Survival on the California Frontier*, 132–34.

6. Bancroft, 30:186; Beckham, *Requiem*, 73; Howard C. Brooks and Len Ramp, *Gold and Silver in Oregon*, 167.

7. Skinner to Dart, 26 July 1852, in United States, House, *Message from the President of the United States*, 32nd Cong., 2nd sess., 1852, H. Ex. Doc. No. 1, Serial 673, 455. For another account see Steele to Office of Indian Affairs, 27 May 1873, in United States, *Letters Received by the Office of Indian Affairs, 1824–81*, NAM 234X, Roll 608, 5–13.

8. *Statesman*, 14 August 1852, quoted in Beckham, *Requiem*, 79, and in Terence O'Donnell, *An Arrow in the Earth: General Joel Palmer and the Indians of Oregon*, 141.

9. Johnson and Malone, eds., *Dictionary of American Biography*, 8:186–87.

10. Robert A. Trennert, Jr., *Alternative to Extinction: Federal Indian Policy and the Beginnings of the Reservation System, 1846–51*, 30–31.

11. Trennert, 50, 56, 59–60.

12. Trennert, 93, 129.

13. Manypenny to McClelland, 26 November 1853, in United States, House, *Message from the President of the United States*, 33rd Cong., 1st sess., 1853, H. Ex. Doc. 1, Serial 710, 256–57.

14. For a critical account of Eliot's enterprise, see Francis Jennings, *The Invasion of America: Indians, Colonialism, and the Cant of Conquest*, 230–53.

15. For an account of the California missions, see Castillo, "Impact of Euro-American Exploration and Settlement," in Robert F. Heizer, ed., *Handbook of American Indians: California*, 8:99–105.

16. Manypenny to McClelland, 26 November 1855, in United States, Senate, *Message from the President of the United States*, 34th Cong, 1st sess., 1855, S. Ex. Doc. 1, Serial 810, 338.

17. Palmer to Manypenny, 23 June 1853, in United States, Office of Indian Affairs, *Records of the Oregon Superintendency of Indian Affairs*, NAM 2, quoted in O'Donnell, 145–56.

18. *Oregon Statesman* (Oregon City), 30 April 1853.

19. *Oregon Statesman*, 4 June 1853.

20. Bancroft, 30:310.

21. Joseph Lane, "Autobiography," 63.

22. Daniel Ream, "Autobiographical Dictation," Ms. C-D 954, Bancroft Library, University of California at Berkeley, 115; Palmer to Mannypenny, 8 July 1853, in NAM 234, Roll 608; *Oregon Statesman*, 28 June 1853.

23. *Oregon Statesman*, 30 August 1853.

24. *Oregon Statesman*, 23 August 1853.

25. *Oregon Statesman*, 30 August 1853.

26. *Oregon Statesman*, 23 August 1853.

27. Alden to Adjutant General, 18 October 1853, in House, *Message*, 1853, 41–42.

28. *Oregon Statesman*, 30 August 1853, 23 August 1853.

29. Alden to Adjutant General, 18 October 1853, in House, *Message*, 1853, 42–43.

30. After the Rogue River valley people were removed to the Coast Reservation (later the Siletz Reservation), Klamaths were linked in reservation records with people identified as Chasta and Scoton or Shasta Scoton Indians. Ethnologist Cora Du Bois said in the 1930s that informants told her that "the term Klamath is used on the Siletz Reservation for Shasta Indians." See "Minutes of a Council held at Siletz Agency, Oregon, December 15, 1873" in United States, Senate, *Letter from the Acting Secretary of the Interior*, 43rd Cong., 1st sess., 1874, S. Mis. Doc. 65, Serial 1584, 4; United States, House, *Report of the Secretary of the Interior*, 44th Cong., 2nd sess., 1876, H. Ex. Doc. 1, Part 5, Serial 1749, 622; "Census Roll," 20 August 1877, NAM 234, Roll 756; Cora Du Bois, "The 1870 Ghost Dance," *University of California Publications in Anthropological Records* 3 (1946): 27.

31. *Oregon Statesman*, 11 October 1853.

32. George Minot, ed., *Statutes at Large and Treaties of the United States of America*, (1855) 10:1118–20.

33. *Oregon Statesman*, 11 October 1853.

34. *Oregon Statesman*, 27 September 1853.

35. James W. Nesmith, "A Reminiscence of the Indian War, 1853," *Quarterly of the Oregon Historical Society* 7 (1906): 217–18.

36. Browne to Denver, 17 November 1957, in United States, House, *Indian Affairs in the Territories of Oregon and Washington*, 35th Cong., 1st sess., 1858, H. Ex. Doc. 39, Serial 955, 27–28.

37. Minot, 1018–20.

38. Ambrose to Palmer, 20 October 1855, in United States, House, *Indian Hostilities*, 1856, Serial 858, 88–90.

The identity of John or Tecumtum is confirmed by his signing in November 1854 of amendments to the 1853 treaty. John or Tecumtum, translated as Elk Killer, was listed fourth among the signers after Apserkahar, Toquahear, and a man called Sambo. Another man named John signed one of the amendments— Hart-tish or Applegate John—but he seems to have been less important; his was the eighth name on a list of eleven, apparently arranged by rank. (Minot, 1021, 1120.)

Frances Fuller Victor said that Tecumtum, when he was considering surrender in 1856, identified his home as being on Deer Creek, presumably the creek by that name that rises in the hills between the Applegate and the Illinois and flows into the Illinois (Bancroft, 406). The conventional linguistic division given for southwestern Oregon would make him an Athapascan speaker on that basis. See William G. Loy, ed., *Atlas of Oregon*, 6–7. A modern Shasta account, however, claims Tecumtum as a Shasta and identifies him as one of the sons of Toquahear and the nephew of Apserkahar. See Betty L. Hall, "Faces of the Shasta People: Who We Were and Who We Are, the Shasta Nation," 137.

39. "Stipulations of a Treaty made and entered into at Table Rock . . . ," 10 September 1853, NAM 234, Roll 608.

40. *Oregon Statesman*, 27 September 1853.

41. *Oregon Statesman*, 11 October 1853.

42. *Oregon Statesman*, 24 August 1853.

43. Palmer to Manypenny, 8 October 1853, in House, *Message*, 1853.

44. *Statesman*, 18 October 1853; United States, House, *Message from the President of the United States*, 33rd Cong., 1st sess., 1853, H. Ex. Doc. 1, Serial 710, 122–23, quoted in Beckham, *Requiem*, 127.

45. Wool to Cooper, 14 March 1854, in United States, House, *Correspondence Between the Late Secretary of War and General Wool*, 35th Cong., 1st sess., 1858, H. Ex. Doc. 88, Serial 956, 13.

46. C. A. Spreen, "A History of Placer Gold Mining in Oregon, 1850–1870," M.A. thesis, University of Oregon, 1939, 11.

47. Smith to Palmer, 5 February 1854, in United States, House, *Message from the President of the United States*, 33rd Cong., 2nd sess., 1854, H. Ex. Doc. 1, Serial 777, 476.

48. Soap to Smith, 27 January 1854, in House, *Message*, 1854, 481.

49. Abbott to Smith, 28 January 1854, in House, *Message*, 1854, 481.

50. Smith to Palmer, 5 February 1854, in House, *Message*, 1854, 477–79.

51. Palmer to Manypenny, 11 September 1854, in United States, Senate, *Letter from the Secretary of the Interior*, 53rd Cong., 1st sess., 1893, S. Ex. Doc. 25, Serial 3144, 26–27.

52. Culver to Palmer, 20 July 1854, in United States, House, *Message*, 1854, 503–504.

53. Palmer to Manypenny, 11 September 1854, in Senate, *Letter*, 1893, Serial 3144, 24–26.

54. *History of Southern Oregon Comprising Jackson, Josephine, Douglas, Curry and Coos Counties*, 211.

55. Palmer to Manypenny, 11 September 1854, in Senate, *Letter*, 1893, Serial 3144, 25; Bonneycastle to Wool, 28 May 1854, in House, *Correspondence*, 78–81.

56. Ambrose to Palmer, 12 June 1854, NAM 234, Roll 608.

57. Bancroft, 30:406.

58. Ambrose to Palmer, 12 June 1854, NAM 234, Roll 608.

59. *Oregon Statesman*, 19 September 1854.

60. Deady to Nesmith, 2 November 1854, in Deady Letters, 1853–1854, Ms. 577, Oregon Historical Society, Portland.

61. Bancroft, 30:423.

4. Motivation for War

1. Palmer to Manypenny, 11 September 1854, in United States, Senate, *Letter from the Secretary of the Interior*, 53rd Cong., 1st sess., 1893, S. Ex. Doc. 25, Serial 3144, 27–28.

2. George Minot, ed., *Statutes at Large and Treaties of the United States of America*, (1855), 10:1020–21.

3. Minot, *Statutes*, 1119–21.

4. *Oregon Statesman* (Corvallis), 28 July 1855.

5. Terence O'Donnell, *An Arrow in the Earth: General Joel Palmer and the Indians of Oregon*, 184.

6. Minot, *Statutes*, 1122–24. Palmer's September 10, 1853, Rogue River treaty was signed by President Pierce on February 5. The November 15, 1854, Rogue River treaty was signed April 7. The November 18, 1854, treaty with the Chastas, Scotons, and Grave Creek Umpquas was signed April 10. See Minot, *Statutes*, 1018–21, 1119–24.

7. *Oregon Statesman*, 28 July 1855.

8. Minot, *Statutes*, 1120.

9. See Wright to Palmer, 19 November 1854, in Ms. AX57/1/7, Palmer Papers, University of Oregon Library.

10. Hitchcock to Cooper, 31 March 1853, in United States, House, *Indian Affairs on the Pacific*, 34th Cong., 3rd sess., 1857, H. Ex. Doc. 1, Serial 906, 78; Josiah L. Parrish, "Anecdotes of Intercourse with the Indians," Ms. P-A 59, Bancroft Library, University of California at Berkeley, 89.

11. Palmer to Manypenny, 16 March 1855, in Senate, *Letter*, 1893, Serial 3144, 33.

12. O'Donnell, 191–92.

13. In the winter of 1855, for example, Wright expressed concern over the killings of Indians in nearby coastal northern California and said that he had kept "the Exterminators" from attacking the Chetcos. See Wright to Palmer, 8 January 1855, and Wright to Palmer, 5 February 1855, in 1/8, Palmer Papers.

14. Wright to Palmer, 19 November 1854, in Senate, *Letter*, 1893, Serial 3144, 34.

15. Palmer to Manypenny, 11 September 1854, in Senate, *Letter*, 1893, Serial 3144, 27.

16. David Alan Johnson, *Founding the Far West: California, Oregon, and Nevada, 1840–1890*, 58–59.

17. *Oregon Statesman*, 21 November 1854.

18. Priscilla Knuth, "Oregon Know Nothing Pamphlet Illustrates Early Politics," *Oregon Historical Quarterly* 54 (March 1953): 52.

David Alan Johnson quoted Bush's statement in the *Statesman* for December 12, the day after the territorial house of representatives passed the viva voce law, that men of prominence and influence who had supported the "damning conspiracy" would all be exposed within six months and that they were "doomed men." Bush was correct, according to Johnson (Johnson, Founding, 60–61).

19. Stanley S. Spaid, "Joel Palmer and Indian Affairs in Oregon," Ph.D. thesis, University of Oregon, June 1950, 233–34; Knuth, 49. Palmer biographer Terence O'Donnell concluded that Palmer probably was a Know-Nothing. Palmer was a likely candidate for the nativist movement, O'Donnell said, because he probably felt threatened by the increasing population of Catholic foreigners in Indiana in the early 1840s. O'Donnell found significance in Palmer having left Indiana for Oregon in the same year the first Catholic church was opened in his vicinity. See O'Donnell, 187–89.

20. Miller, Taylor, Ambrose, and Jackson to Palmer, 30 September 1854, Palmer Papers, 1/6.

21. O'Donnell, 184.

22. Skinner to Dart, 26 July 1852, in United States, House, *Message from the President of the United States*, 32nd Cong., 2nd sess., 1852, H. Ex. Doc. No. 1, Serial 673, 455.

23. *Oregon Statesman*, 27 October 1855. This letter, signed Miner, was revealed as the work of Ambrose by A. G. Henry in a speech December 3, 1855. See A. G. Henry, *Speech of A. G. Henry of Yambill delivered before the citizens of Corvallis on the evening of Dec. 3rd, 1855, on the subject of the pending Rogue River War*, 4.

24. Miller, Taylor, Ambrose, and Jackson to Palmer, 30 September 1854, Palmer Papers, 1/6.

25. Ambrose to Palmer, 14 April 1855, in United States, Office of Indian Affairs, *Letters Received by the Office of Indian Affairs*, 1824–81, 234 NAM 234, Roll 608. "Bill" is identified as Konechequot, without a translation, in the November 18 "Treaty with the Chastas, &c." See Minot, 1122–24.

26. *Oregonian* (Portland), 23 June 1855.

27. *Oregon Statesman*, 7 July 1855.

28. United States, House, *Message from the President of the United States*, 34th Cong., 1st sess., 1856, H. Ex. Doc. 1, Serial 841, 171; United States, House, *Message from the President of the United States*, 34th Cong., 3rd sess., 1857, H. Ex. Doc. 1, Serial 894, 260; United States, House, *Letter from the Secretary of War*, 34th Cong., 1st sess., 1856, H. Ex. Doc. 15, Serial 851, 7; United States, House, *Letter from the Secretary of War*, 34th Cong., 3rd sess., 1857, H. Ex. Doc. 23, Serial 897, 9; *History of Southern Oregon Comprising Jackson, Josephine, Douglas, Curry and Coos Counties*, 232.

29. Oregon Territory, *Journal of the Proceedings of the Council of the Legislative Assembly of Oregon Territory*, 9th sess., 1857, 15–18.

30. Bancroft, 30:324–25, 322.

31. Bancroft, 30:325.

32. "I, William Martin . . . ," 9 November 1853, NAM 234, Roll 608.

33. *Oregon Statesman*, 2 June 1855.

34. *Oregonian*, 30 June 1855.

35. *Oregon Statesman*, 21 July 1855.

36. See Drew to Stark, 11 November 1855, in B[enjamin] F. Dowell, "Oregon Indian Wars of 1855–6 in Southern Oregon, Volume 2," Ms. P-A 138, Bancroft Library, University of California at Berkeley.

37. *Oregon Statesman*, 13 October 1855.

38. *Oregonian*, 30 June 1855.

39. Bancroft, 30:358.

40. *Oregon Statesman*, 7 July 1855.

41. *Oregonian*, 30 June 1855.

42. *History of Southern Oregon*, 243.

43. Browne to Commissioner of Indian Affairs, 4 December 1857, NAM 234, Roll 611. The phrase used is in Chinook Jargon and would more properly be spelled "Polaklie Illahee."

44. *Oregon Statesman*, 18 August 1855.

45. *Oregon Statesman*, 25 August 1855.

46. *Oregon Statesman*, 15 September 1855.

47. *Oregonian*, 25 August 1855.

48. *Oregonian*, 8 September 1855.

49. *Oregonian*, 4 August 1855.

50. See chapter 3.

51. "Articles of Agreement," August and September, 1855, in Senate, *Letter*, 1893, Serial 3144, 8–15.

52. Rodney Glisan, *Journal of Army Life*, 244–45.

53. *Oregon Statesman*, 15 September 1855.

54. Glisan, *Journal*, 244–45.

55. "Articles of Agreement," August and September 1855, in Senate, *Letter*, 1893, Serial 3144, 8–15. Because of the war that was about to begin, the Indian Office would delay submitting the treaty with the coast tribes for ratification by the Senate, and when the war was over, by a later Indian Office account, the treaty was "accidentally overlooked." It would never be ratified. (Armstrong to Secretary of the Interior, 5 October 1893, in Senate, *Letter*, 1893, Serial 3144, 3.)

56. *Oregonian*, 13 October 1855.

57. Ambrose to Palmer, 30 September 1855, in United States, House, *Indian Hostilities*, 1856, Serial 858, 62–64.

58. United States, Senate, *Communication from C. S. Drew*, 36th Cong., 1st sess., 1860, S. Misc. Doc. 59, Serial 1038, 26–28.

59. Clifford E. Trafzer and Richard D. Scheuerman, *Renegade Tribe: The Palouse Indians and the Invasion of the Inland Pacific Northwest*, 62–64; Bancroft, 31:108–13; Kent D. Richards, *Isaac I. Stevens: Young Man in a Hurry*, 240–41.

60. See Trafzer and Scheuerman, Renegade, 46–47.

61. Trafzer and Scheuerman, *Renegade*, 46–59; Richards, *Isaac I. Stevens*, 215–25.

62. Trafzer and Scheuerman, *Renegade*, 33, 57–58, 65–66; Richards, *Isaac I. Stevens*, 221.

63. Richards, *Isaac I. Stevens*, 224, 235–36; Trafzer and Scheuerman, *Renegade*, 61–62.

64. United States, Senate, *Communication from C. S. Drew*, 36th Cong., 1st sess., 1860, S. Misc. Doc. 59, Serial 1038, 26–28.

65. Palmer to Manypenny, 9 October 1855, in House, *Indian Hostilities*, 1856, Serial 858, 59.

66. "Regulation for the Guidance of Agents," 13 October 1855, in House, *Indian Hostilities*, 1856, Serial 858, 72–73.

67. John Beeson, *A Plea for the Indians*, 47–52.

68. *Crescent City Herald* (Crescent City, Calif.), 12 October 1855 (extra), quoted in *National Intelligencer* (Washington), 14 November 1855.

69. Beeson, *Plea*, 53–54.

70. Senate, *Communication*, 28–29.

71. Beeson, *Plea*, 54–55.

72. Palmer to Manypenny, 20 October 1855, in House, *Indian Hostilities*, 1856, Serial 858, 75–76.

73. Ambrose to Palmer, 9 October 1855, in House, *Indian Hostilities*, 1856, Serial 858, 66–67; Ambrose to Palmer, 20 October 1855, in House, *Indian Hostilities*, 1856, Serial 858, 89.

74. Ambrose to Palmer, 9 October 1855, in House, *Indian Hostilities*, 1856, Serial 858, 67.

75. *Oregon Statesman*, 20 October 1855.

76. Bancroft, 30:207.

77. *Oregon Statesman*, 20 October 1855.

78. *Oregon Statesman*, 27 October 1855. This letter is identified as Ambrose's work both by its parallels with his October 9 report and by the statement of A. G. Henry, said to have been authorized by Ambrose, in a pro-war speech December 3, 1855. See A. G. Henry, *Speech of A. G. Henry*, 4.

79. *Oregonian*, 20 October 1855.

80. *Oregonian*, 20 October 1855.

5. The War Within a War

1. *Oregon Statesman* (Corvallis), 20 October 1855. The attack on the Waggoner or Wagoner farm may have been revenge for the burning and killings in 1854 at the mouth of the Chetco River. Joel Palmer had named a "J. Wagoner" as one of the men he wanted arrested for the Chetco affair (Palmer to Parrish, 15 May 1854, in United States, Office of Indian Affairs, *Letters Received by the Office of Indian Affairs*, 1824–1881, NAM 234, Roll 608). Frances Fuller Victor said that the man whose farm was burned, J. B. Wagoner (as she spelled his name), survived his wife and child and became an express rider for the volunteers (Bancroft, 30:379).

If the Wagoner farm was attacked for revenge, then in a certain sense the idea "prevalent among the white population that there is a combination among all the Indians," mentioned by George Ambrose in a report in September, was correct; at least there had been some discussion of mutual grievances that included not only people in the valley but also people on the coast. See Ambrose to Palmer, 30 September 1855, in United States, House, *Indian Hostilities*, 1856, Serial 858, 64.

2. George Riddle, *Early Days in Oregon*, 92; Holt, "Shasta Ethnography," 313–14. Using women as go-betweens and appearing for negotiations prepared for combat were described by Holt in a Shasta context, but customs of warfare and diplomacy were similar throughout the region.

3. Riddle, *Early Days*, 93–94.

4. Bancroft, 30:377–78.

5. Bancroft, 30:379.

6. See *Oregon Statesman*, 24 December 1855.

7. *Oregon Statesman*, 20 October 1855.

8. "General Order No. 10," 20 October 1855, in United States, House, *Indian Affairs on the Pacific*, 34th Cong., 3rd sess., 1856, H. Ex. Doc. No. 76, Serial 906, 156–57.

9. Ambrose to Palmer, 4 November 1855, in House, *Indian Hostilities*, 1856, Serial 858, 93.

10. *Oregon Statesman*, 3 November 1855.

11. Palmer to Manypenny, 25 October 1855, in House, *Indian Hostilities*, 1856, Serial 858, 84–85, 87.

12. Dunbar to Palmer, 19 November 1854, in United States, Senate, *Letter from the Secretary of the Interior*, 53rd Cong., 1st sess., 1893, S. Ex. Doc. 25, Serial 3144, 42.

13. Bancroft, 30:392–93.

14. Dunbar to Palmer, 19 November 1854, in Senate, *Letter*, 1893, Serial 3144, 42.

15. Harvey Robbins, "Journal of the Rogue River War," *Oregon Historical Quarterly* 34 (December 1933): 346–47.

16. Bancroft, 31:118–24; Kent D. Richards, *Isaac I. Stevens*, 256–57.

17. Robbins, "Journal," 345–47.

18. Mulkey, "Eighty-One Years," 65.

19. Robbins, "Journal," 347–48.

20. Ambrose to Palmer, 4 November 1855, in House, *Indian Hostilities*, 1856, Serial 858, 93–94.

21. Robbins, "Journal," 348–49.

22. Bancroft, 30, 382–84.

23. *Oregon Statesman*, 24 November 1855.

24. Mulkey, "Eighty-One Years," 66–67.

25. *Oregon Statesman*, 24 November 1855.

26. Mulkey, "Eighty-One Years," 68–69; O'Donnell, 228.

27. Mulkey, "Eighty-One Years," 71.

28. *Oregon Statesman*, 24 November 1855.

29. Palmer to Wool, 1 November 1855, in House, *Indian Hostilities*, 1856, Serial 858, 112–13.

30. Johnson and Malone, eds., *Dictionary of American Biography*, 513–14; Prucha, 1:239–40.

31. *Oregon Statesman*, 3 November 1855, 17 November 1855. Terence O'Donnell speculated that the mention of Know Nothings was a reference to Palmer's long-time friend and frequent employee Cris Taylor (O'Donnell, 57–58, 223).

32. Joel Palmer later reported that Bruce had taken part in the Lupton expedition. (Palmer to Commissioner, 27 April 1856, in NAM 234, Roll 609.) A man

by named Bruce was reported to have commanded eleven men in the October 8 attack (*Crescent City* [Calif.] *Herald*, 12 October 1855, quoted in *National Intelligencer* [Washington], 14 November 1855).

33. *Oregon Statesman*, 24 November 1855.

34. *Oregon Statesman*, 21 November 1854.

35. *Oregon Statesman*, 24 November 1855.

36. Robbins, "Journal," 349–52.

37. *Oregon Statesman*, 24 November 1855.

38. Bancroft, 30:386.

39. Robbins, "Journal," 352–54.

40. *Oregon Statesman* (Salem), 8 April 1856.

41. Bancroft, 30:386–87.

42. *Oregon Statesman* (Corvallis), 8 December 1855.

43. Ambrose to Palmer, 2 December 1855, in House, *Indian Hostilities*, 1856, Serial 858, 120.

44. Henry, *Speech of A. G. Henry*, 7–8.

45. *Oregon Statesman*, 8 December 1855.

46. Robbins, "Journal," 355.

47. Bancroft, 30:387.

48. *Crescent City Herald*, 12 October 1855, quoted in *National Intelligencer*, 14 November 1855.

49. *Alta California* (San Francisco), 19 September 1854.

50. Robbins, "Journal," 355–57.

51. Bancroft, 30:389.

52. Trafzer and Scheuerman, *Renegade*, 67–69.

53. *Oregon Statesman* (Salem), 15 January 1856.

54. *Oregon Statesman*, 27 May 1856.

55. *Oregon Statesman*, 27 May 1856.

56. *Oregon Statesman*, 26 February 1856.

57. *Oregon Statesman*, 15 January 1856, 23 August 1853.

58. *Oregon Statesman*, 15 January 1856.

59. Smith et al. to Pierce, 8 January 1856, in House, *Indian Hostilities*, 1856, Serial 858, 134.

60. Palmer to Manypenny, 22 January 1856, in House, *Indian Hostilities*, 1856, Serial 858, 132.

61. *Oregon Statesman*, 5 February 1856.

62. Richards, *Isaac I. Stevens*, 260; Bancroft, 31:125–33.

63. Dennison and Smith to the President, 30 January 1856, in United States, House, *Indian Hostilities in Oregon and Washington Territories*, 34th Cong., 1st sess., 1856, H. Ex. Doc. 118, Serial 859, 31–32.

64. *Oregon Statesman* (Corvallis), 8 December 1855.

65. Bancroft, 30:390.

66. *Oregon Statesman* (Salem), 5 February 1856.

67. *Oregonian* (Portland), 13 December 1885.

68. *Oregon Statesman*, 19 February 1856.

69. *Oregonian*, 2 February 1856.

6. Undefeated

1. Palmer to Manypenny, 8 March 1856, in United States, Senate, *Letter from the Secretary of the Interior*, 53rd Cong., 1st sess., 1893, S. Ex. Doc. 25, Serial 3144, 45–46.

2. Palmer to Manypenny, 25 October 1855, in United States, House, *Indian Hostilities*, 34th Cong., 1st sess., 1856, Serial 858, 84–85.

3. Reynolds was a West Point graduate who had fought in the battles of Monterey and Buena Vista during the Mexican War and would fight as a major-general of Union volunteers at Chancellorsville, Fredericksburg, and Gettysburg during the Civil War. He would be killed by a sniper during the battle at Gettysburg. (Johnson and Malone, eds., *Dictionary of American Biography*, 8:520.)

4. Palmer to Manypenny, 8 March 1856, in Senate, *Letter*, 1893, Serial 3144, 44–45.

5. Dunbar to Palmer, 24 February 1856, in Senate, *Letter*, 1893, Serial 3144, 46.

6. Cora A. Du Bois, "General Ethnographic Notes on the Tututni (Rogue River) Indians," Ethnological Documents, Museum of Anthropology Archives, CU-23-1, Item 6, Bancroft Library, University of California at Berkeley.

7. Palmer to Manypenny, 8 March 1856, in Senate, *Letter*, 1893, Serial 3144, 45. Concerning Wright and the Modocs, see Hitchcock to Cooper, 31 March 1853, in United States, House, *Indian Affairs on the Pacific*, 34th Cong., 3rd sess., 1857, H. Ex. Doc. 1, Serial 906, 78.

Palmer biographer Terence O'Donnell maintained that Wright was not hostile toward Indians after he became subagent, "but, indeed, the reverse," and cited Charles S. Drew and Rodney Glisan as character witnesses. See O'Donnell, *Arrow in the Earth*, 181. Drew was using Palmer's approval of Wright as an argument against accusations that Wright had murdered the Modocs. His purpose was to justify payment of war claims. See United States, Senate, *Communication from C. S. Drew*, 36th Cong., 1st sess., 1860, S. Mis. Doc. 59, Serial 1038, 36–38.

Any statement by Drew on any subject should be viewed with suspicion. On the other hand, Glisan, an army doctor, seems to have been a good observer and had no known reason to misrepresent Wright. See Glisan, *Journal of Army Life*.

The most convincing evidence apart from the obvious hostility toward Wright of the people who killed him, however, has already been described, and it was provided by Wright himself in 1854 when he defended the character of the man Joel Palmer held most responsible for killing and burning out the Chetcos and in 1855 when he gave the Coquilles over to the dubious mercy of a man who had been on his way to attack the them.

8. Bancroft (Victor), *Works of Hubert Howe Bancroft*, 30:393–94.

9. A[lexander] W. Chase, "Siletz, or 'Lo' Reconstructed," *Overland Monthly* 2 (May 1869): 431–32, quoted in Lyman, "Alexander W. Chase," 11.

10. *Oregon Statesman* (Salem), 18 March 1856.

11. Richard, *Isaac I. Stevens*, 263, 265; Bancroft, 31:163–65, 170–71.

12. *Oregon Statesman*, 11 March 1856.

13. Palmer to Manypenny, 8 March 1856, in Senate, *Letter*, 1893, Serial 3144, 45.

14. *Oregon Statesman*, 13 March 1856. Buchanan had taken part in the initial battles of the Mexican War. During the Civil War he became a brigadier general of volunteers in 1862 and commanded a brigade in the battles of Antietam and Fredericksburg; his commission expired after four months and was not renewed, however, and he was made a garrison commander. Near the end of the war he was given the temporary rank of major general. He was later involved in Reconstruction in Louisiana. (Johnson and Malone, *Dictionary*, 2, 217–18.)

15. Beckham, *Requiem*, 179. Ord had fought Seminoles in Florida and would later take part in the expedition against John Brown at Harper's Ferry, Virginia. Ord became a major general of volunteers during the Civil War. (Johnson and Malone, *Dictionary*, 7:48–49.)

16. [E. O. C. Ord], "Soldiering in Oregon," *Harper's New Monthly Magazine* 13 (August 1856): 522.

17. *Oregon Statesman*, 11 March 1856.

18. *Oregon Statesman*, 29 April 1856. Augur, a West Point graduate in the class that included Ulysses Grant, had been involved in the initial battles of the

Mexican War and was commandant of West Point before becoming a major general of Union volunteers during the Civil War. He was involved as a departmental commander from 1867 until 1885 in Reconstruction and the wars on the Plains. (Johnson and Malone, *Dictionary*, 1:427–28.)

19. [Ord], "Soldiering," 523.

20. Chase, "Shell Mounds of Lat. 42° 02', 42° 05', & 42° 15'," quoted in Lyman, 35.

21. [Ord], "Soldiering," 523.

22. *Oregon Statesman*, 29 April 1856.

23. *Oregon Statesman*, 1 April 1856. Waymire had already expressed similar sentiments in the debate in the legislature's Democratic caucus over asking President Pierce to dismiss Palmer. A defender of Palmer, George Brown, had argued that it was the policy of the government that was wrong, not the conduct of Palmer in carrying out that policy. Waymire responded that Palmer was accused of being a Know-Nothing and appointing Know-Nothings. See O'Donnell, 238–40.

24. *Oregon Statesman*, 27 May 1856.

25. *Oregon Statesman*, 8 April 1856.

26. Ord to Buchanan, 27 March 1856, in War Department, *Records of the Office of the Secretary of War*, NAM 689, Roll 567.

27. [Ord], "Soldiering," 526.

28. *Democratic Standard* (Portland), 16 May 1856.

29. *Oregon Statesman*, 27 May 1856.

30. *Oregon Statesman*, 8 April 1856.

31. *Oregon Statesman*, 8 April 1856.

32. *Oregon Statesman*, 27 May 1856.

33. *Democratic Standard*, 16 May 1856.

34. *Pittsburgh* [Pa.] *Gazette*, 1 April 1856.

35. *Oregon Statesman*, 27 May 1856.

36. *Congressional Globe*, 34th Cong., 1st sess., 789, quoted Hendrickson, *Joe Lane*, 130.

37. *Oregon Statesman*, 15 April 1856.

38. *National Intelligencer* (Washington), 2 May 1856.

39. *Oregon Statesman*, 8 April 1856.

40. *Oregon Statesman*, 8 April 1856.

41. Bancroft, 30:402–3.

42. *Oregonian* (Portland), 26 April 1856.

43. *Statesman*, 15 April 1856. Terence O'Donnell suggested that "W" was Fred Waymire, a strident critic of Palmer within the Democratic leadership. See O'Donnell, 237, 238, 239–40, 242.

44. *Oregon Statesman*, 29 April 1856; Spaid, "Joel Palmer and Indian Affairs in Oregon." For a discussion of Henry's politics see *Oregon Statesman* (Corvallis), 8 December 1855.

45. Terence O'Donnell, for whom Palmer's apparent good character often seems sufficient evidence against any argument that Palmer was capable of crass behavior, implicitly denied that Palmer had surrounded himself with Know-Nothing employees by contending that he doubted Palmer would have either hired or rejected a man because he was a Know-Nothing. In addition, "it seems unlikely" to O'Donnell that Palmer was still a Know-Nothing by the spring of 1856. See O'Donnell, 266.

46. *Oregon Statesman*, 29 April 1856.

47. *Oregonian*, 24 May 1856.

48. Joel Palmer, "Joel Palmer Diary for 1856," tms., State Library, Salem, Oregon, 6. Lieutenant Sheridan would become a famous cavalry general during the Civil War, command armies in the Plains Indian Wars, and succeed William T. Sherman as commander-in-chief of the U.S. Army in 1884. See Johnson and Malone, *Dictionary*, 9:79–81.

49. *Oregonian*, 26 April 1856.

50. *Oregonian*, 26 April 1856.

7. The War Ends

1. *Oregon Sentinel* (Jacksonville), 17 May 1856.

2. *Oregonian* (Portland), 24 May 1856.

3. *Oregon Sentinel*, 17 May 1856.

4. *Oregonian*, 24 May 1856.

5. *Chicago Daily Tribune*, 26 April 1856.

6. *National Intelligencer* (Washington), 30 April 1856.

7. *National Intelligencer*, 2 May 1856.

8. *Oregonian*, 3 May 1856.

9. *National Intelligencer*, 13 May 1856.

10. *Oregonian*, 24 May 1856.

11. Buchanan to Jones, 22 May 1856, in United States, War Department, *Records of the Secretary of War*, NAM 689, Roll 567.

12. Joel Palmer, "Joel Palmer Diary for 1856," 7.

13. Buchanan to Jones, 22 May 1856, NAM 689, Roll 567.

14. Bancroft, 30:406.

15. See Minot, ed., *Statutes at Large and Treaties* (1855), 10:1124.

16. Rector to Dole, 24 May 1862, in United States, Office of Indian Affairs, *Letters Received by the Office of Indian Affairs, 1824–1881*, NAM 234, Roll 613.

17. "Sketch of the Battle of Big Bend" (initialed "E. O. C. O____"), undated, NAM 689, Roll 567.

18. Buchanan to Jones, 22 May 1856, NAM 689, Roll 567. Buchanan's statement that the people from Galice Creek and Applegate Creek were prepared to come in and Old John would then be left only with his own band supports the assertion that Old John was not Applegate John or Hartish but rather Tecumtum.

19. Smith to Chambers, 30 May 1856, NAM 689, Roll 567.

20. Buchanan to Jones, 30 May 1856, NAM 689, Roll 567.

21. Smith to Chambers, 30 May 1856, NAM 689, Roll 567.

22. Palmer to Manypenny, 3 July 1855, in United States, Senate, *Letters from the Secretary of the Interior*, 53rd Cong., 1st sess., 1893, S. Ex. Doc. 25, Serial 3144, 51.

23. Palmer, "Diary," 18.

24. Buchanan to Jones, 30 May 1856, NAM 689, Roll 567.

25. Palmer to Manypenny, 3 July 1856, in Senate, *Letter*, 1893, 51–52.

26. Smith to Chambers, 30 May 1856, NAM 689, Roll 567.

27. Buchanan to Jones, 30 May 1856, NAM 689, Roll 567.

28. Palmer, "Diary," 7, 18; *Oregon Statesman* (Salem), 24 June 1856.

29. Palmer, "Diary," 18.

30. Augur to Chandler, 30 May 1856, NAM 689, Roll 567.

31. Palmer, "Diary," 18.

32. *Oregon Statesman*, 17 June 1856; Buchanan to Jones, 30 May 1856, NAM 689, Roll 567; Rinearson to Palmer, 3 June 1856, in Ms. AX57/2/2, Palmer Papers, University of Oregon Library.

Terence O'Donnell, Palmer's biographer, doubted that Palmer took an active part in the battle and suggested that the author of the Orford letter, who may have been Palmer's friend R. W. Dunbar, "seeking to deflect criticism of Palmer, was at pains to tout his bravery, even though in this instance it had not been exercised." See O'Donnell, 271–72. That does not, however, explain Buchanan's official report or Rinearson's personal letter.

33. Buchanan to Jones, 30 May 1856, NAM 689, Roll 567.

34. *Democratic Standard* (Portland, Ore.), 3 July 1856.

35. *Oregon Statesman*, 17 June 1856.

36. See "Metsker's Map of Curry County, State of Oregon" (Tacoma, Wash.: Metsker Maps, undated).

37. *Oregon Statesman*, 24 July 1856.

38. The identity of the bands was confirmed by Latshaw when he claimed after the attack that the volunteers had almost captured Cholcultah and Lympe. See *Oregon Statesman*, 17 June 1856. It was also confirmed by reports and messages brought to Palmer. See Palmer, "Diary," 19. Cholcultah and Lympe told Palmer they had been kept by Tecumtum from coming in to surrender. (Palmer to Manypenny, 3 July 1856, in Senate, *Letter*, 1893, Serial 3144, 52.)

39. *Oregon Statesman*, 17 June 1856.

40. *Oregon Statesman*, 24 July 1856.

41. *Oregonian*, 21 June 1856.

42. Palmer to Manypenny, 3 July 1856, in Senate, *Letter*, 1893, Serial 3144, 52.

43. Palmer, "Diary," 9.

44. Palmer, "Diary," 19.

45. Palmer, "Diary," 9; Palmer to Manypenny, 3 July 1856, in Senate, *Letter*, 1893, Serial 3144, 52.

46. *Oregon Statesman*, 24 June 1856.

47. Palmer to Manypenny, 3 July 1856, in Senate, *Letter*, 1893, Serial 3144, 53.

48. Palmer to Manypenny, 3 July 1856, in Senate, *Letter*, 1893, Serial 3144, 53.

49. *Oregon Statesman*, 24 June 1856.

50. Palmer to Manypenny, 3 July 1856, in Senate, *Letter*, 1893, Serial 3144, 53–54; Palmer, "Diary," 11.

51. *Oregon Statesman*, 22 July 1856.

52. *Oregon Statesman*, 8 July 1856.

53. Palmer, "Diary," 11; Palmer to Manypenny, 3 July 1856, in Senate, *Letter*, 1893, Serial 3144, 54; *Oregonian*, 28 February 1857.

54. Palmer, "Diary," 11–12; Palmer to Manypenny, 3 July 1856, in Senate, *Letter*, 1893, Serial 3144, 49–50, 54.

55. *Oregon Statesman*, 8 July 1856; Palmer to Walker, 1 July 1856, NAM 234, Roll 610.

56. Palmer to Manypenny, 3 July 1856, in Senate, *Letter*, 1893, Serial 3144, 55.

57. Chandler to Palmer, 4 July 1856, in United States, Senate, *Message from the President of the United States*, 34th Cong., 3rd sess., 1856, S. Ex. Doc. 5, Serial 875, 774.

8. Unsatisfactory Results

1. Bancroft, 30:439–40.

2. Beckham, *Requiem*, 9.

3. Metcalfe to Nesmith, 15 July 1857, in United States, House, *Message from the President of the United States*, 35th Cong., 1st sess., 1857, H. Ex. Doc. 2, Serial 942, 645; Miller to Nesmith, 20 July 1857, in House, *Message*, 1857, Serial 942, 649.

4. Chandler to Palmer, 4 July 1856, in United States, Senate, *Message from the President of the United States*, 34th Cong., 3rd sess., 1856, S. Ex. Doc. 5, Serial 875, 774; *Oregon Statesman* (Salem), 15 July 1856.

5. Miller to Nesmith, 20 July 1857, in House, *Message*, 1857, 649–50.

6. Tichenor to Nesmith, 3 August 1857, in House, *Message*, 1857, 669–70.

7. Drew to Nesmith, 30 June 1858, in United States, Senate, *Message from the President of the United States*, 35th Cong., 1st sess., 1858, S. Ex. Doc. 1, Serial 974, 608.

8. Tichenor to Drew, 30 June 1858, in Senate, *Message*, 1858, 609–11.

9. Swanton, *Indian Tribes of North America*, 456.

10. Wallace Turner, "Trip with Medicine Man Up Rogue River to Agness," *Oregonian* (Portland), 5 January 1947, Sunday magazine, 3; Bancroft, 30:393.

11. Browne to Denver, 17 November 1857, in United States, House, *Indian Affairs in the Territories of Oregon and Washington*, 35th Cong., 1st sess., 1858, H. Ex. Doc. 39, Serial 955, 44–47.

12. Glisan, *Journal of Army Life*, 391–92.

13. "Letter of Colonel T. Morris, May 7, 1858," quoted in Oscar Winslow Hoop, "History of Fort Hoskins, 1856–65," *Oregon Historical Quarterly* 30 (December 1929): 357.

14. Glisan, *Journal*, 399.

15. *Oregonian*, 26 June 1858.

16. Glisan, *Journal*, 405.

17. United States, Office of Indian Affairs, *Report of the Commissioner of Indian Affairs for the Year 1862*, 255.

18. Royal A. Bensell, *All Quiet on the Yambill: The Civil War in Oregon*, ed. Gunther Barth, 21, 24. Bensell was a volunteer soldier from California whose company was sent to Oregon when regular troops were withdrawn from the forts around the reservation so they could be sent east for the Civil War. See Bensell, *All Quiet*, viii–ix.

19. *Oregonian*, 15 June 1864.

20. Browne to Commissioner of Indian Affairs, 4 December 1857, in United States, Office of Indian Affairs, *Letters Received by the Office of Indian Affairs, 1824–81*, NAM 234, Roll 611.

21. Bancroft, 31:119, 171–74; Richards, *Isaac I. Stevens*, 308–309, 311–12.

22. Richards, *Isaac I. Stevens*, 387.

23. Trafzer and Scheuerman, *Renegade*, 84–88, 93–95, 101.

24. *Oregon Statesman*, 1 July 1856.

25. *Oregon Statesman*, 1 July 1856.

26. Joel Palmer, "Joel Palmer Diary for 1856," tms., State Library, Salem, Oregon, 14.

27. "We, the undersigned, Joel Palmer . . . ," 20 September 1856, in NAM 234, Roll 609; Hedges to Manypenny, 7 November 1856, NAM 234, Roll 609.

28. *Oregonian*, 8 April 1870, quoted in Stanley S. Spaid, "The Later Life and Activities of General Joel Palmer," *Oregon Historical Quarterly* 55 (December 1954): 326–27.

29. Spaid, "Later Life," 328–29.

30. Hams to Parker, 14 January 1871, NAM 234, Roll 616; Meacham to Commissioner, 25 October 1871, in United States, House, *Report of the Secretary of the Interior*, 42nd Cong., 2nd sess., 1871, H. Ex. Doc. 1, Part 5, Serial 1505, 731.

31. *Richmond* [Va.] *Enquirer*, 30 May 1856.

32. Hendrickson, *Joe Lane*, 131.

33. Bancroft, 30:432, 440–41.

34. Hendrickson, *Joe Lane*, 226–30.

35. Bancroft, 30:30, 450–51. According to James E. Hendrickson, "Although there appears to be no good evidence that Lane ever countenanced the scheme,

it was natural for his political opponents to identify him with it." See Hendrickson, *Joe Lane*, 249.

36. United States, Census Bureau, *Historical Statistics of the United States from Colonial Times to 1957*, 689.

37. Bancroft, 30:433, 439–40.

38. *Oregonian*, 27 February 1861.

39. Bancroft, 30:455–56.

40. Hendrickson, *Joe Lane*, 257.

41. Smith, Ingalls, and Grover to Floyd, 10 October 1857, in United States, House, *Expenses of the Indian Wars in Washington and Oregon Territories*, 35th Cong., 1st sess., 1858, H. Ex. Doc. 45, Serial 955, 9.

42. Atkinson to Pennington, 7 February 1860, in United States, House, *Claims Growing Out of Indian Hostilities in Oregon and Washington in 1855 and 1856*, 36th Cong., 1st sess., 1860. H. Ex. Doc. 11, Serial 1046, 44–47, 51–52.

43. United States, Senate, *Expenses Incurred in Suppression of Indian Hostilities in Certain Territories*, 42nd Cong., 3rd sess., 1872, S. Ex. Doc. 24, Serial 1545, 39–48.

44. *Oregonian*, 22 May 1888, 3.

9. The Coast Reservation

1. United States, House, *Eighteenth Annual Report of the Bureau of American Ethnology*, Part 2, 56th Cong., 1st sess., 1899, S. Doc. 736, Serial 4015, 814, Map 51; United States, Congress, *Joint Hearings Before the Subcommittees of the Committees on Interior and Insular Affairs . . . on S. 2746 and H.R. 7317, February 17, 1954*, 140.

2. Manypenny to McClelland, 26 November 1853, in United States, House, *Message from the President of the United States*, 33rd Cong., 1st sess., 1853, H. Ex. Doc. 1, Serial 710, 256–57.

3. Manypenny to McClelland, 26 November 1855, in United States, Senate, *Message from the President of the United States*, 34th Cong, 1st sess., 1855, S. Ex. Doc. 1, Serial 810, 338.

4. "To Whom It May Concern," 18 May 1854, in AX57/1/5, Palmer Papers, University of Oregon Library.

5. Bensell, *All Quiet*, 206–207, 213.

6. Browne to Denver, 17 November 1857, in United States, House, *Indian Affairs in the Territories of Oregon and Washington*, 35th Cong., 1st sess., 1858,

H. Ex. Doc. 39, Serial 955, 39–40; Metcalfe to Nesmith, 15 July 1857, in United States, House, *Message from the President of the United States*, 35th Cong., 1st sess., 1857, H. Ex. Doc. 2, Serial 919, 644.

7. Palmer, "Joel Palmer Diary," 11–12. Grand Ronde became a separate reservation in 1857. See United States, Senate, *Indian Affairs. Law and Treaties*, 1:886.

8. Browne to Denver, 17 November 1857, in House, *Indian Affairs*, 1858, Serial 955, 40, 47–48.

9. Frances Fuller Victor, *The Early Indian Wars of Oregon*, 416.

10. Odeneal to Walker, 27 January 1873, in Office of Indian Affairs, *Letters Received by the Office of Indian Affairs, 1824–81*, NAM 234, Roll 618.

11. T. W. Davenport, "Recollections of an Indian Agent," *Quarterly of the Oregon Historical Society* 8 (March 1907): 18–19.

12. Hedges to Manypenny, 7 November 1856, NAM 234, Roll 609.

13. Hedges to Manypenny, 19 December 1856, NAM 234, Roll 610.

14. Browne to Denver, 17 November 1857, in House, *Indian Affairs*, 1858, Serial 955, 40–41.

15. Hedges to Manypenny, 19 December 1856, NAM 234, Roll 610.

16. Sheridan to Augur, 4 February 1857, in War Department, *Records of the Office of the Secretary of War*, RG 393, Box 11, National Archives, Washington.

17. Augur to Mackall, 16 February 1857, RG 393, Box 11.

18. Sheridan to Augur, 13 April 1857, in House, *Indian Affairs in Oregon and Washington Territories, &c.*, 35th Cong., 1st sess., 1858, H. Ex. Doc. 112, Serial 958, 17.

19. Metcalfe to Sheridan, 14 April 1857, in House, *Indian Affairs*, 1858, Serial 958, 17.

20. Sheridan to Metcalfe, 14 April 1857, in House, *Indian Affairs*, 1858, Serial 958, 18.

21. Metcalfe to Augur, 15 April 1857, in House, *Indian Affairs*, 1858, Serial 958, 19–20.

22. Sheridan to Augur, 15 April 1857, in House, *Indian Affairs*, 1858, Serial 958, 18–19.

23. Metcalfe to Nesmith, 15 July 1857, in House, *Message*, 1857, 645–47.

24. Browne to Denver, 17 November 1857, in House, *Indian Affairs*, 1858, Serial 955, 32.

25. Nesmith to Denver, 1 September 1857, in House, *Message*, 1857, 604, 607.

26. Browne to Denver, 17 November 1857, in House, *Indian Affairs*, 1858, Serial 955, 43.

27. Metcalfe to Nesmith, 15 July 1857, in House, *Message*, 1857, 645.

28. Metcalfe to Nesmith, 27 July 1858, in United States, Senate, *Message from the President of the United States*, 35th Cong., 1st sess., 1858, S. Ex. Doc. 1, Serial 974, 603.

29. Metcalfe to Nesmith, 27 July 1858, in Senate, *Message*, 1858, 605.

30. Nesmith to Mix, 20 August 1858, NAM 234, Roll 611.

31. Mott to Mix, 11 February 1859, NAM 234, Roll 611. The coastal tribes got no annuities—that is, payments for their land in the form of goods—because their treaties had not been ratified. See Metcalfe to Nesmith, 1 September 1857, in House, *Message*, 1857, 64

32. Mix to Thompson, 6 November 1858, in Senate, *Message*, 1858, 357.

33. See Rector to Dole, 23 January 1863, NAM 234, Roll 613, and Hendrickson, *Joe Lane*, 208.

34. Geary to Mix, 10 May 1859, NAM 234, Roll 611.

35. Palmer to Manypenny, 22 January 1856, in United States, House, *Indian Hostilities in Oregon and Washington*, 34th Cong., 1st sess., 1856. H. Ex. Doc. 93, Serial 858, 132.

36. Geary to Commissioner of Indian Affairs, 20 July 1859, NAM 234, Roll 611.

37. Bancroft, 30:423, 432, 438.

38. *Crescent City Herald* (Extra), 9 October 1856, quoted in *National Intelligencer*, 14 November 1856.

39. Newcomb to Geary, 15 August 1860, in United States, Senate, *Message from the President of the United States*, 36th Cong., 2nd sess., 1860, S. Ex. Doc. 1, Serial 1078, 435.

40. Newcomb to Geary, 15 August 1860, in Senate, *Message*, 1860, 437.

41. Sykes to Geary, 12 July 1860, in Senate, *Message*, 1860, 438–39.

42. Secretary of the Interior to Dole, 13 June 1861, NAM 234, Roll 612.

43. Rector to Dole, 24 September 1861, NAM 234, Roll 612.

44. Biddle to Rector, August 13, 1862, in United States, Office of Indian Affairs, *Report of the Commissioner of Indian Affairs for the Year 1862*, 272–73.

45. Browne to Commissioner of Indian Affairs, 12 November 1861, NAM 234, Roll 612.

46. Dent to Rector, 30 September 1861, NAM 234, Roll 612.

47. "Report of the Speeches made by the Chiefs and Head Men," 24 May 1862, NAM 234, Roll 613.

48. Biddle to Rector, 13 August 1862, in Office of Indian Affairs, *Report for 1862*, 276.

49. Newcomb to Geary, 15 August 1860, in Senate, *Message*, 1860, 437

50. Rector to Dole, 2 September 1862, in Office of Indian Affairs, *Report for 1862*, 256.

51. Biddle to Dole, June 30, 1862, in United States, House, *Message from the President of the United States*, 38th Cong., 1st sess., 1863, H. Ex. Doc. 1, Serial 1182, 178.

52. Rector to Dole, 7 June 1862, NAM 234, Roll 613.

53. Biddle to Rector, 13 August 1862, in Office of Indian Affairs, *Report for 1862* (1863), 273–74.

54. Biddle to Dole, 23 October 1862, NAM 234, Roll 613.

55. Rector to Dole, 11 November 1862, NAM 234, Roll 613.

56. Nesmith and Harding to Dole, 24 December 1862, NAM 234, Roll 613.

57. *Oregon Statesman* (Salem), 26 January 1863.

58. Chief Clerk to Dole, 11 January 1863, NAM 234, Roll 613.

59. Rector to Dole, 3 April 1863, NAM 234, Roll 613.

60. David Newsom, *David Newsom: The Western Observer, 1805–1882*, 282.

61. Rector to Simpson, 14 March 1863, NAM 234, Roll 613.

62. Bensell, *All Quiet*, 128.

63. Fairchild to Smith, 1 September 1875, in United States, House, *Report of the Secretary of the Interior*, 44th Cong., 1st sess., 1875, H. Ex. Doc. 1, Part 5, Serial 1680, 853.

64. A[lexander] W. Chase, "Siletz, or 'Lo' Reconstructed," in Lyman, 8–9.

65. Chase, "Siletz," 425, in Lyman, "Alexander W. Chase," 6; Chase, "Siletz," 428, in Lyman, "Alexander W. Chase," 9.

66. Chase, "Siletz," 429–30, in Lyman, "Alexander W. Chase," 9–10.

67. *Oregon Journal* (Portland), 4 July 1937, 6.

68. Chase, "Siletz," 433, in Lyman, "Alexander W. Chase," 13.

69. Bensell, *All Quiet*, 183–84.

70. Simpson to Huntington, 20 August 1863, in United States, House, *Message from the President of the United States*, 38th Cong., 1st sess., 1863,. H. Ex. Doc. 1, Serial 1182., 185–86.

71. Hedges to Manypenny, 7 November 1856, NAM 234, Roll 609.

72. Nesmith to Mix, 20 August 1858, Senate, *Message*, 1858, 569.

73. Huntington to Dole, 28 March 1864, NAM 234, Roll 613.

74. Huntington to Dole, 28 March 1864, NAM 234, Roll 613.

75. Huntington to Dole, 19 December 1863, NAM 234, Roll 613.

76. Bensell, *All Quiet*, 124–27.

77. Huntington to Dole, 28 March 1864, NAM 234, Roll 613.

78. *Oregon Statesman*, 28 November 1864.

79. Simpson to Huntington, 12 September 1864, in United States, Office of Indian Affairs, *Report of the Commissioner of Indian Affairs for the Year 1864*, 104.

80. Huntington to Dole, 6 September 1864, in Office of Indian Affairs, *Report for 1864*, 83–84.

81. Huntington to Usher, 12 December 1864, in United States, House, *Message from the President of the United States*, 39th Cong., 1st sess., 1865, H. Ex. Doc. 1, Serial 1248, 273–277.

82. Newsom, *David Newsom*, 277.

83. Bayley to Simpson, 31 July 1863, in House, *Message*, 1863, 187–188.

84. *Corvallis* (Ore.) *Gazette* (Corvallis, Oregon), 22 November 1872.

85. *Inventory of County Archives of Oregon, Benton County* (Historical Records Survey, Portland, 1942) A-48, quoted in Newsom, 282.

86. Bancroft, 30:453–54.

87. Senate, *Law and Treaties*, 891. The number of acres lost to the reservation was estimated using Map 51 in House, *Eighteenth Annual Report*.

88. Huntington to Cooley, 8 January 1866, NAM 234, Roll 615.

89. Huntington to Cooley, 16 January 1866, NAM 234, Roll 615.

90. Huntington to Wilson, 15 October 1866, in United States, House, *Message from the President of the United States*, 39th Cong., 2nd sess., 1866, H. Ex. Doc. 1, Serial 1284, 74.

91. David D. Fagan, *History of Benton County, Oregon* (Portland: David D. Fagan, 1885), 479, 482.

92. *Corvallis Gazette*, 14 July 1866.

93. Leslie M. Scott, "The Yaquina Railroad, the Tale of a Great Fiasco," *Quarterly of the Oregon Historical Society* 16 (September 1915): 229.

94. Wells to Commissioner of Indian Affairs, 7 January 1867, in United States, Office of Indian Affairs, *Letters Received by the Office of Indian Affairs, 1824–81*, NAM 234, Roll 615.

95. Palmer to Meacham, 9 September 1871, in United States, House, *Report of the Secretary of the Interior*, 42nd Cong., 2nd sess., 1871, H. Ex. Doc. 1, Part 5, Serial 1505, 735.

96. J. Owen Dorsey, "The Gentile System of the Siletz Tribes," *Journal of American Folklore* 3 (January–March 1890): 228–29.

97. Megginson to Biddle, 1 August 1862; Allen to Biddle, 30 June 1862; Hill to Biddle, 1 August 1862, in United States, Office of Indian Affairs, *Report of the Commissioner of Indian Affairs for the Year 1862*, 272, 280–83; map of Siletz Reservation in NAM 234, Roll 622.

The tribes into which the Indian Service divided the reservation population were not identical with the villages Palmer mentioned; in an 1877 census, only two or perhaps three of the eleven groups listed were then small enough to fit into one village of the kind that Palmer described. See "Census Roll of Indians belonging to the Siletz Agency, 1877," in NAM 234, Roll 624.

98. "We the undersigned Chiefs," 3 September 1874, in NAM 234, Roll 619.

99. Wells to Commissioner of Indian Affairs, 7 January 1867, in NAM 234, Roll 615.

100. *Corvallis* (Ore.) *Gazette*, 26 October 1867.

101. *Corvallis Gazette*, 23 November 1867. Bensell's letter was one of many during this period which he signed "Rialto." He was identified as Rialto in the *Corvallis Gazette*, 24 October 1879.

102. *Corvallis Gazette*, 1 February 1868.

103. United States, House, *Report of the Secretary of the Interior*, 41st Cong., 2nd sess., 1869, H. Ex. Doc. 1, Pt. 3, Serial 1414, 902, 918.

104. Simpson to Meacham, 30 September 1870, in United States, House, *Report of the Secretary of the Interior*, 41st Cong., 3rd sess., 1870, H. Ex. Doc. 1, Part 4, Serial 1449, 853–54.

105. Fay and Hayden to the Senate and House, 7 October 1870, in United States, House, "Siletz Indian Reservation, " *Memorial of the Legislative Assembly of the State of Oregon*, 41st Cong., 3rd sess., 1871, H. Mis. Doc. 19, Serial 1462, 1; House, *Report*, 1870, 795.

106. House, *Report*, 1870, 795.

107. Hams to Parker, 14 January 1871, in NAM 234, Roll 616.

108. Meacham to Commissioner, 25 October 1871, in House, *Report*, 1871, 731.

109. Newsom, 284; Simpson to Mitchell, 29 June 1874, in NAM 234, Roll 619.

10. Dancers, Dissenters, Refugees, and Methodists

1. Prucha, 1:482, 512.

2. Robert H. Keller, Jr., *American Protestantism and United States Indian Policy, 1869–82*, 123–24, 210.

3. Fairchild to Smith, 1 September 1875, in United States, House, *Report of the Secretary of the Interior*, 44th Cong., 1st sess., 1875, H. Ex. Doc. 1, Part 5, Serial 1680, 853.

4. Palmer to Meacham, 6 November 1871, in United States, Office of Indian Affairs, *Records of the Oregon Superintendency of Indian Affairs*, NAM 2, Roll 27.

5. See Gray, *Takelma*, 41, 59.

6. Palmer to Meacham, 9 September 1871, in United States, House, *Report of the Secretary of the Interior*, 42nd Cong., 2nd sess., 1871, H. Ex. Doc. 1, Part 5, Serial 1505, 735.

7. Palmer to Meacham, 9 September 1871, in House, *Report*, 1871, 735–38.

8. Meacham to Drummond, 28 March 1872, in United States, Office of Indian Affairs, *Letters Received by the Office of Indian Affairs, 1824–81*, NAM 234, Roll 617.

9. T. W. Davenport, 242–43. Also see Fairchild to Smith, 26 July 1875, in NAM 234, Roll 621.

10. Fairchild to Clum, 18 August 1873, in NAM 234, Roll 617; Palmer to Odeneal, 28 September 1872, in House, *Report of the Secretary of the Interior*, 42nd Cong., 3rd sess., 1872, H. Ex. Doc. 1, Part 5, Serial 1560, 753.

11. "Minutes of Council," 15 December 1873, in United States, Senate, *Letter from the Acting Secretary of the Interior*, 43rd Cong., 1st sess., 1874, S. Mis. Doc. 65, Serial 1584, 4–7; "We the undersigned Chiefs," 3 September 1874, in NAM 234, Roll 619.

12. Fairchild to Clum, 18 August 1873, in NAM 234, Roll 617.

13. Palmer to Meacham, 9 September 1871, in House, *Report*, 1871, 736.

14. O'Donnell, 293–94; *Pacific Christian Advocate*, 17 October 1872, quoted in O'Donnell, 293; Palmer to Parrish, 14 November 1872, in NAM 2, Roll 27.

15. Vittorio Lanternari, *The Religions of the Oppressed: A Study of Modern Messianic Cults*, 301.

16. Lanternari, *Religions*, 131–32.

17. Sixes George attended the 1873 council and was described as a former chief. He was quoted as saying, "Now I am awaking. For a long time I have been asleep." Depoe also was not listed as a chief at the 1873 council but was described as "one of the most influential Indians on the reservation." He was quoted as saying, "Church-members have come here and taught us, and now we are all trying to be good." Both men were listed as chiefs on an 1874 document

concerning a grazing lease, Sixes George as chief of the Sixes and Depoe as chief of the Joshuas. ("Minutes of Council," 15 December 1873, in Senate, *Letter*, Serial 1584, 5–6); "We the undersigned Chiefs," 3 September 1874, in NAM 234, Roll 619.

Depoe's deep involvement in the Ghost Dance before and after 1873 suggests that his remark at the 1873 council was meant to be ironic.

18. Cora Du Bois, "The 1870 Ghost Dance," 25.

19. Odeneal to Walker, 27 January 1873, in NAM 234, Roll 618.

20. *Corvallis Gazette*, 8 February 1873, quoted in DuBois, "1870 Ghost Dance," 26.

21. Du Bois, "1870 Ghost Dance," 27.

22. Odeneal to Smith, 30 May 1873, in NAM 234, Roll 618.

23. Fairchild to Smith, 29 September 1873, in NAM 234, Roll 617.

24. Fairchild to Smith, 16 October 1873, in NAM 234, Roll 617.

25. Fairchild to Smith, 18 October 1873, in NAM 234, Roll 617.

26. "Minutes of Council," 15 December 1873, in Senate, *Letter*, Serial 1584, 4–6.

27. Kemble to Smith, 7 January 1874, in Senate, Letter, 1874, 3.

28. E. A. Schwartz, "Sick Hearts: Indian Removal on the Oregon Coast, 1875–1881," 233–34; Johnson and Malone, eds., 7:54; John Messing, "Public Lands, Politics, and Progressives: The Oregon Land Fraud Trials, 1903–1910," *Pacific Historical Review* 35 (1966), 56.

29. Mitchell to Delano, 2 January 1874, in NAM 234, Roll 619

30. Newsom, 284; Simpson to Mitchell, 29 June 1874, in NAM 234, Roll 619.

31. Bagley to Smith, 15 September 1876, in NAM 234, Roll 622.

32. Fairchild to Smith, 28 January 1874, in NAM 234, Roll 619.

33. Delano to Smith, 5 January 1874, in NAM 234, Roll 619.

34. Litchfield to Smith, 10 February 1874, in NAM 234, Roll 619.

35. Simpson to Mitchell, 29 June 1874, in NAM 234, Roll 619.

36. *Corvallis Gazette*, 13 December 1878.

37. Fairchild to Smith, 11 June 1875, in NAM 234, Roll 621.

38. Harney to Smith, 24 December 1875, in NAM 234, Roll 622.

39. Fairchild to Smith, 22 April 1875, in NAM 234, Roll 622.

40. Fairchild to Smith, 4 December 1874, in NAM 234, Roll 619.

41. *Congressional Record*, 26 January 1875, 729–30.

42. *Congressional Record*, 20 February 1875, 1528–29.

43. Fairchild to Smith, 17 May 1875, in NAM 234, Roll 621.

44. "Minutes of Council held with the Tillamook and other bands," 1 June 1875, in NAM 234, Roll 621.

45. Fairchild to Smith, 4 June 1875, in NAM 234, Roll 621.

46. Fairchild to Smith, 5 June 1875, in NAM 234, Roll 621.

47. "Proceedings of a Council held June 17th, 1875," in NAM 234, Roll 621.

48. Smith to Simpson, 17 July 1875, in NAM 234, Roll 621.

49. Simpson to Commissioner, 27 August 1875, in NAM 234, Roll 621.

50. See Chapman to Fairchild, 8 September 1875, in NAM 234, Roll 620.

51. Simpson to Smith, 27 August 1875, in NAM 234, Roll 621.

52. Chapman to Fairchild, 8 September 1875, in NAM 234, Roll 620.

53. Litchfield to Smith, 27 August 1875, in NAM 234, Roll 621

54. Fairchild to Smith, 2 September 1875, in NAM 234, Roll 621. Fairchild was incorrect when he said that the three men from Siletz and the leading men on the Alsea Reservation spoke the same language, unless he was referring to Chinook Jargon, which was also spoken by many whites. The men from Siletz were members of southern Oregon bands who spoke at least two distinct mother tongues, and the people on the Alsea Reservation spoke at least three more. See Beckham, *Requiem*, 36–38; Swanton, *Indian Tribes of North America*, 469, 473.

55. Fairchild to Smith, 30 September 1875, in NAM 234, Roll 621.

56. United States, Senate, *Indian Affairs*, 1:157.

57. Fairchild to Smith, 30 October 1875, in NAM 234, Roll 621.

58. Fairchild to Smith, 21 September 1875, NAM 234, Roll 621. Fairchild was later involved in a coastal real estate speculation. On September 23, 1876, Fairchild and six other people sold 52 acres in the vicinity of Yaquina Bay for $6,000, or a little more than $115 an acre (roughly $2,300 an acre in 1990s dollars). How they had acquired this property is not clear from existing records. The buyer was the Union Real Estate Association of San Francisco. In February 1877, Fairchild was listed as the secretary of the association. Fairchild and the others were also listed as creditors of a milling company owned by the association. The milling company was sold off in February, and Fairchild and the others were in bankruptcy in October. See Lincoln County, Oregon, County Clerk, Deed Records Book A, 200, 228, 268.

59. Fairchild to Smith, 31 March 1877, NAM 234, Roll 623.

60. Bagley to Commissioner, 20 August 1876, in United States, House, *Report of the Secretary of the Interior*, 44th Cong., 2nd sess., 1876, H. Ex. Doc. 1, Part 5, Serial 1749, 526.

61. Wallis Nash, *Oregon: There and Back in 1877*, v–viii, 181.

62. Fairchild to Smith, 1 November 1875, NAM 234, Roll 621.

63. Fairchild to Simpson, 11 November 1875, NAM 234, Roll 621.

64. Harney to Smith, 24 December 1874, NAM 234, Roll 622. This letter was witnessed as being the true statement of George Harney by R. A. Bensell and Joseph Howard.

65. United States, House, *Report of the Secretary of the Interior*, 42nd Cong., 3rd sess., 1872, H. Ex. Doc. 1, Part 5, Serial 1560, 796–97.

66. United States, House, *Report of the Secretary of the Interior*, 43rd Cong., 2nd sess., 1874, H. Ex. Doc. 1, Part 5, Serial 1639, 430.

67. House, *Report*, 1876, 636–37.

68. Bagley to Smith, 24 December 1875, NAM 234, Roll 622.

69. Secretary of the Interior to Commissioner of Indian Affairs, 3 March 1876, NAM 234, Roll 622.

70. *Corvallis Gazette*, 7 April 1876.

71. Bagley to Smith, 1 June 1876, NAM 234, Roll 622.

72. House, *Report*, 1876, 636, 622.

73. Bagley to Smith, 15 September 1876, NAM 234, Roll 622.

74. *Corvallis Gazette*, 6 October 1876.

75. Bagley to Smith, 4 August 1877, NAM 234, Roll 624.

76. "Census Roll of Indians Belonging to the Siletz Agency," 20 August 1877, NAM 234, Roll 624.

77. *Corvallis Gazette*, 7 September 1877.

78. *Corvallis Gazette*, 21 September 1877.

79. *San Francisco Chronicle*, 12 October 1877.

80. *Corvallis Gazette*, 9 November 1877.

81. Bagley to Hayt, 26 November 1877, in NAM 234.

82. Bagley to Hayt, 24 November 1877, NAM 234, Roll 624.

83. Bagley to Hayt, 24 November 1877, NAM 234, Roll 624. Perhaps Bagley neglected to mention Harney by name because, thanks to his visit to the East with Alfred B. Meacham, he was known to Indian Service officials who might have questioned whether such a prominent example of the civilizing influence of the reservation policy could have so readily reverted to savagery.

84. Bagley reported that this conflict involved two white men, brothers Perry and Elon Dodson, who had driven off two bulls belonging to the reservation. On Saturday, June 15, 1878, Bagley said, Sam, the chief of the Nestuccas (and the man whose name was first on the petition against Bagley) had gone to the Dodson

place on the north side of the Salmon River to talk about the stolen bulls. "Hard words passed between them for some time, when Perry Dodson kicked an Indian in the breast," Bagley said. The man who had been assaulted grabbed Dodson, who drew a revolver from his pocket and shot the man. As he lay dying, he called to his friends to kill Dodson; his brother responded by striking Dodson three times with a hatchet and then took a gun from another Indian and shot Dodson.

Tourists who were camped nearby were assured by the Indians, Bagley added, "that no danger attended their remaining in their camps, as the Indians did not, nor had they at any time desired to fight." Elon Dodson "thought the Indians came to kill his brother, though he admitted his brother commenced the combat." The Dodsons, Bagley said, "were, and had been, much prejudiced against Indians," and he added that Elon Dodson had told him "the Indians were not human but brutes." (*New York Times*, 11 July 1878, 5.)

85. Samuel and others to Starr, 7 August 1878, NAM 234, Roll 628.

86. "Census Roll of Indians belonging to the Siletz Agency, 1877," 20 August 1877, in NAM 234, Roll 624. This census shows 299 men over twenty and fourteen tribes, not including the Siuslaws, Cooses, and Umpquas.

87 Bagley to Hayt, 5 September 1878, NAM 234, Roll 628.

88. McCain to Secretary of the Interior, 26 September 1878, in NAM 234, Roll 628.

89. Watkins to Hayt, 28 December 1878, in NAM 234, Roll 628.

90. Bagley to Hayt, 8 November 1878, NAM 234, Roll 625.

91. Du Bois, "1870 Ghost Dance," 117, 125.

92. Bagley to Hayt, 11 February 1879, NAM 234, Roll 627.

93. Du Bois, "1870 Ghost Dance," 126.

94. Bagley to Hayt, 11 February 1879, NAM 234, Roll 627.

95. Chief Clerk of the Department of the Interior to Hayt, 14 June 1879, NAM 234, Roll 627.

96. Schurz to Bagley, 14 June 1879, NAM 234, Roll 627.

97. Swan to Hayt, 17 June 1879, NAM 234, Roll 628.

98. Swan to Trowbridge, 31 August 1880, NAM 234, Roll 630.

99. Swan to Hayt, 31 July 1879, NAM 234, Roll 628.

100. Swan to Hayt, 29 November 1879, NAM 234, Roll 628.

101. Swan to Hayt, 13 December 1879, NAM 234, Roll 629.

102. S. 202, March 26, 1879, NAM 234, Roll 629; Bancroft 30:675.

103. Slater to Schurz, 26 December 1879, NAM 234, Roll 629.

104. Swan to Hayt, 13 January 1880, NAM 234, Roll 630.

105. Carl Schurz, who became interior secretary in 1877 in the administration of Rutherford B. Hayes, said he had favored consolidation of agencies at first but had come to see that leaving people on their own lands was more likely produce their successful conversion to farming and herding. See Prucha, 1:577.

106. *Corvallis Gazette*, 19 September 1879.

107. Swan to Trowbridge, 23 August 1880, NAM 234, Roll 630.

108. Swan to Commissioner of Indian Affairs, 18 August 1881, in United States, Office of Indian Affairs, *Annual Report of the Commissioner of Indian Affairs to the Secretary of the Interior for the Year 1881*, 147.

109. Swan to Commissioner, 28 August 1882, in United States, Interior Department, *Report of the Secretary of the Interior* (1882), 2:202.

110. United States, Interior Department, *Report of the Secretary of the Interior* (1879), 1:237–39.

111. Office of Indian Affairs, *Annual Report for 1881*, 147.

112. Office of Indian Affairs, *Annual Report for 1881*, 304–5.

113. United States, Interior Department, *Report of the Secretary of the Interior* (1883), 2:356–57.

114. Lane to Commissioner, 20 August 1888, in United States, Interior Department, *Report of the Secretary of the Interior* (1888), 210.

115. See Fairchild to Clum, 18 August 1873, NAM 234, Roll 617; Bagley to Smith, 1 June 1876, NAM 234, Roll 622.

116. Swan to Commissioner, 18 August 1881, in Office of Indian Affairs, *Annual Report for 1881*, 304.

117. Swan to Commissioner, 28 August 1882, in Interior Department, *Report* (1882), 199. Only twenty-six allotments were listed in the statistical report (see Interior Department, *Report* [1882], 420), but in the context of Swan's optimistic narrative report, this seems to be a typographical error, or perhaps the number of allotments made during the year rather than the total number.

118. Price to Swan, 9 August 1881, Siletz Reservation Collection, Oregon Historical Society, Portland.

119. See Prucha, 2:663–65.

120. United States, Interior Department, *Report*, (1879), 346.

121. United States, Office of Indian Affairs, *Annual Report of the Commissioner of Indian Affairs to the Secretary of the Interior for the Year 1880* (1880), 250; Office of Indian Affairs, *Annual Report for 1881*, 284; Interior Department, *Report* (1882), 400; Interior Department, *Report* (1883), 336.

122. United States, Interior Department, *Report of the Secretary of the Interior* (1886), 1:622–23.

123. Nash, *Two Years in Oregon*, 137, 139.

124. Swan to Commissioner, 28 August 1882, in Interior Department, *Report* (1882), 2:199.

125. Swan to Trowbridge, 18 June 1880, NAM 234, Roll 630.

126. Swan to Trowbridge, 31 August 1880, NAM 234, Roll 630.

127. Wadsworth to Commissioner, 13 August 1883, in Interior Department, *Report* (1883), 188.

128. Prucha, 1:527.

129. Wadsworth to Commissioner, 12 August 1883, in Interior Department, *Report* (1883), 189.

130. Wadsworth to Commissioner, 20 August 1884, in United States, Interior Department, *Report* (1884), 2:190.

131. See Wadsworth to Commissioner, 10 August 1885, in United States, Interior Department, *Report* (1885), 2:392–94.

132. Wadsworth to Commissioner, 12 August 1886, in Interior Department, *Report* (1886), 1:434.

133. The reported oats crop went from 25,000 bushels in 1883 to an estimated 20,000 bushels in 1886. Hay production, estimated at 769 tons in 1883, dipped to 438 in 1884 but was expected to be 530 tons in 1886. Vegetable production peaked at 28,125 bushels in 1884 and declined to an estimated 16,250 bushels in 1886. See Interior Department, *Report* (1883), 2:356–57; Interior Department, *Report* (1884), 2:358–59; Interior Department, *Report* (1885), 2:604–605; Interior Department, *Report* (1886), 1:652–53.

134. Wadsworth reported making six allotments in 1885, when he said 450 people were living on allotments, and five more in 1886, when, as has been noted, he claimed that all the 612 people he counted on the reservation were living on allotments. See Interior Department, *Report* (1885), 2:575; Interior Department, *Report* (1886), 1:623.

135. Interior Department, *Report* (1883), 2:336; Interior Department, *Report* (1884), 2:340; Interior Department, *Report* (1885), 2:574; Interior Department, *Report* (1886), 1:622.

136. Wadsworth to Commissioner, 12 August 1883, in Interior Department, *Report* (1883), 2:190.

137. Lane to Commissioner, 15 August 1887, in United States, Interior Department, *Report* (1887), 2:270–71.

138. Lane to Atkins, 11 June 1886, in United States, Bureau of Indian Affairs, Records of the Bureau of Indian Affairs, RG 75, National Archives.

11. Achievements of Allotment

1. The text of the act is in *United States Statutes at Large*, 24:388–91, and also in Wilcomb E. Washburn, *The Assault on Indian Tribalism: The General Allotment Law (Dawes Act) of 1887*, 68–73.

2. Hoxie, *Final Promise*, viii.

3. United States, Interior Department, *Report* (1886), 1:692.

4. See Hoxie, *Final Promise*, 77.

5. Interior, *Report* (1886), 992.

6. Interior, *Report* (1886), 996.

7. United States, Interior Department, *Report*, (1887), 2:994.

8. Prucha, 2:895.

9. Janet A. McDonnell, *The Dispossession of the American Indian, 1887–1934*, 124.

10. McDonnell, *Dispossession*, 124.

11. McDonnell, *Dispossession*, 121.

12. *Congressional Record* (29 January 1881), 11:1031.

13. *Congressional Record* (25 January 1887), 19:974. Dolph spoke several times on allotment during the debates of the 1880s, but aside from Slater, no other member of Oregon's congressional delegation made any recorded remarks on the subject from the floor.

14. Lane to Commissioner, 20 August 1888, in United States, Interior Department, *Report*, (1888), 2:211.

15. Atkins to Lane, 13 January 1888, in Siletz Reservation Collection, Ms. 442, Oregon Historical Society, Portland (hereafter cited as Siletz Reservation Collection).

16. Lane to Atkins, 8 February 1888, in United States, Bureau of Indian Affairs, Records of the Bureau of Indian Affairs, RG 75 (hereafter cited as RG 75), National Archives, Washington.

17. Atkins to Lane, 24 February 1888, Siletz Reservation Collection.

18. Belt to Gaither, 25 April 1889, Siletz Reservation Collection.

19. Belt to Gaither, 21 May 1889, Siletz Reservation Collection.

20. *Lincoln County Leader* (Toledo, Ore.), 4 May 1893.

21. Buford to Commissioner, 12 August 1891, in United States, House, *Report of the Secretary of the Interior*, 52nd Cong., 1st sess., 1891, H. Ex. Doc. 1, Part 5, Serial 2933, 376.

22. Buford to Commissioner, 15 August 1892, in United States, House, *Report of the Secretary of the Interior*, 52nd Cong., 2nd sess., 1892, H. Ex. Doc. 1, Part 5, Serial 3088, 416.

23. Morgan to Boies [*sic*], Odell, and Harding, 22 August 1892, Docket 239, Box 361, in United States, Indian Claims Commission, Records of the Indian Claims Commission, RG 279 (hereafter cited as RG 279), National Archives, Washington.

24. Boise, Odell, and Harding to Noble and Morgan, 9 November 1892, in United States, Senate, *Letter from the Secretary of the Interior*, 52nd Cong., 2nd sess., 1893, S. Ex. Doc. 39, Serial 3056, 5-6.

25. "On this 17th Day of October" (Defendant's Exhibit 17), Docket 239, Box 361, RG 279, National Archives, Washington, 13-14.

26. Boise, Odell, and Harding to Noble and Morgan, 9 November 1892, in Senate, *Letter*, 1893, Serial 3056, 5-6; "On this 17th Day of October" (Defendant's Exhibit 17), Docket 239, Box 361, RG 279, National Archives, Washington, 20-21.

27. "The Indians of the Siletz" (Defendant's Exhibit 18), Docket 239, Box 361, RG 279, National Archives, Washington, 1, 3.

28. "Journal, October 6th, 1892" (Defendant's Exhibit 16), Docket 239, Box 361, RG 279, National Archives, Washington.

29. Senate, *Letter*, 1893, Serial 3056, 10-11.

30. Boise, Odell, and Harding to Noble and Morgan, 9 November 1892, in Senate, *Letter*, 1893, Serial 3056, 6.

31. United States, House, *Agreement with Indians on the Siletz Reservation*, 53rd Cong., 2nd sess., 1894, H. Rpt. 527, Serial 3270, 1-2.

32. Lincoln County, Oregon, County Clerk, Deed Records Book A.

33. United States, Bureau of Indian Affairs, *Proposed Withdrawal of Federal Responsibilities over the Property and Affairs of the Indians of Western Oregon*, December 1953, 2.

34. Interior, *Report* (1887), 448-75; United States, House, *Annual Reports of the Department of the Interior . . . 1904: Indian Affairs, Part I* (1905), 544-65, 616-31.

35. United States, House, *Eighteenth Annual Report of the Bureau of American Ethnology*, Part 2, 56th Cong., 1st sess., 1899, H. Doc. 736, Serial 4015, 948.

36. *Lincoln County Leader*, 14 July 1895, 9.

37. George L. Curry, Jr., "Much Good Land Left," *Oregonian* (Portland), 27 July 1895, 9.

38. Stephen A. D. Puter, *Looters of the Public Domain*, 471–72. Three men went to trial in 1905 for the Siletz land fraud scheme described by Stephen A. D. Puter. The federal government accused one of the three, Willard N, Jones, of having organized the fraudulent acquisition of former reservation land by hiring "dummy entrymen" who would take claims under his direction and sell the claims to him as soon as they had title (Puter, *Looters*, 471–72). Jones and another man were convicted in October. Ira Wade, the Lincoln County clerk, was tried with them but acquitted. (*Oregonian*, 15 October 1905, 1). Wade denied that he had knowingly helped register false claims. He admitted building cabins for Jones, which Jones had used to prove that his dummy entrymen had made the improvements required to get the titles they registered with Wade. But Wade claimed that he had not realized why Jones wanted the cabins (*Oregonian*, 13 October 1905, 12).

39. Gaither to Commissioner, 24 August 1894, United States, Office of Indian Affairs, *Annual Report of the Commissioner of Indian Affairs, 1894* (1895), 266.

40. United States, Interior Department, *Annual Reports . . . 1897*, 506.

41. United States, Interior Department, *Annual Reports . . . 1899*, 592.

42. House, *Annual Reports . . . 1904*, 626.

43. House, *Report* (1892), 812.

44. United States, House, *Report* (1893), H. Ex. Doc. 1, Part 5, Serial 4748, 718.

45. Interior, *Annual Reports . . . 1899*, 592.

46. House, *Annual Reports . . . 1904*, 626.

47. Buford to Commissioner, 14 August 1899, in Interior, *Annual Reports . . . 1899*, 318.

48. Buford to Commissioner, 10 August 1900, in United States, House, *Annual Reports of the Department of the Interior . . . 1900*, 56th Cong., 2nd sess., 1900, H. Doc. 5, Serial 4100, 361.

49. Buford to Commissioner, 5 August 1901, in United States, House, *Annual Reports of the Department of the Interior . . . 1901*, 57th Cong., 1st sess., 1901, H. Doc. 5, Serial 4289, 350.

50. McArthur to Commissioner, 4 August 1902, in United States, Interior Department, *Annual Reports of the Department of the Interior . . . 1902*, Indian Affairs, Part I (1904), 319.

51. Interior, *Report* (1887), 448–75; House, *Annual Reports . . . 1904*, Serial 4792, 544–65, 616–31. These calculations do not include the Five Civilized Tribes, Malheur, Uintah Valley, St. Regis, Oil Springs, Kansas Chippewa and Munsee and Vermillion Lake, Red Lake, Mille Lac and Isabella Chippewa.

52. Gaither to Commissioner, 20 August 1897, in Interior, *Annual Reports . . . 1897*, 254.

53. See Hoxie, 159–60, and Donald J. Berthrong, *The Cheyenne and Arapaho Ordeal: Reservation and Agency Life in the Indian Territory, 1875–1907*, 280.

54. *Lincoln County Leader*, 29 July 1904, 1.

55. "Report of Superintendent," 18 August 1905, in United States, House, *Annual Reports of the Department of the Interior . . . 1905*, 59th Cong., 1st sess., 1905. H. Doc. 5, Serial 4959, 326.

56. "Report of Superintendent," 6 August 1906, in United States, Interior Department, *Annual Reports . . . 1906* (1907), 333.

57. Brown and 76 others to Roosevelt, 6 December 1907 (Defendant's Exhibit 50), Docket 239, Box 361, RG 279, National Archives.

58. United States, House, *Sale of Certain Lands on the Siletz Indian Reservation*, 61st Cong., 2nd sess., 1910, H. Rpt. 1098, Serial 5592, 1.

59. Pierce to Clapp, 15 February 1908, in United States, Senate, *Sale of Certain Lands on Siletz Reservation, Oregon*, 60th Cong, 1st sess., 1908, S. Rpt. 305, Serial 5218, 1–2.

60. *United States Statutes at Large* (1911), 36:367–68.

61. At termination the Confederated Tribes still owned 2,695.28 acres of the 3,200 acres of timber retained after allotment. See United States, Congress, *Joint Hearings Before the Subcommittees of the Committees on Interior and Insular Affairs . . . on S. 2746 and H.R. 7317, February 17, 1954*, 143.

62. Leupp to Secretary of the Interior, 30 September 1908, in United States, Office of Indian Affairs, *Report . . . 1908* (1909), 128–29.

63. Egbert to Commissioner, 15 July 1909, RG 75, Box 29, National Archives, Seattle.

64. Egbert to Commissioner, 10 September 1909, RG 75, Box 29, National Archives, Seattle.

65. "Report of Siletz Agency," 16 September 1910, in United States, Bureau of Indian Affairs, *Annual Narrative and Statistical Reports from Field Jurisdictions of the Bureau of Indian Affairs, 1907–1938*, NAM M-1011, Roll 139, 7.

66. "Report of Siletz Agency," 16 September 1910, in NAM M-1011, Roll 139, 4.

67. "Report of Siletz Agency," 16 September 1910, in NAM M-1011, Roll 139, 1.

68. Egbert to Commissioner, 11 October 1909, RG 75, Box 29, National Archives, Seattle.

69. "Report of Siletz Agency," 16 September 1910, in NAM M-1011, Roll 139, 10.

70. Donald L. Parman, *Indians and the American West in the Twentieth Century*, 12–13.

71. "Report of Siletz Agency," 16 September 1910, in NAM M-1011, Roll 139, 29–30.

72. "Report of Siletz Agency," 16 September 1910, in NAM M-1011, Roll 139, 7.

73. United States, Interior Department, *Reports . . . 1911* (1912), 2:99, 125, 119. Statistics in annual reports from 1911 through 1918 supposedly lump Grand Ronde Indians, left under the jurisdiction of the Siletz agency after the closure of their own agency, with Siletz Indians. That supposition is apparently incorrect, however. The 1910 reports shows 437 "Siletz (Confederated)" Indians and only 43 people belonging to groups present at Grand Ronde. The 1911 report shows a total for both of 434. In 1912, the joint total is 429 and in 1916 it is 416. The figure for 1918 is 446, but the table mentions only "Confederated Siletz" Indians, leaving out Grand Ronde groups. Those groups finally reappear in the 1919 statistics, which show 335 Grand Ronde Indians and 434 Siletz Indians. (United States, Interior Department, *Reports . . . 1910* [1911], 2:65; Interior, *Reports . . . 1911* (1912), 64; United States, Interior Department, *Reports . . . 1912*, vol. 2 [1913], 2:81; United States, Interior Department, *Reports . . . 1916*, [1917] 2:80; United States, Interior Department, *Reports . . . 1918* [1919], 2:76; United States, Interior Department, *Reports . . . 1919*, [1920], 2:74.)

74. Congress, *Joint Hearings*, 141.

75. Interior, *Reports . . . 1911*, 69, 99. Statistics for the Roseburg agency are confused because it had jurisdiction over scattered Indians in both Oregon and northern California and the numbers given are obviously estimates. Although the 1911 population table shows 3,000 people in the Roseburg jurisdiction, the table of vital statistics lists 8,150 people. (Interior, *Reports . . . 1911*, 148.) According to the 1912 report, which showed 8,000 people in the Roseburg jurisdiction, about 5,000 of them were in northern California. (Interior, *Reports . . . 1912*, 87.) In 1919, these public domain Indians were divided statistically into two groups, one of 389 "Fourth Section Allottees" and the other of 2,200 people described

as, "Scattered Indians formerly under Roseburg, on public domain." (The fourth section of the General Allotment Act authorized public domain allotments.) The 1919 table of allotted and unallotted Indians shows the 2,200 scattered people as having no allotments. (Interior, *Reports... 1919*, 75, 79.)

76. United States, Senate, *Survey of Conditions of Indians in the United States*, Part 21 (1931), 11734–35, 11742–43. A 1954 pretermination report stated, without elaboration, that 273 allotments and 18 Indian homesteads were granted in southwestern Oregon and, "As time elapsed, many allotments and homesteads were either cancelled, fee patented, or sold" (Congress, *Joint Hearings*, 141.)

77. "Annual Report, 1919," Siletz Reservation Collection.

78. Robert P. Tom, ed., *Siletz Restoration Days, 1st Annual, November 1977*, 19.

79. *Oregonian*, 11 May 1919, 9; "Register," 4–5, Siletz Reservation Collection.

80. Interior, *Reports... 1918*, 90, 98, 94, 413. The statistical tables in this report do not mention Grand Ronde in any context, but in the 1917 report the table of Indian population lists 437 people under the jurisdiction of the Siletz superintendent and identifies them as "Clackamas, Rogue River, Santiam, Siletz, Grande [*sic*] Ronde, Umpqua, etc." See United States, Interior Department, *Reports... 1917*, (1918), 2:76. On the other hand, the 1920 statistics reported 432 "Confederated Siletz" Indians and 318 Grand Ronde Indians plus 387 people with allotments on the public domain under the jurisdiction of the Siletz superintendent. See United States, Interior Department, *Reports... 1920*, (1920), 2:71.

81. Interior, *Reports 1920*, 133, 138.

82. Hoxie, *Final Promise*, 175–76.

83. Hoxie, *Final Promise*, 179–82.

84. *Oregonian*, 11 May 1919, 9.

85. Circular No. 892, August 10, 1914, OIA Circulars, National Archives Microform 1121, Reel 10, quoted in Prucha, 2:879; Prucha, 2:879, 883.

86. Senate, *Survey of Conditions*, 11726–28. Simmons was in his early twenties when allotments were made. See "Register," 13–14, Siletz Reservation Collection.

87. Senate, *Survey of Conditions*, 11726–28. Simmons's grandson, Manuel Rilatos, a member of the Siletz Council in 1991, told me that Hoxie Simmons took the loan in question knowing that he could not pay it back and he would lose the land. Another one of Simmons's grandsons, Phil Rilatos, would serve as general manager for the Confederated Tribes of Siletz Indians in the 1980s. (Manuel Rilatos interview, 4 July 1991, Siletz, Oregon.)

88. United States, Census Bureau, *Historical Statistics of the United States from Colonial Times to 1957*, 283, 279, 278.

89. Senate, *Survey of Conditions*, 11721–22.

90. Chalcraft to Conley, 2 May 1921, Siletz Reservation Collection.

91. Interior, *Reports . . . 1920*, 172.

92. Lee Sackett, "The Siletz Shaker Church," *Pacific Northwest Quarterly* 64 (July 1973): 121–22.

93. Cora Du Bois, "The 1870 Ghost Dance," 25.

94. Sackett, "Siletz Indian Shaker Church," 122–24.

95. *Yaquina Bay News* (Newport, Ore.), 12 November 1925, 1.

96. Simmons to Secretary of the Interior, 7 December 1925 (Defendant's Exhibit 56), Docket 239, Box 361, RG 279, National Archives, Washington.

97. Lane to Commissioner of Indian Affairs, 1 June 1929 (Defendant's Exhibit 57), Box 361, Docket 239, RG 279, National Archives, Washington.

98. Senate, *Survey of Conditions; Prucha*, 2:923; *Oregonian*, 31 May 1931, 6.

99. Senate, *Survey of Conditions*, 11713–14.

100. Senate, *Survey of Conditions*, 11716–17.

101. Senate, *Survey of Conditions*, 11722–24.

102. Senate, *Survey of Conditions*, 11728–29.

103. Senate, *Survey of Conditions*, 11731.

104. Prucha, 2:955, 797–99, 951. Graham D. Taylor described Collier's position on assimilation as "deliberately enigmatic" and suggested that Collier's "basic orientation was toward groups and communities, not individuals, as the building blocks of society." See Graham D. Taylor, *The New Deal and American Indian Tribalism*, 23.

105. Prucha, 2:941, 955–58; Taylor, *New Deal*, 20–21.

106. Vine Deloria, Jr., and Clifford M. Lytle, *The Nations Within: The Past and Future of American Indian Sovereignty*, 92–95.

107. See chapter 1 for a discussion of the organization of Indian society in southwestern Oregon prior to intense contact with American society.

108. Taylor, *New Deal*, 21–22.

109. Prucha, 2:959; Taylor, *New Deal*, 25.

110. *Oregonian*, 9 March 1934, 1.

111. *Oregonian*, 9 March 1934, 1.

112. *Oregon Statesman* (Salem), 10 March 1934, 2.

113. *Oregonian*, 9 March 1934, 1; *Oregon Statesman*, 9 March 1934, 2.

114. *Oregon Statesman*, 10 March 1934, 2.

115. "Proceedings of the Conference at Chemawa, Oregon, April 8 and 9 [1934] to Discuss with the Indians the Howard-Wheeler Bill," Box 257, RG 75, National Archives, Seattle, 60.

116. "Proceedings," RG 75, 62.

117. "Proceedings," RG 75, 80.

118. *Oregonian*, 10 March 1934, 1; *Oregon Statesman*, 10 March 1934, 1.

119. Prucha, 2:961–63; Deloria and Lytle, *Nations*, 172.

120. See Lawrence C. Kelly, "The Indian Reorganization Act: The Dream and the Reality," in Roger L. Nichols, ed., *The American Indian, Past and Present*, 3rd ed. 248–49.

121. Kelly, "Indian Reorganization Act," 250.

122. Kelly, "Indian Reorganization Act," 250.

123. Deloria and Lytle, Nations, 172–73.

124. "Indian Referendum Ballots," Box 2, Siletz Reservation Collection.

125. "Narrative Report, 1934–35," Box 50, RG 75, National Archives, Seattle. The people on the Grand Ronde Reservation would later reorganize themselves under the Indian Reorganization Act into the Grand Ronde community. The principal advantages of their new status apparently were restoration of about 537 acres of land and the creation of a loan fund for housing rehabilitation. The Siletz people who had turned the act down also got housing rehabilitation loan money but did not get back any of their lost lands. See Congress, *Joint Hearings*, 142.

126. "1934 Statistical Report," Box 50, RG 75, National Archives, Seattle, 16.

127. "Narrative Report, 1934–35," Box 50, RG 75, National Archives, Seattle, 4.

128. "Absentee Ballots Mailed March 19, 1935," Box 3, and Council Minutes, 12 March 1950, Roll 1, Siletz Reservation Collection.

129. Towner later found a measure of national recognition when, calling himself Chief Red Cloud and wearing a feathered headdress featuring beaded swastikas, he became a leader of the anti-Collier American Indian Federation and a sympathizer with the pro-Nazi German-American Bund. He called Collier a "Jew-loving Pink Red" and said that he wanted Jews eliminated from the Indian Office. See Kenneth R. Philp, *John Collier's Crusade for Indian Reform, 1920–1954*, 201–203.

In 1950, Towner was chosen chair of the tribal council, but his tenure was brief. When his pre-war political career was exposed, he was recalled. One man said, "Mr. Towner had so much education if you put your trust in him, he will sting you and sting you." (Council Minutes, 16 April 1950 and 21 November 1948, Roll 1, in Ms. 442, Siletz Reservation Collection.)

130. Towner to Collier, 14 March 1934, Box 50, RG 75, National Archives, Seattle.

131. The hypothesis that concern over trust allotments was a significant reason for opposition to the Indian Reorganization Act is not a new idea. Many accounts of the development of the Indian Reorganization Act have mentioned Indian expressions of concern. For example, Francis Paul Prucha took note of the "fears about allotments belonging to individuals who wanted to keep them," which were expressed at the regional congresses on the original Wheeler-Howard bill held in 1934 (Prucha, 2:959.)

Graham D. Taylor suggested that Collier arranged the congresses because anthropologists Franz Boas and Ralph Linton "felt that holders of allotments in trust would be reluctant to part with them voluntarily in view of their previous experience with bureau maladministration." (Taylor, New Deal, 24–25.)

Vine Deloria, Jr., and Clifford Lytle mentioned that at committee hearings, even before the congresses, some Indian spokespersons expressed misgivings about Collier's property rights proposals. They were concerned that landless people would get together to take property away from the people who had managed to keep it. (Deloria and Lytle, *Nations Within*, 92–95.)

Kenneth R. Philp noted several negative responses to Collier's circular "Indian Self-Government," dated January 20, 1934, in which he proposed transferring individual control of property to tribal corporations. Those responses included a petition from fifty-two Wind River Arapahoes opposing communal ownership of property and a statement by "the Assiniboine and Atsina Indians . . . that they would refuse to relinquish their allotments without suitable financial reimbursements." See Philp, Crusade, 137–40.

Philp also implied that much of the opposition expressed at the congresses came "from those who viewed the reservation as a prison, where they were held captives, instead of a viable community. They disliked the bill because it destroyed their heirship rights and confiscated their allotted land to give to poor Indians." (Philp, *Crusade*, 145.)

12. Claims, Termination, Salmon, and Restoration

1. United States, Congress, *Joint Hearings*, 147.

2. *Oregonian* (Portland), 1 November 1925, 27.

3. Congress, *Joint Hearings*, 147.

4. United States, House, *Authorizing Adjudication of Claims of the Coos (Kowes) Bay, Lower Umpqua (Kalawatset), and Siuslaw Tribes of Indians of Oregon*, 70th Cong., 2nd sess., 1929, H. Rpt. 2209, Serial 8979, 3.

5. Work to Leavitt, 24 May 1928, in House, *Authorizing Adjudication*, 3.

6. United States, Senate, *Letter from the Secretary of the Interior*, 52nd Cong., 2nd sess., 1893, S. Ex. Doc. 25, Serial 3144, 8–15; Armstrong to Secretary of the Interior, 5 October 1893, Senate, *Letter*, 1893, Serial 3144, 3.

7. Rhoads to Secretary of the Interior, 24 February 1930, in United States, Senate, *Conferring Jurisdiction upon Court of Claims to Hear Claims of Certain Oregon Indians*, 71st Cong., 3rd sess., 1931, S. Rpt. 1361, Serial 9323, 2–3; Prucha, 2:923.

8. Prucha, 2:939, 926.

9. *Congressional Record*, 72:1051–53, quoted in Prucha, 2:926.

10. Rhoads to Secretary of the Interior, 24 February 1930, in United States, House, *Court of Claims to Adjudicate Claims of Certain Bands of Indians in Oregon*, 71st Cong., 3rd sess., 1931, H. Rpt. 2758, Serial 9327, 2–3.

11. Rhoads to Secretary of the Interior, 26 January 1932, in United States, Senate, *Court of Claims to Hear and Determine Claims of Certain Bands, Nations, or Tribes of Indians Residing in the State of Oregon*, 72nd Cong., 1st sess., 1932, S. Rpt. 430, Serial 9487, 2.

12. Congress, *Joint Hearings*, 146.

13. Congress, *Joint Hearings*, 147.

14. United States, Bureau of Indian Affairs, Grand Ronde-Siletz Agency, *Ten-Year Program, 1946–1955*, Siletz, Oregon, Salem, Oregon, March 1944, 4. The combined Grand Ronde–Siletz Agency was established July 1, 1938, and head-quartered in Salem. See Bureau of Indian Affairs, *Ten-Year Program*, 13, 32.

15. Bureau of Indian Affairs, *Ten-Year Program*, 21.

16. Bureau of Indian Affairs, *Ten-Year Program*, 4, 25.

17. Bureau of Indian Affairs, *Ten-Year Program*, 4, 8, 10.

18. Bureau of Indian Affairs, *Ten-Year Program*, 8, 23, 22.

19. Bureau of Indian Affairs, *Ten-Year Program*, 23.

20. Bureau of Indian Affairs, *Ten-Year Program*, 8.

21. "Testimony of Pauline Ricks on S. 2801" in United States, Senate, *Hearings Before the Subcommittee on Indian Affairs of the Committee on Interior and Insular Affairs, United States Senate, Ninety-Fourth Congress, Second Session, on S. 2801*, 128.

22. Congress, *Joint Hearings*, 145–46.

23. Congress, *Joint Hearings*, 145–46; *Oregonian*, 26 November 1946, 1; *Oregonian*, 27 November 1946, 1.

24. *Oregonian*, 29 November 1946, 2.

25. *Oregonian*, 21 October 1947, 14.

26. Wallace Turner, "Lands Ruling Gives Indians Lift," *Oregonian*, 1 December 1948, 21.

27. *Oregonian*, 4 January 1950, 1; *Oregonian*, 10 April 1951, 1; *Oregonian*, 27 April 1951, 14; Congress, *Joint Hearings*, 146.

28. Congress, *Joint Hearings*, 146–47; United States, Bureau of Indian Affairs, *A Profile of the Confederated Tribes of Siletz Indians of Oregon on February 18, 1978*, Report 264, 3, 6.

29. "Testimony of Robert P. Rilatos on S. 2801" in United States, Senate, *Hearings on S. 2801*, 143–44.

30. See Prucha, 2:993–1005, 1019.

31. Donald Fixico, *Termination and Relocation: Federal Indian Policy, 1945–1960*, 29.

32. Prucha, 2:1026.

33. Prucha, 2:1030.

34. Prucha, 2:1033, 1040, 1044.

35. E. Morgan Pryse testimony, 17 February 1954, in United States, Congress, *Joint Hearings*, 180.

36. "Resolution," 29 August 1951, Congress, *Joint Hearings*, 162–63; Congress, *Joint Hearings*, 141.

37. "Resolution," 29 July 1951, Congress, *Joint Hearings*, 166–67.

38. "Resolution," 12 November [1951], Congress, *Joint Hearings*, 159–61.

39. *Oregonian* (Portland), 17 January 1952, 13.

40. E. Morgan Pryse testimony, 17 February 1954, Congress, *Joint Hearings*, 187.

41. "Resolution . . . April 15, 1951," Congress, *Joint Hearings*, 162–63.

42. Wallace Turner, "Indian Office Faces Inquiry in Land Deal," *Oregonian* 25 January 1952, 1; *Oregonian*, 8 October 1952, 14.

43. Wallace Turner, "Court Lists Jail, Fines for Fraud," *Oregonian* 13 May 1953, 1; *Oregonian*, 8 October 1952, 14.

44. *Oregonian*, 25 January 1952, 8.

45. "Testimony of Pauline Ricks on S. 2801," Senate, *Hearings on S. 2801*, 127.

46. "Testimony of Siletz Tribal Council on S. 2801," Senate, *Hearings on S. 2801*, 136–37.

47. During World War II, forty-seven men who were members of the Confederated Siletz Tribes served in the armed forces. They included Joe Lane, who would become a significant figure in the tribal government more than thirty years later, and Phil Rilatos, who would be general manager for the tribes in the 1980s. See Tom, ed., *Siletz Restoration Days*, 19–20; Philp, Crusade, 201–203.

48. Hardy Simmons statement, 14 March 1976, Senate, *Hearings on S. 2801*, 140.

49. Lindsay John statement, 14 March 1976, Senate, *Hearings on S. 2801*, 142.

50. See Congress, *Joint Hearings*, 177–89.

51. *United States Statutes at Large*, Vol. 68, pt. 1 (1955), 724–28.

52. *Oregonian*, 15 August 1956, 1.

53. "Testimony of Pauline Ricks on S. 2801," Senate, *Hearings on S. 2801*, 128.

54. Lindsay John statement, March 14, 1976, Senate, *Hearings on S. 2801*, 142.

55. "Testimony of Robert P. Rilatos on S. 2801," Senate, *Hearings on S. 2801*, 144.

56. Prucha, 2:1015.

57. William Zimmerman's plan made this explicit by dividing tribes into three groups: one of tribes that could be considered ready for immediate withdrawal, one of tribes that could be severed from the government within ten years, and a third of tribes that would have to be prepared further for withdrawal. See Prucha, Vol. 2, 1026. Assistant Interior Secretary Orme Lewis, commenting on the Siletz termination bill, explained that the Siletz people no longer needed "special assistance" because their long association with whites had resulted in their integration into white society, "where they are accepted without discrimination" (Lewis to Nixon, 4 January 1954, Congress, *Joint Hearings*, 134).

58. Prucha, 2:1055–56.

59. Fixico, *Termination*, 176–80.

60. Prucha, 2:1056–59.

61. Fixico, *Termination*, 181.

62. See United States, American Indian Policy Review Commission, *Report on Terminated and Nonfederally Recognized Indians*, 64, 35–36.

63. "Statistical Profile," Senate, *Hearings on S. 2801*, 203, 201, 205.

64. "Testimony of Joseph H. Lane on S. 2801," Senate, *Hearings on S. 2801*, 166–68; *Oregon Journal* (Portland), 3 October 1973, J20.

65. "Testimony of Arthur S. Bensell on S. 2801," Senate, *Hearings on S. 2801*, 180.

66. "Testimony of Joseph H. Lane on S. 2801," Senate, *Hearings on S. 2801*, 168–70.

67. Les AuCoin, "Special Wildlife Rights Not in Bill to Restore Siletz Tribal Status," *Oregonian*, 12 July 1977, B1.

68. Senate, *Hearings on S. 2801*, 3.

69. United States, Senate, *Siletz Indian Tribe Restoration Act*, 95th Cong., 1st sess., 1977, S. Rpt. 95-386, Serial 13168-8, 3.

70. *Congressional Record* (December 17, 1975), Vol. 121, Pt. 32, 41231–32.

71. Lincoln County Board of Commissioners to Hatfield, 13 October 1975, in *Congressional Record* (December 17, 1975), Vol. 121, Pt. 32, 41234.

72. United States, Senate, *Survey of Conditions of Indians in the United States*, pt. 21 (1931), 11716–17, 11722–23.

73. Prucha, 2:1183–85.

74. Hatfield and AuCoin to Straub, 4 December 1975, *Congressional Record* (December 17, 1975), Vol. 121, pt. 32, 41232.

75. Senate, *Hearings on S. 2801*, 68–69.

76. "A bill to restore federal recognition," Senate, *Hearings on S. 2801*, 16.

77. Senate, *Hearings on S. 2801*, 68–69.

78. Senate, *Hearings on S. 2801*, 26–30.

79. Senate, *Hearings on S. 2801*, 77.

80. Art Bensell interview, 16 August 1986, Siletz, Oregon; Senate, *Hearings on S. 2801*, 59–60.

81. Senate, *Hearings on S. 2801*, 70–71, 67.

82. Senate, *Hearings on S. 2801*, 81, 90.

83. United States, House, *Restoring the Confederated Tribes of Siletz Indians of Oregon as a Federally Recognized Sovereign Indian Tribe*, 95th Cong., 1st sess., 1977, S. Rpt. 95-623, Serial 13172-10, 3; Robert Olmos, "Siletz Indian Bill Gets Mixed Reaction from Leaders, Youth," *Oregonian*, 12 June 1977, F1.

84. "A bill to restore the Confederated Tribes of Siletz Indians" in United States, Senate, *Hearing Before the United States Senate Select Committee on Indian Affairs, Ninety-Fifth Congress, on S. 1560*, 5, 9.

85. Les AuCoin, "Special Wildlife Rights Not in Bill to Restore Siletz Tribal Status," *Oregonian*, 12 July 1977, B1.

86. Herbert Lundy, "Right of Regulation at Issue for State," *Oregonian*, 12 July 1977, B1.

87. "Statement of John R. Donaldson, Director, Oregon Fish and Wildlife Department," Senate, *Hearing on S. 1560*, 27–29.

88. "Proposed Siletz Health, Education and Welfare Act by Oregon Fish and Wildlife Commission, July 10, 1977," Senate, *Hearing on S. 1560*, 34–39.

89. United States, Senate, *Siletz Indian Tribe Restoration Act*, 95th Cong., 1st sess., 1977, Rpt. 95-386, Serial 13168-8, 3–4.

90. *United States Statutes at Large*, vol. 91 (1980), 1415–19; *Oregonian*, 4 November 1977, A1.

91. *Oregonian*, 3 June 1979, C3.

92. Dave Peden, "Siletz Voters OK Transfer of City Land to Tribe," *Oregonian*, 3 November 1979, A18; Phillip Johnson, "The Siletz Fight for Their Reservation," *Willamette Week* (Portland, Ore.), 12 November 1979, 7.

93. Johnson, *Siletz Fight*, 10–11; United States, House, *Establishing a Reservation for the Confederated Tribes of Siletz Indians of Oregon*, 96th Cong., 2nd sess., 1980, H. Rpt. 96-1159, Serial 13372, 2–4; Jim Hill, "Judge Signs Decree on Siletz Hunting," *Oregonian*, 3 May 1980, A8.

94. Don Holm, "Siletz Submit Plan for Tribal Hunting, Fishing Rights on Coast Lands," *Oregonian*, 15 December 1979, C8; Tom McAllister, "Siletz Tribe Seeks Fishing, Hunting Rights," *Oregon Journal* (Portland), 15 December 1979, 1.

95. Dick Johnston, "Siletz Reservation Voted by Senate," *Oregonian*, 21 March 1980, A1.

96. Jim Kadera, "Settlement Spells Out Tribe Rights," *Oregonian*, 22 April 1980, C1; Hill, "Judge Signs Decree." Darrelle Dean Butler had been involved in July 1975 in a gunfight on the Pine Ridge Reservation in South Dakota in which two agents of the Federal Bureau of Investigation were killed. The following year he and another AIM member, Bob Robideau, were tried for murder and acquitted. In 1977 a third AIM member indicted in the killings of the agents, Leonard Peltier, was convicted. See Peter Matthiessen, *In the Spirit of Crazy Horse* (New York: Viking, 1991).

In 1985, Butler and a cousin, Gary Butler, were tried in Portland for murder in the 1981 killing of a Toledo millworker who was involved in digging up Indian graves in the Siletz area to get salable artifacts. I covered their trial as a correspondent for the *Statesman-Journal* of Salem. They were acquitted.

97. Hill, "Judge Signs Decree;" United States, House, *Establishing a Reservation*, 4.

98. Dick Johnston, "Siletz Reservation Bill Wins House Approval," *Oregonian*, 19 August 1980, B5; *Oregonian*, 6 September 1980, A1.

99. E. A. Schwartz, "Siletz Argue for Land," *Statesman-Journal* (Salem, Ore.), 18 September 1985, 3C.

100. Confederated Tribes of Siletz Indians, "Impact Statement: Land Acquisition Effort, Confederated Tribes of Siletz Indians of Oregon," undated, distributed to Lincoln County Board of Commissioners 17 September 1985.

101. *Statesman-Journal*, 2 November 1986, 2C.

102. E. A. Schwartz, "Tribe Looks Both Ways," *Statesman-Journal*, 16 November 1986, 1A.

Bibliography

General

Alcea Band of Tillamooks et al. v. United States. 59 Federal Supplement. St. Paul: West Publishing Co., 1945.

Alta California. San Francisco. 1851–56.

AuCoin, Les. "Special Wildlife Rights Not in Bill to Restore Siletz Tribal Status." *Oregonian*, 12 July 1977, B1.

Bancroft, Hubert Howe (Frances Fuller Victor). *The Works of Hubert Howe Bancroft*. Vol. 29, *History of Oregon, 1834–1848*. Vol. 30, *History of Oregon, 1848–1883*. San Francisco: History Co., Publishers, 1888.

———. *The Works of Hubert Howe Bancroft*. Vol. 31, *History of Idaho, Washington, and Montana, 1845–1889*. San Francisco: History Co., Publishers, 1890.

Beckham, Stephen Dow. *The Indians of Western Oregon: This Land Was Theirs*. Coos Bay, Ore.: Arago Books, 1977.

325

———. *Land of the Umpqua: A History of Douglas County, Oregon*. Roseburg, Ore.: Douglas County Commissioners, 1986.

———. *Requiem for a People: The Rogue Indians and the Frontiersmen*. Norman: Univ. of Oklahoma Press, 1971.

Beeson, John. *A Plea for the Indians*. Fairfield, Wash.: Ye Galleon Press, 1982.

Bensell, Arthur. Interview, 16 August 1986, Siletz, Ore.

Bensell, Royal A. *All Quiet on the Yamhill: The Civil War in Oregon*. Edited by Gunther Barth. Eugene: Univ. of Oregon Books, 1959.

Berthrong, Donald J. *The Cheyenne and Arapaho Ordeal: Reservation and Agency Life in the Indian Territory, 1875–1907*. Norman: Univ. of Oklahoma Press, 1976.

Boyd, Robert T. "Demographic History, 1774–1874." In Wayne Suttles, ed., *Handbook of North American Indians*, 7. Washington: Smithsonian Institution, 1990.

Brooks, Howard C., and Len Ramp. *Gold and Silver in Oregon*. Portland: State of Oregon Department of Geology and Mineral Industries, 1968.

Capital Journal (Salem, Ore.), 8–9 March 1934.

Cardwell, James A. "Emigrant Company." Ms. P-A 15. Bancroft Library, Univ. of California at Berkeley.

Carey, Charles H. *History of Oregon*. Chicago: Pioneer Historical Publishing Co., 1922.

———. Historical note in W. Lansford Hastings, *Emigrants' Guide to Oregon and California*. Princeton: Princeton Univ. Press, 1932.

Castillo, Edward D. "The Impact of Euro-American Exploration and Settlement." In Robert F. Heizer, ed., *Handbook of American Indians: California*, 8: 99–127. Washington: Smithsonian Institution, 1978.

Chicago Daily Tribune (Chicago, Ill.), 1856.

Clark, Robert Carlton. "Military History of Oregon, 1849–59." *Oregon Historical Quarterly* 36 (March 1935): 14–59.

Coan, C. F. "The Adoption of the Reservation Policy in Pacific Northwest, 1853–55." *Quarterly of the Oregon Historical Society* 23 (March 1922): 1–38.

Confederated Tribes of Siletz Indians. "Impact Statement: Land Acquisition Effort, Confederated Tribes of Siletz Indians of Oregon." Undated. Distributed to Lincoln County Board of Commissioners, 17 September 1985.

Corning, Howard McKinley. *Dictionary of Oregon History*. Portland: Binford and Mort, 1956.

Corvallis Gazette (Corvallis, Ore.), 1866–80.

Cresap, Bernarr. "Captain Edward O. C. Ord in the Rogue River Indian War." *Oregon Historical Quarterly* 54 (June 1953): 83–90.

Curry, George L., Jr. "Much Good Land Left." *Oregonian*, 27 July 1895, 9.

Davenport, T. W. "Recollections of an Indian Agent." *Quarterly of the Oregon Historical Society* 8 (March 1907): 1–41; (June 1907): 95–128; (September 1907): 231–64; (December 1907): 353–74.

Deady, Matthew. Deady Letters, 1853–1854. Ms. 577, Oregon Historical Society, Portland.

Deloria, Vine, Jr., and Clifford M. Lytle. *The Nations Within: The Past and Future of American Indian Sovereignty*. New York: Pantheon Books, 1984.

Democratic Standard (Portland, Ore.), May 1856.

Dicken, Samuel N., and Emily Dicken, *The Making of Oregon: A Study in Historical Geography*. Portland: Oregon Historical Society, 1979.

Dodge, Orvil. *Pioneer History of Coos and Curry Counties, Oregon*. Salem: Capital Printing Co., 1898.

Dorsey, J. Owen. "Indians of Siletz Reservation, Oregon." *American Anthropologist* 2 (January 1889): 55–61.

———. "The Gentile System of the Siletz Tribes." *Journal of American Folk-Lore* 3 (January–March 1890): 227–37.

Douthit, Nathan. "The Hudson's Bay Company and the Indians of Southern Oregon." *Oregon Historical Quarterly* 93 (Summer 1992): 25–64.

Dowell, B[enjamin] F. "Oregon Indian Wars of 1855–6 in Southern Oregon, Volume 2." Ms. P-A 138, Bancroft Library, Univ. of California at Berkeley.

Drucker, Philip. *Cultures of the North Pacific Coast*. San Francisco: Chandler Publishing Co., 1965.

———. "The Tolowa and Their Southwest Oregon Kin." *University of California Publications in American Archeology and Ethnology* 36 (1943): 221–300.

Du Bois, Cora A. "General Ethnographic Notes on the Tututni (Rogue River) Indians." Ethnological Documents, Museum of Anthropology Archives, CU-23-1, Item 6. Bancroft Library, Univ. of California at Berkeley.

———. "The 1870 Ghost Dance." *University of California Publications in Anthropological Records* 3 (1946): 1–152.

Elliot, T. C., ed. "The Oregon Coast as Seen by Vancouver in 1792." *Oregon Historical Quarterly* 30 (March 1929): 33–42.

Fagan, David D. *History of Benton County, Oregon.* Portland: David D. Fagan, 1885.

Fixico, Donald. *Termination and Relocation: Federal Indian Policy, 1945-1960.* Albuquerque: Univ. of New Mexico Press, 1986.

Geer, T. T. *Fifty Years in Oregon.* New York: Neale Publishing Co., 1916.

Gienapp, William R. *The Origins of the Republican Party, 1852-1856.* New York: Oxford Univ. Press, 1987.

Glisan, Rodney. *Journal of Army Life.* San Francisco: A. L. Bancroft Co., 1874.

Gray, Dennis J. *The Takelma and Their Athapascan Neighbors: A New Ethnographic Synthesis for the Upper Rogue River Area of Southwestern Oregon.* University of Oregon Anthropological Papers, no. 37 (1987).

Hall, Betty L. "Faces of the Shasta People: Who We Were and Who We Are, the Shasta Nation." In *Living With the Land: The Indians of Southwest Oregon,* edited by Nan Hannon and Richard K. Olmo. Medford, Ore.: Southern Oregon Historical Society, 1990.

Harvison, Robert Guy. "The Indian Reorganization Act of 1934 and the Indians of Oregon and Their Land." M.A. thesis. Univ. of Oregon, 1970.

Haskell, J. Loring. *Southern Athapascan Migration A.D. 200-1750.* Tsaile, Ariz.: Navajo Community College Press, 1987.

Hastings, W. Lansford. *Emigrants' Guide to Oregon and California.* Princeton: Princeton Univ. Press, 1932.

Hendrickson, James E. *Joe Lane of Oregon: Machine Politics and the Sectional Crisis, 1849-1861.* New Haven: Yale Univ. Press, 1967.

Henry, A. G. *Speech of A. G. Henry of Yamhill delivered before the citizens of Corvallis on the evening of Dec. 3rd, 1855, on the subject of the pending Rogue River War.* Corvallis, Ore.: *Oregon Argus,* 1855.

Hill, Jim. "Judge Signs Decree on Siletz Hunting." *Oregonian,* 3 May 1980, A8.

History of Southern Oregon Comprising Jackson, Josephine, Douglas, Curry and Coos Counties. Portland: A. G. Walling, 1884.

Holm, Don. "Siletz Submit Plan for Tribal Hunting, Fishing Rights on Coast Lands." *Oregonian,* 15 December 1979, C8.

Holt, Catharine. "Shasta Ethnography." *University of California Publications in Anthropological Records,* 3, no. 4. Berkeley: Univ. of California Press, 1946.

Hoop, Oscar Winslow. "History of Fort Hoskins, 1856-65." *Oregon Historical Quarterly* 30 (December 1929): 346-61.

Hoxie, Frederick E. *A Final Promise: The Campaign to Assimilate the Indians, 1880-1920.* Cambridge: Cambridge Univ. Press, 1984.

————. "Indian-White Relations: 1790–1900." In *Scholars and the Indian Experience*, edited by W. R. Swagerty. Bloomington: Indiana Univ. Press, 1984.

Hurtado, Albert O. *Indian Survival on the California Frontier*. New Haven: Yale Univ. Press, 1988.

Jennings, Francis. *The Invasion of America: Indians, Colonialism, and the Cant of Conquest*. New York: W. W. Norton and Co., 1976.

Johnson, Allen, and Dumas Malone, eds. *Dictionary of American Biography*. New York: Charles Scribner's Sons, 1964.

Johnson, David Alan. *Founding the Far West: California, Oregon, and Nevada, 1840–1890*. Berkeley: Univ. of California Press, 1992.

Johnson, Overton, and William H. Winter. "Route across the Rocky Mountains with Description of Oregon and California, Etc., 1843." *Quarterly of the Oregon Historical Society* 7 (June 1906): 163–210.

Johnson, Phillip. "The Siletz Fight for Their Reservation." *Willamette Week*, 12 November 1979, 7, 10–11.

Johnston, Dick. "Siletz Reservation Bill Wins House Approval." *Oregonian*, 19 August 1980, B5.

————. "Siletz Reservation Voted by Senate." *Oregonian*, 21 March 1980, A1.

Kadera, Jim. "Settlement Spells Out Tribe Rights." *Oregonian*, 22 April 1980, C1.

Kane, Paul. *Wanderings of an Artist Among the Indians of North America*. Edmonton, Alberta: M. G. Hurtig, Ltd., 1968.

Kasner, Leone Letson. *Survival of an Artifact*. Dallas, Ore.: Itemizer-Observer, 1976.

Keller, Robert H., Jr. *American Protestantism and United States Indian Policy, 1869–82*. Lincoln: Univ. of Nebraska Press, 1983.

Kelly, Lawrence C. "The Indian Reorganization Act: The Dream and the Reality." In *The American Indian, Past and Present*, 3rd ed., edited by Roger L. Nichols. New York: Alfred L. Knopf, 1986.

Kent, William Eugene. *The Siletz Indian Reservation, 1855–1900*. Newport, Ore.: Lincoln County Historical Society, 1977.

Kirkpatrick, J. M. *Heroes of Battle Rock, or the Miners' Reward*. Edited by Orvil Dodge. Myrtle Point, Ore.: 1904.

Knuth, Priscilla. "Oregon Know Nothing Pamphlet Illustrates Early Politics." *Oregon Historical Quarterly* 54 (March 1953): 40–53.

LaLande, Jeff. "The Indians of Southwestern Oregon: An Ethnohistorical Review." In *Living With the Land: The Indians of Southwest Oregon*, edited by Nan Hannon and Richard K. Olmo. Medford, Ore.: Southern Oregon Historical Society, 1990.

Lane, Joseph. "Autobiography." Ms. P-A 43, Bancroft Library, Univ. of California at Berkeley.

Lanternari, Vittorio. *The Religions of the Oppressed: A Study of Modern Messianic Cults*. New York: Alfred A. Knopf, 1963.

Lincoln County Leader (Toledo, Ore.), 1893–1925.

Lincoln County, Newport, Ore., County Clerk. Deed Records Book A.

————. Planning Department. "Zoning Maps," circa 1989.

————. Planning Department. "Zoning Summary," circa 1989.

Loy, William G., ed. *Atlas of Oregon*. Eugene: Univ. of Oregon Books, 1976.

Lundy, Herbert. "Right of Regulation at Issue for State." *Oregonian*, 12 July 1977, B1.

Lyman, R. Lee. "Alexander W. Chase and the 19th Century Archeology and Ethnography of the Southern Oregon and Northern California Coast." Tms. Univ. of Missouri-Columbia Anthropology Department, undated.

McAllister, Tom. "Siletz Tribe Seeks Fishing, Hunting Rights." *Oregon Journal*, 15 December 1979, 1.

McDonnell, Janet A. *The Dispossession of the American Indian, 1887–1934*. Bloomington: Indiana Univ. Press, 1991.

Mercury (Salem, Ore.), June 13 and June 20, 1873.

Messing, John. "Public Lands, Politics, and Progressives: The Oregon Land Fraud Trials, 1903–1910." *Pacific Historical Review* 35 (1966): 35–66.

Mills, Hazel Emery. "The Emergence of Frances Fuller Victor—Historian." *Oregon Historical Quarterly* 62 (December 1961): 309–36.

Minot, George, ed. *Statutes at Large and Treaties of the United States of America* 10. Boston: Little, Brown and Co., 1855.

Mulkey, Cyrenius. "Eighty-One Years of Frontier Life." Ms. 981, Oregon Historical Society, Portland.

Murray, Keith A. *The Modocs and Their War*. Norman: Univ. of Oklahoma Press, 1959.

Nash, Wallis. *Oregon: There and Back in 1877*. Corvallis: Oregon State Univ. Press, 1976.

————. *Two Years in Oregon*. New York: D. Appleton and Co., 1882.

National Intelligencer (Washington, D.C.), 1855–56.

Nesmith, James W. "A Reminiscence of the Indian War, 1853." *Quarterly of the Oregon Historical Society* 7 (1906): 213–21.

New York Times, 1878, 1905.

Newsom, David. *David Newsom: The Western Observer, 1805–1882*. Portland: Oregon Historical Society, 1972.

O'Donnell, Terence. *An Arrow in the Earth: General Joel Palmer and the Indians of Oregon*. Portland: Oregon Historical Society, 1991.

Oak, Henry L. *"Literary Industries" in a New Light*. San Francisco: Bacon Printing Co., 1893.

Olmos, Robert. "Siletz Indian Bill Gets Mixed Reaction from Leaders, Youth." *Oregonian*, 12 June 1977, F1.

Onstad, Preston E. "The Fort of the Luckiamute: A Resurvey of Fort Hoskins." *Oregon Historical Quarterly* 65 (June 1964): 173–97.

"The Oregon Indians." *The Overland Monthly* 7 (October 1871): 344–52.

Oregonian (Portland), 1854–1986.

Oregon Journal (Portland), 1968–79.

Oregon Sentinel (Jacksonville), 1856 and 1873.

Oregon Spectator !Oregon City), 1848–53.

Oregon Statesman (Corvallis and Salem), 1851–1934.

Oregon Territory. *Journal of the Proceedings of the Council of the Legislative Assembly of Oregon Territory*, 9th sess., 1857.

Palmer, Joel. "Joel Palmer Diary for 1856." Tms., State Library, Salem, Ore.

———. *Journal of Travels over the Rocky Mountains*. Cincinnati: J. A. and U. P. James, 1847.

Palmer Papers. Ms. AX57, Univ. of Oregon Library, Eugene.

Parman, Donald L. *Indians and the American West in the Twentieth Century*. Bloomington: Indiana Univ. Press, 1994.

Parrish, Josiah L. "Anecdotes of Intercourse with the Indians." Ms. P-A 59, Bancroft Library, Univ. of California at Berkeley.

Peden, Dave. "Siletz Voters OK Transfer of City Land to Tribe." *Oregonian* (Portland), 3 November 1979, A18.

Philp, Kenneth R. *John Collier's Crusade for Indian Reform, 1920–1954*. Tucson: Univ. of Arizona Press, 1977.

Pittsburgh Gazette (Pittsburgh, Pa.), 1856.

Price, Richard L. *Newport, Oregon, 1866–1936: Portrait of a Coastal Resort*. Newport: Lincoln County Historical Society, 1975.

Prucha, Francis Paul. *The Great Father: The United States Government and the American Indians*, 2 vols. Lincoln: Univ. of Nebraska Press, 1984.

Puter, Stephen A. D. *Looters of the Public Domain*. Portland, Ore.: Portland Printing House, 1908.

Rawls, James J. *Indians of California: The Changing Image*. Norman: Univ. of Oklahoma Press, 1984.

Ream, Daniel. "Autobiographical Dictation." Ms. C-D 954, Bancroft Library, Univ. of California at Berkeley.

Richards, Kent D. *Isaac I. Stevens: Young Man in a Hurry*. Pullman: Washington State Univ. Press, 1993.

Richmond Enquirer (Richmond, Va.), 1856.

Riddle, George. *Early Days in Oregon*. Riddle, Ore.: Riddle Parent Teacher Association, 1953.

Rilatos, Manuel. Interview, 4 July 1991, Siletz, Ore.

Robbins, Harvey. "Journal of the Rogue River War." *Oregon Historical Quarterly* 34 (December 1933): 345–58.

Rogue River Tribe of Indians et. al. v. United States. 89 Federal Supplement. St. Paul, Minn.: West Publishing Co., 1950.

Sackett, Lee. "The Siletz Shaker Church." *Pacific Northwest Quarterly* 64 (July 1973): 120–27.

San Francisco Chronicle, 18 May 1873, 12 October 1877.

Sapir, Edward. "Notes on the Takelma Indians of Southwestern Oregon." *American Anthropologist* 9 (April–June 1907): 251–75.

Schwartz, E. A. "Blood Money: The Rogue River Indian War and Its Aftermath, 1850–1986." Ph.D. dissertation, Univ. of Missouri-Columbia, 1991.

———. *"Polaklie Illahee:* The Siletz Reservation and U.S. Indian Policy, 1855–1925." M.A. thesis, Univ. of Missouri-Columbia, 1988.

———. "Sick Hearts: Indian Removal on the Oregon Coast, 1875–1881." *Oregon Historical Quarterly* 92 (Fall 1991): 228–64.

———. "Siletz Argue for Land." *Statesman-Journal* (Salem, Ore.): 18 September 1985, 3C.

———. "Tribe Looks Both Ways." *Statesman-Journal* (Salem, Ore.): 16 November 1986, 1A.

Scott, Leslie M. "Indian Diseases as Aids to Pacific Northwest Settlement." *Oregon Historical Quarterly* 26 (June 1925): 144–61.

————. "The Yaquina Railroad, the Tale of a Great Fiasco." *Quarterly of the Oregon Historical Society* 16 (September 1915): 228–45.

Siletz Reservation Collection. Ms. 442, Oregon Historical Society, Portland.

Smith, Marian W. *Indians of the Urban Northwest*. New York: Columbia Univ. Press, 1949.

Smith, Thomas. "Rogue River Indian Wars of 1853 and 1856." Ms., Bancroft Library, Univ. of California at Berkeley.

[Ord, E. O. C.] "Soldiering in Oregon." *Harper's New Monthly Magazine* 13 (August 1856): 522–26.

Spaid, Stanley S. "Joel Palmer and Indian Affairs in Oregon." Ph.D. thesis, Univ. of Oregon, 1950.

————. "The Later Life and Activities of General Joel Palmer." *Oregon Historical Quarterly* 55 (December 1954): 311–32.

Spreen, C. A. "A History of Placer Gold Mining in Oregon, 1850–1870." M.A. thesis, Univ. of Oregon, 1939.

Statesman-Journal (Salem, Ore.), 1985–86.

Starr, Kevin. *Americans and the California Dream, 1850–1915*. New York: Oxford Univ. Press, 1973.

Stuart, James. "White Man's Guardianship of Indian to End After 100 Years." *Oregonian* (Portland), 24 February 1952, 21.

Swanton, John R. *Indian Tribes of North America*. Washington: Government Printing Office, 1952.

Table Rock Sentinel. See *Oregon Sentinel*.

Taylor, Graham D. *The New Deal and American Indian Tribalism*. Lincoln: Univ. of Nebraska Press, 1980.

Telegram (Portland, Ore.), 1916, 1925.

Thomas, Edward Harper. *Chinook: A History and Dictionary of the Northwest Coast Trade Jargon*. Portland, Ore.: Binford and Mort, 1970.

Thornton, Russell. *American Indian Holocaust and Survival*. Norman: Univ. of Oklahoma Press, 1987.

Tom, Robert P., ed. *Siletz Restoration Days, 1st Annual, November 1977*. Siletz, Ore.: Confederated Tribes of Siletz Indians, 1977.

Trafzer, Clifford E., and Richard D. Scheuerman. *Renegade Tribe: The Palouse Indians and the Invasion of the Inland Pacific Northwest*. Pullman: Washington State Univ. Press, 1986.

Trennert, Robert A., Jr. *Alternative to Extinction: Federal Indian Policy and the*

Beginnings of the Reservation System, 1846–51. Philadelphia: Temple Univ. Press, 1975.

Turner, Wallace. "Court Lists Jail, Fines for Fraud." *Oregonian* (Portland), 13 May 1953, 1.

———. "Lands Ruling Gives Indians Lift." *Oregonian* (Portland), 1 December 1948.

———. "Indian Office Faces Inquiry in Land Deal." *Oregonian* (Portland), 25 January 1952, 1.

———. "Trip with Medicine Man up Rogue River to Agness." *Oregonian* (Portland), Sunday magazine, 5 January 1947, 3.

Unruh, John D. Jr. *The Plains Across: The Overland Emigrants and the Trans-Mississippi West, 1840–60.* Urbana: Univ. of Illinois Press, 1979.

Utley, Robert M. *Frontiersmen in Blue: The United States Army and the Indian, 1848–1865.* Lincoln: Univ. of Nebraska Press, 1967.

Van Pelt, Sam. "Before the White Man: An Indian's Story." *Oregonian* (Portland), Sunday magazine, 5 February 1939, 8.

Victor, Frances Fuller. *The Early Indian Wars of Oregon.* Salem, Ore.: Frank C. Baker, State Printer, 1894.

Washburn, Wilcomb E. *The Assault on Indian Tribalism: The General Allotment Law (Dawes Act) of 1887.* Philadelphia: J. B. Lippincott Co., 1975.

Weatherford, Mark. "Rogue River Indian War." Ms., Multnomah County Library, Portland, Ore.

Webster, G. "The Rogue River Indian War of 1855–'56." *Overland Monthly* 4 (September 1884): 235–40.

Williams, George H. "Political History of Oregon from 1853 to 1865." *Quarterly of the Oregon Historical Society* 2 (March 1901): 1–35.

Williams, Lorin L. "First Settlements in Southwestern Oregon. T'Vault's Expedition." Ms. P-A 77, Bancroft Library, Univ. of California at Berkeley.

Yaquina Bay News (Newport, Ore.), 1925.

Federal Documents

American Indian Policy Review Commission. *Report on Terminated and Non-federally Recognized Indians.* Washington: Government Printing Office, 1976.

Bureau of American Ethnology. *See* authors in "General" listings above.

Bureau of Indian Affairs. *Also see* Office of Indian Affairs.

——. *Annual Narrative and Statistical Reports from Field Jurisdictions of the Bureau of Indian Affairs, 1907–1938.* Records of the Bureau of Indian Affairs, National Archives. Microcopy 1011, Roll 139.

——. Grand Ronde–Siletz Agency. *Ten-Year Program, 1946–1955, Siletz, Oregon.* Salem, Ore., March 1944.

——. *A Profile of the Confederated Tribes of Siletz Indians of Oregon on February 18, 1978.* Report 264.

——. *Proposed Withdrawal of Federal Responsibilities over the Property and Affairs of the Indians of Western Oregon.* December 1953.

——. Records of the Bureau of Indian Affairs. RG 75, National Archives, Washington, D.C., and Seattle Branch.

Bureau of Topographical Engineers. "Map of the State of Oregon and Washington Territory." 1859.

Census Bureau. *Historical Statistics of the United States from Colonial Times to 1957.* Washington: Government Printing Office, 1960.

Congress. *Joint Hearings Before the Subcommittees of the Committees on Interior and Insular Affairs . . . on S. 2746 and H.R. 7317, February 17, 1954. Congressional Record.* Washington: Government Printing Office, 1954.

Court of Claims. *Coos (Kowes) Bay, Lower Umpqua (or Kalawatset), and Siuslaw Indian Tribes v. United States* in *Cases Decided in the Court of Claims of the United States,* Vol. 87. Washington: Government Printing Office, 1939.

House. *Agreement with Indians on the Siletz Reservation.* 53rd Cong., 2nd sess., 1894. H. Rpt. 527, Serial 3270.

——. *Annual Reports of the Department of the Interior for the Fiscal Year Ended June 30, 1900.* 56th Cong., 2nd sess., 1900. H. Doc. 5, Serial 4100.

——. *Annual Reports of the Department of the Interior for the Fiscal Year Ended June 30, 1901.* 57th Cong., 1st sess., 1901. H. Doc. 5, Serial 4289.

——. *Annual Reports of the Department of the Interior for the Fiscal Year Ended June 30, 1904: Indian Affairs, Part I.* 58th Cong., 3rd sess., 1904. H. Doc. 5, Serial 4792.

——. *Annual Reports of the Department of the Interior for the Fiscal Year Ended June 30, 1905.* 59th Cong., 1st sess., 1905. H. Doc. 5, Serial 4959.

——. *Authorizing Adjudication of Claims of the Coos (Kowes) Bay, Lower Umpqua (Kalawatset), and Siuslaw Tribes of Indians of Oregon.* 70th Cong., 2nd sess., 1929. H. Rpt. 2209, Serial 8979.

————. *Canal Through Siletz Indian Reservation, Oreg.* 59th Cong., 1st sess., 1906. H. Rpt. 1552, Serial 4906.

————. *Claims Growing Out of Indian Hostilities in Oregon and Washington in 1855 and 1856.* 36th Cong., 1st sess., 1860. H. Ex. Doc. 11, Serial 1046.

————. *Claims of Certain Indian Tribes to Lands in Oregon.* 72nd Cong., 1st sess., 1932. H. Rpt. 1289, Serial 9493.

————. *Correspondence Between the Late Secretary of War and General Wool.* 35th Cong., 1st sess., 1858. H. Ex. Doc. 88, Serial 956.

————. *Court of Claims to Adjudicate Claims of Certain Bands of Indians in Oregon.* 71st Cong., 3rd sess., 1931. H. Rpt. 2758, Serial 9327.

————. *Distribution of Funds to Indians.* 64th Cong., 1st sess., 1916. H. Rpt. 298, Serial 6903.

————. *Eighteenth Annual Report of the Bureau of American Ethnology.* Part 2. 56th Cong., 1st sess., 1899. H. Doc. 736. Serial 4015.

————. *Establishing a Reservation for the Confederated Tribes of Siletz Indians of Oregon.* 96th Cong., 2nd sess., 1980. H. Rpt. 96-1159, Serial 13372.

————. *Expenses of the Indian Wars in Washington and Oregon Territories.* 35th Cong., 1st sess., 1858. H. Ex. Doc. 45, Serial 955.

————. *Indian Affairs in Oregon and Washington Territories, &c.* 35th Cong., 1st sess., 1858. H. Ex. Doc. 112, Serial 958.

————. *Indian Affairs in the Territories of Oregon and Washington.* 35th Cong., 1st sess., 1858. H. Ex. Doc. 39, Serial 955.

————. *Indian Affairs on the Pacific.* 34th Cong., 3rd sess., 1857. H. Ex. Doc. 76, Serial 906.

————. *Indian Hostilities in Oregon and Washington.* 34th Cong., 1st sess., 1856. H. Ex. Doc. 93, Serial 858.

————. *Indian Hostilities in Oregon and Washington Territories.* 34th Cong., 1st sess., 1856. H. Ex. Doc. 118, Serial 859.

————. *Letter from the Secretary of War.* 34th Cong., 1st sess., 1856. H. Ex. Doc. 15, Serial 851.

————. *Letter from the Secretary of War.* 34th Cong., 3rd sess., 1857. H. Ex. Doc. 23, Serial 897.

————. *Memorial of the Legislative Assembly of the State of Oregon,* 41st Cong., 3rd sess., 1871, H. Mis. Doc. 19, Serial 1462.

————. *Memorial of the Legislative Assembly of the State of Oregon.* 41st Cong., 3rd sess., 1871. H. Mis. Doc. 77, Serial 1462.

————. *Memorial of the Legislature of Oregon*. 44th Cong., 2nd sess., 1876. H. Mis. Doc. 22, Serial 1762.

————. *Message from the President of the United States*. 32nd Cong., 1st sess., 1851. H. Ex. Doc. 2, Serial 634.

————. *Message from the President of the United States*. 32nd Cong., 2nd sess., 1852. H. Ex. Doc. 1. Serial 673.

————. *Message from the President of the United States*. 33rd Cong., 1st sess., 1853. H. Doc. 1, Serial 710.

————. *Message from the President of the United States*. 33rd Cong., 2nd sess., 1854. H. Ex. Doc. 1, Serial 777.

————. *Message from the President of the United States*. 34th Cong., 1st sess., 1856. H. Ex. Doc. 1, Serial 841.

————. *Message from the President of the United States*. 34th Cong., 3rd sess., 1857. H. Ex. Doc. 1, Serial 894.

————. *Message from the President of the United States*. 35th Cong., 1st sess., 1857. H. Ex. Doc. 2, Serial 942.

————. *Message from the President of the United States*. 35th Cong., 1st sess., 1858. H. Ex. Doc. 112, Serial 958.

————. *Message from the President of the United States*. 38th Cong., 1st sess., 1863. H. Ex. Doc. 1, Serial 1182.

————. *Message of the President of the United States*. 39th Cong., 1st sess., 1865. H. Ex. Doc. 1, Serial 1248.

————. *Message of the President of the United States*. 39th Cong., 2nd sess., 1866. H. Ex. Doc. 1, Serial 1284.

————. *Message of the President of the United States*. 40th Cong., 2nd sess., 1867. H. Ex. Doc. 1, Serial 1326.

————. *Message of the President of the United States*. 40th Cong., 3rd sess., 1868. H. Ex. Doc. 1, Serial 1366.

————. *Report of the Secretary of the Interior*. 41st Cong., 2nd sess., 1869. H. Ex. Doc. 1, Part 3, Serial 1414.

————. *Report of the Secretary of the Interior*. 41st Cong., 3rd sess., 1870. H. Ex. Doc. 1, Part 4, Serial 1449.

————. *Report of the Secretary of the Interior*. 42nd Cong., 2nd sess., 1871. H. Ex. Doc. 1, Part 5, Serial 1505.

————. *Report of the Secretary of the Interior*. 42nd Cong., 3rd sess., 1872. H. Ex. Doc. 1, Part 5, Serial 1560.

——. *Report of the Secretary of the Interior.* 43rd Cong., 1st sess., 1873. H. Ex. Doc. 1, Part 5, Serial 1601.

——. *Report of the Secretary of the Interior.* 43rd Cong., 2nd sess., 1874. H. Ex. Doc. 1, Part 5, Serial 1639.

——. *Report of the Secretary of the Interior.* 44th Cong., 1st sess., 1875. H. Ex. Doc. 1, Part 5. Serial 1680.

——. *Report of the Secretary of the Interior.* 44th Cong., 2nd sess., 1876. H. Ex. Doc. 1, Part 5, Serial 1749.

——. *Report of the Secretary of the Interior.* 52nd Cong., 1st sess., 1891. H. Ex. Doc. 1, Part 5, Serial 2933.

——. *Report of the Secretary of the Interior.* 52nd Cong., 2nd sess., 1892. H. Ex. Doc. 1, Part 5, Serial 3088.

——. *Report of the Secretary of the Interior.* 53rd Cong., 2nd sess., 1893. H. Doc. 1, Part 5, Serial 4748.

——. *Report of the Secretary of the Interior.* 54th Cong., 2nd sess., 1896. H. Doc. 1, Part 5, Serial 3489.

——. *Restoring the Confederated Tribes of Siletz Indians of Oregon as a Federally Recognized Sovereign Indian Tribe.* 95th Cong., 1st sess., 1977. H. Rpt. 95-623, Serial 13172-10.

——. *Sale of Certain Lands on the Siletz Indian Reservation.* 61st Cong., 2nd sess., 1910. H. Rpt. 1098, Serial 5592.

——. *Sale of Certain Lands on the Siletz Indian Reservation.* 63rd Cong., 2nd sess., 1914. H. Rpt. 909, Serial 6560.

Indian Claims Commission. *Final Report.* Washington: Government Printing Office, 1980.

——. Records of the Indian Claims Commission. RG 279, National Archives.

Interior Department. *Annual Reports of the Department of the Interior for the Fiscal Year Ended June 30, 1897.* Report of the Commissioner of Indian Affairs. Washington: Government Printing Office, 1897.

——. *Annual Reports of the Department of the Interior for the Fiscal Year Ended June 30, 1898.* Report of the Commissioner of Indian Affairs. Washington: Government Printing Office, 1898.

——. *Annual Reports of the Department of the Interior for the Fiscal Year Ended June 30, 1899.* Report of the Commissioner of Indian Affairs. Washington: Government Printing Office, 1899.

——. *Annual Reports of the Department of the Interior for the Fiscal Year Ended*

June 30, 1902. Indian Affairs. Part I. Washington: Government Printing Office, 1904.

———. *Annual Reports of the Department of the Interior. 1906.* Indian Affairs. Washington: Government Printing Office, 1907.

———. *Report of the Secretary of the Interior,* Vol. 1. Washington: Government Printing Office, 1879.

———. *Report of the Secretary of the Interior,* Vol. 2. Washington: Government Printing Office, 1882.

———. *Report of the Secretary of the Interior,* Vol. 2. Washington: Government Printing Office, 1883.

———. *Report of the Secretary of the Interior,* Vol. 2. Washington: Government Printing Office, 1884.

———. *Report of the Secretary of the Interior,* Vol. 2. Washington: Government Printing Office, 1885.

———. *Report of the Secretary of the Interior,* Vol. 1. Washington: Government Printing Office, 1886.

———. *Report of the Secretary of the Interior,* Vol. 2. Washington: Government Printing Office, 1887.

———. *Report of the Secretary of the Interior,* Vol. 2. Washington: Government Printing Office, 1888.

———. *Report of the Secretary of the Interior,* Vol. 2. Washington: Government Printing Office, 1890.

———. *Reports of the Department of the Interior for the Fiscal Year Ended June 30, 1909,* Vol. 2. Washington: Government Printing Office, 1910.

———. *Reports of the Department of the Interior for the Fiscal Year Ended June 30, 1910,* Vol. 2. Washington: Government Printing Office, 1911.

———. *Reports of the Department of the Interior for the Fiscal Year Ended June 30, 1911,* Vol. 2. Washington: Government Printing Office, 1912.

———. *Reports of the Department of the Interior for the Fiscal Year Ended June 30, 1912,* Vol. 2. Washington: Government Printing Office, 1913.

———. *Reports of the Department of the Interior for the Fiscal Year Ended June 30, 1914,* Vol. 2. Washington: Government Printing Office, 1915.

———. *Reports of the Department of the Interior for the Fiscal Year Ended June 30, 1915,* Vol. 2. Washington: Government Printing Office, 1916.

———. *Reports of the Department of the Interior for the Fiscal Year Ended June 30, 1916,* Vol. 2. Washington: Government Printing Office, 1917.

————. *Reports of the Department of the Interior for the Fiscal Year Ended June 30, 1917*, Vol. 2. Washington: Government Printing Office, 1918.

————. *Reports of the Department of the Interior for the Fiscal Year Ended June 30, 1918*, Vol. 2. Washington: Government Printing Office, 1919.

————. *Reports of the Department of the Interior for the Fiscal Year Ended June 30, 1919*, Vol. 2. Washington: Government Printing Office, 1920.

————. *Reports of the Department of the Interior for the Fiscal Year Ended June 30, 1920*, Vol. 2. Washington: Government Printing Office, 1920.

Library of Congress. *Journals of the Continental Congress, 1774–1789*, Vol. 32. Edited by Roscoe R. Hill. Washington: Government Printing Office, 1936.

NAM M-1011. *See* Office of Indian Affairs.

NAM 2. *See* Office of Indian Affairs.

NAM 234. *See* Office of Indian Affairs.

NAM 689. *See* War Department.

Office of Indian Affairs. *Annual Report of the Commissioner of Indian Affairs to the Secretary of the Interior for the Year 1877*. Washington: Government Printing Office, 1877.

————. *Annual Report of the Commissioner of Indian Affairs to the Secretary of the Interior for the Year 1878*. Washington: Government Printing Office, 1878.

————. *Annual Report of the Commissioner of Indian Affairs to the Secretary of the Interior for the Year 1880*. Washington: Government Printing Office, 1880.

————. *Annual Report of the Commissioner of Indian Affairs to the Secretary of the Interior for the Year 1881*. Washington: Government Printing Office, 1881.

————. *Annual Report of the Commissioner of Indian Affairs. 1894*. Washington: Government Printing Office, 1895.

————. *Letters Received by the Office of Indian Affairs, 1824–81*. National Archives Microcopy 234 (cited as NAM 234).

————. *Records of the Oregon Superintendency of Indian Affairs*. National Archives Microcopy 2 (cited as NAM 2).

————. *Report of the Commissioner of Indian Affairs for the Year 1862*. Washington: Government Printing Office, 1863.

————. *Report of the Commissioner of Indian Affairs for the Year 1864*. Washington: Government Printing Office, 1865.

————. *Report of the Commissioner of Indian Affairs to the Secretary of the Interior, 1908*. Washington: Government Printing Office, 1909.

RG 75. *See* Bureau of Indian Affairs.

RG 279. *See* Indian Claims Commission.

RG 393. *See* War Department.

Senate. *Authorizing Adjudication of Claims of the Coos (Kowes) Bay, Lower Umpqua (Kalawatset) and Siuslaw Tribes of Indians of Oregon*. 70th Cong., 2nd sess., 1929. S. Rpt. 1631, Serial 8977.

————. *Canal Through Siletz Indian Reservation, Oreg.* 61st Cong., 2nd sess., 1910. S. Rpt. 714, Serial 5584.

————. *Communication from C. S. Drew.* 36th Cong., 1st sess., 1860. S. Mis. Doc. 59, Serial 1038.

————. *Conferring Jurisdiction upon Court of Claims to Hear Claims of Certain Oregon Indians*. 71st Cong., 3rd sess., 1931. S. Rpt. 1361, Serial 9323.

————. *Correspondence of General Wool with the Government*. S. Ex. Doc. 16, Serial 751.

————. *Court of Claims to Hear and Determine Claims of Certain Bands, Nations, or Tribes of Indians Residing in the State of Oregon*. 72nd Cong., 1st sess., 1932. S. Rpt. 430, Serial 9487.

————. *Expenses Incurred in Suppression of Indian Hostilities in Certain Territories*. 42nd Cong., 3rd sess., 1872. S. Ex. Doc. 24, Serial 1545.

————. *Fee-Simple Patents to Indians of Siletz Reservation*. 57th Cong., 1st sess., 1901. S. Doc. 80, Serial 4226.

————. *Hearing Before the United States Senate Select Committee on Indian Affairs, Ninety-Fifth Congress, on S. 1560*. Washington: Government Printing Office, 1977.

————. *Hearings Before the Subcommittee on Indian Affairs of the Committee on Interior and Insular Affairs, United States Senate, Ninety-Fourth Congress, Second Session, on S. 2801*. Washington: Government Printing Office, 1976.

————. *Indian Affairs. Law and Treaties*, Vol. 1. Edited by Charles J. Kappler. 58th Cong., 2nd sess., 1904. S. Doc. 319. Serial 4623.

————. *Letter from the Acting Secretary of the Interior*. 43rd Cong., 1st sess., 1874. S. Mis. Doc. 65, Serial 1584.

————. *Letter from the Secretary of the Interior*. 52nd Cong., 2nd sess., 1893. S. Ex. Doc. 39, Serial 3056.

———. *Letter from the Secretary of the Interior.* 53rd Cong., 1st sess., 1893. S. Ex. Doc. 25, Serial 3144.

———. *Message from the President of the United States.* 34th Cong., 1st sess., 1855. S. Ex. Doc. 1, Serial 810.

———. *Message from the President of the United States.* 34th Cong., 3rd sess., 1856. S. Ex. Doc. 5, Serial 875.

———. *Message from the President of the United States.* 35th Cong., 1st sess., 1858. S. Ex. Doc. 1, Serial 974.

———. *Message from the President of the United States.* 36th Cong., 1st sess., 1859. S. Ex. Doc. 2, Serial 1023.

———. *Message from the President of the United States.* 36th Cong., 2nd sess., 1860. S. Ex. Doc. 1, Serial 1078.

———. *Message from the President of the United States.* 37th Cong., 2nd sess., 1861. S. Ex. Doc. 1, Serial 1117.

———. *Report of the Secretary of the Interior,* 32nd Cong., spec. sess., 1853, S. Ex. Doc. 4, Serial 688.

———. *Right of Way for Water Ditch or Canal Through Siletz Indian Reservation, Oreg.* 59th Cong., 1st sess., 1906. S. Rpt. 4905.

———. *Sale of Certain Lands on Siletz Indian Reservation, Oreg.* 61st Cong., 2nd sess., 1910. S. Rpt. 119, Serial 5582.

———. *Sale of Certain Lands on Siletz Reservation, Oregon.* 60th Cong., 1st sess., 1908. S. Rpt. 305, Serial 5218.

———. *Siletz Indian Tribe Restoration Act.* 95th Cong., 1st sess., 1977. S. Rpt. 95-386, Serial 13168-8.

———. *Survey of Conditions of Indians in the United States,* Part 21. Washington: Government Printing Office, 1931.

United States Statutes at Large, Vol. 36, Pt. 1. Washington: Government Printing Office, 1911.

United States Statutes at Large, Vol. 39, Pt. 1. Washington: Government Printing Office, 1917.

United States Statutes at Large, Vol. 68, Pt. 1. Washington: Government Printing Office, 1955.

United States Statutes at Large, Vol. 91. Washington: Government Printing Office, 1980.

United States Statutes at Large, Vol. 94, Pt. 1. Washington: Government Printing Office, 1981.

War Department. Records of the Office of the Secretary of War. RG 393, National Archives.

War Department. *Records of the Office of the Secretary of War*. National Archives Microcopy 689.

Athapascan speakers, 9–10, 13, 17, 18, 23, 166
AuCoin, Les, 260, 263–66
Augur, Christopher, 118, 138–40, 143–44, 163, 165–66

Bagley, William, 198–205, 208
Bailey, Joseph, 110
Baker, See-nee-nis, 175, 268
Bancroft, Hubert Howe. *See* Victor, Frances Fuller
Barkwell, M. C., 119–20
Barnes, Captain, 141
Barnum, E. M., 93, 104
Battle Rock, 6, 33–35
Bayley, James R., 177, 179
Bear Creek, 6, 22, 32
Beaver, as food, 22–24
Beckham, Stephen Dow, 149
Beeson, John, 85–86
Benecia, Calif., 123
Bensell, Arthur, 263, 265
Bensell, Royal A., 175, 176–77, 179, 182, 194, 296n
Biddle, B. R., 170–72, 177, 179
Big Bar, camp near, 48
Big Bend of the Rogue River, 41, 47, 114, 136–43
Big Head Dance, 204–5
Big Meadows. *See* Meadows
Bigler, John, 45
Bill. *See* Konechequot
Blakely (officer of volunteers), 141
Boas, Franz, 318n
Bogus Tom, 191
Boldt, George, 261–62
Breckinridge, John, 156
Brooks, Preston, 155
Brophy, William, 252
Browne, J. Ross, 78–79, 151, 164, 167, 168
Bruce, James, 57, 102–4, 119, 131–32, 145; in Lupton massacres, 286–87n
Buchanan, Robert C., 117–18, 125, 134–40, 141, 143–46, 290n
Buena Vista, Battle of, 100
Buford, T. Jay, 218, 223
Buoy, Laban, 119
Burlingame, Anson W., 155
Burns, James, 265

Bush, Asahel, 32, 39–40, 52–53, 58; extermination too costly, 60, 71–72, 101, 103, 106, 158, 169
Butler, Darrelle Dean, 265, 323n
Butler, Gary, 323n
Butler, Jane, 237
Butte Creek people, or Jake's band, 47, 85, 8[

California, 51, 79; gold rush, 26, 44–45, 81; reservations, 169; state government bonds f[Indian wars, 45–46
Californians, 35, 48, 66, 75
Camp Stewart, 55
Cannibalism, alleged, 115
Cape Lookout, 161, 162
Cardwell, James, 3
Carson, Frank, 238
Carter, F. M., 203
Cascade Mountains, 8
Case, Samuel, 179
Casey, Silas, 42, 116
Cayuse Indians, 29
Cayuse War, 50
Chalcraft, Edwin, 228, 231, 234
Chapman, M. N., 196–97
Chapman, W. W., 125
Chase, Alexander W., 174–75
Chastacostas (Shasta Costas), 7, 9–10, 202
Chemawa Indian School, 236, 240, 256
Cherokee Indians, 100
Chetco Jenny, 70, 115
Chetco River, 6, 62–63, 118
Chetco Indians, 7, 9, 10, 13–14, 18–19, 63, 66, 71, 135, 147, 149, 253, 254, 282n, 290n
Chettanne, or Chettannene (village), 9; attacke[63
Chief Tom (Cow Creek Indian), 92
Chinook Jargon, 30, 58, 66, 165, 305n
Cholcultah (George), 69, 87, 135, 136–37, 141–43, 146–47, 151, 294n
Church policy. *See* Grant Peace Policy
Cictaqwutmetunne. *See* Umpqua Indians, Upp[
Cistakwusta (village), 9–10, 150
Civil War, 156, 170
Clarendon (pseudonym), 76–78, 80–81, 89
Cluggage, James, 46
Coast Ranges, 8

Coast Reservation, 47, 69, 89–90, 135, 136, 149, 154; established, 161; on map, 162, 163; reduction proposed, 178
Coast Station, on Coast Reservation, 162
Collier, John, 238–39, 241, 242, 244, 252; enigmatic concerning assimilation, 316n, 318n
Columbia (steamship), 42, 117, 134, 146, 149, 151, 164
Columbia River peoples, 60
Competency commissions, 230–31, 233–34, 235
Connelly, M. C., 218
Cooper, Frank, 172
Coos Bay, 6, 47, 95
Coos Indians, 7, 169, 196, 200, 212; land claims, 245–48
Coos River, 34, 60
Cooter, J. E., 233–34, 236–37
Coquille Indians (Mishikhwutmetunne), 7, 10, 41, 42; attacked by miners, 61, 62, 95, 117, 202, 290n
Coquille River (Mishikhwutme), 6, 34, 41–42, 47, 123
Cornelia Terry (schooner), 176
Corruption, 73, 164, 165, 172, 175
Corvallis, Ore., 106, 162
Corvallis and Yaquina Bay Wagon Road Co., 177–80
Courts, on reservation, 186, 201
Cow Creek, 88, 102, 125
Cow Creek band (Nahankuotana), 10, 92, 137
Crawford, E. L., 249
Crescent City, Calif., 47
Cultus Jim, 151
Culver, Samuel, 61, 63–64, 74, 73, 126
Curry, George L., 75, 78, 80, 87, 93, 103, 104, 106, 108, 111, 112, 123, 127–29, 144
Curry, George L., Jr., 222
Custer, George Armstrong, 200

Dakubetede Indians, 7, 10
Dance houses, 191
Danforth, Lucius, 102
Dart, Anson, 34–39, 41, 49
Davenport, J. W., 49
Davenport, T. W., 164, 187–88
Davis, Jefferson, 100
Davis, John W., 75, 77
Dawes, Henry, 216

Dayton, Ore., 145, 162, 164
Dead Indian Act, 225
Deady, Matthew, 67, 73, 77–78
Decatur (sloop), 96, 110–11
Deer Creek (home of Tecumtum), 47, 61, 66, 135, 280n
Deloria, Vine, Jr., 242, 318n
Democratic Party, 50, 52, 71, 72, 75, 76, 78, 80, 109; pro-slavery faction, 156, 169
Dent, Frederick, 170
Depoe, Charles (Depot Charlie), 190, 192–93, 196–97, 203, 204, 206, 207, 219, 225, 229, 303–4n
Depoe, Robert, 229
Depot Slough (Yaquina Bay tributary), 179
Dilley, David, 32–33
Dilomi (village), 12
Diseases, 12, 17, 18, 22, 51, 64, 162
Dodson brothers, 306–7n
Dolph, Joseph N., 218
Dorsey, J. Owen, 18, 181
Douglas, Stephen A., 50, 156
Douthit, Nathan, 22
Dowell, Benjamin F., 75, 76–78, 158–59
Drew, Charles S., 75, 76–78, 83–86, 93, 101–2, 106, 158, 289–90n
Drew, E. P., 149
Drucker, Philip, 14
Dryer, Thomas J., 74, 127, 132–33
Du Bois, Cora, 190
Dunbar, R. W., 95, 114, 154, 293n
Duncan, Joseph, 195

Education. *See* Schools
Edwards (homicide victim), 53
Egbert, Knott, 225, 226–27
Eliot, John, 51
Elk City, Ore. Terr., 162
Employment, during World War II, 248, 251. *See also* Migratory labor
Er-ches-sa, 171
Etnemitane. *See* Umpqua Indians, Upper
Eugene, Ore., 95, 162
Evans Creek, 56, 151
Ewald (correspondent), 38

Fairchild, J. H., 192–98, 201, 207; bankrupted, 305n

Feather dances, 226
Fillmore, Millard, 128
First Salmon Ceremony, 14
Fishing, 14–15, 16, 64, 168, 169
Fishing and hunting rights, 261–63
Foods, 13, 15, 16, 19, 22–24
Fort Hoskins, 162, 163, 166, 168, 170
Fort Jones, 55, 66
Fort Lamerick, 144
Fort Lane, established, 60, 86, 105, 113, 124
Fort Orford, 123
Fort Umpqua (Hudson's Bay Company), 24
Fort Umpqua (U.S. Army), 162, 163, 168
Fort Yamhill, 162, 163, 168
Foster, Charles, 115, 140, 150
Franciscans, 51
Frank (Big Head dancer), 204
Franklin (steamship), 127
Frazier, Lynn, 236
Fry, Edna, 150
Fur traders, 20–21

Gaines, John, 29; negotiations in 1851–39, 38, 52
Gaither, Beal, 218, 223
Galice Creek people (Taltushtuntude), 10, 13, 17, 82, 137, 142, 202
Gambling, 16
Games, 16–17
Geary, Edward R., 109–10, 169, 170
General Allotment Act (Dawes Act), 209–10, 214–17, 219, 269n
George. *See* Cholcultah
Ghost Dance, 189–91, 202–3, 206, 207, 212, 234, 304n
Glisan, Rodney, 81, 151, 289–90n
Gold, traded by Indian people in California, 276n
Gold Beach, Ore., 47, 114, 149
Grand Ronde, 113, 164
Grand Ronde agency, 162
Grand Ronde Reservation, 40, 121–22, 126, 127, 144, 152, 154, 164; and Ghost Dance, 190; and Indian Reorganization Act, 243–44, 317n; population, 314n, 315n
Grant Peace Policy, 183–84, 185–86, 197, 201, 210–12
Grave Creek, 47, 58

Grave Creek House, 101
Grave Creek people, and 1854 treaty, 282n
Gray, Dennis J., 22–23
Greenwood (pseudonym), 104
Gwin, William, 156

Hall, Beverly B., 262, 263
Harding, H. H., 219
Harjo, Suzan, 263
Harlan, James, 178
Harney, George, 187, 192, 194, 196–98, 200–206, 207, 219, 306n
Hart-tish (Applegate John), 280n
Hastings, W. Lansford, 25–26
Hatfield, Mark, 260–66
Hawley, Luther, 98, 100
Hedges, Absalom, 154, 165, 176
Heirship cases, 234
Henry, A. G., 88, 102, 105–6, 111, 126, 286n
Hillyer, Richard, 176–77
Hitchcock, Ethan Allan, 42
Hokan speakers, 11
Holladay, Ben, 173, 193
Homestead Act, 196
House Concurrent Resolution 108, 253
Housing, 13, 15, 59, 167, 178, 182, 195, 226
Howard, John, 189
Howard, Joseph, 198
Hoxie, Frederick E., 215, 269n
Hudson's Bay Company, 21–24, 71
Humbug (mining camp), 79
Humbug John, 204
Hungry Hill (Grave Creek Hills), Battle of, 97, 99–100, 101, 117, 124–25
Hunting, 16, 168
Huntington, J. W. Perit, 172, 177–79

Ikirukatsu (Rogue River Valley Shastas), 11
Illinois River, 6, 74; miners, 31, 47, 70, 134, 150
Illinois River people, 66
Illinois River valley, 74
Indian conferences on Indian Reorganization Act, 240
Indian New Deal, 215, 240
Indian policy, 266–67. *See also* Reservation policy; Grant Peace Policy

Martin, William, 77, 79–80, 97, 101–3, 106, 125, 154, 155
Mary (Shasta), 40
Massachusetts "praying towns," 51
Massacres: at Battle Rock in 1851, 34; of Chetcos, 19–20, 63, 66; and Rogue River War, 85–89, 91; Whitman, 29; Gen. Wool on, 123, 133
Massey (officer of volunteers), 141
McArthur, Duncan, 223–24
McBride, James, 32
McCain, J. S., 203, 211
McDonnell, Janet A., 217
McKee, Reddick, 45
McLeod, Alexander, 22
Meacham, Alfred B., 188, 194, 306n
Meadows (Big Meadows), 47, 116, 125, 127, 131, 133–34, 141
Medicine, traditional Native, 17–18
Medill, William, 50
Mesquakie Indians, 259
Metcalf, Lucy, 114
Metcalfe, Robert, 57, 73, 126, 143, 151, 163–67, 169
Methodists, 155, 183–84, 186, 202, 203, 205, 206, 210–12
Mexican-American War, 27, 28
Migratory food production, 13–14, 19
Migratory labor, 171, 180–81, 187, 191, 199–200
Mikonotunne (village), 9, 120
Miller, A. F., 63, 71, 95, 118
Mining, 6, 30; Illinois River, 31, 44, 61, 63, 74–75, 84
Mishikhwutme. See Coquille River
Mishikhwutmetunne. See Coquille Indians
Mitchell, John H., 173, 193–95, 197, 199, 266
Mix, Charles E., 169
Modoc Indians, 70, 114, 290n
Modoc War, 34
Mollie (Warm House dancer), 191
Morality, of Rogue River War, 132–33, 172, 186, 195, 212
Mott, C. H., 168
Mount McLoughlin, 6
Mulkey, Cyrenius, 26–27, 97, 99
Myer, Dillon S., 252–53
Myrtle (pseudonym), 119

Nahankuotana. See Cow Creek band
Nash, Wallis, 198
National Congress of American Indians, 263
Native American Rights Fund, 260
Navajos, and Indian New Deal, 242
Negutretun (sub-village), 9
Nesmith, James W., 72–73, 167, 172, 176, 178
Nestucca band, 195, 196, 202
Newcomb, Daniel, 169, 170, 171
Newport, Ore., 162, 179
Nez Perce War, 200
Noland, Rhodes, 54
Northwest Coast culture area, 8

Oak Flat, camps at, 134–35, 137, 138
Odell, W. H., 219
Odeneal, Thomas B., 177, 190, 191–92
O'Donnell, Terence, 70, 289–90n, 292n, 293n
Ogden, Peter Skene, 12, 22–24
Old Joshua (Rogue River leader), 135
Olney, Nathan, 134, 139–40, 145
O'Meara, James, 156
Omnibus Act of 1910, 230
Ord, Edward O. C., 117–18, 120, 135, 290n
Oregon-California Trail, 6, 26, 46, 47
Oregon City, Ore., 29
Oregon Fish and Wildlife Commission, 262, 263–65
Oregonian (newspaper), 112
Oregon Spectator (newspaper), 33
Oregon state constitution, 67
Oregon Statesman (newspaper), 32, 54, 67, 71, 77, 78, 87–89, 112, 172
Owen, Captain, 58
Oyster piracy, 176–77

Pacific Mail Steamship Line, 33
Pacific Republic accusation, 156–57
Packwood, Bob, 263
Palmer, Joel, 28, 49–50, 52, 60, 63–70, 71–73 81, 83–85, 89–90, 94–95, 97, 100–101, 109–10, 113, 116–17, 119, 121, 126–27, 130, 134, 138–40, 142–43, 145–46, 151, 153–55, 159, 162–65, 183; in Big Bend battle, 293n; on Ghost Dance 190–91, 195, 210; and Know-Nothings, 283n, 289–90n, 291n, 292n; on Rogue River people, 4–5; at Siletz as agent, 186–89

Tatretun (sub-village), 9
Tattoos, 40
Taylor (lynching victim), 53
Taylor, Cris, 286n
Taylor, Graham D., 318n
Taylor, Zachary, 29
Taylor's Indians, 58
Tcetci'wut (sub-village), 10, 150
Tecumtum (John or Elk Killer): identity of, 293n, 294n; signed 1853 treaty, 59, 66, 69, 82, 86–87, 90, 113, 125, 135–37, 141, 144, 146, 149, 151–52; signed 1854 treaty amendments, 280n
Teller, Henry M., 211
Termination: and fishing and hunting rights, 262; meetings in 1948, 253–59
Texas reservations, 169
Thompson, Coquille, 190, 191, 204–5
Thurston, Samuel, 88
Tichenor, William, 33, 35–36, 39, 106, 115, 149–50, 154
Tillamook County, 191
Tillamook Indians, 195, 199, 200
Tillamook River, 60
Timber, improperly sold, 255. *See also* Logging
Tipsu Tyee (Bearded Chief), 3, 31, 64–66, 270n
Tleatti'ntun (sub-village), 10, 150
Tobacco, 15–16
Toledo, Ore., 162, 179
Tolowa Indians, 7, 9; and Ghost Dance, 190, 207, 234
Tom, Robert Paul, 263
Toppenish Creek, 83
Toquahear, 11, 39, 40, 46, 48, 49, 57–59, 66, 69, 74, 87, 90, 105, 116; signed 1853 treaty, 59; signed 1854 treaty amendments, 280n
To-toot-na Jenny (Chetco Jenny), 70, 115
Tourists, assured of safety after killings, 307n
Towner, Elwood A., 231, 241, 244
Traders, 20–24, 26; Klickitat, 29
Transportation, 165, 172, 177, 204–8, 226–27, 231; to reservation, 116, 146, 149–50
Trappers, 20–22
Treaties: with coastal peoples, 246–47, 284n, 299n; 1850 unofficial, 30–31; 1851 coastal, 41–42; 1853, 57–59, 64, 65; 1854, 61, 67, 69–70, 81–82, 83, 282n; informal with Gaines, 39; personal with Tipsu Tyee, 31

Trennert, Robert A., Jr., 50
Tribes, 181; not necessarily traditional, 239
Truman, Harry S., 252
Tuqwetatunne, collective term for south coast peoples, 9
Turner, Wallace, 255
Tututni Indians (Tututunnes), 7, 9, 10, 202; land claims, 247
Tututunne, or Tututun (village), 9, 114
T'Vault, William G., 33, 35, 40–41, 42, 46
Ty-gon-ee-shee, 168

Umatilla Indians, 107
Umatilla Reservation, 164
Umpqua Indians, Lower (Kalawatsets), 10, 15, 169, 196, 200, 212; land claims, 245–48
Umpqua Indians, Upper (Etnemitane), 7, 10, 11, 24, 64
Umpqua River, 5, 6, 34, 38, 41, 47, 149, 161, 162, 163
Umpqua River valley, 8, 36, 53, 74
United Brethren Church, 211
Upper Farm, Siletz Reservation, 181, 191, 210

Valentine, Robert, 230
Vancouver, George, 21–22
Van Pelt, Sam, 13, 18–19, 62
Van Pelt, Thomas, 13, 18, 273n
Victor, Frances Fuller, 53, 107, 110, 135, 148, 164, 274n
Villages, 5, 6, 181; and allotment, resistance to, 187–88; at Alsea and Yachats River mouths, 200, 210; different from tribes on reservation, 302n
Vive Voce Law, 72, 282n
Volkman, John, 260

W (pseudonym), 126
Wade, Ira, 312n
Wadsworth, F. M., 211–12
Wagoner (or Waggoner), Jacob B., 91, 286n
Walker, Courtney M., 126
Walker, I. G., 126
Walker, Jesse, 75; expedition, 75, 77
Walla Walla Indians, 107
Walla Walla River, 107
War claims, 1853 paid, 75, 76, 77, 81, 88, 95, 118, 121, 122–23, 148, 157, 158–59

Warfare, 3–4, 270–71n
Warm House Dance, 191, 192, 204, 234
Warm Springs Reservation, 164
Washington fishing controversy, 261–62
Washington Territory, 93
Wasson, George, 228, 241
Watkins, E. C., 203
Waymire, Fred, 119, 291n
Wells, John W., 180, 181
Wheeler, Burton K., 236
Whig Party, 52, 53, 71, 72, 78; and A. G.
    Henry, 88
Whiskey Run, on Coquille River, 61
White River valley, 96, 116
Whitman Massacre, 29
Wilkinson, Charles, 265
Willamette River, 162
Willamette Valley peoples, 60
William (Alsea leader), 196
Williams, Bob, 58, 106–7, 116
Williams, Lorin L., 41
Willow Springs, on Bear Creek, 32
Wilson, Henry, 155
Winant, J. J, 201
Winchuck River, 13, 18
Winter, William H., 26
Wodziwob (Ghost Dance prophet), 189–90
Women: as fighters and negotiators, 4; and
    fishing, 16; in precontact societies, 17, 286n

Woods, J. G., 87–88
Wool, John E., 100, 108; criticized by
    legislators, 111, 117, 123–24, 128, 133, 134
    153, 154
Work, Hubert, 246
Work, John, 24
World War I, 228–29
World War II, 248–49, 321n
Wright, Benjamin, 70–71, 81, 95, 114–15, 134
    139, 282n, 289–90n
Wright, W. H., 139–40
Wyatt, Wendell, 260

Yakima Indians, 84
Yakima War, 79, 83, 93, 107, 127, 153
Yamhill River, 94, 162
Yaquina Bay, 162, 165, 176–80, 200–201
Yaquina River, 178
Ya-su-chah band, mentioned in treaty, 42
Yellowtail, Robert, 259
Young, Ewing, 20–21, 24, 24
Youqueechee band, mentioned in treaty, 41
Yoyotan band, mentioned in treaty, 41
Yreka, Calif., 6, 33, 47, 55, 80
Yreka Herald (newspaper), 54
Yurok Indians, 234

Z (pseudonym), 104–5
Zimmerman, William, 252, 321n